ABSTRACTS OF
FAUQUIER COUNTY, VIRGINIA

Wills, Inventories and Accounts
1759-1800

By
JOHN K. GOTT

CLEARFIELD

Reprinted for
Clearfield Company, Inc. by
Genealogical Publishing Co., Inc.
Baltimore, Maryland
1994, 1999

Originally Published: Arlington, Virginia, 1976
Reprinted: Genealogical Publishing Co., Inc.
Baltimore, 1980
Library of Congress Catalogue Card Number 80-67141
International Standard Book Number 0-8063-0898-2
Made in the United States of America

TO

S. A. Z.

FAUQUIER COUNTY
VIRGINIA

FORMATION

Fauquier County was established May 1, 1759, by an Act of Assembly passed February 22 of that year, dividing Prince William "into two distinct counties, that is to say: All that part of the said county that lies above a line to be run from the head of Bull run, and along the top of the Bull run mountains, to Chapman's mill, in Broad run thoroughfare, from thence by a direct line to the head of Dorrel's run, and from thence by a direct line till it intersects the nearest part of the line dividing Stafford and Prince William counties, shall be one distinct county, and called and known by the name of Fauquier; and All that other part thereof below the said bounds shall be one other distinct county, and retain the name of Prince William."

Prince William had been taken from the counties of King George and Stafford in 1730, and King George from Richmond in 1720. Old Rappahannock County, formed from Lancaster in 1656, had passed out of existence on its division into the counties of Richmond and Essex in 1692. Lancaster existed as a county in 1652 and was probably taken from Northumberland, the original name of which was Chicawane. Northumberland, first mentioned in 1646, was established as a county in 1648, at which time it was declared to contain the "neck of land between Rappahannock River and Potomack River." Prince William's other parent, Stafford, was taken from Westmoreland in 1675, and Westmoreland from Northumberland prior to 1653, although its boundaries were not defined until that year.

Fauquier County was named for Francis Fauquier, Lieutenant-Governor of the colony of Virginia from 1758 until his death in 1767. According to Mr. Jefferson he was the most intelligent and best beloved of the colonial governors.

ORGANIZATION

The organization of the county was effected May 24, 1759. On this date certain of the gentry of the new county, to whom commissions had been issued, assembled at the house of John Duncan. Commissions of the Peace under the seal of the colony, bearing date at Williamsburg "the seventh day of May last," to Thomas Harrison, Joseph Blackwell, John Wright, William Blackwell, John Trogg, John Bell, William Eustace, John Churchill, William Grant, John Crump, Duff Green, Yelverton Peyton, Thomas Marshall, George Lambkin, Wharton Ransdell, Elias Edmonds, Thomas McClennahan and Richard Foote, Gent., were first read. Thomas Harrison, John Wright, William Blackwell, William Eustace, John Churchill, William Grant, Yelverton Peyton, Thomas Marshall and George Lambkin being present, the oath appointed by Act of Parliament, entitled "An Act for the Further Security of his Majesty's Person and Government and the Succession of the Crown in the heirs of the late Princess Sophia, being Protestants, and for extinguishing the hopes of the pretended Prince of Wales and his open and secret Abettors," was taken. The persons aforesaid having severally subscribed the "test," the oaths of a Justice of the Peace and of a Justice of the County Court in Chancery were administered, and the first court for Fauquier County was convened.

Of this court Humphrey Brooke was commissioned clerk and Joseph Blackwell qualified as sheriff, with Martin Pickett and Rhodham Tullos as under sheriffs.

Henry Churchill took the oath as county lieutenant, and William Elbzey, James Keith and Cuthbert Bullit, Gent., were sworn as attorneys to practice law in the county.

Thomas Marshall, Gent., then produced a commission "from under the hands and seals of the President and masters of the College of William and Mary," appointing him to be surveyor of the county and the following persons were appointed surveyors of the roads: George Cosby, of the road "from Town Run to the county line;" John Catlett, "from Brent Town to the Stafford line," and Alexander Bradford, "from Marr's Bridge to Coventons." Other matters being disposed of, the court adjourned.

COUNTY SEAT AND OTHER SETTLEMENTS

On the records of the first court the following minute appears: "It being the opinion of the court that the plantation of John Duncan is the most proper and convenient place for the Court House of this county to be established on, it is ordered that it be certified to His Honor the Governor." In this recommendation, however, the governor apparently did not concur, for in a writ dated June 13, 1759, under the seal of the colony, he directed that the next court for the county be held "in the house of William Jones, on the lands of Richard Henry Lee, Esquire, in the Parish of Hamilton, in the said county." At this court (June 28, 1759), it was ordered that the sheriff advertise that the court at its next session would "agree with workmen" to build a court house of wood, and further that John Bell, William Eustace and Yelverton Peyton, or any two of them, should receive bids for building a prison for the use of the county of the same dimensions as the prison of Stafford County. A site for the proposed buildings was provided at the next court when John Bell and Yelverton Peyton were appointed " to lay off two acres of land belonging to Richard Henry Lee for the court house and prison of this county to be erected on." After the sheriff, at the same court, had " protested against the court for want of a sufficient prison," Elias Edmonds undertook to construct such a building of wood, to be 12 feet square in the clear, with a brick or stone chimney, for the sum of seventy-three pounds and fifteen shillings, and to complete the same within three months. This building was accepted April 24, 1760, and although there is no mention of a court house being contracted for, a small temporary structure was evidently built, as on August 29 of the same year the sheriff was directed to pay John Bell twenty-four pounds, eighteen shillings and four pence, " being the sum the Court House was built for." In the meantime the construction of a permanent court house was under consideration and on June 27 the sheriff gave notice that at the August court, the court would agree with an " undertaker " to build a court house of brick, to be 36 feet long and 20 feet wide in the clear. Subsequently the advisability of erecting a frame building was considered and at the next court John Wright and John Bell were appointed to receive bids for a court house of clapboards, to be 24 feet long, 16 feet wide and 10 feet pitch, with a partition of 10 feet at one end, and to have a bench and a bar. Eventually, however, the justices decided to build a court house of brick and August 29, 1760, John Bell undertook to construct a building of this material, " 26 feet long and 20 feet wide in the clear; the walls to be 18 feet high from the surface and 18 inches thick from the water table; 6 sash windows below, 14 lights in each, 12 by 10; two dormers, 18 lights in each, 12 by 10; a partition of 12 feet at one end for a justices' room, with a chimney; the plank used to be of pine, and shingles of chestnut, sapped; the doors to have good locks and hinges and in all other respects to be finished in a complete and workmanlike manner, after the manner of the court house of Lancaster County;" all for the consideration of three hundred and thirty-nine pounds, and to be finished by November 20, 1762. If this building was not completed in 1762 it was at least ready for use by the justices in 1764, for in July of that year they ordered John Bell to provide curtains for three of its windows. This court house stood on the land now occupied by the residence of Mr. Lucien Keith on Culpeper Street, while the first court house and prison were built at a point between the present residence of Mr. Moses M. Green and the cemetery. The house of William Jones, to which court was adjourned June 28, 1759, also stood within, or close to, the limits of the present town of Warrenton, and the house of John Duncan, at which the first court for the county was held, was probably situated at Fayetteville.

The location chosen for the court houses was approximately the intersection of the old road from Winchester to Falmouth, with the post road from Charlottesville to Alexandria. As this point was a convenient stopping place for teams and travellers, a tavern, a store or two and a blacksmith shop were built, a few houses sprang up and the locality, under the name of Fauquier Court House, soon became a thriving cross roads settlement.

The brick court house built in 1762 sufficed for public needs until after the Revolution, when, as the business of the county grew, new buildings became necessary and the Justices of the County, May 26, 1790, purchased the present site from Thomas Maddux, Thomas Nelson and Joseph Nelson, " for the purpose of erecting thereon a Court House, Prison, Pillory, whipping-post and stocks, and for no other use, intent or purpose whatsoever." These buildings when completed were said to be "spacious and handsome and erected at an expense estimated at $30,000." The court house on this site has been twice destroyed by fire and twice rebuilt, once in 1853 and again in 1889.

Fauquier Court House, on the petition of its citizens, was laid off to comprise seventy-one acres of land and incorporated as a town January 5, 1810, under the name of Warrenton, in honor of General Joseph Warren of early Revolutionary fame. In this petition reference is made to the "stores and manufactories" of the place.

In 1835 Warrenton is described as containing "200 neat and closely built dwelling houses, 3 houses of public worship, Methodist, Presbyterian and Episcopalian, 4 primary schools, 3 taverns, 4 private boarding houses, 2 printing offices, each issuing a weekly paper, 4 wheelwrights, 1 coach maker, 3 saddlers, 1 hatter, 2 boot and shoe factories, 2 cabinet makers, 5 house carpenters, 4 blacksmith shops, 2 tailors, 2 clock and watch makers, 3 bakers, 1 tanner and currier, 3 breweries, 1 tin plate worker, 2 milliners, 1 mantuamaker, 1 house and sign painter and 2 plow manufactories. The village had a regular market, which was held in a neat little building, the upper part of which was used as a Town Hall. Population 1300; of whom 3 were resident ministers, 9 attorneys and 8 physicians."

The first settlement in Fauquier County, then a part of Stafford, was probably that made by some German Protestants at a place on Licking Run, about eight miles south of Warrenton, which afterwards became known as Germantown (see map). These colonists were iron workers from Westphalia, in Germany, and were engaged by Governor Spotswood, through the Baron de Graffenreid, to operate his iron furnaces in Orange, then Essex County. They arrived in Virginia in April, 1714, and settled at Germanna, from which place they removed to Germantown about the year 1720. In 1724, 1800 acres of land on Licking Run were granted to them by Lord Fairfax, proprietor of the Northern Neck.

Settlements were made on the Rappahannock River early in the history of the county, many of which have long since ceased to exist. Among these was a town at Norman's Ford (see map), called Carolandville, chartered in 1788 to comprise fifty-one acres on land owned by Landon Carter.

Salem (now Marshall) was established by Act of Assembly in 1796. It was situated on the post road from Winchester to Falmouth and had a stage service between these points three times a week. There was also a cross mail three times a week to Buckland, in Prince William County.

Upperville, on the Ashby's Gap turnpike from Winchester to Alexandria, was an early post village and was incorporated as a town March 31, 1852.

Towns recently incorporated are Remington, March 3, 1890, and The Plains, April 26, 1910.

PARISHES

Under the colonial government the Church of England was "established" in Virginia, that is a compulsory tax for its support was levied upon all persons subject to taxation regardless of sect or creed. For this purpose the country was laid off in ecclesiastical divisions called parishes, and the vestry of each parish assessed the taxes out of which the salaries of minister and clerk were paid, the church buildings kept in repair and the poor of the parish cared for. The original boundaries of the parishes covering the territory now occupied by Fauquier County, and their subsequent subdivision, may be traced as follows:

Prince William County was formed March 25, 1730, to include all the land " on the heads " of the counties of

Stafford and King George, lying "above Chopawansick creek, on Potomac river, and Deep Run, on Rappahannock river, and a southwest line to be made from the head of the north branch of the said creek, to the head of the said Deep Run." All of this territory was originally included in Overwharton Parish, in Stafford County. By an Act of Assembly which took effect January 1, of the year prior to the formation of Prince William County, Overwharton Parish was divided by practically the same line which afterwards served as a boundary between the counties of Prince William and Stafford, and a new parish was created under the name of Hamilton, to include all of Prince William County.

"By reason of the large extent of the Parish of Hamilton" and for the purpose of alleviating the resulting difficulties under which the minister and inhabitants labored, the parish was divided April 25, 1745, by a line "run from the dividing line of Stafford and Prince William counties, a straight course to the head of Dorrel's run; thence down the said run to Cedar run; thence to the fork of Broad run, near the lower line of colonel Charles Carter's tract called Broad run tract; thence to the mouth of Bull Lick run, opposite Jacob Smith's in Fairfax County," that part of it lying below this line to be known as the Parish of Dettingen, and that other part lying above the line to retain the name Hamilton. When Fauquier County, therefore, was formed from Prince William in 1759, it absorbed the greater part of Hamilton Parish together with that part of Dettingen Parish lying between the eastern boundary of the new county and Dorrel's Run.

On May 1, 1769, Hamilton Parish was again divided and the Parish of Leeds created, the latter to include that portion of Hamilton lying above "a straight line, to begin at the north fork of Broad run at an angle made by the

line that divides the said Parish of Hamilton from the
Parish of Dettingen and to end at two red oaks on the
bank of the north fork of Rappahannock river in the plantation of Jesse Williams."

Fauquier County was thus, ten years after the date of
its formation, definitely divided into two parishes, the
northern division forming the Parish of Leeds, while the
southern was comprised in that of Hamilton.

COLONIAL CHURCHES

The first church in that portion of Hamilton Parish
which afterwards became a part of this county, was St.
Mary's, a wooden building better known as "the old Turkey
Run Church." This church was situated on Turkey Run
about one mile below the present court house and was
probably built soon after Hamilton Parish was created from
Overwharton in 1730. It was used for many years, but was
finally abandoned on account of its inconvenience. In
1816 a new frame church was built on the Alexandria road
in Warrenton, to which the name St. James' was given,
and which served the needs of the parish until 1850. In
that year a brick church was built on Culpeper Street, which
was also called St. James' and which stood until 1910, when
it was destroyed by fire. This church was rebuilt and
enlarged in 1912.

Another early church in this parish was a substantial
brick building of cruciform design known as "the Elk
Run Church," situated on the Fredericksburg road about
fifteen miles below Fauquier Court House (see map). The
history of this church is not known, but Bishop Meade
states that it had fallen into decay and been abandoned
prior to 1811.

In the Parish of Leeds were Taylor's Church, not very
far from Warrenton; Goose Creek Church, near Marshall,

then Salem; old Bull Run Church, and Piper's Church, all
frame buildings of which no trace now remains.

Among the early churches of other sects was the Broad
Run Baptist Church. The first minute of this congregation
states, that "the church was constituted Dec. 3, 1762,
consisting of the ten following members, being near Broad
Run, in Fauquier County in the State of Virginia: Edmond
Hayes, Peter Cornwell, Joshua Dodson, Thomas Dodson,
William Stamps, Elizabeth Hayes, Sara Cornwell, Ruth
Dodson, Elizabeth Dodson, Betty Bennett." An organization of the members of this sect had, however, been effected
prior to 1762 under the name of "Ye Society of Baptists
on Broad Run." The first church house, situated on
Barker's Branch, near Broad Run, was used until 1798,
when a new church was built in the same locality. The
present site, near New Baltimore, was devised to the congregation by William Hunton in 1838, at which time a church
was already standing on the property. This third church
was demolished by Federal soldiers in 1862, but was rebuilt
on the same site in 1870 and dedicated October, 1871. The
records of this congregation show that among its early
members were Nancy Hanks, admitted in 1778, and Luke
Hanks, admitted in 1779, and that this pair left the neigh-
borhood in 1785. It seems likely that these were the parents
of Abraham Lincoln's mother, Nancy Hanks, who was born
in Virginia in 1783.

FAUQUIER COUNTY, VIRGINIA

WILL BOOK NO. 1

1759 - 1783

Pages 1-2*: WILLIAM BROOKS "of Fauquier County &
 Hamilton Parish" (Will)
Date: 10 January 1767
Dau.: Sarah - what she has already received
Dau.: Hannah - what she has already received
Dau.: Dauchers (or Danckus) - what she has
 already received
Dau.: Mary - what she has already received
Dau.: Ann - what she has already received
Dau.: Elizabeth - have an equal portion with
 the rest of her sisters except one bed
Wife: Ann - the plantation and lands and the
 movables during her natural life.
Son : Thomas - be content with what he had
 until his mother's death - then to have
 plantation - one-half of the movables -
 except dau. Elizabeth's bed
Son : William - the other plantation and one-
 half the movables - a mare and colt
Exor: Son Thomas.
Wit.: Peter Conway, George Theldkild, Thomas
 Conway.
Signed: William (his M mark) Brooks
Proved: 23 March 1767 by o. of George Theldkild
 and Peter Conway. Thomas Brooks took
 o. as Executor.

Page 2: JOHN SMITH "... of Hamilton Parish ..." (Will)
Date: 3 September 1776
Sister: Mary Manrony - 160 a. in County of Dunmore
Mother: Jane Smith - remainder of tract in Dunmore
 County and tract she now lives on in
 Hamilton Parish, during her life - then

*These two pages are attached in the front of
W. B. No. 1.

```
           equally divided between sister Hannah
           Smith and her son, Lewis Smith
Signed:    John (X) Smith
Wit.:      Augustine Smith, James Smith, William
           Smith
Proved:    24 March 1777, by o. of Augustine
           Smith and James Smith.  Jane Smith
           appointed admrx.

Pages 3-5: BENJAMIN BULLITT (Appraisement)
Date:      9 January 1767
App'd. by: Jonathan Gibson, James Murrey, William
           Roussaw
Total eval.: L 212.13.6
Ret.:      23 March 1767

Page 1:    RICHARD TULLOS (Will)
Date:      13 July 1758
           Peter Laurence - horse
           Edward Laurence, Jr. - clothes
           Jeanny Laurence - money in Martin Hardin's
           hand
           Sister's oldest son to have remainder
           of estate - L40 in the hands of William
           Shumate - my crop at Seaton's
Exor.:     John Markham
Wit.:      William Marshall, Thomas Conway
Signed:    Richard (h. R m.) Tullos
Proved:    24 May 1759 by o. of William Marshall
           John Markham refused to be executor -
           Edward Laurence took o. with Joseph
           Hudnal and James Foley as his securities.

              (Humphrey Brooke, Clerk)

Pages 1-4: GEORGE FOOTE (Will) ... of the parish of
           Hamilton ...
Date:      31 May 1759
Wife:      Mary Foote - during her life the plantation
           whereon I now live
Son:       William - plantation after death of wife
Son:       Richard - if William should have no heirs,
           plantation
Son:       Gilson - if Richard should have no heirs,
           plantation
Son:       Henry - 100 a. adjoining land already given
           him
```

- 3 -

Son:	George - 365 a. whereon he now lives
Son:	Gilson - 648 a. commonly known as Cullins's - part of which said land lying in Prince William and other part in Fauquier
Son:	Richard - 556 a. on Champes run & Cedar run
Son:	William - to have the 556 a. if Richard leaves no heirs, and then to son Gilson
Wife:	Mary - during her life - lent four Negroes to descend to sons: Richard & William and heirs, but should they not have heirs to <u>Daus</u>: Elizabeth, Frances and Behethelem
Son:	Henry - Negroes: Sarah & son Ely and all cattle and hogs raised on place.
Son:	George:- Negro man and girl, all cattle on plantation and one-half hoggs
Son:	Gilson - Negro man & woman - 2 cows & calves, one heifer and a steer and one-half hoggs at my son George's and 2 young sows from my home plantation
Dau.:	Elizabeth - Negro man and L50
Dau.:	Frances - Negro man and L50
Dau.:	Behethelon - Negro wench and child
Son :	Richard - Negro boy & girl, to William in case of default of heirs
Son :	William - 2 Negro girls, or to Richard or to Gilson
Wife, 3 Daus. and two youngest Sons: Mary, Elizabeth, Frances and Behethelon, Richard & William - all cattle, horses, mares & hoggs to be divided equally between them
Wife, 3 Daus., Sons: Gilson, Richard & William - all household furniture & sheep to be equally divided
Sons:	Richard & William's slaves to be left until they are 19 (the sons) and that Richard let William live on his land till the decease of his mother, Mary
Sons:	Richard & William to be educated as mother sees fit
Signed:	George Foote
Wit.:	Bereton Jones, William (X) Fletcher, John (X) Burditt, George (X) Bussell

```
Exors:  Wife, George and Gilson Foote,
        Richard and Wm. Foote
Proved: 28 June 1759, by o. of Brereton
        Jones, William Fletcher, John
        Burditt and George Bussell.
        Gilson Foote appointed Executor,
        John Ashby & Bereton Jones his
        securities.
```

Page 4:   RICHARD TULLOS (Appraisement)
```
    Date:   8 June 1759
    App'd. by:  Richard Lutteril, Clement Norman,
        George Crosby
    Total Eval.: L7.15.6
    Ret.:   28 June 1759
```

Pages 4-5: RICHARD REDMAN (Appraisement)
```
    Date:   28 June 1759
    App'd by:  Wm. Underwood, Joseph Smith,
        Henry Maffett
    Total Eval.: L14.10.3
    Ret.:   23 August 1759
```

Pages 5-6: JOHN SHADRACK (Will)
```
    Date:   11 August 1759
    Wife:   Elizabeth - Negro boy, cash, household
        goods and crops
        Thomas Johnston - who now lives with me
        my Tract of land lying in Culpeper County -
        460 a. purchased from William Hand - his
        mother's ring
    Exors:  wife, loving friend Charles Morehead.
    Signed: John (Z) Shadrach
    Wit.:   Sam'l. Earle, Will'm Bradford, Mary
        Bradford.
        Negro Joe never to go into the service
        of Charles Martin.
    Proved: 27 September 1759, exhibited by
        Elizabeth Shadrack, who was appointed
        exectrix. Prov. by Samuel Earle and
        Mary Bradford.
```

Page 7:   JOHN SHADRACK (Appraisement)
```
    Date:   27 September 1759
    App'd. by: Sam Earle, Edm'd. Basyè, Simon
        Morgan, sworn before Yelverton Peyton,
        Gent.
```

No total.
Ret.:   28 February 1760

Pages 8-9:   WILLIAM BRADFORD   (Will)
Date: 30 September 1759
Son: Henry - 206 a. I now live on
Unborn child, if male, to have one-half of
the 206 a.
Dau.:   Anne - one Negro woman
Unborn child, if female, to have one-half
issue of said Negro woman
Wife: Mary - use of estate, real & personal
for her natural life
Exors: wife, Mary and brother, Daniel Bradford,
sole executors
Signed: William Bradford
Wit.:   Alexander Bradford, Henry Rector, Laz.
Taylor
Prov.:   28 February 1760, exhibited by Alexander
Bradford and Lazarus Taylor. Mary
Bradford made oath according to law.

Pages 9-10:   JAMES McCORMICK   (Appraisement)
Date: 28 June 1759
App'd. by: John Duncan, Edward Willbourn,
Tran's. Tennill
Total Eval.: L47.7.10½
Ret.:   28 February 1760

Pages 10-13: JACOB HOLTZCLAW (Will) "... of the
Parish of Hamilton and County of Prince
William ..."
Date: 15 January 1759
Son :   Joseph - 374 a. bought of Warner Toward,
in case of default of heirs, etc., to
Son :   Jacob
Son :   Jacob - 200 a. on Licking Run where he
now lives, including 40 a. bought of
Harman Kemper, also 40 a. bought of
Harman Button - 150 a. in Prince William
bought of Thomas Barton, reserving to son
Joseph the liberty of taking as much
timber off of the said 150 a. for building
a dwelling house for himself.
Son: Harman - 200 a. bought of Thomas Stone,
whereon son Harman now lives - 100 a.
being part of a tract of 337 a. on the

branches of Hunger Run in Prince
William County and hereafter given to
my grandsons Henry and Joseph Holtzcalw

Dau.:   Eve Wiley, wife of Allen Wiley - 300 a.
in Loudoun Co. on Goose Creek granted
by Patent in 1750 - should she die
without heirs to son Jacob

Dau.:   Alice Katherine Hitt, wife of Henry
Hitt - 300 a. where sd. Henry Hitt now
lives, being part of a Tract in Culpeper Co. containing 1300 a. granted
by patent dated 1748 - in case of no
heirs to son Jacob and his heirs

Dau.:   Elizabeth Miller, wife of Harman Miller -
300 a. on which sd. H. Miller now lives,
part of above 1300 a., to son Jacob if
she leaves no heirs.

Son: H enry - 200 a. where he now lives, part
of 496 a. on Broad Run, taken up in
1724 and "at his Death to fall to his
son Jacob Holtzclaw and his heirs", in
case of default to son Jacob.

Gr.son: H enry Holtzclaw, son of son John, 100 a.
on Branches of Hunger Run, part of tract
containing 337 a.

Gr.son: Joseph Darnall, son of Jer're Darnall -
305 a. in Loudoun County near Williams'
Gap joining the land of George Carter

Dau.:   Katharine Darnal, wife of Jeremiah
Darnal - 362 a. in Pr. Wm. Co. joining
the Land of the Heirs of John Fishback

Son: Joseph Holtzclaw - one Negro woman, one
feather bed & furniture, one cow & calf,
one pewter dish and bason and two plates
and one desk

Son: Jacob - one Negro boy, one feather bed &
furniture, one clothes press, one cow &
calf, one pewter dish & bason, two plates

Dau.:   Eve Wiley - one Negro girl now in possession of Allen Wiley her husband

Dau.:   Alice Katharine Hitt - one Negro boy

Dau.:   Elizabeth Miller - one Negro boy, now in
possession of Harman Miller her husband

Son: Harman Holtzclaw - one Negro Wench - now
in his possession

```
Son:        Henry - one Negro boy now in his
            possession
Gr.son:     Jacob Fishback, son to Frederick
            Fishback - one Negro boy
Dau.:       Katharine Darnal - one Negro man,
            one feather bed & furniture, one
            warming pan
Gr.son:     John Fishback, son to Frederick
            Fishback - 177a. in Loudoun Co. on
            Goose Creek being the remaining part
            of tract set aside for dau. Eve Wiley.
            511 a. in Augusta County in two patents,
            together with all my personal estate not
            herein before mentioned be sold at public
            auction and after paying my just Debts
            to be divided between my children.
Son-in-law: Jeremiah Darnal and son, Jacob, to
            be executors.
Signed:     Jacob Holtzclaw
Wit.:       Peter (X) Hitt, Thos. Marshall, Henry
            Kamper
Proved:     29 February 1760, by Thomas Marshall and
            Henry Kamper. Jeremiah Darnal made
            motion to be recorded & granted cert.
```

Pages 13-14: TILMAN WEAVER (Will)
```
Date:       14 December 1759
Wife:       Anne Elizabeth Weaver - the use of my
            Plantation and Land adjacent whereon I
            now live and one containing 111 a. being
            land I had of Martin Hardin and taken up
            by John Hardin
Son:        Tilman Weaver - to get all land at death
            of wife
Wife:       use of slaves and after her death to sons
            Tilman and John and dau. Susanah Weaver -
            each to have one, in case they should have
            no heirs to go to son Tilman
Wife:       all household furniture to be divided
            according to what she can spare as the
            children are married, 4 cows & calves,
            4 large stears & all Hoggs - to be
            divided among children at her death. One
            Negroe girl, to go to son Tilman at her
            death
Dau.:       Anne Kemper, wife to John Kemper, one
            Negro woman and Negro child now in posses-
```

|Dau.:|Mary Hitt, wife of Harmon Hitt - one tract of land in Culpeper County, 400 a. to be equally divided. Eight Dubloons cash to buy a Negro with in room of one given her before by me which Died.|

Dau.: sion of John Kemper, her husband, and with

Dau.: Mary Hitt, wife of Harmon Hitt - one tract of land in Culpeper County, 400 a. to be equally divided. Eight Dubloons cash to buy a Negro with in room of one given her before by me which Died.

Dau.: Eve Porter - wife to Samuel Porter - 150 a. same bought of Charles Taylor, also 8 Doubloons

Son: Jacob Weaver - one tract 221 a. on Crummies Run, one Negro boy and one Negro girl

Dau.: Elizabeth Weaver - 150 a. lying on Crummies Run and being part of a Tract containing 539 acres, one Negro woman one Negro boy.

Dau.: Catharine Weaver - 150 a. part of tract of 539 a. above, one Negro man and one Negro girl.

Son: John Weaver - 150 a. on Crummie's Run, part of above 539 a., one Negro girl.

Son: Tilman Weaver - one Negro boy.

Dau.: Susanna Weaver - the remainder of above tract of land containing 539 a., being 89 a.
The remainder to be distributed among wife and children except my crop which is to be left in the hands of wife for her benefit and small children.

Exors: Wife, Anne Elizabeth, son Jacob, and son-in-law Samuel Porter.

Signed: Tilman Weaver

Wit.: William (his W mark) Norman, Tilman Martin, Thos. Marshall

Proved: 27 March 1760 by Tilman Martin and Thomas Marshall. Elizabeth Weaver and Jacob Weaver made motion & granted cert.

Pages 14-16: GEORGE FOOTE (Inventory & Appraisement)
Date: 28 June 1759
App'd by: Benj'a. Bullitt, James Seaton, John Catlett.
No total.
Ret.: 27 March 1760

Pages 16-18: JOSEPH WRIGHT (Will)
Date: 5 November 1759
Son :   (John - written in pencil) Wright
Daus: Hester Jackman
         Mary Russell
         Catharine Bailey
         All my whole Estate both real and per-
         sonal to be equally divided to them and
         their heirs forever
Exors: frieðds, William Russell and Thomas Jackman
Signed: Jos. (+) Wright
Wit.:   Lazarus Taylor, Richard McPherson, Elizabeth
         (X) Butler.
Codicil: 5 November 1759
Children: John Wright, Hester Jackman, Mary
         Russell and Catharine Bailey - all my
         real estate and "personal and remembering
         on Information by sundry of my neigh-
         bours that my son John had made a Con-
         veyance Deed to Capt. Elias Edmonds for
         that part of the land I now live on which
         he says he held by a Deed of Gift that I
         made to him some years past which I
         utterly disallow, revoke and deny that
         ever I made a Deed to him for any Land,
         except it was for that part which he
         lived on as far as the Division Lane as
         we formerly made" Declared to be a
         Recollection of Memory.
Prov.:   27 March 1760, by o. of Lazarus Taylor and
         Richard McPherson. William Russell and
         Thomas Jackman granted bond and cert.

Pages 18-19: EDWARD TWENTYMEN (Will) ... of Prince
              William County ...
Date: 20 April 1759
Wife: Elizabeth - land during her life
Son :   Benjamin - 200 a. in Prince William
Son :   John - home plantation & 200 a. adjoining
Dau.:   Alender - all my stock and household
         furniture, excepting one bed belonging to
         my son John
No executors named.
Wit.:   William Jett, William Threlkeld, Jesse
         Threlkeld

Signed: Edw'd. (+) Twentymen
Proved: 22 May 1760, by o. of William Jett and Jesse
Thraitkill. Letters of admr. obtained by
John Twentymen.

Page 19: JOHN COOK (Will)
Date: 5 January 1760
Dau: Elizabeth Page - one Weather
Dau.: Jane Pritchett - one ewe
Dau..: Sarah Cook - the rest of my estate, real
& personal and to be executrix
Signed: John (X) Cook
Wit.: Johnson, Isaac (X) Spark, William Marshall
Proved: 22 May 1760, on o. by John Son, Isaac
Sparks and William Marshall. Sarah Cook
made o. and obt. bond.

Page 20: WILLIAM BRADFORD (Appraisement)
Date: 28 February 1760
App'd. by: Alex'r. Bradford, Tran's. Day, John
Jones, sworn before Wm. Eustace, a justice
Not totalled.
Ret.: 26 June 1760

Page 21: JACOB SPILMAN (Inventory)
Date: 2 May 1760
App'd. by: Jacob Wever, Henry Utterback, Jacob
Holtzclaw
Total: L22.6.9
Retn: 24 July 1760

Pages 21-22: TIMOTHY REDDIN (Appraisement)
No date.
App'd. by: Dan'l. Bradford, Jeremiah Darnall,
Alex'r. Bradford
Total: L51.4.3
Ret.: 28 August 1760

Pages 22-23: JACOB SPILMAN (Sale of Estate)
Date: 3 May 1760
Admr.: Daniel Floweree
Total: L23.2
Purchasers: Dan'l. Floweree, John Morgan, Wm.
Reding, Humphrey Brook, John Churchill,
Elizabeth Spilman (bought nearly every-
thing), Mary Gent, Mrs. Keith, Peter Hitt,
Henry Utterback.
Retn.: 28 August 1760

Pages
24-25: JOHN CORDER (Inventory)
No date. Appr'd. by: William Dulin, David
Darnel. No. total.
Retn.: 25 September 1760

Pages
25-27: JOSEPH WRIGHT (Inventory)
No date. Appr'd. by: Thomas Porter, Jos. Hitt,
Hermon Hitt, sworn before Col. John Bell.
No total. Ordered by Court, 1760.
Retn.: 27 November 1761.

Page
27: JOHN COOKE (Inventory)
No date. Appr'd. by: Charles Morgan, Daniel
Bradford, Alexander Bradford, sworn before
William Grant. Total eval.: L64.11.3
Retn.: 26 February 1761

Pages
28-29: JOHN BROWN (Will) ... of Prince William
and Parish of Hamilton ...
Date: 1 October 1744
Son: John — one-half land
Son: Dixon - other half ... land to be equally
divided between the above named son - right
across the run called Brown's Run
Son: John - one featherbed and boulster
Exors: son, John and William Parnal
Signed: John Brown
Wit.: Lazarus Taylor (X), Wm (W) Delany, John
(£) Corder - 26 Feb. 1761.
Proved: 26 February 1761, exhibited by Lazarus Taylor
and William Dulany. Dixon Brown appointed
administrator.

Pages
29-30: JOHN ALLEN (Will)
Date: 3 November 1759
Son: John - all land in the Marsh Neck above
the Indian Spring Savannah - 3 slaves
Son: Thomas - all land below the Indian Spring
Savannah to the Great Savannah, a tract of
land in Culpeper Co. which John Frogg, gent.,
and myself took up - 2 Negroes

Son: William Allen - tract of land bought of John Hopper
          where Gerrad Edwards now lives - 2 Negroes - one
          feather bed and furniture - 2 cows and calves
Sons: Joseph and James - the land where I know live if
          they arrive to the age of 21 years - survivor to
          have it in case of one's death; if both should die
          to go to Son: William
Son: Joseph - 2 Negroes - 2 cows & claves - one feather
          bed and furniture
Son: James - 2 Negroes - 2 cows & calves - one feather
          bed and furniture
Dau.:   Ann Allen - 2 Negroes - 2 cows & calves - one
          feather bed and furniture
Wife: Ursila Allen - 9 Negroes and all the rest of estate
          for her life, then to be divided between 3 sons:
          William, Joseph, James and dau.: Ann
Exors: Wife, Ursila, and son, Thomas
Signed: John Allen
Wit.:   George Crump (X), Benjamin Crump (X), William
          Mcdanel (X)
Proved: 26 March 1761, by o. of George Crump, Benjamin
          Crump and William McDaniel. Cert. to obt. probate
          issued to Ursila Allen and Thomas Allen

Pages
30-31   JOHN FINNIE (Will)
              Date: 14 August 1760
Wife: Ann Finney - all and every part of my Estate both
          real and Personal during her life and after her
          decease to my Dau: Hannah
Exors.:   Wife, Ann Finney and loving friend, John James
Signed: John (his J mark) Finney
Wit.:   Alex. Parker, Daniel Newlan, Jane (I) Newlan
Proved: 27 November 1760, by Jane Newlan, presented by
          John James and Ann Finney. Further proved 26
          March 1761 by Daniel Newland

Pages
31-32:   DAVENPEART LEGG (Inventory)
              Order of Court dated 26 Febr. 1761
App'd. by: Absolem Ramey, James Hogain, William Hogain
Total eval.: L6.6.3
Ret.:   26 March 1761

- 13 -

Page
32:                JOHN CORDER (Addition to Inventory)
                   No date
Admin'x.:   Patience Corder. No evaluation.
Ret.:   28 May 1761

Pages
32-33:   DAVENPORT LEGG (Estate Account)
                   No date
Adm'r.: Daniel Hogan
Details: 18 Jan. 1761: To burying your Husband:
                   3½ yds of Linnen for a Burying
                   Shirt - 10s
                   To a Sheet for D⁰ - 10s
                   To a Coffin   10s
                   To 5 qts Rum at 8/- 10s
                   To 2 qts Brandy   3s
                   To Diging the Grave 5s
Ret.:   28 May 1761

Pages
33-35:   JACOB HOLTZCLAW (Inventory)
                   No date
App'd. by: John Duncan, John Wright, John Sinkler
No total
Ret.:   25 June 1761

Page
35:                RICHARD TULLOS (Remainder of Estate)
                   No date
Admr.:   Edward Larrance
Details: To cash - L11.4.1
                   To Tobacco - 520
Ret.:   23 October 1760

Page
36:                RICHARD REDMAN (Account of Administrator)
                   No date
Admr.:   Jos'h. Neavill
Details: To Mr. Humphrey Brooke Clk - 72 Tob.
         " Mr. Ben Waller   32 Tobo.
         " Mr. Samuel Earle   L2.4.3½
         " a Rent to Fairfax   L2.10
Ret.:   25 June 1761

Pages
36-37:   EDWARD TWENTYMEN (Inventory)
                   Order of Court dated 21 May 1760
App'd by: Wm. Dulany, Lott Hackley, Charles (X) Duncan
Total eval.: L32.9.2
Ret.:   25 June 1761

Pages
37-38:   WILLIAM WYAT   (Inventory)
                   No date
App'd by: John Syars, Jas. Foley, John Obanion.
No total
Retn: 23 July 1761

Page
38:             JOHN BROWN (Appraisement)
                   Court Order dated 25 June 1761
App'd by: Alexander Bradford, John Butler, Thos. Smith
Total eval: L80.8.0
Ret.:   27 August 1761

Page
39:             JOSEPH WRIGHT (Estate Account)
                   No date, no administrator named.
Details: TO PAID: Capt. Elias Edmonds, Harman Hitt, Karr
         Bayley, Joseph Hudnall, John Reddish, William
         Robinson, Henry Moffett, Samuel Earle, Col. William
         Blackwell, Edward Ball, Thomas Jackman, William
         Russell
Ret.:   27 August 1761

Pages
39-40:   ALEXANDER SMITH (Appraisement)
                   Court Order dated 26 March 1761
App'd by: William Reading, David Holder, William Preston
Total Eval: L80.9.11
Ret.:   25 September 1761

Page
40:             WILLIAM WYAT (Inventory - part of Estate)
                   No date
App'd by: John Obanian, Jas. Foley, Jno. Syars
Total: L1.18.6
Ret.:   26 November 1761

Pages
41-43:   BRYAN OBANON (Will)
                      Date: 4 September 1760
Son: John Obanon - plantation whereon he now lives,
              212 a. - Negro woman Judy, after death of son
              John and his wife Sarah, sd. Negro (if living)
              to granddaughter Sarah, dau. of John - "the said
              Negroe Judy shall after my Decease be Totally
              Exempted from Labouring without Doors during her
              Natural life." Still and young unbroken horse.
Son: William - plantation on which he lives, 212 a.
Son: Samuel - plantation and lands in King George
              County, 300 a. - L100 - all wearing apparel
Dau.:   Elizabeth Ambrose - L60 - chair & horses
Dau.:   Ann Miller - L100
Gr.son: Thos. Obanon, son of son John - "plantation
              whereon I now live", 220 a., "on this side of
              Broad run ..."
Gr.son: Wm. Obanon, son of my son Wm. Obannon - "remaining
              tract of Land I now live on lying Chiefly on the
              North side of the said Broad run."
Gr.son: Bryan Obanon - son of my son John Obanon - negro
              girl, Lucy
Gr.son: Bryan Obanon, son of my son, Wm. Obanon - negro
              girl, Cate
              "... to Each my Grand Children both Male & Female
              being twenty-seven in Number the sum of Ten
              pounds Current Each ..."
Natural
Children: Aron Johnston and Francis Johnston, children of
              Margaret Johnston - plantation and lands in
              Frederick County, 257a. - should they die before
              they come of age or marry the part of one to go
              to the survivor, if both should die, the bequest
              to go to Bryan Obanon, Grandson, son of son
              John OBanon." "... direct & Appoint my son-in-law,
              Jacob Hite, my Grand Daughter Elizabeth Hite to
              have the Care & Managemt of the said Children..."
              To Francis Johnston - "500 lbs. tobacco to be
              yearly paid to Margaret Johnston - Mother of the
              aforesaid Francis for the support & maintenance of
              the said Francis during the space of four years."
Exors: Sons, John and William; son-in-law, Jacob Hite
Signed: Bryan (x) Obanon
Wit.:   Elias Edmonds, Sam'l. Earle, Jas. Rogers
Proved: 25 February 1762, by o. of Elias Edmonds, Sam'l.
              Earle, Jas. Rogers.

Pages
43-47:   JOHN ALLEN   (Inventory)
          Court Order dated 21 March 1761
App'd by: Daniel Bradford, Alexander Bradford, George
          Crump
Total: L1283.15.5
Ret.:   25 March 1762

Pages
47-48:   ANDREW BEARD   (Inventory)
          Court Order dated 26 November 1761
App'd by: Edward Humston, John Ashby, Maximillian Berryman
Total: L8.17.4
Ret.:   25 March 1762

Pages
48-50:   BRYAN OBANON   (Inventory)
          Court Order dated 25 February 1762
App'd by: George Lamkin, John Rector, William Edmonds,
          William Wright
Total: L863.6.2
Ret.:   27 March 1762

Pages
51:       WILLIAM WIAT   (Added Inventory)
          Date: 27 May 1762
App'd by: John Siers, Jas. Foley, John Obanon
Total: 18s. 6d.
Ret.:   27 May 1762

Pages
51-52:   JACOB HOLTZCLAW   (Estate Account)
          no date. No administrator listed
Details: To going twice to Frederick to make Sale of
          the Land - 3 days each time at 7/6 per day
          To paid Land Tax of 2489 at 2/3
          To paid the Dutch parson for burying the dec'd - 1L
          To paid for the coffin — 7s.6d.
Retn: 29 May 1762

Pages
52-54:   TILMAN WEAVER   (Inventory)
          No date
App'd by: John Wright, Jeremiah Darnal, John Sincklear
No total. Returned: 24 June 1762.

Pages
54-55:   JOHN FINNIE   (Inventory)
              Court Order dated 27 November 1760
App'd by: Geo. Crump, Edw'd. Humston, Dan'l. Bradford
No total. Returned: 22 July 1762

Page
56:           JACOB SPILMAN   (Estate Account)
Admr.:   Daniel Flowers
Ret.:.   22 July 1762

Page
56:           THOMAS SEAMAN   (Inventory)
              No date
App'd by: E. E. Home, Martin Hardin
Retn: 26 August 1762

Pages
57-58:   HENRY CHURCHILL, ESQ.   (Inventory)
              No date
App'd by: H. Brooke, Thos. McClanaham, Whart'n Ransdell
Total: L239.3.7½
Ret.:   27 August 1762
              Then follows the sale of the estate, listing
              many titles of books sold and equipment, etc.
              pages 58-62. Retn: 27 August 1762

Pages
63:           HENRY CHURCHILL, ESQ.   (Estate Account)
              No date
Adm'r.:   John Churchill
Details: To Alexander Woodrows Acct for Funeral
              expenses - L9.5.10½
              To Hen ry Brinkers do L10
              To Mr. Wm Ellzey for lawyers fees
              To paid Colo. Armistead Churchill
              By Cash rec'd of Parson Clug
Ret.:   27 August 1762

Pages
63-64:   ALEXANDER BEECH   (Will) .. of Hamilton Parish ..
              Date: 11 March 1762
Dau.:   Elizabeth Butler - 1s. sterling & what she has already
Son :   Peter - 1s. sterling & what he has already
Son :   William - 1s. sterling & what he has already
Dau.:   Mary Beach (sic) tract of land where I now dwell

Wife: Margaret Beach - all the rest of my estate, to
             be divided among: son, Alexander, son Thomas and
             dau. Sarah Beach.
Exor.:   John Barber
Signed: Alexander (B) Beach
Wit: Henry Smith, Henry Morless, George Smith
Proved: 24 September 1762, by o. of Henry Smith and
             George Smith.

Page
65:                 THOMAS SEAMONS (Inventory)
                    No date
App'd by: Edward Humston, Dan'l. Delashumate, Edward Humston, Jr.
Total: L7.17.1½
Ret.:   24 September 1762

Page
65:                 HENRY MAHORNER (Estate Account)
                    No date
Admr.:   Jean Mahorner
Details: Burying my husband and expenses
Ret.:   24 March 1763

Page
66:                 HENRY MAHORNER (Inventory)
                    Court Order dated October, 1762
App'd by: Maxill'n Berryman, Francis Fennell, William Keirns
Total: L3.8.3
Ret.:   24 March 1763

Pages
66-67:   RICHARD REDMAN (Estate Account)
                    No date
Admr.:   Jos'h. Neavill
Details: To pd. Capt. George Neavill his Rent
          Benjamin Waller
Ret.:   24 March 1763

Page
67:                 GEORGE WHEATLEY (Division of Estate)
                    Date: 27 November 1762
Admrs.:   John Duncan, Nath'l. Dodd, Paul Williams
Div.:   To Joseph Wheatley - 2 Negroes - he paying
          L5 to his brother William Wheatley
Ret.:   24 March 1763

Pages
67-71:   THOMAS STAMPS (Will)
                 Date: 28 July 1761
Son: Timothy - piece or parcel of land whereon he
                 now lives, 150 a. more or less - it being part
                 of the land purchased of the Rev. Lawrence
                 Debuts of the province of Maryland
Son: John - the remainder of the above land
                 The survivor of each to have the entire tract.
Gr.Dau.: Molly Stamps, dau. of my son, Thomas, dec'd.,
                 L15, when she arrives to the age of 18
Gr.Dau.: Hannah Stamps, dau. of my son, Thomas, dec'd.,
                 L15, when she arrives to the age of 18
                 If neither of them should live to come of age
                 the money to be divided among the children
                 then living.
Son :   William - tract of land at the Walnut branch,
                 631a. - feather bed & furniture - 5 head cattle
Son :   George - parcel of land purchased of Lewis
                 Tackett, 142½ a. - 5 head cattle - feather bed
                 and furniture.
Dau.:   Elizabeth Tackett (heirs of) - the 142½ a. should
                 George Stamps die without heirs
Dau.:   Elizabeth Tackett - L10
Dau.:   Mary Shackleford - L10 & 800 lbs. tobacco
Wife: Mary - use of all my moveable estate both Negroes
                 and stock of all kinds, as long as she remains a
                 widow, if she marries to be divided among the
                 children.
                 "If my dau. Mary Shackleford should die without
                 any more children lawfully begotten of her Body
                 or that shall not arrive at Lawful Age that her
                 part of my Moveable Estate may fall to her two
                 children she had by James Allen to be equally
                 divided among them.
Exors: Sons, Timothy, John and William
Wit.:   Archibald Allen, Mary Rhodas, James Stewart, Jun'r.
Signed: Thomas Stamps
Proved: 26 May 1763, by Archibald Allen, Mary Rhodas, &
                 James Stewart, Jun'r. Above exors. qualified.

Pages
71-72:   ROBERT WOOD (Inventory)
                 Date: 25 May 1763
App'd by: John O'Banon, Jas. Foley, George Berry
Total: L25.6.6
Ret.:   26 May 1763

- 20 -

Pages
72-73:   WILLIAM HAND   (Inventory)
        No date
App'd by: Wm. Roberts, Benjamin Ashby, Francis Burgess
Total: L48.12.2
Ret.:   26 May 1763

Pages
73-75:   TIMOTHY READING (Estate Account)
        No date
Admr.: William Reading
Details: CASH TO: Mr. Darnall, Cryer-5s.; Henry Utter-
back for burying Timothy Reading & wife-1L;
Martin Hardin, William Pickett, Martin Pickett,
William Cunninghame, William Norman, Mary Gent,
Elizabeth Marr, Mr. Brooke, Peter Hitt, Mr.
Jeremiah Darnall, Mr. William Ellrey, schooling
two children, John Rector Orphan the ballance
of the Estate due him 6L, Nathaniel Rector
Orphan of Do upon Account of his part of his
fathers Estate L11.3.1½.
Ret.:   26 May 1763

Pages
75-76:   JOHN COPPEDGE (Division of Estate)
        Date: 29 March 1763
Divided by: Gilson Foote, James Seaton, James Murray
Details: Widow Elizabeth - Negroes - L14.19.3; William
Coppedge - 2 Negroes - cash L2.9.6.3 farthings
(delivered to John Catlett, gdn. to sd. Wm.)
Sally Coppedge - Negro girl, cash L9.19.6.3
Elizabeth Coppedge - 2 Negroes - Cash L17.9.3f.
John Coppedge - Negro - Cash L3.9.6.3f.
Ret.:   23 June 1763

Pages
76-77:   ROBERT WOOD (Inventory) (Addition)
        Date: 4 June 1763
App'd by: John O'Banon, James Foley, George Berry
Total: L3.12.9
Ret.:   23 June 1763

Pages
77-78:   ROBERT WOOD (Sale of Estate)
        Date: 4 June 1763
Made by: John Willoughby and John Laws
Some Purchasers: George Berry, Sarah Wood, Benjamin Willoughby,

Simon Miller, John Willoughby, John Neavill,
John Sias, Richard Healey, John Laws, Alexander
Farrow, John Cornwell, Henry Berry, Yelverton
Peyton, Samuel Simpson, Evan'Griffith, Thomas
Hogain, Joshua Joinianse, William Owens, Joseph
Morin, James Sias, John Chapman.
Total: L37.13.7
Ret.:   23 June 1763

Pages
78-79:   THOMAS STAMPS (Inventory)
                   Order of Court: 26 May 1763
App'd by: Rich'd. Hampton, Archibald Allen, Pamach George
No total. Ret.: 25 August 1763

Page
80:                JAMES HARRILL (Inventory)
                   No date
App'd by: Nicholas George, John Shumate, George Turberville
          Kenner
Total: L50
Ret.:   27 October 1763

Page
80-81:   JOHN GARNER (Inventory)
                   Court Order dated 22 July 1762
App'd by: James Arnold, Wm. Morgan, Paul Williams
Total: L160.7.6
Ret.:   23 March 1764

Pages
81-82:   JAMES HARRILL (Estate Account)
                   No date
Admr.:   Daniel Harrill
Details: PAID TO: Alexander Cunninghame, Howson Kenner,
          Martin Hardin, John Harrill, James Wood, Clement
          Norman, John & Moses Harrill
Estate sold: L32.12.11
Ret.:   23 February 1764

Pages
83-85:   JOHN MAUZY, JR. (Will)
                   Date: 20 February 1764
Wife: Betty - slaves, land whereon I now live during her
          widowhood
Dau.:   Peggy - at the time when she reaches 18, one-half
          of lan d given to wife, but if she should remarry

all the estate of 321 acres to go to dau.
Margaret and <u>dau.</u> Molly

Dau.: Peggy - slaves - equal share of stock and
household furniture at the time of her
marriage or 18 years of age.

Dau.: Molly - 22 a. of land in Culpeper, 300 a.
about 5 miles from Winchester which is my
property for which I have sued Jonathan
Parkins for in Chancery in the General
Court - Negroes - equal part of estate at
the time of her marriage or 18 years of age.

Dau.: Betty - 164 a. bought of Robert Jackson
lying on a Branch of Cherry's Branch above
the mouth of Back Creek in Frederick County -
198 a. in Hampshire County lying on a Branch
of the Maple Bottom branch of Crooked Run a
Branch of the No. River of Cacaphon - 254 a.
of land at the end of the Spring Gap Mountain -
78 a. of Patented Land on the north side of
the Sandy Ridge in Hampshire which I desire
may be sold & the money to be Delivered her
at her age or marriage.
If all should die before becoming of age
without heirs the entire estate, except 2
slaves given to wife, to be divided between "my
nephews John Roussau, William Roussau & Henry
Roussau ..."

Signed: Jno. Mauzy
Exors: Wife Betty, brothers Henry and Peter Mauzy and
William Roussau.
Wit.: Thomas Conway, John Edge, John Luttrell
Codicil: Dau. Molly to have Negro Ginn if widow should
remarry, and two entries of Land in Hampshire
County - 400 a. on the head of the Sick branch
of Sleepy Creek about two miles from David
Whites - 200 a. at the Grass Licks or Spaw
Water Springs. Dau. Margaret - 50 a. in this
county joyning Furr's & Brents Patents & Thomas
Railey.
Proved: 26 July 1764, by Thomas Conway, John Edge and
John Luttrell. Cert. to obtain probate granted
to Betty Mauzy, Henry Mauzy and Henry Roussau.

Page 85: RICHARD FOOTE, Dr. in Acct. with Mary Foote,
Gdn. of Said Richard.
Date: 2 August 1764
Details: Board and clothing from December 1760 to 1764, L2.1.1
Ret.: 23 August 1764

Page
85:        GEORGE BEARD   (Inventory)
           Date: 4 September 1764
App'd by: James Young, Geo. Neavil, Edw'd. Dickeson
Total: L8.13   Ret.: 27 September 1764.

Page
86:        JOHN MAUZY   (Inventory)
           No date
App'd by: Houson Kenner, Thos. Raley, Jonathan Gibson
Total: L431.14
Ret.:   28 September 1764

Pages
87-88:   JOHN GLASCOCK   (Will)
           Date: 8 March 1765
Wife: Mary - half of estate, real and personal
Dau.:   Frances - other half
Signed: John Glascock
Exors: wife Mary Glascock and Thomas Glascock
Wit.:   Gregory Glascock, Aaron Drummond, John Hendren
Proved:.   22 April 1765, by o. of Aaron Drummond and John
           Hendren. Thomas Glascock gave bond and was
           granted cert. to obt. probate.

Pages
88-89:   JOHN GLASCOCK   (Inventory)
           Court order dated 27 May 1765
App'd by: Simon Miller, John Obanon, William Obannon
Total: L40.8.9
Ret.:   24 Jun e 1765

Pages
89-90:   WILLIAM WYATT   (Estate Account)
           No date
Admr.:   Winifred Sparks
Details: PAID TO: Archibald Henderson; appraisers, Jno.
           Obanion, Jno. Scias, Jr., James Foley; James
           Douglass; Mark Canton; Benj. Willoughby in part
           of his wife's share of the estate; Thomas Leach-
           man & Wife for do; Samuel Baylis; John Glascock;
           John Metalf; Simon Miller; Thomas Dodson; Richard
           Cundiff; Wm. Ellsey.
Ret.:   23 July 1765

Pages
91-92:
 DANIEL FRAZIER (Will)
 Date: 28 May 1765 ... of Hamilton Parish ...
 Samuel Anderson Joiner "my chest at Reuben
 Berrys and all thats in it ..."
 Catherine Thatcher - "the remainder of my estate..
 if she is living if dead to .. Charles Haynies
 Eldest son ... Mary Bradford to "keep my mare till
 August next and then deliver to Catherine Thatcher
 Exor.: Charles Haynie
 Signed: Daniel (X) Frazier
 Wit.: Dan'l. Bradford, Alex'r. Bradford, Jo's. Morgan
 Proved: 26 August 1765, by o. of Daniel Bradford and
 Alexander Bradford. On oath of Catherine Thatcher
 cert. of admr. granted, the named exor. refused.

Pages
92-93:
 ROBERT WOOD (Administrator's Account)
 No date
 Admr.: John Law and John Willoughby
 Details: CASH PAID BY: Colo. John Baylis, Joshua Morgan,
 Marg't. Coming, Even Grifis, John Allison,
 Dan'l. Payne, Capt. George Neavil.
 Ret.: 26 August 1765

Pages
93-94:
 JOHN MAUZEY (Estate Account)
 Exor.: Henry Mauzey
 Details: TO PAID: William Lambert, John Knox, Alexander
 Cunninghame, John Lockart, Thomas Railey, John
 Peters, Clemmount Norman, Nimrod Ashby, Addam
 Haymaker, to the office for Bryan Bruin's W't,
 To the office for six warrants for Sam'l.
 Prickett, John Ashby, Richard Mynatt for George
 Roling, Jacob Adams for Thomas Triplett, George
 Lamkin, Gabriel Jones for a clerk's note, Gavin
 Lawson, Gavin Lawson for Docter Mich'e Wallice,
 Robert Brent, Charles Porter, Charles Morgan,
 John Ralls, Colo. Martin for John Rausau's W't,
 Robert Downman for attendance at C't., James
 Stuart for Do, Colo. John Bell for Quitrents,
 Original Young, Henry Mauzey's exp's attending
 Fred'k. Court Nov'r & Decem. 1764 & March &
 Aprill, May & July 1765, Bruton Jones, Wm. Waite,
 Dinah James, Henry Neff, Rodum Tullos

RECEIVED OF: John Roberson, William Miller,
Maj'r. Jerrard Fookes, William Murray, William
Pickring, Randol Kinnerly, my Lord Fairfax,
Samuel Prichett, John Capper, Rich'd Colyer,
Cap't. John Gibson for Moses Hays, Sheriff of
Fred'k for Geo. Hogg, Elias Edmonds for William
Miller, James Scott on the Act of Robt. Scott,
Moses Hayes, Charles Smith, John Moffett for
Joseph Edwards.
Ret.: 23 September 1765

Pages
94-95:   JAMES MORGAN (Inventory)
         No date
App'd. by: Fras. Bronaugh, Vinson (X) Garner, Wm. (his
         H mark) Settle
Total: L55.0.3
Ret.: 24 September 1765

Pages:
95-97:   RICHARD LUTTRELL (Will)
         Date: 10 September 1764
Son: Michael - 70 a. whereon he now lives, on the same
side of the run James lives on, bounded by me
Son: James - 70 a. whereon he now lives
Son: Samuel - 70 a., where John Colliers formerly lived
and bounded by me
Son: John - 70 a. whereon he now lives & bounded by me
Son: Richard - "my new Patent of land containing 58 a.
whereon he now lives"
Dau.: Unstiss Luttrell - part of land bought of George
Crump lying on the south side of Rock run that
Rins from John Nelsons old field to William
Rousaws mill Bounded by Woods line Forsyths Line
and Dearmons line .. 80 a.
Dau.: Mary - land on the West side of said run bounded
by Woods line, Dearmons line and Peters line and
the Ridge Path that goes from John Combses to
John Nelsons, 80 a.
Dau.: Susanna - the rest of said land on the west side
of said Path, 80 a.
Son: Robert - plantation whereon I now live and remaining
part of my said land adjoining to my said Plantation
74a., one feather bed & furniture, new Gunn, sword
& Cotuchbox.
Dau.: Catharine Corum - L5
Dau.: Sarah - L5 and young bay Mare Branded on the near
buttock I L to be delivered to her at the age of

```
                18 or marryed.
Gr.Dau.:        Mary Coram - L5
Wife:           Mary - all the rest of my moveable Estate to be
                hers for her natural life, and equally divided
                among children after her death.
Exors.:         Wife Mary and son Richard
Signed:         Richard (R) Luttrell
Wit.:           Edward (his E mark) Larrance Sen'r., Edward
                Larrance, Richard Larrance.
Proved:         26 May 1766 by o. of witnesses named above.
                Cert. granted to Richard and Robert Luttrell
                to obt. probate.
```

Pages
97-99:   RICHARD LUTTRELL (Inventory)
                Date: 14 June 1766
App'd by: Edward (E) Larrance, William Rousau, Thomas
                Raily.
Total: Ret.: 23 June 1766

Pages
99-100:   JAMES DRUMMOND (Inventory)
                Court Order dated June, 1766
App'd by: Rich'd. Luttrell, Thos. Priest, John Cattlett
Total: L19.19.6
Ret.:   28 July 1766

Pages
100-105:   DUFF GREEN (Inventory)
                Date: 9 & 10 June 1766
App'd by: John Bell, Whart'n Ransdell, J. Brooke
Admrs.:   William Green, John Green
Total: L1196.14.2½
Ret.:   29 July 1766

Page
105   MORGAN DARNALL, JR. (Noncupative Will)
                Date: 30 September 1765
Bro.:   Isaac Darnall - land and plantation of 150 a.,
                horse, bridle and saddle, all wearing apparrell,
                all debts due me in Carrolina
Bro.:   Waugh Darnall - L5 due for rent of my plantation
                Mother and Bro. Waugh's wife all my money in my
                Pocket Book in Equal Partition
                John Wood, son of Samuel Wood as much money out of
                my Estate as will pay for one years Schooling
Bro.:   John Darnall - Rifle gun
Exor.:   Father, Morgan Darnall

- 27 -

Wit.:   Jean (her X mark) Darnall, Jeames Wheatly,
          Eliz. Darnall
Proved: 29 July 1766, by o. of Elizabeth Darnall and
          Jane Darnall. Morgan Darnall granted cert.

Page
106:          ALEXANDER SMITH (Estate Account)
              No date
Admr.:   Jane Smith
Ret.:   29 July 1766

Page
106:          MORGAN DARNALL, JR. (Inventory)
              Order or Court dated July 1766
App'd by: Nathaniel Todd, James Arnold, Paul Williams
Total eval.: L26.12s.6d.   Retn: 26 August 1766

Page
107:          CHARLES MORGAN, SEN'R (Will)
              Date: 5 December 1758 .. of Hamilton Parish
          in Prince William County ..
Children: Seven of my children has had and received their
          full parts in purportion of my Estate - the
          Seven Children before spoken of and above mentioned
          is (viz): Charles, Simon, William, Benjamin,
          James, Alice and Mary Morgan.
Wife: Anne - 1/3 part of personal estate
Son :   John - 2/3 remaining part
Exor: Son, John Morgan
Signed: Charles Morgan
Wit: John Edwards, Ganet (X) Edwards, James (X) Edwards
Proved: 26 September 1766, by o. of John Edwards, Gerrard
          Edward and James Edwards. John Morgan granted cert.

Pages
108-109:   BENJAMIN BULLITT (Will) of Hamilton Pr.
              Date: 3 May 1766
Son: Joseph - all in his possession & 2s. 6p. sterling
Son: Thomas - 2 tracts of land in Province of Maryland
          and Situate the one in a fork of Mattioman Creek
          Purchased of one Hutcherson and where my father
          Joseph Bullitt was buried, the other lying on
          Daniels Branch and was Surveyed by one Lomax &
          1s.6d.
Dau.:   Seth Combs - all that is in the possession of sd.
          Seth & John Combs & 1s.6d. Sterling
Son :   Cuthbert - 1s.6d., besides what he has deeds for ..

Dau.:   Elizabeth Bullitt - one Negro girl named Sarah &
her child named Charles - and her increase to
Elizabeth's heirs lawfully begotten of her body and
in default of such heirs to be equally divided

Son s: between my Six sons: William Burditt alias Bullitt,
John Bullitt, George Bullitt, Benoni Bullitt,
Parmanus Bullitt and Burwell Bullitt, also ten
silver teaspoons, one feather bed - to be rec'd.
at the age of 18 or the day of marriage.

Wife: Sarah - and 6 sons - 3 Negroes, one mulatto, one
servant boy and one mulatto woman.
The rest of the estate not mentioned to be used
to support the above 6 sons and wife, and after
her death to be divided among them equally.

Exors: Sons, Thomas and Cuthbert and wife Sarah.

Signed:.   Benjamin (his B mark) Bullitt

Wit.:   Jon'a Gibson, William Conway, Alex. Parker

Proved: 27 October 1766, by o. of Jonathan Gibson, William
Conway. Thomas & Cuthbert Bullitt granted cert.
of Probate.

Pages
109-110:   JOHN MAUZY   (Estate Account)
           No date.

Admr.:   Henry Mauzy

Details: TO PAID:. Colo. Martin, Colo. John Bell, Martin
Pickett, Colo. Tho: Martin, Capt. John Greenfield,
Colo. Tho.: Martin for a deed issued out in Betty
Mauzey & Margaret Mauzy's name, (Same) for a Deed
in Betty Mauzy's name Daughter of John Mauzey's
dec'd., John Keith, Jacob Hite, William Love for
Woodron & Nelson, Expences at Frederick Court,
Gavin Lawson. BY RECEIVED OF: Sheriff of Frederick
James Keith, James Withers, Moses Hayes, my bro.
John Mauzy's Estate for one sett of Surveying
Instruments & Books, Rich'd Collar, Mr. Lawson.

Retn: 28 October 1766

Pages
110-112:   WILLIAM PICKETT   (Will)
           Date: 26 September 1766

Dau.:   Sarah Pickett - Negro girl, one featherbed & furniture, one cow & calf at the day she marries or
when 18 years.

Wife: Elizabeth - all estate both real and personal except lands held in Caroline & Culpeper counties.

Son: Ruben - "the land I hold in Culpepper County and

Caroline County shall be sold in that year that
Ruben Pickett shall arrive to the age of twenty-
one years or as soon as can be conveynanly sold
to the best advantage by my Exb'r ... my intent
is that the land I hold in Caroline County after
my mothers death and the money arising from the
sale of the Lands of Each County be disposed of in
manner and form following, first it is my desire
that my Executors pay Maryann Marshall out of the
Land of Culpeper and Caroline L50 .. pay my dau.
Sarah Pickett L70 .. out of the Sales .. it is
also my desire the residue of the money arising
from the sale of the land in Culpeper and Caroline
Countys shall be equally divided between my two
sons George Pickett and Ruben Pickett ... after
the death of my wife .. Elizabeth .. that all my
Estate both real & personal .. shall be sold ..
to be equally divided among my three sons John
Pickett, Martin Pickett and William Pickett.

Exors.:	Wife Elizabeth, sons: Martin and William
Signed:	Wm. Pickett
Wit.:	Henry Kamper, James (X) Peney, Philliee (her X mark) Kamper, Sarah (X) Peney.
Proved:	24 November 1766 by o. of James Penny and Henry Kamper. Martin and William Pickett granted cert. for obtaining probate.

**Page
112:**

JOHN FINNEY (Additional Inventory)
No date.

App'd by: Geo. Crump, Dan'l. Bradford, Edward Humston.
Retn: 25 November 1766

**Pages
112-114:**

RICHARD HAMPTON (Will)
Date: 24 November 1766

Wife:	Martha - house, plantation, Negroes & household furniture during her widowhood
Dau.:	Elizabeth - after marriage or death of wife - a Negro boy, Negro girl, wench, one silver Castor
Dau.:	Sarah - tract of land on Goose Creek in the Co. of Fauquier - 200 a. - 4 slaves after death or marriage of wife - silver soup spoon.
Dau.:	Martha - 5 slaves, after death or marriage of wife - 3 silver tablespoons & 3 teaspoons
Son:	William - 5s. sterling
Son:	Richard - 5s. sterling

Gr.Son: Richard Hampton, son of William, after death or
          marriage of wife - 2 Negroes
Gr.Son: Gale Hampton, son of Richard, after death or
          marriage of wife - 1 Negro
          After death or marriage of wife all household
          furniture to be divided among three daughters.
          Land in Hampshire and my waggon sold immediately
          after my decease and money used to pay just debts.
          After death of wife & debts paid the land where-
          on I now live be Sold by sons William and Richard
          and the money used to be laid out in land at their
          discretion and be equally divided between their
          two sons Richard and Gale Hampton, "but my will is
          that my two sons have the liberty of living on the
          Lands Purchased during their lives."
Wife: (Martha) - riding Chair and Harness
Exors: Wife, son William and son-in-law Richard Lingham
          Hall.
Signed: Ric'd. Hampton
Wit: Charles Morehead, Sarah Sinkler, John Bell
Proved: 22 December 1766, by o. of Charles Morehead and
          John Bell. Martha Hampton granted Cert. for
          obtaining probate.

Pages
114-115:   THOMAS SEMAN (SEAMAN) (Estate Account)
                 No date
Admr.:   Martin Hardin
Details: TO: John Morehead, Colo. William Blackwell, Moses
          Seaman, Rhodam Tullos, Messr's. Woodron & Nelson
Retn.:   26 May 1767

Pages
115-118:   RICHARD HAMPTON (Inventory)
                 Court Order dated December 1766
App'd by: Whart'n Ransdell, Wm. Ransdell, Edmond Basye
Total eval.: L657.5.10
Retn.:   22 June 1767

Pages
118-120:   ROBERT MATTHIS (Inventory)
                 No date.
App'd by: George Rogers, James Bayley, John Tomlin.
No total. Retn.: 22 June 1767

Pages
120-121:   MARGARET HOGAN (Will)
                 Date: 20 November 1767

Son: Charles Hogan - one bed and furniture, 2 iron
            pots, 3 plates, 1 dish, 4 Basons, 4 head cattle,
            2 wheels, 2 tables, 6 chairs, and "all the rest
            of my Lumbers"
"Grate grand Child'? Frances Banester - one bed and Rugg
            one small Pott
Dau.:   Mary Banester - one large chest
Signature: Margret (X) Hogan
Wit.:   Joh Williams, Ann (X) Williams, Fra Moore.
Proved: 23 June 1767, by o. of John Williams and Ann
            Williams. Charles Hogain granted cert. for
            obtaining Letters of Adm'r.

Pages
121-123:   MARGRET HOGAIN   (Inventory)
                Date: Crt. Order June 1767
App'd by: John Jett, William Triplett, John Williams, sworn
            before Mr. Gilson Foote, gentleman one of his
            majisties Justices for the said County
Total eval.:   L17.10.4
Ret.:   27 July 1767

Pages
123-125:   CHARLES MORGAN   (Inventory)
                Court Order dated September 1766
App'd by: Alexander Bradford, John Jones, Benjamin Snelling
Total eval.:   L76.7.6, Cash: L1.10.7
Ret.:   27 July 1767

Page
125:            JOHN GRANT (Will)
                Date: 5 October 1767
                "It my Will and pleasher is to leave my howle
                Estate which God hath Blest me with to James
                Duff his heirs and assines Being weak and low
                But has my Sencies."
Signed: John Grant
Wit.:   Charles Martin, John Colvin
Proved: 23 November 1767 by o. of Charles Martin & John
            Colvin. James Duff made o. and granted cert. for
            obtaining Letters of Administration.

Pages
125-126:   JOHN NEAVILL (Will) ... of Hamilton Parish ..
                Date: 24 April 1767
Son: John - 1s. sterling
Son: Robert - 1s. sterling

Son:	Gabriel - 1s. sterling
Son:	Henry - 1s. sterling
Dau.:	Kitty Fitzgerald - 1s. sterling
Dau.:	Ann Fishback - 1s. sterling
Dau.:	Elizabeth Taylor - 1s. sterling
Dau.:	Sarah Redman - 1s. sterling
Dau.:	Mary Neavill - 1s. sterling
Son:	Thomas - "all the rest of my Estate, both real & personall .."
Signed:	John (his J mark) Neavill
Exors.:	friends, George Neavill and John Buchanan and gdns. of son Thomas till he comes to the age of 21 years
Wit.:	James Young, Mary Barrott, Alex'r. Parker
Proved:	25 April 1768, by o. of James Young and Alexander Parker. William Carr made o., cert. granted him for obtaining letters of adm'r ... "it appearing that the Executors therein named refused to take upon them the Execution thereof."

Pages
126-130: MRS. MARY TYLER (Inventory)
Court Order dated: 22 August 1766
App'd by: Thomas Priest, Richard Luttrill, William Rousau
No total. Retn: 25 April 1768.

Pages
130-131: PETER PEARCE (Will)
Date: 8 February 1768

Son:	John - 1 Negro boy
Daus. & Son:	Roseannah and Susannah Pearce, and John - one Negroe girl and "her increase in equal partition to be divided when the youngest viz. Susannah shall become of age .."
Wife:	Lidya - land and plantation bought of William Waugh during her natural life, also tract bought of John Ferguson for same term and at her death to go his heirs at law, she to pay the taxes annually. Enough livestock and moveable estate sold to pay debts - the remainder divided between 2 daus., except one feather bed & furniture to son John at coming of age.
Son:	John - tract of land bought of John Morgan
Exors:	Wife, brothers: John and Jacob Garrison Pearce
Wit.:	James Craig, Joseph Morgan, Wm. Sturdy, Elizabeth (X) Morgan
Proved:	27 June 1768, by o. of Elizabeth Morgan and Joseph Morgan. Lydia Pierce and John Pierce granted cert. for obtaining probate.
Signed:	Peter Pearce

Page
131:                JOHN LEE (Inventory)
                    Date: 3 November 1766
App'd by: Wm. Robertson, Jo's. Williams, John Russell,
          "being first sworn before Joseph Hudnall Gent."
Total eval.: L7.4.3
Ret.:   29 June 1768

Pages
131-132:   MARY LEE (Inventory)
                    Date: 29 October 1767
App'd by: John Blackwell, Thomas Bronaugh, James Arnold
Total eval.: No total. Retn.: 30 June 1768

Pages
132-133:   MARY LEE (Sale of Estate)
                    Date: 27 November 1767
Purchasers: Hancock Lee, John Lear, Willis Lee, Ann Garner,
                    Bennit Brown, Sarah Alexander Lee, Francis
                    Atwell, Isaac Roberts, Patterson Fletcher,
                    John Blackwell, Tolliver Bodes, Francis
                    Bronaugh, Nathaniel Williams, John Lee.
Ret.:   30 June 1768

Pages
133-134:   GEORGE FOOTE (Estate Account)
                    Date: 9 June 1759
Exor.:   Gillson Foote
Details: CASH PAID TO: Moses Fletcher, Daniel Payne, George
          Foote, overseer, Miss Eliz'a. Foote, Mr. Henderson,
          Lewis Reno, Dr. Michael Wallace, Doctor Parker,
          Rev'd. James Scott, Willoughby Jones, Martin Pickett,
          Geo: Brown, Geo: Bussle, Miss Frances Foote, Wm.
          Carr, Thomas Ramey, Mrs. Mary Foote's dower.
          CASH OF: Dan'l. Payne, James Cullins, Doctor Parker,
          Geo. Foote, Wm Rousau, Maj'r. Wm. Eustace, Geo.
          Bussle, Wm. Carr, Miss Eliz'a. Foote, Miss Frances
          Foote, Mrs. Mary Foote.
Ret.:   26 September 1768

Pages
135-136:   ABRAHAM DODSON (Will)
                    Date: 17 June 1767
Wife: Barbary Dodson - slaves, household goods and stock
          during her natural life
Dau.:   Milly Holtzclaw - 1 slave for her life, then to go
          to her heirs, begotten of her body, or to her bros.
          and sisters.

Dau.:	Tabitha Dodson - 1 slave
Son:	Enoch Dodson - 1 slave
Son:	Greenham Dodson - 1 slave
Dau.:	Molly Dodson - 1 slave
Exors:	Jacob Holtzclaw, wife, Barbary Dodson
Wit.:	Absalom Cornelius, Elijha Dodson, John Bennitt
Proved:	25 October 1768, by o. of Absalom Cornelius and John Bennitt. Jacob Holtzclaw and Barbary Dodson made oaths & granted cert. for obt. a probate.

Pages 136-138: JOHN MOREHEAD (Will)
Date: 22 June 1768

Dau.:	Hannah Johnson - 5 shillings
Son:	Charles Morehead - 5 shillings
Son:	Joseph - 5 shillings
Son:	John Morehead - 5 shillings
Son:	Alexander Morehead - 5 shillings - slaves
Son:	William Morehead - L15
Dau.:	Mary Lawrance - 5 shillings
Dau.:	Elizabeth Brigham - 5 shillings
Son:	Samuel Morehead - tract of land, 90 a., adjoining Rhodam Tillis, Joseph Blackwell & Brooks, and another tract containing 50 a. adjoining the land my son Joseph sold to Edward West. After wife's death the land he lives on to go to 3 sons: Alexander, William and Presly. All rest of estate to be divided between wife, sons Samuel and Presley Morehead.
Exors:	Sons: Charles, Alexander and William Morehead
Signed:	John Morehead
Wit.:	John Jett, William Drim, Joseph Stocklan
Proved:	24 October 1768, by o. of John Jett and William Drim. Cert. to obtain probate granted to Charles, Alexander and William Morehead.

Pages 138-139: JAMES MORGAN (Estate Account)
No date.

Adm'r.:	Henry Mauzy
Details:	TO PAID: Bennitt Price, Francis Bronaugh, Vincent Garner, Richard Mynatt, Benj'a. Waller, Richard Covington, Benjamin Settle, Woodrow & Neilson, Benjamin Morgan, Thomas Ayres, William Morgan.
Ret.:	25 October 1768

Pages 139-140: THOMAS DAVIS (Inventory)
No date.

- 35 -

App'd by: Stephen McCormack, John Bell, James Freeman
No total. Ret.: 28 November 1768.

Pages
140-141:   JOHN MOREHEAD (Inventory)
                No date
App'd by: Edward Humston, John Ashby, Nicholas George.
Total eval.: L392.12.9
Ret.:   28 November 1768

Pages
141-142:   JOHN RENNOLD   (Inventory)
                Date: 21 January 1769
App'd by: Thom Marshall, John Keith, William Seaton
Total Eval.: L39.7.11½   Ret.: 27 March 1769

Pages
142-143:   JOHN MAUZY (Division of Estate)
                Date: 7 April 1769
By: Thomas Harrison, Jonathan Gibson, Howsen Kinner
          (done by lot to widow and children, not named)
Ret.:   24 April 1769

Pages
143-144:   PETER PEARCE (Inventory)
                Court order: June 1768
App'd by: Charles Morgan, Charles Martin, Alex'r. Bradford
No total. Ret.: 24 April 1769

Page
145:            MARTIN SETTLE (Inventory)
                Court Order: August 1768
App'd by: Thomas Withers, Wm. Withers, Vincent Garner
Total eval.: L24.18.6   Ret.: 24 April 1769

Pages
146-147:   ABRAHAM DODSON (Inventory)
                Date: 29 November 1768
App'd by: None listed. No total. Ret.: 22 June 1769

Pages
147-149:   THOS. WATTS (Inventory)
                Date: 22 July 1769
App'd by: Robert (his R mark) Ashby, Wm. Harrison, John
          Southard
Total eval.: L127.4.9
Ret.:   28 August 1769

Pages
149-150:   ROBERT MATTHIS   (Will) ... of the County
            of Prince William ...
            Date: 30 November 1766
Wife: Elizabeth Matthews (sic) - land whereon I now
            hold by a lease from the Rev'd. Mr. William
            Stuart of Stafford County - two Negro men &
            one Negro woman
Son: Dudly Matthis - that parcel of Land in Prince
            William County which was left to me by the last
            Will and Testament of my Brother Griffin Matthis
Son :   Chitchester Matthis - the land I purchased of
            Benjamin Morriel in Fauquier County containing
            127 acres
Son: Robert Matthis - one Negro girl
Dau.:   Alice Matthis - one Negro girl
Dau.:   Sarah Matthis - one Negro girl
            I have owing to me from Capt. James Lane of
            Loudoun Coun ty which is L39.14s. I order to
            the payment of the Debt I owe to Benjamin Morriel
            for the land I purchased of him.
Daus.:   Elizabeth, Anna, Nancy - rest of my Estate debts
            to me divided among my three Youngest daus. ...
            at the time when they come of age or at the day
            of their Respective Marriages, (also the property
            left his wife, at-her death)
Signed: Robert Matthis
Exors: Capt. James Lane, Newman Matthis, Elizabeth Matthis
            Matthis (sic)
Wit.:   Cornelius Kincheloe, James Hardwick, Maximillian
            Haynie
Proved: 23 February 1767, by o. of Maximillian Haynie,
            Newman Matthis and Elizabeth Matthis made motion
            and granted bonds.

Page
151:        MALACHI CUMMINGS   (Inventory)
            Date: 14 August 1769
App'd by: William Kincheloe, Jno. Fishback, Thomas Bartlett
Total eval.: L69.7.0   Ret.: 25 September 1769

Page
152:        MARY MAUZEY   (Will)
            Date: 10 February 1769
Dau.:   Sally - 2 Negroes, if no heirs to go to:
            brother, John Mauzey and brother, Peter Mauzey -
            cash due me which is ten pounds in the hands of my
            brother Peter Mauzy, the cash in the hands of Mrs.

Mary Doniphan, .. John Robertson which was for
the hire of my Negroe wench ...

Exor.:   Uncle Thomas Conway
Signed: Mary (X) Mauzy
Wit.:   Susannah Kenner, Betty Rousaw, J. Markham
Proved: 23 September 1769, by o. of John Markham -
         23 October 1769, by o. of Betty Rousau.
         Thomas Conway granted cert. to obt. probate.

Pages
152-153:   ROBERT MATTHIS (Estate Account)
           No date.
Exor.:   Newman Matthis
Details: PAID TO: Coffin - 10s., 1 gallon of rum for the
         funeral - 5s., Wm. Parsons, John Matthews,
         Abraham Raws, Benja. Morris, Dan'l. Payne, Dan'l.
         Loflan e, John Riddell, Doct. George Graham,
         Ann White, admr. of Wm. White, Cuthbert Bullitt,
         James Lane, Dodson, Morrison, Eliz'a. Hall.
         BY: Capt. James Lane, Jno. Riddell
Ret.:   23 October 1769

Page
154:         PLEASANT WHITE (Will) .. of the Parish of
         Hamilton .. Date: 21 November 1769
         Ann Parker - sum of L5
Sister: Misniah Jeffries - all the rest of my estate real
         or personal
Extrix: Misniah Jefferies
Signed: Pleasant (P) White
Wit.:   Alex. Parker, William Parker, Jr., Richard Parker,
         Jr.
Proved: 27 November 1769, by o. of William Parker. Cert.
         granted Alexander Jeffries and Misniah his wife.

Pages
154-155:   JOHN ETHERINGTON (Inventory)
         Court Order: October 1769
App'd by: John Wright, John Sinckler, Augustine Jennings,
         sworn before Jeremiah Darnall.
Eval.:   L64.15.2   Returned: 26 February 1770

Pages
155-156:   SIMON MILLER (Will)
         Date: 26 March 1769
Gr.dau.: Ann Edmonds - dwelling plantation with the land
         annexed also my part of the Tract I hold on the

Top of the Piggnut Ridge also 139 a. Joining
Jeremiah Darnall also what Land I have Joining
formerly the Ewells on Goose Creek lying all
in this County likewise the half of a Tract in
Fauquier & Loudoun the other half Granted to
William Furr lying where Joshua Yeates lives ...
all my household furniture except one Feather
Bed and furniture she must Give her sister
Judith also one Bed and furniture to her sister
Betty ...

Gr.dau.: Judith Edmonds - the place where George Ford is
Overseer with 600 a. of Land ... Negroes ...

Gr.dau.: Betty Edmonds - remaining part of the Tract of
Land after Judith part is Given her also Neroes ...

Gr.son: Elias Edmonds - a horse - 200 a. of Land in King
George

Dau.: Betty - two Negroes

Bro.: John - all my wearing cloathes - two Gunns

_____: Jean Hughes - 100L to be paid her on her day of
Marriage or when she is 18 years of age.
Anything not mentioned to be sold and equally
divided among my three grand-daughters.

Exors: Elias Edmonds, William Edmonds, John Obannion
son of William and George Bennitt

Signed: Simon Miller

Wit.: James Craig, Thomas Mackie, Robert Scott

Proved: 26 February 1770, by o. of James Craig and
Thomas Mackie. Cert. granted Elias Edmonds

Page
157:        THOMAS WATTS (Inventory)
            Date: 24 March 1770
App'd by: Wm. Harrison, Robt. Ashby, John Southard
Total eval.: L34.5.6
Retun: 26 March 1770

Pages
157-159:   FRANCIS BURGESS (Will)
            Date: 5 November 1767

Wife: Jane Burgess - the use of all my whole estate

Dau.: Jane Burgess - one horse and saddle, one feather
bed and furniture

Dau.: Ruth - one feather bed and furniture

Dau.: Ann - one feather bed and furniture - to her when
whe shall arrive to 20 years of age or on the day
of marriage

Dau.:   Elinor Elliott - wife to Wm. Elliott - 20s. to
                buy her a gold ring and no more

Son: Dawson - the Lease of Land whereon I now live and
                one Negro man - one mulatto

Gr.dau.:   Sarah Elliott - to share in division of sale of
                Negroes with three daus., if son Dawson should
                die without heirs

Gr.dau.:   Anne Elliott - should enjoy all that part of my
                estate aforementioned which would have been in-
                herited by the said Sarah.

Exor.:   friends, John Suddoth and Francis Tupman

Signed: Francis (X) Burgess

Wit.:   Thom. Marshall, John Southard, Benjamin Elliott,
                Moses (his M mark) Congrove.

Proved: 26 March 1770, by o. of Benj. Elliott and Moses
                Congrove. Cert. granted John Suddoth.

Pages
159-160:   FRANCIS WATTS (Will) ... Francis Watts of
                South Carolina, Craven County ...
                      Date: 23 October 1753

Son: Thomas - one Negro woman Cate and her Increase to
                him and his heirs forever - best feather Bed
                Bolster - a pair of Blancketts and a rugg - no
                more of my estate neither real nor Personal

Wife: Ann - Negro girl -"after my wife's decease my will
                and desire is that the Negro Girl and her Increase
                should ____?____ to Ann Dergan two Cows and
                Calves"
                "Land unto my beloved wife the use and Profitts of
                all my real and Personall Estate for and during her
                natural life ... after the decease of my wife that
                my Granson Francis Watts should have my negro boy
                James ..."
                Rest of estate to be divided among grandchildren -
                not named.

Exor.:   Wife - "if my wife should die in this province that
                Benjamin Stone ..."

Signed: Francis (X) Watts

Wit.:   John Dergan, Benjamin Stone, Ann (X) Dargan
                "Secretary's Office - A True Copy taken from the
                Record & Examined - Geo. Murray, pro Secretary"

Page
160:           FRANCIS WATTS (Inventory)
                   Date: 29 May 1754

App'd. by: Benjamin Stone, Edward Barwick, Benjamin Walker,
                William Heatly

Total eval.: L1397.17.6

"Secretarys Office a true Copy taken from the Original & Examined. Geo. Murray, pro. Secretary"
"So. Carolina -- By the Honourable William Bull, Esq. Lieut. Governor & Commander in Chief in and over the said Province - (certifies that the above two documents are true copies) Signed: Wm. Bull, 28 October 1769.

Proved: Both will & inventory: 27 March 1770. Ltrs. of Admr. granted to John Watts.

Pages
162-164:   FRANCIS BURGESS (Inventory)
Date: 4 April 1770
App'd by: Wm Harrison, Rob't. Ashby, George Bennitt.
No total. Details: To 1 bed & furniture (a legacy to Jane Burgess) - L7; To 1 bed & furniture (a legacy to Ruth Burgess - L7; To 1 bay horse (a legacy to Jane Burgess - L7.10.0; To 1 mans saddle & smooth Gun - a legacy to Dawson Burgess - L1.0.0; To 1 Gray horse (a legacy to Ann Burgess) - L8.0.0; To 1 Negro man (a legacy to Dawson Burgess - L70.
Ret.: 28 May 1770

Page
164:   PLEASANT WHITE (Inventory)
No date.
App'd by: Edward Ball, William Ball, Wm. Smith
Total eval.: L14.17.0
Ret.: 28 May 1770

Page
165:   MARY MAUZEY (Inventory)
Date: 18 November 1769
App'd by: W. Blackwell, Rhodam Tullos, Joshua Tullos
Total eval.: L53.17.0
Ret.: 28 May 1770

Pages
165-167:   JAMES DRUMMOND (Estate Account)
"Dr. James Drummonds Estate in Acc't. with Daniel Payne for Mess'rs. William Cunningham & Company"
Details: TO: Colo. Rich'd Foote, Sen., A. Fletcher, Lewis, Rense, Peter How, Esq., Mr. Brooke, Aaron Fletcher, Carr & Chapman, Priest for apprais'g the estate.

BY CASH OF: A. Fletcher, Ann Drummond, Wm.
Bannister, Aaron Fletcher, John Wood, James
Luttrill, Nancy Drummond, Mr. Riddell, Nathaniel
Williams, Capt. Lynaugh Helm, Burton
Ret.:   28 May 1770

Page
167:       MISS MARY MAUZEY (Estate Account)
          No date.
Admr.:   Thomas Conway
Details: To the trouble & expenses in her sickness -
         L2.10.0; To funeral expenses - L3.10.0; To the
         keeping her child 14 months & 27 days - 10s.;
         To pd. Mrs. Dinah James for bringing her to
         bed - 10s.
Ret.:   29 May 1770

Pages
168-170:   GILSON FOOTE (Invencory)
          No date
App'd by: Richard Foote, jr., Will'm Alexander, Lynaugh
         Helm - being first sworn before William Grant,
         Gent'n. No total. Ret.: 22 October 1770.

Pages
171-176:   JOHN MAUZY (Estate. Account)
          Date: Begins 19 June 1768
No admr. named.
Details: TO PAID: Carr, John N elson, Sen'r. for smith's
         work; Messrs. Keith & Bhckwell; Peter Conway for
         Schooling Pegy Mauzy; Cathrine Stark, Henry Mauzy;
         Jno. Brahawn; Colo. Harrison; Ann Catlett; Wm.
         Smith; shoes for Betty Mauzy; John Ashby for whiskey;
         shoes for Moley Mauzy; Jno. Luttrell, Jno. Nelson,
         Jun'r. for smith's work; Howen Kenner; John Nelson
         E.. Run for weaving; John Ralls; Carty Wells; W.
         Brent; W. Wate; Ralph Murry for schooling Pegy,
         Moley - 109 days - 12s.; Jas. Luttrell; Saley
         Wood; Knoxes Exors for William Hedgman; Carr &
         Chapman; James Peters Overseer; Messrs. Carr,
         Lawson & Peters.
         BY: Francis Hanners; Joseph Combs; Rod. Tulless;
         Brewen Jones; Nem Wood; William Miller; William
         Lambert; Thomas Brooks; Colo. William Eustace;
         Chris Young; James Luttrell; Peter Wood; Capt.
         Carr; Jno. Rusaw; William Conway; James Duff.
Ret.:   26 November 1770

Page
176:     JOHN HOGANS (Inventory)
         No date.
App'd by: Henry Peyton, James Foley, John Obannon
Total eval.: L42.7.2
Ret.:   27 November 1771

Pages
177-178:   CHARLES MORGAN (Inventory)
           Court Order dated: April 1770
App'd by: William Eustace, Daniel Bradford, Alexander
          Bradford. No total.
Ret.:   25 March 1771

Pages
178-179:   JOHN SINCLEAR (Will)
           Date: 21 January 1767
Son: William Sinclear - one Negro man
Son: John - one Negro woman
Son: James - 213 a. of Land the Land that I now live
       on - one cow and fore hoggs and all my white ware
Son: Robert - one Negro Boy - Bed & furniture - one
       cow and calf
Son: Daniel - One Negro girl - one bed & furniture -
       one cow and calf
Dau: Charity - one bed and furniture - one cow and
       calf and five pounds cash
Dau: Jimmie Sinclear - one feather bed and furniture
       one cow and calf and five pounds Cash
       "... the rest of my estate to be equily Divided
       Between My five daughters that Sarah, Mary,
       Eliz'h, Charitie, Jemime ... if any of the above
       Mentioned Sons John, James, Robert, Daniel should
       die without heir it is my desire that there Estate
       should be equally divided between my Two daughters
       Charity and Jemime
Exors: Sons William and John Sincler
Signed: John Sinclear
Wit.:   John Wright, John (X) Kerns, William (X) Preston
        "As for my Land which My Son John Sinclear Lives
        on at the manor I desire Shall be Equally Divided
        between my son John and Robert"
Proved: 22 April 1771, by o. of John Wright, John Kurnes,
        William Preston, Witnesses William Sinclear and
        John Sinclear made o. and were granted cert. for
        probate.

Pages
179-180:   JOHN EDRINGTON, SEN'R. (Inventory)
                  No date
App'd by: Charles Deane, Thomas King, William Pearse
Total eval.: L512.15.8   Ret.: 27 May 1771

Pages
181-182:   CARR BAILEY (Will)
                  Date: 6 October 1770
Wife: Mary - "my whole Estate real and personal during
          her widowhood and after her marriage or decease
          my desire is that my Land may be sold and the
          money arising therefrom be equally divided among
          all my Children ..."
Son: James - after the marriage or decease of his mother,
          one Negro boy named Solomon
Son: Joseph - (as above) - Negro boy named Daniel
Dau.:   Betty - (as above) - Negro girl named Lucy
Son: Carr - (as above) - Negro boy named Tom
Son: Minter - (as above) - Negro boy named Bacchus
Son: William - (as above) - Negro woman named Sarah
Son: John - (as above) - one Negro Girl named Pursley
          "... as the boy Solomon before devised to my son
          James is sickly my will and desire is that in case
          the said Negro should die before the division of
          my Estate in that case I give and devise to my
          said son James one Negro Man named Bob ..."
Exors: Wife Mary and friends, George Rogers and Joseph
          Minter, Jun'r.
Signed: Carr (X) Bailey
Wit.:   Humphrey Brooke, William Hampton, Charles Morehead
          John Baley
Proved: 28 May 1771, by o. of William Hampton, Charles
          Morehead. Cert. granted Mary Bailey and Joseph
          Minter, Ju'r. George Rogers refused to take upon
          him the burthen of the Execution.

Page
182:         SIMON CUMMINGS (Will)
                  Date: 19 April 1771
Son: Alexander - plantation whereon I now live all the
          land that I hold in Fauquier County .. bounded as
          follows that is beginning at the head of the
          kuptree branch thence down the said Branch to Medle
          Run thence from the said Run to Howson Kenners line
Wife: (not named) - may dwell and Quietly possess the said
          plantation whereon I now live during her natural
          life

Son:	John - one young stear of 2 years old
Dau.:	Sarah Mynatt - one young heffer of 2 years old
Dau.:	Siety Edge - one young heffer of 2 years old
Dau.:	Conney Biruram - one bed and furniture and a cow
Wife:	(Elizabeth ?) all the remainder of my parshonal Estate during her naturall life and in Case she should marry then to Be Divide between my wife and Peter Cummings and my Daughter Elizabeth Cummings
Exor:	Wife and son John Cummings and Alexander Cummings
Wit.:	Daniel Harrill, John Edge
Proved:	24 Jun e 1771, by o. of Daniel Harrel and John Edge. Cert. of probate granted to Elizabeth Cummings and Alexander Cummings

Page
183:           CAPT. SIMON MILLER (Inventory)
                 Date: 24 July 1770
App'd by: John Basye, Will'm. Obanon, James Foley
No total. Ret.: 27 June 1771

Page
183:           FRANCES BURGES (Additional Inventory)
                 Date: 26 August 1771
App'd by: William Harrison, Robert Ashby, Geo. Bennett
Total eval: L2.5   Ret.: 26 August 1771

Page
184:           (MARY MAUZEY ?) (Estate Account)
                 No date. Note from: Minute Book 1768-1772,
                 p. 320, 26 August 1771: Thomas Conway Guardian
                 of Sally Mauzy returned and made oath to an
                 account of the Profits of his Wards estate which
                 is ordered to be recorded.
Admr.:.   Thomas Conway
Details: Salley Mazy The Alphins Estate - Dr.
           Cash paid by Henry Mauzy, Cash paid by John
           Robertson, Cash paid by Mrs. Doniphan.
Ret.:   26 August 1771

Pages
184-185::   BENJ. BLAND (inventory)
                 Date: 24 August 1771
App'd by: John Metcalfe, Thomas Hughs, George Sullavin
Total eval.: L145.10.4   Ret.: 26 August 1771

Pages
185-187: CARR BAILEY (Inventory)
              No date
App'd by: Wharton Ransdell, Charles Morehead, John Cooke
Total eval.: L548.9d.
Ret.:. 27 August 1771

Page
187   WILLIAM DARNALL (Will)
              Date: 28 August 1771
_____: Hannah Lear - L10, also my Saddle and bridle
_____: Saly Rile - L10
Exor.:   Edward Ball
Signed: William (his **S** mark) Darnall
Wit.:   Sarah (X) Jeffries, Alse (X) Robertson
Proved: 23 September 1771, by o. of Sarah Jeffries and
         Alice Robertson. Cert. of probate granted to
         Edward Ball.

Page
188:      JOHN SINCLOR (Inventory)
              No date.
App'd by: James Wright, Abner Phillips
Total eval.: L355.10.4
Ret.:   23 September 1771

Pages
188-189: JAMES NELSON (Inventory)
              Date: 14 November 1771
App'd by: Samuel Grigsby, John Obanon, James Foley
No total. Ret.: 25 November 1771

Page
189-190: JAMES BAILY (Inventory)
              No date
App'd by: Henry Taylor, Parnack George, Samuel Steel
Ret.:   23 March 1772. No total.

Pages
190-193: JOHN GRIGSBY (Inventory)
              Date: 1 January 1772
App'd by: James Foley, John Obannon, John Fishback
Total eval.: L969.11.9   Ret.: 23 March 1772

Page
193:      WILLIAM STAMPS (Will)
              Date: 25 April 1771

Wife: Ann Stamps - the use of all my Estate during
her widowhood - should she think proper to marry
again then my will is that she shall have only one
third part - at my s'd. Wife's Marriage my will
is that two thirds parts of my s'd Estate shall
be Equally divided among all my Children including
the Infant now unborn provided it shall live till
that time

Exors: loving friends, William Hunton, Robert Sanders
Signed: William Stamps
Wit.:   Richard Chichester, Peter Hedengran, Margaret
Metcalf
Proved: 23 March 1772, pro. by Peter Hedengran and Margaret
Metcalf. Cert. of admr. granted William Hunton
and Robert Sanders

Page
194:          WILLIAM DARNALL (Inventory)
Court Order dated: September 1771
Date: 7 January 1772
App'd by: Jos. Smith, Alexander Jeffries, Wm. Smith
Total eval.: L7.6.6 Ret.: 23 March 1772

Pages   FRANCIS WATTS (Division of Estate)
Court Order dated: March 1770
Date: 26 May 1770
Details: To John Watts - Negro and pay devisees L16.5
To Thomas Watts - Negro and pay devisees L15.5
To William Hansbrough, husband of Sarah, Grand
Daughter of the s'd. Dec'd - Negro and pay
devisees L6.5
To: Francis Watts - Negro - L3.15
To Margaret Watts - Negro - to pay devisees L1.5
To Ben nett Watts - Negro - to pay devisees L1.5
To Mason Watts - Negro - to receive L17.10
To Mary Watts - Negro - receives L18.15
Divided by: John Moffett, Wm. Harrison, John Ashby,
Hez'k. Turner
Ret.:   25 March 1772

Pages
195-196:   JOHN NICOLS (Inventory)
Date: 22 March 1772
App'd by: Samuel Harriss, Dickerson Wood, Henry Jones
Total eval.: L115.6.6
Ret.:   27 April 1772

Pages
196-197:   WILLIAM STAMPS (Inventory)
             No date.
App'd by: William Russell, William Ransdell, James Stewart
Total eval.: L86.3.1½   Ret.: 25 May 1772

Page
197:          JOSEPH COCKRELL   (Inventory)
              No date.
App'd by: Charles Morehead, John Hudnall, Absalom Adams
Total eval.: L9.19.6   Ret.: 25 May 1772

Pages
197-198:   THOMAS BOGGESS (Will)
              Date: 11 December 1771
Wife: Hannah - my whole estate, except what is herein-
            after mentioned
Son: Richard - one Negro named Daniel, now in his
            possession
Son: Thomas - Negro named Peter, now in his possession,
            also L10 cash
Son: Jeremiah - Negro woman called Jane - one desk, a
            bed & furniture
Dau.:   Magdalen Jackson - Negro girl named Letty
Dau.:   Elizabeth Maddox - Negro boy called James -
            one feather bed and furniture
Dau.:   Hannah Russ Watts - a Negro Girl called Winny
            All estate not mentioned to be equally divided
            between "my four Youngest Children after the
            Decease of my Wife..."
Exor.:   Wife (Hannah)
Signed: Thomas (X) Boggess
Wit.:   Moses Johnson, Betty (X) Johnson, Eli's. Edmonds
Proved: 25 May 1772, by o. of Moses Johnson and Betty
            Johnson. Hannah Boggess granted cert. of admr.

Pages
199-200:   JOHN LAWS (Inventory)
              No date.
App'd by: Henry Peyton, James Foley, George Berry
Total eval.: L109.4.6   Ret.: 23 June 1772

Page
200:          PETER HITT (Will)
              Date: 23 March 1772
Wife: Elizabeth - estate during her natural life
Son :   John - Negro woman Judy & my Negroe boy George
Son :   Joseph - my Negroe man called Tom
Son: Harmon - my Negro Girl Hannah & my Negroe man

called Old Tom

Son: Peter - my negroe boy called by the name of Ben

Dau.:   Mary Rictor - 100 a. of Land being the plantation whereon I now live and my Negroe boy named Moses

Son: Henry - L100 cash which is all he is to have of my Estate

"... after the decease of my wife all my Estate is not herein mentioned be sold to the highest bider & the money arising .. be Equally divided amongst all my children .. that is to say John, Joseph, Harmon, Peter & Mary."

Exors: Sons, Harmon and Joseph

Signed: Peter (his P mark) Hitt

Wit.:   Harmon (R) Rector, Joseph Taylor, John Morgan, Harmon Rectors

Proved: 27 July 1772, by o. of Harmon Rector, Joseph Taylor. Cert. granted Harmon Hitt and Joseph Hitt.

Page 201:   JOHN CRIMM (Inventory)

Date: 27 June 1772

App'd by: Ach'd. Allen, Sen'r., Jesse Thompson, Chas. Morgan

Total eval.: L199.4.3   Ret.:. 24 August 1772

Page 202:   JOSEPH EMMONS (Estate Account)

Admr.: William Emmons.   Dated 1767

Debit: L20.16.4

Credit: To Cash Paid: Mr. Graven Lawson, Thomas Harwood, Wm. Butler, James Crap, Joseph Odor, Thomas Barber

Ret.:   25 August 1772

Pages 202-204:   THOMAS BOGGESS (Inventory)

No date

App'd by: Henry Peyton, John Obannon, John Obannon, Sen'r.

No total. Ret. 23 November 1772

Pages 204-205:   PETER HITT (Inventory)

Date: 24 September 1772 (also dated 22 Sept.)

App'd by: Max'm. Berryman, Zacharias Lewis, Tilman Wever

No total. Ret. 23 November 1772

- 49 -

```
Pages
205-207:        JOHN RECTOR  (Will)
                Date: 5 July 1772
Wife:           Catherine - the plantation whereon I now dwell
                containing 300 a. of land, for and during her
                natural life
Son:            Henry - all that part or parcel of Land whereon
                Joseph Neil now dwells containing 224 a. - like-
                wise my now dwelling plantation containing 300 a.
                after the decease of my wife Catherine  - one
                negroe man called Old Jack and one negroe Girl
                called Hannah, after the decease of my wife ...
                at which time he shall pay the full sum of Fifty
Son:            pounds to my son Daniel or his heirs
Son:            Charles - all that part or parcel of Land adjoining
                his plantation commonly known by the name of the
                race ground Lott containing 201 a. - one negroe
                woman called Cate & one negroe boy called James
                to him and his Heirs, after the decease of my Wife
Son:            Jacob - one negroe man called Sambo and one
                negro boy called anthony and likewise my clock
                after the decease of my wife - smiths Bellows and
                anvil and Tools of all Kinds
Son:            Benjamin - the plantation whereon he now Dwells
                containing 160 a. - one negroe woman called Jude
                and one negroe Boy called Immanuel
Son:            Frederick - the plantation whereon he now dwells
                lying on Cromwells run containing 200 a. - one
                negroe boy called Jackey
Gr.son:         John Rector, son of my son John, 100 a. of Land
                adjoining my son Frederick's plantation on Cromwell's
                Run
Brother:        Harmon Rector - 100 a. whereon he now Dwells lying
                on licking run
                "... after the decease of my well beloved wife
                Catherine af'sd then all my household & kitchen
                Furniture likewise my stock of all kinds and de-
                nominations also my two distills and all my planta-
                tion Utensils be exposed to publick Sale and the
                amount thereof to be divided into Eight equal parts,
                one Eighth part thereof I Give to my son John, -
                son Dan iel, son Jacob, son Charles, son Benjamin,
                son Frederick, on e Eighth thereof to be equally
                divided among the children of my Daughter Catherine
                deceased, and one Eighth thereof to be equally
                Divided amongst the children of my daughter Elizabeth
                now living
```

Exors:	Wife, Catherine and son Henry to be joint Executrix and Executor
Signed:	John (his R mark) Rector
Wit.:	Henry (IR) Rector, Jacob (IF) Faubion, John Adams
Proved:	22 March 1773, by o. of Henry Rector and John Adams. Cert. granted Catherine Rector and Henry Rector.

Pages
207-208:   JACOB MINTER (Will)
                 Date: 21 November 1772

Wife:	"., the bed my Father gave me - use of my negroe boy Adam and a negroe man named Lewis..."
Son:	_____ - only my son is to have schooling and maintained in reasonable Good manner as shall be thought Proper by my Executors till he comes of age then to have the above negroe boy named Adam
Exors:	William Settle and Hannah Minter
Signed:	Jacob Minter
Wit.:	Franci s Bronaugh, Andrew Anderson, Edward Settle, John Edwards
Proved:	26 April 1773, by o. of Andrew Anderson, Edward Settle, John Edwards. Cert. granted to William Settle and Hannah Minter

Pages
208-209:   RANDLE MORGAN "of the County of Fauquier
                 and parish of Leed" (Will)
                 Date: 13 February 1773

Wife:	Martha - my house and plantation that I now live on as far as the Gap branch over the big road ledding to falmouth during her life in case of her Remaining a widow & at her decease or marriage to
Son:	fall to my youngest son Randle Morgan - if he should die without an heir, the land to be sold & divided among my children that is then living
Sons:	Abel & Enoch - the remainder of my land that lies over the Gap branch Joining Nathaniel Moss and Balls line to be equally divided between them - they paying each of them to their Brother in Law Abraham Morgan ten pounds apiece, within one year of my decease
Son:	Randle - should live with his Mother till he is of Age but if he should Marry or decline living with his Mother then I will that they divide the plantation equally with all the profits of the orchards

```
              stock & all other of the movable Estate that
              the then hold together in possession & at her
              death to have all farther I will that my son
              Randle when he comes to the age of twenty one
              years (which will be on the 25th day of October
Dau.:         1777) pay to his sister Mary the sum of 10L;
Dau.:         that he pay to his dec'd sister Grace  daughter
Gr.dau.:      Sarah Carpenter the sum of ten pounds, when she
              shall arrive to the age of 18 years
Exor.:        loving wife Martha Morgan & two sons Abel &
              Enoch Morgan
Signed:       Randle Morgan
Wit.:         Michael Henrie, Nathan Bewley
Proved:       24 May 1773, by o. of Michael Henry and Nathan
              Bewley.  Cert. of admr. granted to Martha Morgan
              Abel Morgan and Enoch Morgan
```

Pages
209-211:   WILLIAM FOOTE   (Inventory)
                  No date
App'd by: John Catlett, John Nelson, Thos. Priest
No total. Details: Books: 8 vols of the Spectator - 13 s;
                  7 vols. of Swifts works - 13s.
Retn: 24 May 1773

Pages
211-213:   JOHN BALL   (Inventory)
                  No date.
App'd by: Bennett Price, Fra's Attwell, William Jones
Total eval.: L775.19.0   Ret.: 24 May 1773

Pages
213 -214:   WILLIAM BOSWELL   (Inventory)
                  Date: 24 March 1773.
App'd by: Zacharias Lewis, James Blackwell, Henry (X)
                  Griffin. No total.
Ret.:   28 June 1773

Page
214:              JACOB MINTER   (Inventory)
                  No date
App'd by: William Morgan, John Edwards, Thomas Ayres
No total. Ret.: 23 June 1773

Pages
214-215:   RANDLE MORGAN   (Inventory)
                  Date: Saturday, 17 July 1773
App'd by: Daniel Jones, Thomas (X) Stone, Michael (M)
                  Dearman

Detai ls: An Old Bible — 1s.6d.; To Watts Hymns - 2s.6d.
          To Sundry Old Books — 2s.
Ret.:   26 July 1773

Pages
215-216:   JOHN BALL (Inventory of "all the Est'r of Mr.
               John Ball dec'd. in Lancaster.")
No date. App'd by: Henry Towles, Chas. Rogers, Wm.
          Chowning.
Total eval.: L23.9.7½
Details: "Lan'r. Crt. The above was sworn to be a true
          and Just Inventory of all the Estate of Mr.
          John Ball Dec'd in this County that was pre-
          sented to the appraisers before me this 19th of
          July 1773. Ja. Ewell."

          "The within is a true and Just Inventory of all
          the Estate of John Ball dec'd in this County as
          far as I know or believe - Mary Ball, Administrix."
Ret.:   27 July 1773

Pages
216-217:   JOHN CLAYTOR (Inventory)
               No date.
App'd by: R. Kenner, John James, Joseph (X) Strickland
Tot al eval.: L30.8.11
Ret.:   23 August 1773

Page
217:           JOHN RECTOR (Inventory)
               No date.
App'd by: Henry Rector, Joseph Robinson, Reubin Elliott
No total. Ret.: 26 October 1773

Page
218:           ROBERT STEPHENS   (Will) "of the county of
               Loudon and Colony of Virginia"
               Date: 11 December 1771
Wife: Ann my dearly beloved wife - all my Estate Real
          and personal - to be enjoyed untill her marriage or
          Death and after her marriage or Death to be
Son: divided between my Children & hers by son William
          Stephens & William Bartlett
Exors: William Stephens and William Bartlett
Signed: Robert (his. T mark) Stevens
Wit.:   Silas Rose, Isaac Grun (or Green ?) John Leary
          John Metcalf, William Kenton

Proved:. 25 October 1773, in Fauquier County on o. of
John Metcalf and William Kenton. Cert. granted
William Stephens and William Bartlett.

Pages
219-220:   SIMON CUMMINS   (Inventory)
                  Date: 9 November 1771
App'd by: Howson Kenner, Brenton Jones, Daniel Harrill
No total. Ret.: 25 October 1773

Pages
220-221:   BETTY QUARLES   (Will)
                  Date: 9 September 1773
Father-in-law: Thomas Harrison - one Negro woman named
               Alce, servant girl "named Dasias Alias Dark the
               said servant girl to serve him untill he Dies
               and then to be set free if her time of Service
               by her Indenture be not xpired before that time."
____: Thomas Gibson, son of Jonathan Gibson - 1 negro
               boy, Dick Alias Alley
Bro.:   Benjamin Harrison - one Negro boy named George,
               if Benj. should die without lawful heirs to
               descend to Burr Harrison, son of my brother William
               Harrison
Niece: Susannah Humstead - two Negroes, Bennah and Amia
               "Bequeath to Benjamin Harrison my said Brother
               Thomas Gibson son to the said Jonathan Gibson and
               Susannah Humstead - my stock of Cattle and Hogs to
               be equally Divided Amongst them."
___ __: John Gibson, son of Jonathan Gibson - my Young Horse
Nephew: Burr Haarison, son to my Brother William Harrison -
               my Bay Mare
Niece: Susannah Humstead - feather bed and furniture -
               saddle and bridle
Sister: Mary Fwoke - one of my rings
Niece: Ann Harrison Fwokes, dau. of Mary Fwoke, - one
               other ring
Brother: John Quarles - all cash after debts have been paid
Exor.:   "My Loving friend Jonathan Gibson" - no appraisal
               to be made and no security to be required of exor.
Signed:.   Betty Quarles
Wit.:   William Coppedge, John (X) Coppedge, Benjamin (X)
               Jones
Proved: 22 November 1773, by o. of William Coppedge, John
               Coppedge and Benjamin Jones. Jonathan Gibson
               granted cert. to obtain probate.

Pages
221-223:   ROBERT STEPHENS (Inventory)
            No date.
App'd by:. John Fishback, Philip Fishback, Joseph Fishback
No total. Retn.: 22 November 1773

Pages
223-226:   RICHARD FOOTE IN ACC'T. WITH GILSON FOOTE,
            GUARDIAN
Details: 1766, Oct. 6: To rent pd your brother William
            Foote. To cash pd. Mr. Tylers Estate. 2 Dec.:
            To cash pd Mary Bruton for spinning & knitting
            2 pr. stockings. 1767, 8 Feb: To Cash pd. Phillip
            Spiller for Taylors work;. To buckskin bought of
            Rich'd Luttrel. 22 July: To Cash pd. Rich'd Webb
            for working 1 month with the carpenters at the
            Tob'o. house; To Cash pd Joseph Minter for your
            board; To Cash pd Mr. Bailey Washington 1 Tob'o
            house, 1 corn house & prize. 5 Aug.: To Cash pd
            Mary Smith for 1 pr stockings; To Cash pd. Thomas
            Chapman for a felt hat; To Cash pd John Riddle for
            1 pr. shoes; To Cash pd Dan'l. Payne for 1 pr.
            shoes; To Cash pd. Eliz. Wood for knitting 1 pr.
            stockings. 28 Nov.: To Cash pd Phillip Spiller
            for his wife making 4 shirts; To Cash pd Wm.
            Alexander for soleing 1 pr shoes; To Cash pd
            William Foote for timber sufficient to make 2200
            boards for building your Tob'o house & cornhouse;
            Cash pd Mr. John Matthews School master; For
            sundry areares in Francis Moores Rents; Paid Mr.
            John Matthews School master 1 Spelling book -
            1s. 4d.; Cash expended in Gitting you a board to
            go to Col'o. Henry Lee's Matter; Cash pd Aaron
            Fletcher; Cash pd Phillip Spiller; Cash pd Sarah
            Fletcher for mending your shirts. 30 Nov.: Paid
            Mrs. Eliz. Wilkerson for your board six months;
            Paid Eliz. Wood; Paid Perron a Taylor for 2 pr.
            Breeches; Cash of Mrs. Mary Tyler your Guardian
            for your part of your Fathers Estate.
Ret.:   At a Court held for Fauquier County the 22d day
            of Nov. 1773. This account was returned and made
            Oath to by Hannah Foote Administratrix of Gilson
            Foote dec'd. Guardian of the within named Richard
            Foote as a true copy taken from the Books of the
            said Gilson Foote and ordered to be recorded.

Pages
226-228:   Dr. RICHARD FOOTE & WILLIAM FOOTE, INFANTS
            IN ACCOUNT WITH GILSON FOOTE GUARDIAN

Details: 1766, 25 Oct. 1767, 30 June: To cash pd John
            Nelson for smiths work. 7 Aug.: To Cash pd
            William Hogain for Smith work.
Ret.:   22 November 1773, by Hannah Foote, Adm'x. of
            Gilson Foote dec'd, Guardian of the within
            named Richard Foote and William Foote

Pages
228-230:   Dr. WILLIAM FOOTE, INFANT IN ACCOUNT WITH
            GILSON FOOTE, GUARDIAN

Details: 1766, Oct. 6: To Cash pd John Burditt for making
            1 pr shoes; To cash pd William Foote for your
            board; To cash pd Mary Bruton. 1767: To cash pd.
            Phillip Spiller, Thomas Chapman, Eliz. Wood, Aaron
            Fletcher, Joseph Minter, Mr. John Riddle, Sarah
            Ellis, Priss Spiller, Mrs. Cook for board, John
            Newman for board. 23 Dec.: Pd Thomas Carver for
            Schooling; pd. Edward Person Taylor. 1767 By Cash
            of Mrs. Mary Tyler your late Guardian being your
            part of your fathers personal estate; By Cash for
            your part of your mothers Estate.
Ret.:   22 November 1773, by Hannah Foote Adm'r. of Gilson
            Foote dec'd, Guardian of within named William Foote.

Pages
230-231:   BETTY QUARLES (Inventory)
            Date: 24 November 1773
No total.   "November 24th 1773. Then Received of Mr.
            Jonathan Gibson Executor of Betty Quarles Dec'd.
            Twenty three pounds five shillings and six
            pence also 1 Gold stone Ring, the Ring being left
            to my daughter Elizabeth Minors Quarles by Will.
            John Quarles, P. W."
Ret.:   25 January 1774

Pages
231-232:   THOMAS HARRISON (Will)
            Date: 26 September 1773
Son: William - four negroes - also one half of the Land
            whereon I now have a Quarter purchased of Elias
            Edmonds to be equally divided between him and his
Son: brother Burr Harrison also one other small piece

Land lying on the right hand side of the road
leading through Ashby's Gap and part of a tract
land I purchased of Mr. Mercer to be divided
like manner - one other Negro called Dublin

Son: Thomas - one tract Land I took up, 409 a., except what I have sold out of the same to Joseph
Kelly and Edmond Homes - one other tract land
which I took up Joining the above mentioned
land being 344 a. Also my Will and desire is
that my said son Thomas do sell the several parts
of the said Land to the Persons I have already
agreed with and make them Good and Lawfull Deeds
from him and his heirs - Money due from Edmond
Homes for his bond - Negroes - and all my wearing
Boddy Cloaths.

Son: Burr - 408 a. I bought of John Mercer, Gent.
Deceased with the Plantation thereon lying
between the land of William Harrison & Dixon's
Quarter laid off and Surveyed by John Moffett -
four Negroes

Gr.son: Benjamin Harrison, son of Burr Harrison, one
Negro boy

Dau.: Susannah Gibson - five Negroes - L200 Virginia
Curren cy - one large Chest draws, My Clock and
one large Looking Glass

Dau.: Mary Fowke - four Negroes now in her possession -
L150 Virginia currency

Dau.: Ann Gillison - two Negroes - L150 Virginia Currency
to be left in the hands of Mr. Jonathan Gibson to
pay my sd. dau. annually and every year the Lawfully Interest for the above - for the only support
of her and Children as above described. Also one
Feather Bed and Furniture

Gr.son: Thomas Gibson the Plantation whereon my son
Benjamin Harrison now lives part of the Tract of
Land I purchased of Bertrand Ewell Begining on
the Westerly Branch of Goose run where John Orear
Crosses the said Branch and Extending thence up
the sd. run opposite the plantation to the mouth
of a small Branch thence up the said branch to the
head thereof or pond to the dividing Line of Helm
and myself thence along the said line to the line
of Cuthbert Harrison formerly Tidwells then down
the sd. line to John Orears Corner thence with the
line of Orear to the Beginning - one Negroe boy
named Adam

Gr.son: John Gibson - two Negro boys

Gr.dau.:   Ann Harrison Fowke - one negro girl
Son-in-law: Jonathan Gibson - the sum of Money he is
             indebted to me per account L79.2.5
Son-in-law: Chandler Fowke - sum of money lent him -
             about L70
Gr.son: Thomas Harrison Fowke - 1 negro boy
Gr.son: John Gillison - one negro girl
Gr.son: Burr Harrison - one negro called Norfolk Tom
             my will and desire is that my said Son do sell
             the said Negroe slave to pay his Debts
Gr.dau: Lucy Harrison, dau. of William, - one Negro girl
Gr.dau: Ann Grayson Gibson - one negro girl
Gr.son: Jonathan Catlett Gibson - one negro boy
Son: Benjamin - the Old plantation mill & land there-
             unto belonging which sd land I purchased of my
             Father lying on Cedar Run below the mouth of
             Darrells run - also the Land I purchased of
             Thomas Whittedge lying on the upper side of
             Goose run and Joining the afs'd. tract of Land -
             also the Plantation and land whereon I now live
             formerly the Glebe of Hamilton Parish Joining
             the aforesaid Land - also, the Land I purchased
             of Bertrand Ewell Joining the afs'd Land Except
             what part I have already given away by this will
             of the said Tract of Land (to Thomas Gibson with
             the house & plantation thereon)
Son: Benjamin - 17 Negroes - if Benjamin should die
             without lawful issue the land and Negroes above
             shall descend to my three Grandsons namely Thomas
             Gibson, Burr Harrison son of William Harrison and
             Thomas Harrison Fowke - all my Household furniture -
             live stock, those excepted at my Quarter at the
             Mountains and fifty head Sheep - oxen - also all my
             right and Title & claim to one negroe Slave called
             Peter that is now in dispute between me and the
             Garners
Nephew: and friend: Cuthbert Harrison - 25s. to purchase
             him a Mourning Ring
Nieces: Seth Harrison, Francis Harrison, Ann Harrison and
             Sarah Harrison - 20s. each to buy mourning rings
Sons: William, Thomas and Burr - all stock I have at my
             plantation at the Mountains equally divided also
             slaves to be equally divided
             Desire that my Estate may not be brought to an
             appraisement but that my Executors hereafter men-
             tioned Return a just Inventory of my whole Estate
             to Court
Son-in-law: Jonathan Gibson - one dark bay horse now at the
             Mountains

Exors: Sons, William, Benjamin and Jonathan Gibson
Signed: Thomas Harrison
Wit.:   Originald Young, John Peters, John (x) Shumate,
         Sen'r., John (X) Coppage
Proved: 25 Jan uary 1774, by o. of Originald Young, John
         Peters, John Shumate, Sen'r. and John Coppage.
         William Harrison, Benjamin Harrison and Jonathan
         Gibson granted cert. for obtaining a probate.

Page
235:              THOMAS BOLT   (Inventory)
                 No date
App'd by: Samuel (his D mark),Davis, William (X) Taylor,
         Jekil (X) Jeonkins.
No total. Ret.: 23 November 1773

Pages
236-237:   CAPT. WILLIAM BALL   (Inventory)
                 No date.
Adm'r.: John Moffett, Gent.
App'd by: Henry Allan, William Elliott, William Holton
Total eval.: L247.1.9
Ret.:   28 March 1774

Pages
237-239:   JOHN OBANON   (Will) of the County of
                 Fauquier planter
                 Date: 18 November 1773
Wife: Sarah - use and benefit of the plantation where-
         on I now live - use of all my houshold furniture
         with the Plantation utensils for & during her
         natural life
Son: William - the Plantation and Lands on the East
         side of the Pignutt Ridge it being the same
         whereon he formerly lived - one negroe woman
         named Jean and all her children born since she
         has been in his possession in lieu of a legacy
         left him by his Grand Father Bryant Obanon (the
         said Lands containing 189 acres)
Son: John - one negroe boy named Tom
Son: James - a Good Suit of Cloaths to be purchased
         out of my Crop
Son: Thomas - one suit Cloaths to be also purchased
         as them of James'
Son: Samuel - the following tract of Land Viz. Beginning
         at Nelson's third Corner and binding on the Lines

- 59 -

of the said Nelson, the Rev'd. Mr. Scott &
Gibon Line, 150 yards above old ford on Broad
Run thence a straight Line to the Begining
containing 139 a. - one negroe girl called
Hannah

Son: Andrew - in Lieu of all Legacies bequeathed him
by his Grand Father Bryant Obanon One negroe
man named Frank

Son: Joseph - in lieu of fifty pounds part of a legacy
left him by his Grand Father Bryant Obanon One
negroe boy named Moses

Son: George - in full of all legacies left him by his
Grandfather Bryant Obanon one negroe man named
James

Son: Bryant - my Riding Horse - Saddle and Bridle - in
lieu of his dividend of his Grand Fathers Estate -
after the death of his mother the plantation
whereon I now live to contain 100 acres.

Son: Benjamin - a new saddle and bridle - in lieu of his
dividend of his Grand Father's Estate the remainder of all my Lands not yet bequeathed but not be
possessed therewith til after the death of his
mother

Dau.: Sarah Foley - a negroe boy named Will now in her
Possession

Dau.: Caty Nelson - one negroe girl named Jude now in
her Possession
... after the death of my said wife all my negroes
not being named in this will together with the
livestock houshold furniture & plantation utensils
be equally divided between by then surviving sons
and my further will & desire is that my wife have
the use & benefit of the negroes which are not otherwise bequeathed by this will and my further will &
desire is that if any of my sons refuse to take the
Legacies or legacy by this will devised them in
lieu of their dividend of their Grand Fathers
Estate that then in such Case such son or sons
shall only receive one shilling sterling instead
of the legacies devised them by this will

Exors: Loving son William, Samuel and John
Signed: John Obanon
Wit.: Thomas Elliott, Ben jamin Elliott, John Moffett
Proved: 28 March 1774, by o. of the witnesses above.
And on the motion of William Obanon who made o.
and executed and acknowledged bond as the Law
directs cert. is granted him for obtaining probate

- 60 -

Pages
239-242:   CAPT. NIMROD ASHBY (Inventory)
                     Date: 29 June 1764 at Goose Creek
App'd by: William Love, Enoch Berry, John Rector, Sen'r.
Total eval.: L248.15.9

                     Another Inventory dated: 25 July 1764
App'd by: Wm. Love, Enoch Berry, John Rector, Sen'r.
Total eval.: L23.13.9 Virginia currency

                     Another Inventory dated: 4 July 1764
App'd by: Taliaferro Stripling, Humphrey Wills and Edward
          Snickers - being in Frederick County
Total eval.: L244.18.6
                     Two more articles were appraised by Thomas
                     Colson, William Love and Richard Jacksnan,
                     sworn before Capt. Charles Smith
Admr!   Alexander Wodron
Ret.:   28 March 1774

Page
242:   THOMAS CONWAY'S GUARDIAN ACC'T. OF
                     SALLY MAUZY
                     Dates: 1769-1773
Ret.:   28 March 1774 - This account was returned and
         made Oath to by Thomas Conway & ordered to be
         Recorded.

Pages
243-245:   NIMROD ASHBY (Estate Account)
Admr.:   Alexander Wodron
Details: TO: Capt. William Grant, Mr. John Knox, Peter
         Grant, John Moffett, Cuthbert Bullett, Robert
         Ashby, Alexander Cummins, Charles Morgan, Thomas
         Conner, Reginald Young, Benjamin Wood, Richard
         Higgins, Ephraim Furr, Benjamin Neil, Francis
         Howell, Wm. Scott, Jacob Wease, James Wood, James
         Withers, Jun'r., Joseph Blackmore, Edward Snickers,
         John Foreman, George Yoakum, Capt. Van Sweringen,
         John Crim, Andrew Cockrane & Co., Nathaniel S.
         White, David Scott, Edmund Godfrey, Colonel Adam
         Stephens, Rosanna Noland, Benjamin Tutt, Edw'd.
         Kemp, George Arnold, William Cochran, Alexander
         Farrow, George Wright, Samuel Moore, David Barton,
         James Catlett, Col. Abraham Hite, Frederick Conrad,
         John Healey, Maj'r. John Field, Michael Hoover,
         Joshua Tullos, James Kerr, Edward Rogers, William

- 61 -

wood, George Lamkin, Patrick Kirk, John Lamby,
Peter Catlett, John Owens, John Blackmore, Edwin
Young, Baylis Earle, William Scale, John Kerr,
John Anderson, Jacob Hite, Bayley Johnson, Thomas
Wood, Humphrey Wills, Aron Chambling, William
Foreman, John Churchhill, James Gallant, Samuel
Harris, John Rector, Henry Brinker, Daniel
Frowerce, Joseph Berry, John Russan, Charles
Lineh, James Winn, Lewis Powell, Wodron & Neilson,
Wodron Neilson & Foster, Heronomos Algiers,
Taliaferro Striblin g, William Heartwell, Joseph
Stephens, George Farrow, Edward Blackburn, Col.
George Mercer, William West, Martin Pickett, John
Riddle, James Barnett, John Obanon, Michael Hombey,
Adam Haymaker, John Jones, Charles Barker, David
Ashby.

Examined: Falmouth, 20 April 1774 .. examined by Arthur
Morson, James Buchanan
Ret.: 25 April 1774

Pages
245-246: NIMROD ASHBY (Estate Account)
Admr.: Alexander Wodron
Details: Debts due to be paid by the Administrator "when
the Administrator is in cash from said Estate":
Laurence Snap, Col. John Hite, Francis Heronomos,
Joseph Watson, James Mercer, Joseph Settle, John
Wilton, George Bennett, Thomas Attwell, Foushee
Tebbs, John Grigsby, James Lindsay, Stephen
Donaldson, Robert Allan, Jun'r., Michael Thorn,
John Smearer, Peter Hogg, Bryant Brien, Thomas
Edmondson, Jacob Troutvine, Estate of Wm. Bayles,
dec'd., William Allan, George Tebbs, Thomas Prichard,
Benjamin Hampton, Robert Rutherford, M. Rowler
ass'ee of Strickler, Peter How White Haven, John
Howard, Francis Edzar, G. Banks.
King George County S'ct. Alexander Wodron came
before me one of his Majesties Justices of the
Peace for said County .. 22 April 1774 .. James
Buchanan. 25 April 1774 Informed of a Judgment
Agt. Estate of N. Ashby obtained by Francis Triplett
for L9.5. Alexander Wodron.
Ret.: 25 April 1774

Page CAPT. NIMROD ASHBY (Sale of Estate)
Date: 5 March 1765
Purchasers: David Barton, Edward Godfrey, Edward Garrett,

Thomas Williams, John Settle, John Moffett,
George Farrow, Capt. Robt. Ashby, Capt. Thomas
Marshall, Rose Conner, John Winn, Mrs. Francis
(Ashby) Obannion, James Barnel, David Ashby,
Daniel Morgan, Speake & Kennedy, Wodrow & Neilson,
William Ashby, Jacob Bowman, John Jimmons, James
Davis, Abraham Kenkendal, Simon Taylor, John
Grigsby, Francis Dade. Everything sold belonging
to the Estate appraised to L517.17.6 Except a
Negroe Girl named Catte & her since ofspring re-
tained by Robert Ashby after the said Girl was
appraised and included in the above L517.17.6
the total of the appraisement. Alex'r. Wodron.

Ret.:   April 1774

Page
248:                HERMAN KEMPER (Inventory)
                    Date: Tuesday, 29 March 1774
App'd by: Peter Kemper, Sen'r., John Kemper, Sen'r., Peter
           Kemper son to Peter.
Total eval.: L79.16   Ret.: 25 April 1774

Pages
249-250:   FRANCIS ASH (Will)
                    Date: 21 February 1774
Son: George - eleven negroes, all now in his possession
Wife: Elizabeth - one old negroe called Ralph and 3 others
Son: Francis (the oldest surviving son of my wife Eliza-
           beth) - negroes - all my Blacksmiths Tools - the
           Land I now live on being the Land I purchased of
           Benjamin Ashby and the said Ashby has not made deeds
           to me for the same it is my will and desire that the
           Ballance of the purchase Money may be paid to the
           said Ashby as soon as the same can be raised out
           of my Estate
Dau.:   Dorothy Alsup - one negroe girl
Son: James - one negroe man
Dau.:   Elizabeth - one negroe boy
Son: Uriel - one negroe girl
Dau.:   Eon - one negroe girl
Son: Littleton - one negroe boy
Dau.:   Peggy Newble - one negroe boy
Son: William - one negroe boy
Dau.:   Molly - one negroe boy
Wife: Elizabeth - all my houshold & Kitchen furniture like-
           wise all my livestock of every kind and denomination
           as also all my plantation Uttensils of every sort

- 63 -

either to retain for her own use or to dis-
tribute among our Children to supply their
nesseties as far as she can spare and all
those negroes given to my wife Elizabeth as
above after her decease I give them amongs my
nine children last above mentioned .. namely
Dorothy Alsup, James, Elizabeth, Uriel, Elon,
Littleton, Peggy Newble, William & Molly
Exor.:   Son, Francis Ash
Signed: Francis Ash
Wit.:   "the mark of R Robert Ashby," John Adams,
              Enoch Adams
Proved:.   25 April 1774, by o. of above witnesses.
              Francis Ash granted cert. to obtain probate.

Pages
250-253:   GEORGE NEAVIL   (Will)
                  Date: 26 February 1774
Wife: Mary - a Mulatto woman named Betty Burk & four
              other Negroes together with the Land whereon I
              now live to the dividing Line between my daus.
Daus: Joanna Hathaway and Judith Barnett hereafter
              mentioned (except the Mill & ten acres of Land
              adjoining and also one third of all my Stock &
              household furniture and all my cash on hand also
              my will is that my said wife shall have one sixth
              part of the profit arising from the labour of my
              Carpenter Will during her said natural life
Wife &
Sons-in-law: Mary Neavil, John Rosser, Solomon Jones,
              Ambrose Barnett, and James Hathaway - my Mill
              on Cedar Run with the appurtenances thereto
              Belonging with ten Acres of Land adjoining as
              Tenants in common and not as Joint Tenants
Sons-in-law: (those above) and Richard Hampton - all the
              debt that may be due on my books at the time
              of my death
Dau.:   Mary Rosser - Negroes
Son-in-law: John Rosser - L25 - to be paid out of my Book
              debts, instead of building for him as I've done
              for all the rest of my sons-in-law
Dau.:   Betty Jones - Negroes - all my tract of land on
              the Bull Run Mountain - during her life and then
              to be equally divided between my two Grandsons
              George Jones and William Jones

Dau.: Lucy Calmes - 125 acres being the Land she now
has in possession the Land to Extend to the back
line - provision made for a child to be born to
his daughter Lucy Calmes

Dau.: Ann Blackmore - the Land whereon she now lives the
same Lying on the Northside and adjoining the Land
given to my daughter Lucy Calmes... Negro woman

Dau.: Milly Barnett - the Land whereon she now lives on
the Southside and adjoining the Land given to my
dau. Lucy Calmes - Negro woman

Gr.son: John Barnett, son of James Barnett - L20 to be
paid him when he arrives at the age of 21 years
out of my Book Debts

Dau.: Letty Helm - Negroes

Gr.dau.: Ann Helm - L20 to be paid at the day of Marriage
or age of 21 years out of my book Debts

Dau.: Susanna Hampton - the tract of Land she now lives
on during her natural life, then to my two
Grand Daughters Charlotte & Joanna Hampton -
Negroes

Dau.: Joanna Hathaway - the upper part of the tract of
Land whereon I now live bounded as followeth
Beginning at a double Sycamore standing on the
bank of Cedar Run below a piece of Low grounds
called Churchhills Oat Patch Extending thence ..
to a Red Oak in Carters Line thence with Carters
Line .. to Baldwins Chesnut corner thence with
Baldwins Line .. to a white Oak standing on the
north side of the main Road .. to a white Oak
Corner to Duff Green dec'd and my own Land standing
on the northside of Cedar Run, 241 acres - a pair
of Hand mill stones

Dau.: Judith Barnett - after my wifes decease the residue
of the Land whereon I now live - Negroes
... the profit arising from the labour of my
Carpenter Will (after my wifes sixth part taken
out) be annually and equally divided among John
Rosser, Solomon Jones, James Hathaway and Ambrose
Barnett, James Hathaway and Richard Hampton.

Signed: George Neavill

Wit.: Richard Chichester, Sarah Chichester, Samuel
Pharis, John Shurley, James (his * mark) Shurley

Exors: Wife Mary & sons-in-law John Rosser, Solomon
Jones, James Hathaway & Ambrose Barnett

Proved: 27 June 1774, by the o. of Richard Chichester,
Samuel Pharis and John Shurley. James Hathaway
& Ambrose Barnett granted cert. for obt. probate.

Page
253:                    BENJAMIN SNELLING   (Will)   of Hamilton Parish
                       Date: 8 November 1773
Wife: Elizabeth Snelling - the land whereon I now live
                       during her Widowhood and after her Marriage or
                       death to fall to my son
Son: Benjamin - all property to be left in her hands
                       until Death or marriage when it is to be equally
                       divided among all my children
Exor.:   Wife Elizabeth
Signed: Benj'a. Snelling
Wit.:   Dan'l. Bradford, Edw'd. Humston, Alex'r. Bradford
Proved: 27 June 1774, by o. of Dan'l. Bradford and Edward
                       Humstead. Cert. for obtaining probate granted
                       Elizabeth Snelling.

Pages
253-254:   JOSEPH MINTER   of Leeds Parish   (Will)
                       Date: 12 December 1772
Wife: Mary - all estate during her natural life
Sons: John and Joseph - to divide the land as follows:
                       John to have the part of land whereon I now live,
                       son Joseph to have the part he now lives on ad-
                       joining South Run - all other property to be
                       appraised and divided between the sons at the
                       death of wife
Gr.son: William Minter, son of Jacob Minter, dec'd, the
                       sum of L25 from sons John and Joseph apiece
                       within twelve months after they have been in
                       possession of the above bequested lands
Exors: son Joseph Minter and William Chilton
Signed: Joseph (his-M-mark) Minter
Wit.:   Will. Chilton, John Chilton
Proved: 27 June 1774, by o. of John Chilton. Joseph
                       Minter made o. and granted cert. to obt. probate

Pages:
254-256:   THOMAS HARRISON   (Inventory)
                       No date
App'd by: Benj'a. Harrison, Jonathan Gibson
No total. Ret.: 27 June 1774

Pages
257-259:   RICHARD HALL   (Will)
                       Date: 1 March 1774
                       ... my will and desire that all my negroes remain
                       on the Marsh plantation belonging to Mrs. Hannah
                       Corbin if she be willing thereto untill my debts

be paid .. if the creditors will not wait ..
that then my Executors sell the Track of Land
in Fauquier County which I Purchased of Richard
and William Hampton ..

Son: Elisha Hall Corbin, born of Mrs. Hannah Corbin -
the tract of Land above mentioned

Dau.: Martha Corbin, born of Mrs. Hannah Corbin - to
have the tract above mentioned if Elisha should
die before he comes of age or without heirs -
Negroes

Sister: Mary Williamson - to have tract of land if both
of the above should die

Nephew: James Williamson - Negro

Nieces: Martha Williamson, Elizabeth, Mary and Hannah -
Negroes

____: Mrs. Hannah Corbin - my bay horse Sterling and it
is my will and desire that he be sent down to her
at my death - that Mrs. Hannah Corbin receive all
debts due from anyone in the County of Richmond or
the adjacent counties and that out of the money
collected on those accounts she pay Mr. Hugh Hamilton
his Just demand and to Mr. Thomas Blain the sum for
which I stand engaged to him

Sister: Mary Williamson -riding chair, feather bed & furniture and that her husband shall have no part of
it - my will and desire that the assortment of
medacine I now have by me in Fauquier of which I
leave a Schedule may be sold by my Executors
either at private or public Sale

Exor: Mrs. Hannah Corbin - so far as my regard my
Estate debts or other connextions I have in the
County of Richmond or the adjacent Counties
Friends: Wharton Ransdell, James Scott, Thomas
Marshall and John Chilton - so far as relates to
my Estate in Fauquier

Signed: Rich'd. Hall

Wit.: Thom. Marshall, Charles Morehead, Samuel Lingan,
Turner Morehead

Codocil: No date. Mrs. Hannah Corbin - negroes mentioned
in a deed of Gift recorded in Westmoreland Court
from her the said Hannah to my son Elisha and
Daughter Martha above mentioned with Reversion
to me recorded in the County Court of Richmond.
Mrs. Hannah Corbin - all the horses, mares and
Colts in Westmoreland County during her life

Wit.: James Thompson, Wharton Ransdell, Charles Morehead, Christopher Sutphin. 28 March 1774.

Proved: 25 July 1774, by o. of Turner Morehead, Charles

Morehead and Wharton Ransdell. Thomas
Marshall and John Chilton granted cert. to
obtain probate.

Pages
259-261:   JOSEPH MINTER   (Inventory)
                     Date: 23 July 1774
App'd by: Charles Chilton, John Tomlin, John Cooke
Total eval.: L437.17.7
Ret.:   25 July 1774

Pages
261-262:   JEREMIAH OWENS (Will)
                     Date: 26 November 1772
Youngest son: Jeremiah Owens - negro girl - if he should
               die without heirs then said Negro girl and her
               increase to be equally divided among the re-
               mainder of my Children then living.
Wife: Jane - remainder of my Estate - to be equally
               divided Between Jane my beloved wife and the
               remainder of children
Signed: Jeremiah (x) Owens
Wit.:   Evan Griffiths, William Berry, John Owens, John
               (his - mark) Kenton
Proved: 23 August 1773 by o. of Evan Griffith and Wm.
               Berry

Pages
262-263:   WILLIAM BLACKWELL (Will)
                     Date: 20 September 1772
Son: William - all the land I Bought of Alexander
               Clement, Christopher Marr, Humphrey Evan and
               Thomas Hudnall, with some other Lands I had of
               Col. William Eustace, on my said son William
Son: giving to my son Joseph 700 acres of Land out
               of the Deed I acknowledged to my said son William
               in Fauquier Court but if he should refuse so to
               do, then I give all the above mentioned Land to
               William, to my son Joseph - if Joseph should die
               all land to William
Children: The track of Land given me by his Hon'r. John
               Tayloe Esq'r. I desire may be sold and the Cash
               to be equally divided between my Children here-
               after named, to wit: Samuel, John, William, Joseph,
               Hannah, Sarah and Lucy.
Son: William - land I had of John Crump - if any
               damages should happen against Estate by a bond I

	am Security in with the said Crump to William H ambleton
Wife:	Elizabeth - have the use of all my Negroes & personal Estate during her life or widowhood only my son William to have his choice of any one of my Negroes at anytime when he shall demand it - all the furniture of my Hall
Son:	John - L50 - after wife's death all property to be divided among the following: Samuel, William, Joseph, Hannah, Sarah & Lucy, my other children that is married off is excluded from having any part of my Estate except the L50 to John they having their parts paid off
Exors:	wife Elizabeth, sons John and William
Signed:	W Blackwell
Codicil:	No date. The land I left above to be sold I give to my son Samuel.
Proved:	26 September 1774, This will was presented in Court and the Identity of the Testators hand being proved by the o. of William Grant, John Green and William Nelson and the Court being also satisfied that the same is in the Testators own hand writing was ordered to be recorded. Elizabeth Blackwell granted cert. to obtain probate.

Pages
264-266:   CAPT. GEORGE NEAVIL (Inventory)
                 No date.
App'd by: Fran's. Whiting, Richard Chichester, J.
              Brooke
Total eval.: L865.8.9½
Ret.:   24 October 1774

Pages
266-267   WILLIAM GRUBBS (Inventory)
                 No date.
App'd by: Ambrose Barnett, Samuel Steele, John Cooke
Total eval.: L21.5.6
Ret.:   24 October 1774

Pages
267-268:   JOHN RECTOR (Inventory)
                 Date: 4 June 1773
App'd by: Daniel Flowree, John Utterback, John Weaver
No total. Ret.: 28 November 1774

- 69 -

Pages
268-269:.   ANNA STEPTOE LAWSON   (Will)
             Date: 1 June 1774
Bro.:   Epaphroditus Lawson - all my Negroes in consideration
             of his paying the Legacies hereafter named
Bro.:   John Lawson & wife Ann - L10 in goods & Give it to
             them yearly - each a Suit of Mourning
Uncle;   Joseph Blackwell - a suit of mourning
Aunt:.   Lucy Blackwell - a suit of mourning
Cousin: Betty Chilton - a Suit of Worked Muslin not yet
             quite finished.
Cousin: Judy Blackwell - my Stone Ring
Cousins: Elizabeth Lawson, Anne Steptoe Lawson, Mary Lawson
             and Elizabeth Gilbert - all my wearing Cloaths to
             be divided among them by the discretion of my dear
Sister: Sister Mary Lawson
             ... Brick Wall Round my Fathers & Mothers Graves
Exor.:   Brother Epaphroditus Lawson
Signed: Anne Steptoe Lawson
Wit.:   Joseph Blackwell, Lucy Blackwell, Sarah Alexander
             Lee, Joseph Blackwell, Jr.
Proved: 28 November 1774, by o. of Joseph Blackwell and
             Joseph Blackwell. Epaphroditus Lawson made o. and
             was granted certificate for obtaining a probate.

Pages:
269-270:   JEREMIAH OWENS (Inventory)
             Date: 18 October 1774
App'd by: Geo. Berry, William Prim, Edward Feagin
Total Eval.: L37.1.6
Ret.:   28 November 1774

Page
270:         NICHOLAS BROWNING (Inventory)
             Date: 19 November 1774, Court Order dated
             October 1774
App'd by: Wm. Edmonds, Francis Attwell, Chas. Bell
Total eval.:   L22.3d.
Ret.:   28 November 1774

Page
271:         FRANCIS ASH (Inventory)
             Date: 28 January 1775
App'd by: Hez'h. Turner, John Adams, John Thomas Chunn
Total eval.: L706.15.5
Ret.:   27 February 1775

Pages
272-273:   JOSEPH LEAVELL (Inventory)
                  Date: 23 March 1775
App'd by: Charles Garner, Paul Williams, Thomas Helm
Total eval.: L242.4.6
Ret.:   27 March 1775

Pages
273-274:   WILLIAM PARKER, JR. (Will)
                  Date: 3 April 1775
Brother: Alexander Parker - bay mare and colt
Brother: Richard Barker - all the land I now possess -
         personal Estate - to maintain my farther &
         Mother as long as they both live and after
         their death to be divided between brother
         Richard Parker & my two sisters Ann Parker
Sisters: and Judith Parker
Exors.: Brothers Alexander Parker & Richard Parker
Signed: William Parker, Jun'r.
Wit.:   James (Σ) Shackelford, William Allen, William
         Hardwick
Proved: 22 May 1775, by o. of James Shackelford and
         William Allen. Alexander Parker and Richard
         Parker the Exors. were granted a cert. to
         obtain probate.

Pages:
274-275:   JOHN HURMONS (Will)
                  Date: 25 April 1775
Son:.   James Hermons - land on the West side of the Great
         branch cald Robinsons Joining Pearle & Carr ...
         when he comes to the age of Twenty one years, I
         likewise desire that he may be educated six years
         in an English school and lastly that he shall have
         five pounds sterling besides one fourth part of
         personal Estate when he comes to the age of 21 yrs.
Wife: Mary Hermons - to have the remainder of the land
         and after her death to be divided between two
         daughters: Susanna and Mary Hurmons, also the re-
         mainder of personal estate and after her death to
         be equally divided between three children
         I likewise desire that each of my Daughters may
         have three years education in an English school.
Dau.:   Susanna Hermons - ¼ part of personal estate when
         she marries or comes of age
Dau.:   Mary Hermons - ¼ part of personal estate when

```
                     she marries or comes of age
Exors:               Wife Mary Hermons and John Kincheloe
Signed:              John Hurmons
Wit.:                John Barker, William Kincheloe, John Kincheloe
Proved:              22 May 1775, by o. of William Kincheloe and
                     John Barker. Mary Hurmons and John Kincheloe
                     granted certificates to obtain probate.
```

Page
275::   JOHN ALLEN   (Inventory)
                     No date
App'd by: Thos. Keith, Wm. Hunton, Rob't. Sanders
Total eval.: L60.5.6
Ret.:   24 May 1775

Page
276::   HENRY ALLEN   (Inventory)
                     Date: 14 April 1775
App'd by: Samuel Grigsby, George Bennett, William Elliott,
          first sworn before John Moffett - Estate shown
          to appraisers by Betty Allen the Adminx Vide
Total eval.:: L29.12.3
Ret.:   22 May 1775

Pages
276-277::   WILLIAM HARRISON   (Inventory)
                     No date.
App'd by: John Thos. Chunn, John Ashby, John Southard -
          sworn first before John Moffett - Estate
          produced by Mrs. Jane Harrison, Adm'x.
Total eval.: L834.8.3
Ret.:   22 May 1775

Page
278:                 JOHN OBANNON   (Inventory)
                     Date: Court order dated 28 April 1774
App'd by: George Bennett, Richard Oldham, Samuel (SP)
          Pepper. No total.
Ret.:   22 May 1775

Page
279:                 JAMES CHAMBERLAYNE   (Inventory)
                     Date: Court Order dated: May 1775
                           26 October 1775
App'd by: Joseph Blackerby, John Metcalf, George Sullivan
No total. Ret.: 23 October 1775 (sic)

Pages
280-281:   BENNETT PRICE (Inventory)
                Date: 15 November 1774
App'd by: Francis Attwell, William Jones, Joseph Bragg
Total Eval.: L490.14.6
Ret.:   23 October 1775

Pages
281-282:   GEORGE FOOTE (Will)
                Date: 15 July 1775
Wife: Celia Foote - 1/3 estate during life, riding horse and mourning ring - if children should die without heirs all the property should go to her to dispose of as she thinks proper
Son: Richard Helm Foote - all lands and 1/2 of my other estate consisting of Negroes & Chattels
Dau.:   Hesther Foote - 1/2 Negroes & chattels - to be divided between them when they come to age or marry - it is my desire that my wife's thirds in Negroes and Chattels at her decease be equally divided between my above mentioned Children and it is my further desire that if my wife should be pregnant with a son, that then he have my Land on the South side of Town Run & an equal proportion of my negroes and Chattels, if a daughter, then only an equal proportion of my negroes and Chattels
Exors: Wife, Celia Foote, Lynaugh Helm, Richard Foote, William Alexander, Thomas Helm, Jun'r.
Signed: Geo. Foote
Wit.:   Hester Helm, Margaret Foote, John Vinnell, John (his I mark) Johnson, James (X) Wood
Proved: 27 November 1775, by o. of John Johnson, James Wood. Celia Foote granted cert. to obtain probate.

Pages
282-283:   JOHN BRAHAN (Will)
                No date.
           ... As it hath pleased Almighty God to spare me on his footstool a tract of time ...
Wife: Lettice - one negroe man named Tom - her proper part of everything else
Son: Thomas - all the tract of Land whereon I live which I desire he should peaceably enjoy after his Mother's decease
Son: John - one Negroe woman named Sarah
Son: William - one Negroe girl named Susanna
Son: James - one Negroe boy named Frank

If son Thomas should die the land he inherited
should "descend to the heir at Law and so down.."
Daus.:   All stock and household furniture to be divided
           among them
Exors.:   Morias Hansbrough and wife, Lettice
Signed: John Brahan
Wit.:   Morias Hansbrough, John Nelson, Edward Ralls
Proved: 27 November 1775, by o. of Edward Ralls. Morias
           Hansbrough and Lettice Brahan granted cert.
           25 March 1776 - proved by o. of John Nelson

Pages
283-284:   WILLIAM PARKER (Inventory)
                Date: 8 June 1775
App'd by: James Shackelford (%), James (x) Young, Benjamin
           Neale
Total eval.: L344.10s. Ret.: 25 March 1776

Pages
284-286:   CHARLES JONES (Inventory)
                Date: 3 October 1775
App'd by: Simon Hefling, Leroy Hughlett, Reubin Payne
Total eval.: L193.4.4
Ret.:   25 March 1776

Page
286:            JAMES RENNOLDS (Will)
                Date: 22 February 1776
Wife: Margaret - all my wordly Estate
Signed: James (X) Rennolds
           "Margaret Rennolds Executor for the same"
Wit.:   Edward Settle, Absalom Isles, Roseanner Settle
Proved: 25 March 1776, by o. of Absalom Isles, Rosanna
           Settle, Margaret Rennolds granted cert.

Page
287:            JOHN HOGAN (Estate Account)
Adm'r.:   John Owens
Details: Cash paid to: John Riddle, George Skinker,
           Silvester Welch. By: Silvester Welch, Benjamin
           Willoughby, John Leachman
Ret.:   27 March 1775

Pages
287-288:   JOHN HERMONS (Inventory)
                Date: 9 September 1775
App'd by: Wm. Kincheloe, Reubin Elliott, John Barker

Details: "To a small quantity of Doctors means;" "To
          Surgeons Instruments," "To a parcel of Doctors
          Means," "To a pr Saddle Bags."
No total. Ret.: 27 May 1776

Pages
288-289:   WILLIAM CHILTON (Inventory)
                     No date.
App'd by: George Rogers, John Tomlin, Ambrose Barnett
Total eval.: L732.16s.
Ret.:   26 August 1776

Pages
289-290:   WILLIAM RANSDELL, SENIOR   (Will)
                     Date: 3 July 1776
Wife: _____ - beloved wife the use of my whole
          Estate during her natural life and after her
          death as follows:
Son: Wharton - my Mansion house and plantation there-
          unto belonging - 1/3 of my whole Tract of Land
Sons: Thomas and William - the remaining part of my
          Tract of Land - my desire that my Mill be kept
          for the use of my plantation and my three sons
          upon the Tract of land
          .... if my son Wharton should die that then the
          Land and plantation devided to him shall devolve
          unto my son Thomas & the land devised unto him be
          equally divided between my two sons Edward &
          Chilton Ransdell
          ... if either of my two sons Thomas or William die
          the Land devised to them be equally divided bet-
          ween my two sons Edward & Chilton Ransdell
          .... all my Negroes, Stock, Houshold furniture to
          be equally divided between all my Children after
          the death of my wife according to Justice and
          Equity
Exors: loving sons: Wharton, Thomas and William
Signed: Will'm Ransdell, Sen'r.
Wit.:   Benj'n. Ashby, John Marshall, Ju., John Ritchie
Proved: 29 October 1776, on o. of John Marshall, Ju.,
          John Ritchie. Cert. to obtain probate granted
          to Thomas and William Ransdell.

Pages
291-293:   JOHN BRAHAWN (or BRAHAN) (Inventory)
                     Date: 19 January 1776
App'd by: Original Young, John Peters, John Wood

Total Eval: L295.18.7 "To half of Still & Tubb in
            partnership with John Nelson"
Ret.:   26 August 1776

Pages
293-295:   PETER CORNWELL (Will)
                    Date: 2 June 1776
Wife: Sarah Ann - the use of all my Estate both real &
            personal for and during her widowhood (except the
            legacies hereinafter mentioned)
Dau.:   Mary - one Good Feather bed & furniture and one
            Cow & Calf to be given up to her at the day of
            Marriage or when she arrives to the Age of Twenty
            one years
Son: Daniel - one dark bay mare commonly called his
Son: Jacob - one horse of the value of twelve or four-
            teen pounds
Son: Simon - the land whereon he lives agreeable to the
            boundaries made between him & myself supposed to be
            about twenty five acres
Son: Jarvice - the land between the Ledge of Rocks and
            his own line also the Land on the South side of
            his path to the Main Road, this Land I agreed for
            and bought of Hector Ross, Gent.
Sons: Daniel & Jacob - all my land at the Pignut Ridge
            except what is already bequeathed - to be held in
            joint tenancy to them and their heirs - if either
            of them die without issue the survivor to have the
            whole - if both should die without issue - the land
            to be sold and the price arising from the sale be
            equally divided between my then surviving children
            ... on death or marriage of wife all slaves &
            personal Estate be equally divided amongst my
            children then living except my two sons Daniel
            & Jacob
Dau.:   Cloe Strange - that such part of my Estate as
            shall become payable to my daughter - shall be
            in trust in the hands of my Executors for her use
Exors: Wife Sarah Ann, son Simon and Mr. William Hunton
Signed: Peter (his D mark) Cornwell
Wit.:   J. Moffett, John Dugarde, Anne (her A mark) Cockrell
Proved: 26 August 1776, by o. of John Moffett and John
            Dugard. Sarah Ann Cornwell and Simon Cornwell
            granted certs. to obtain probate

Page 295:
        JOHN SINKLEAR (Inventory)
        Date: 5 August 1776
App'd by: John Morehead, John Smith, Charles Smith
Total eval.: L93
Ret.: 26 August 1776

Page 296:
        WILLIAM DRUMMOND (Inventory)
        Date: 24 May 1776
App'd by: Hez'h Turner, John Thos. Chunn, John Adams
Total eval.: L29.15.9
Ret.: 26 August 1776

Pages 297-301: JOHN MAUZY (Estate Account)

Adm'r.: Original Young
Exors.: Henry Mauzy and W. Rousaw
Details: TO: Peggy Mauzy's board for 1771; Molly Mauzy's board for 1771; Mr. John Lee, Tho. Carver for Schoolg Pegy, Molly & Betty Mauzey for 1770 - L3; John Ralls; John Catlett; Mr. Gibson, Merchant; James Wood; Thomas Carver; Cuth. Harrison; John Nelson, Senet Young; Doctor Graham; Mr. Vowles; Darkey Carr; Chris. Young; Sam'l. Wood; John Fristoe; Mr. Geo. Johnson; Mr. Martin Pickett; Ben Pope for schooling Molley & Betty Mauzy; Mr. Geo. Laws; James Peters. BY: Peter Wood; William Miller; F. Honers; Jno. Nelson; J. Luttrell; Wm. Lambert; W. Hogins; Wm. Fletcher; James Homes; W. Blackwell; John Neavil, Sheriff; Col. Adam Stephens; Ann Russell; John Combs; Thos. Skinker; William Coppage; Brereton Jones; Howson Kenner; Thomas Whitledge
Ret.: 31 August 1776, by Original Young and the exors. of the Estate of John Mauzy, dec'd.
Signed: Wm. Grant, W. Blackwell

Pages 301-303: JOHN MAUZY (Estate Account)

Admr.: Original Young Dr.: Pegy Mauzy, infant
Date: First entry dated 9 February 1773
Details: CASH PAID TO: John Fristoe, Mr. John Blackwell, Mr. John Litheow, Wm. Rusaw, A. Catlett, Mr. Deall, Mr. Lithgow, Mr. Chapman, Mr. Owens, Peter Crawford, Peggy Nelson, William Vann, Henry Clay, Dr. Neff, Gilbert Attwood, Harman Honer.

REC'D FROM: Stephen Lee for Wm. Lambert, John
Fristoe, William Vann, Josiah Jenkins, Joshua
Fletcher, George Collins
Dated: 31 August 1776, examined by W. Grant and W.
           Blackwell
Ret.:   23 September 1776

Pages
303-304:   JOHN MAUZY (Estate Account)

Gdn.:   Original Young (Molly Mauzy's part of Estate)
Details: PAID TO: Mr. Lithcoe, John Atwood, Mr. Chapman,
           Peggy Nelson, John Blackwell, Wm. Vann, Henry
           Clay, Senett & Young, Harmon Honor. REC'D FROM:
           1/3 part of estate of John Mauzy, John Murray,
           William Pope.
Examined by: W. Grant and W. Blackwell, 31 August 1776
Ret.:   23 September 1776

Pages
304-305:   JoHN MAUZY (Estate Account)

Gdn.:   Original Young (Betty Mauzy, Infant)
Details: PAID TO: John Lithcoe, Chapman, Nath'l. Ashby,
           Peggy Nelson, John Fristoe, Mr. Carr, Gilbert
           Atwood. REC'D.: James Peters, Mr. Seaton at
           Dumfries.
Examined by: W. Grant and W. Blackwell, 31 August 1776
Ret.:   23 September 1776

Pages
305-306:   THOMAS JAMES (Will)
                Date: 9 April 1772
Wife: Mary James - 1/3 part of estate during her natural
           life - that her dower in Lands be set apart to her
           out of the Tract I now live on lying on Deep Run -
           at her death her Dower to descend as followeth:
Sons: George and Thomas - above land to be equally divided
           Between them and the Personal Estate therein to be
           equally divided among all my children that may be
           then living
Daus.:   Molly, Agatha, Margaret and Elizabeth - to each L250
           ... Executors to sell the following tracts and
           lots of land: Land in Spotsylvania County that I
           purchased of George Sharpe, my lot and houses in
           the Town of Fredericksburg, known by the name of
           the long Ordinary and One thousand Acres of the
           land I have purchased of Warner Washington - Money

arising from the sale to be used to pay the sums
devised to daughters. The remainder of the
estate, real and personal, to my said two Sons:
George James and Thomas James

Exors: My friends Charles Bruce, Thomas Hoard, Gerard
Banks and my brother John James.
Signed: Thomas James
Wit.: James Crap, Jun'r., James Allen, John James,
William Delany, Benj'a. Cramp, H. Smith
Codicil: 1 January 1775: In Order to prevent the appear-
ance of a despute be it remembered that whatever
Account I may have against Michael Robinson,
Jun'r. at my death is to be deemed & understood
as so much of my daughter Molly's fortune paid.
Wit.: Ger. Banks Signed: Thomas James
Proved: 26 February 1776, by o. of James Crap, Jr. and
John James. Cert. to obtain probate granted
Charles Bruce, executor.

Page
307: THE ESTATE OF SALLY MAUZEY DAUGHTER OF
MARY MAUZEY, DECEASED
Details: Thomas Conway's account against his ward - first
entry for board and clothing dated 1774.
Ret.: 24 March 1777

Pages
307-308: THOMAS BARBEY (Inventory)
Date: 24 February 1777
App'd by: Garner Burgess, Samuel Luttrell, Matthew Neale
Wit.: James Foley, C. Dulany
Ret.: 24 March 1777

Page
308: RICHARD HALL (Inventory)
Court Order dated: July 1774
"Estate of Richard Hall deceased at the
Marsh Quarter."
App'd by: Jeremiah Darnall, Zach's. Lewis, James Wright
No total. Ret.: 27 January 1777

Page
309: RICHARD LUNGAN HALL (Inventory)
Estate of Richard Lungan Hall deceased as
was produced to us at the house and on the
Plantation where the said Hall died.
Date: Court Order dated: July 1774
App'd by: Whart'n Ransdell, Charles Morehead, John Ransdell
No total.

July 1st 1776

This my will if it Please God to take me out of this
world into an Eternal world. I give to Wm Sinclor my
Negro Fellow Henery and as the Rest of my properties
I give to my two Eldest Sisters and my Eldest Brother
if so be that I Never Come up Again -- I shall be <u>very</u>
Glad if you will be kind Enough to make ---- Best
Advantage of <u>hary</u> Another year. Sir -----

    I have Got the momps a Comeing on me

      I am your most humbled Servent

                  John McLain

Test

Wm Morgin

Vincent Rust

Benjamin Daggitt

This is to certify that John McLain of Capt Ashby's
Company in the 3rd Virg[a] Regt., Died at Mrs. Lefevers
near Carpinder Hall in Philadelphia Jany 1st 1777.

                  Nathl Ashby

                  Saml Waddy

Fauquier To wit The above sworn to before me the
26th February 1777.

                  Jeremiah Darnall

Proved 24th March 1777 by oath of Nathal Ashby. William
Sinclair granted Certificate for obtaining letters of
Administration.

    The above was discovered in the 1777 Will File this
26 April 1954 and filed at the end of Will Book No. 1.

            /s/ T. E. Bartenstein, Clk.

Details: Bond from William Hampton; James Slaughter on
acc't of the Estate of Rich'd Hampton dec'd;
Acc't against Capt. Morehead; do Capt. Elias
Edmonds; do Capt. Wharton Ransdell; do James
Stewart; do William Kirk; do John Russaw; do
William Chilton; do John Cordell
Ret.: 27 January 1777

Page
310: SANFORD CARRELL (Will) of the Parish of Leeds
Date: 8 April 1777
Wife: Elizabeth Carrell - 150 a. of Land jointly with
Silvester Welch the plantation I now live on
during her Widowhood and if she marries the said
Land to be taken away from her by the Executors
and rented out for the children, Anna and Demsey
Porter Carrell and Sally Carrell, children of the
said Sanford Carrell
Wife: Elizabeth - two Negro girls (same conditions as
above) - for the maintenance of my three children:
a Convict Servant man named James James during his
servitude - all the Personal Estate
Exors: beloved wife Elizabeth, Captain John Obanon
Signed: Sanford Carrell
Wit.: Thomas Bartlett, Silvester Welch, James Bartlett
Ret.: 28 July 1777, by o. of Thomas Bartlett, James
Bartlett, Elizabeth Carrell and John Obanon
granted certificate to obtain probate.

Page
311: MR. WILLIAM NELSON (Inventory)
Date: 26 July 1777
App'd by: Ben Harrison, John Peters, George Crosby
Total eval.: L44.2s.
Ret.: 28 July 1777

Pages
311-312: GEORGE O'BANNON (Will)
No date
"Dear mother and brothers i writ to let you know
that i am in good health thanks be to God for it
at this present hoping this lines will find you all
in health. Remember me to all my friends not for-
geting Cuzzen Elizabeth Carle remember my love to
her. I don't expect that i shall write any more
and to let you know that wey are not ben in know
battle yet but we yerepect it every day and night

wey are on a iland about fifteen miles longs two
miles or three miles wide and the innamy is all
round the iland we have know way to get off we
must fit our way off our men is a fiting every day
and night the other night a battle the nue yourk
iland other night at kings Bridge wrothe Town is
on the Island. i am in great hopes that i shawl see
you all again but we expect a battle evere day and
night i am gart hops that the town will be burnt
in a few days the english wod have burnt it before
this time but they want the town for Barricks but
if they dont burn the Town wee Shawll burn the
Town our slves now more at present but you dutiful
son
                      George Obannon
it is my desire that my brother Benjamin Obannon
should have all my astat after my dets is paid i
hop my der brothers you wont think amiss of it for
i think he wont it worse affter my death."

Ret.:   25 August 1777 - handwriting proved by James Foley,
         Jr. Joseph Nelson granted cert. to obtain probate.

Page
312:         GREENHAM DODSON (Will)
                Date: 8 October 1776
Bro.:   Enoch Dodson - slaves
Sister: Tabitha Shumate - slave
Sister: Mary Shumate - above brother & sister to pay Mary
         the sum of L15 each
Mother: Barbary Dodson - "to keep possession of all my
         Estate both real & personal during her natural life."
Exors.: William Hunton and Daniel Shumate
Signed: Greenham Dodson
Wit.:   Johnson Owens, Ayah (X) Shirly
Ret.:   25 August 1777, proved by o. of Johnson Owens and
         Archibald Shirley. Daniel Shumate granted cert.
         to obtain probate.

Page
313:         ELIJAH NASH (Will)
                Date: 1 September 1776
         "Know all Men by these Presents that my will is
         if I never return from the Wars that my Negroe
         Garl that is now living at James Sanders, should
         belong to my sister Elizabeth Sanders and her
         heirs forever."
Signed: Elijah Nash

Wit.:: William Hunton, Judith Hunton, Betty Hunton
Ret.:: 26 May 1777, by o. of William Hunton and Judith
Hunton. John Nash granted cert. to obtain probate.

Pages
313-315:   JAMES BAILEY (Inventory)
               Date: 9 January 1777
App'd by: James McClanahan, William Roach, Parnach George
Details: First section amounted to L484.4.3; the section
          entitled "Mrs. White's third" amounted to L158.
          11s.7d. ... we the Subscribers have appraised upon
          Oath the Estate of James Bailey dec'd. & set apart
          the Widow's dower.
Ret.:   26 May 1777

Pages
315-316:   JOHN RECTOR, JUNIOR (Inventory)
               Date: 24 March 1776
App'd by: Harman Hitt, Jacob Rector, Thomas Glascock
Total eval.: L96.10.6
Ret.:   26 May 1777

Pages
316-317:   CHRISTOPHER MATCALF (Inventory)
               Court Order dated:. March 1777
App'd by: James Murray, John Fields, Uriel Crosby
No total. Ret.: 26 May 1777

Pages
317-318:   SAMUEL WOOD (Inventory)
               No date.
App'd by: Champe Coram, Thomas Railey, James Luttrell
Total eval.: L18.6.3
Ret.:   26 May 1777

Pages
318-319:   SANFORD CARRELL (Inventory)
               No date.
App'd by: John Fishback, Ephraim Hubbard, Sam'l. Grigsby
No total. Ret.: 25 November 1777

Page
319:           JOSEPH SMITH (Inventory)
               Date: 22 November 1777
App'd by: Joseph Taylor, William Nash, Edw'd. Ball
No total. Ret.: 24 November 1777

- 82 -

Page
320:

JOHN CHILTON (Will) "of the Third
Regiment of Virginia Regulars"
Date: 24 August 1776

Children: Joseph, Lucy, George, Nancy - that the land I
purchased of Debutts be sold when my son Thomas
comes to age and the money arising from Sale of
said Land be equally divided between my four
children ...

Son: Thomas - the land given me by my father on which I
lately lived, also my Surveying Instruments. The
small piece of Land joining Shackleford & Parker
I wish to be cleared from the Office and sold and
the money to be laid out at the discretion of my
Executors for the benefit of my Children (previous
provisions for their education and maintenance)

Exors: Major Martin Pickett, Mr. Thomas Keith and Charles
Chilton

Signed: John Chilton

Wit.: Sam'l. Boyd, John Blackwell, Jr., John Ashby, Jun'r.,
Isham Keith, Joseph Blackwell, Jr.

Ret.: 24 November 1777, proved by o. of Samuel Boyd, John
Ashby, Jr., and Isham Keith. Charles Chilton and
Thomas Keith granted cert. to obtain probate.

Pages:
321-322:

THOMAS BULLITT (Will) "Thomas Bullitt, Esq.
of Fauquier County"
Date: 17 September 1775

Bro.: Joseph Bullitt - that my Executor hereinafter named
shall build out of my Estate for my Brother a
house of the price of Twenty pounds to be fixed on
the plantation he now lives on
... direct that my Executor and Devisee shall carry
into execution an Agreement and Bargain entered into
by me with Mr. Cuthbert Combs relative to settling
and improving sundrie Lands &c upon the Kanhawa
River at the mouth of Elk
... to Sarah Bronaunt & her heirs 400 acres of
Land upon the Kanhawa & below the mouth of Elk
... to the said Sarah Bronaunt who is the natural
daughter of Martha Bronaunt, a young Negroe wench,
either one of my own or one purchased by my Executor at his option, provided she is young and likely,
as also I give her L5 annually until she arrives
at the age of 18 years, for her maintenance

Sister: Seth Combs - L15 to purchase her mourning ring

... Mr. Benjamin Harrison - two Colts of the
next Foald the one a horse, the other a Mare,
he is to have his Choice of what are dropt that
season by any of my Mares
... Cuthbert Combs - his next choice of any horse
colt dropt next season from any of my Mares
Bro.: Cuthbert Bullitt - all the rest of my Estate Real
and personal & all my Entries & Interest in any
land whatso ever ... I appoint him Executor.
Signed: Tho's. Bullitt
Wit.: John Blanset, Charles Guy, William Blanset
Proved: 23 February 1778, by o. of Charles Guy, who also
made o. that he saw the other Subscribing
witnesses who are now dead sign the same, being
called upon so to do by the Testator. Cuthbert
Bullitt made o. & was granted cert. to obtain
probabe.

Pages
322-323: JOHN MINTER (Will)
Date: 14 January 1778
Wife: Mary Minter, beloved wife - 1/3 of my Estate
during her natural life and then divided between my children, William, Elizabeth & Jacob
Son: Anthony - my tract of Land whereon I now live
that was left me by my Father Joseph Minter -
my Still and Worm - shall have a good Country
Education and when he shall arrive to age of
Meturity that he shall be bound out by my
Executors to a trade that they shall think will
then sute his Genius and that he shall be ed-
cated from the profit arising from my said Estate.
... to my Children William, Elizabeth and Jacob
Minter, the rest of my Estate to be equally divided
Sons: William and Jacob - when they come to age, that if
my Executors shall think proper, that then they
shall be bound out to such Trade that will best
suit their Genius's
Dau.: Elizabeth - shall be brought up by my sister
Rogers and that she shall be maintained from my
said Estate
Exors: Charles Chilton, Joseph Minter and George Rogers
Signed: John Minter
Wit.:. George Rogers, Mary (x) Baley, William Tomlin
Proved: 23 February 1778, by o. of Mary Bailey and William
Tomlin. Charles Chilton, Joseph Minter and George
Rogers made o. and granted cert. to obtain probate.

- 84 -

Pages
323-324:   ELIZABETH ETHERINGTON (Will)
              Date: 29 November 1776
Devisees: ... Catherine Nelson - one feather bed & furni-
              ture - one Cow & Calf - one Womans side saddle -
              one Walnut Square Table
              ... I lend Betty Allen - one feather bed & furni-
              ture - one Cow & Calf during her natural life then
              I give them to her eldest daughter - all my Wareing
              Cloaths I leave to be divided between Catherine
              Nelson, Betty Allen and Catherine Duncan
              ... Benjamin Russell - one bead & furniture which
              he hath now in his possession
Nephew: ... to my beloved nephew Thomas Obannon, son to
              Samuel Obannon, one still, and it is my desire that
              Capt. John Wright, Sen'r. is to have the use of
              the said tole free during his natural life - one
              negroe Woman named Luse with all her Increase -
              Negroe man named Harry - negroe man named Tom -
              I also give all my goods & Chattels to my beloved
              nephew Thomas O'Bannon, son to Samuel Obannon
Exors: Capt. Elias Edmonds, Sen'r. and Jeremiah Darnall
Signed: Elizabeth (her X mark) Etherington
Wit.:   Harry Bramlett, Berryman Jennings, James Wright
Proved: 23 March 1778, by o. of Berryman Jennings and
              James Wright. And the Executors therein named
              having refused to take upon them the Execution
              thereof On the motion of Thomas Obannon who made
              Oath and executed & acknowledged bond as the law
              directs, Cert. is granted him for obtaining letters
              of administration with the will annexed.

Pages
324-325:   JOHN SHIPP (Will)
              Date: 19 February 1778
Son: Richard Wiatt Shipp - Negroes big Lucy and little
              Lucy
Son: Laban Shipp - negroes Sampson and Judy
Son: Coleby - negroes Tom & Joshua
Dau.:   Suckey Drummond - negroes Hannah & Lancaster
Dau.:   Polly Shipp - negroes Milly & Ben
Dau.:   Betsy Shipp - Negroes Winny & Davie
Dau.:   Nancy Shipp - Negroe Amey - together with L75
              Virginia Currency - the rest of my Estate to be
              equally divided among my Children before men-
              tioned and if any of them die underage and un-
              married that then their parts be equally divided
              among the Survivors

```
Exors:    Sons Richard Wiatt Shipp and Laban Shipp
Signed:   John (his ƚ mark) Shipp
Wit.:     Thomas Lewis, William Donaldson, Thomas James
Proved:   23 March 1778, by o. of William Donaldson and
          Thomas James.  Richard Wiatt Shipp made o. and
          granted cert. to obtain probate
```

Pages
326-327:   JOHN CATLETT, SENIOR of the Parish of
                   Dittingen and County of Fauquier (Will)
                   Date: 3 February 1778
Son: John - 1 shilling sterling
Son: William - a tract of Land on the East side of
         the old Gleib Road Containing 179 a. more or less
Son: Loving son Alexander - the plantation I now live
         on containing 179 a.
Dau.:   Loving daughter Elizabeth Catlett - two white boys
         named John & Henry Henderson until they arrive at
         the age of twenty-one years, which boys was pur-
         chased for me with their Father & Mother of Mr.
         Hector Ross & the Indenture taken in the name of
         Alexander Catlett - also two years Rents of the
         Plantation whereon James Doudle is now Tenant which
         is 3000 pounds of Crop Tobacco - the choice of any
         Cow out of my Flock of Cattle - my Spice mortar &
         pestle and Teakettle - that my said Daughter shall
         not be disturbed for this present year from any
         food or Crop for her support and likewise that she
         may remain undisturbed and enjoy the place she now
         lives at during her natural life and also I give
         the said Elizabeth my black Walnut Chest with
         Drawers
Dau.:   Loving dau. Jane Coppage - my Roan Mare & Colt with
         my Saddle and Bridle and my black Walnut folding
         Table
Gr.dau.: Margret Hume - my Weaving Loom and the gear belong-
         ing to the old Loom
Dau.:   Bersheba Young - bed & furniture I now ly on - the
         remainder of my movable Estate to be Equally divided
         between Maryann Hogans, Elizabeth Catlet, Jane
         Coppage, Bersheba Young, Isbell Summers & Frances
         Priest and that the said Estate shall not be sold
         but be equally divided
Exors: Moses Coppage & John Hogan
Signed: John Catlett, Sen'r.
Wit.:   Origin al Young, James Dowdall, James (x) Holmes
         Wm. Pope

Proved: 23 March 1778, by the o. of Original Young &
James Holmes. Moses Coppage & John Hogan made
oath and granted cert. to obtain probate.

Pages
327-329:   **JOHN BRONAUGH** (Will) of Stafford County &
Parish of Overwharton
Date: 1 July 1777

Wife: Beloved wife, Mary Ann Bronaugh - all my Estate,
Real & Personal for her Natural life provided She
shall not Marry, but in case that she doth Marry
again that then I give her for and in during her
natural life the Dwelling plantation whereon I now
live, and also the following negroes: Lucy, Lettice,
Judah, Bob, George & Stephen and at her death the
aforesaid Tract of Land and negroes to go to my
son William Bronaugh

Son: William - all that tract of Land lying and being in
the County of Prince William on broad Run whereon
now lives John Delgam, William Davis & Meredith Moss

Son: John - 500 a. lying in the County of Loudon (sic)
near the mouth of Goose Creek bequeathed me in the
last Will & Testament of my Aunt, Mrs. Ann Mason,
also four Negroes Viz: big Sam, Jane, Charles and
James

Dau.:   Margaret Bronaugh - negroe Wench named Lydia, also
one Negroe man named Sam - one negroe man named
Griffin

Dau.:   Mary Mason Bronaugh - negroe Wench named Bett

Son :   William - one Negroe boy named Daniel - all that
Tract or parcel of Land lying in Fairfax County
bequeathed me in the last Will & Testament of my
Mother Mrs. Sympha Roseinfield Bronaugh to be sold
and the money arising from the sale to go to the
discharge of my just Debts and the ballance that
shall Remain to be equally Deived amongst my Daughters Marget & Mary Mason Bronaugh - one negroe boy
named Jack

Dau.:   Margret Bronaugh - one negroe girl named Beck (a
child of Liddies)

Exors: Wife Mary Ann Bronaugh, and brother Mr. William
Bronaugh

Signed: John Bronaugh

Proved: 25 May 1778 - Identity of the hand Writing being
proved by William Waite and William Bronaugh it was
Ordered to be recorded. Mary Ann Bronaugh made o.
and granted certificate to obtain probate.

Page
329:
                STEPHEN DONALDSON   (Inventory)
                Date: 8 August 1777
App'd by: Parnick George, Benj'a. Robinson, William Roach
Total eval.: L38.10.0
Ret.:   25 May 1778

Page
330:
                JOHN MINTER   (Inventory)
                Date: 3 February 1778
App'd by: Benj'a. Robinson, John Tomlin, William Roach
Total eval.: L630.13.6
Ret.:   25 May 1778

Page
331:
                ROBERT STEPHENS   (Estate Account)
Admr.:   Wm. Stephens
Details: Items dated 1773 - To my attendance at Court
           from long branch of Little River - Wm. Bartley
           By appraisement of Estate L190.15.0
Ret.:   25 May 1778

Pages
331-332:
                DOCTOR JOHN DUGARD   (Inventory)
                No date.
App'd by: William Norris, Rowley Smith, Jas. Taylor
No total.   Ret.: 25 May 1778

Pages
332-334:
                JOHN JAMES of the Parish of Hamilton and
                County of Fauquier   (Will)
                Date: 6 November 1777
Son: Thomas - all that piece of land lying on the
           Eastermost side of the Spring branch, which Land
           came by his mother, and as there is a small
           quantity of acres of the Land which came by her
           on the other side of the said Spring branch, I
           give to my Said son Thomas in lieu thereof as
           much of my other Lands adjoining the Lands already
           bequeathed (which land I purchased of Griffin) as
           will make with that which came by his mother a
           tract of 500 acres in the whole and binding on
           Capt. Gibson, Capt. Kenners & Rodham Tullos land,
           my siad son Thomas shall not possess the said be-
           quest till after the Decease of his Mother
Son: Benjamin - after his Mothers decease the plantation
           whereon I now live and as much land adjoining as
           will make a Tract of 500 acres bounded as follows:

- 88 -

Begining at the Corner of John Kerr's & my Land
thence up the Spring Branch to the Spring, thence
from a marked White Oak South six degrees east to
the Waggon Road which leads from the Church to
Brereton Jones's the sd 500 acres to lye on both
sides of the sd. Road and joining the Land of John
Crump, Colo. Wm. Eustace & George Crump, also one
Negroe boy named Tom - one feather bed & furniture -
one cow and calf and two Ewes & Lambs - incase of
Benjamin's death the lands to go to son John

Son: John - all my land lying on the South westermost
side of the Waggon Road & Tullos & path containing
by estimation 500 acres - Negroe boy named Moses,
one feather bed and furniture, one cow & calf and
two Ewes & Lambs. If son John should die without
lawful issue the land to be equally divided between
my son Thomas James and my Daughters Sarah Hitt,
Ann Tullos, Hannah Humes, Elizabeth Bradford, Mary
Conway, Dinah Thompson & Susannah James.

Dau.:   Susannah James - a horse - Bridle & Saddle - one
feather bed and furniture - one Cow & Calf and two
Ewes & Lambs

Gr.dau.: Hannah finnie - a bed & furniture - a Cow & Calf
and a horse

Gr.Son: Benjamin James - a horse - bridle and Saddle - one
bed & furniture - one Cow & Calf

Wife: Dinah James - all the residue of my estate both
real & personal during her life & after her decease
all the land not already bequeathed to my Children
I leave to be equally divided among my Daughters
Sarah Hitt, Ann Tullos, Hannah Humes, Eliz'a Bradford, Mary Conway, Dinah Thompson & Susannah James
All the Slaves and their increase lent to his
Children were to be returned after the decease of
his wife and divided with the reat of his Estate.

Exors.:   My dear and loving wife Dinah James and my Sons
Thomas James, Benjamin James & John James.

Signed: John James

Wit.:   Wm. Grant, John Kerr, J. Markham, Marmaduke Brown.

Proved: 25 May 1778, by o. of William Grant, Marmaduke
Brown and John Kerr. Dinah James and Thomas James
made o. and granted cert. to obtain probate.

Pages
334-335:   MARY MARR (Inventory)
          Date: 10 June 1778; Crt. Order dtd.: May 1778
App'd by: James Duncan, Paul Williams, James Wheatley
Total eval.: L102.5.6   Ret.: 22 June 1778

Pages
335-336:   JOHN SHIPP (Inventory)
                Date: 4 March 1778
App'd by: Gregory Glascock, Thomas James, John Dulin,
           Wm. Donaldson. No total.
Ret.:   22 June 1778

Pages
336-337:   SARAH LEWIS of Loudon County (Will)
                Date: 4 February 1768
Dau.:   Sibly West - one mourning Ring
Dau.:   Sarah Manly - one mourning Ring
Dau.:   Mary Peake - all the rest and residue of my
           Estate - during her natural life and after her
           decease to descend to her Children begotten by
           John Peake to be equally among them or to the
           Survivor of Survivors of them
Exor.:   Son-in-law, John Peake
Signed: Sarah (X) Lewis
Wit.:   William Whiteley, Clater Smith
Proved: 22 June 1778, by o. of William Whitley. John
           Peake made o. and was granted cert. to obtain
           probate.

Pages
337-338:   JOHN RUST (Inventory)
                No date.
App'd by: Thos. Nelson, Benjamin Rector, Joseph Robinson.
No total. Ret.: 22 June 1778

Page
339:   PETER CORNWELL (Inventory)
                No date.
App'd by: Thomas Maddux, Thomas Watts & George Kennard,
           "being first sworn before John Moffett, Gent.,
           Justice ..."
Total eval.: L287.0.7 Ret.: 22 June 1778

Pages
340-341:   GEORGE FOOTE (Inventory)
                No date.
App'd by: Benj'a. Harrison, Jon'a. Gibson, John James
Total eval.: L950.2.9 Ret.: 22 June 1778

Pages
341-343:   JOHN CATLETT (Inventory)
                Date: 4 May 1778

App'd by: Richard Luttrell, John Wood, John Peters
Total eval.: L392.12.9
Ret.:   22 June 1778

Pages
343-346:   MINOR WINN (Will)
              Date: 31 July 1775
Wife: Margaret Winn - all my Estate Royl & Personal
           for and during her natural life
Son: William - one Negro man named Godfree and if any
           person whatever should Seas on the said negroe for
           his Debts, then the said Negroe shall be the hole
           & Sole property of my Grandaughter Martha Smith
           and her heirs forever.
Son: John - one Negroe woman named Jean - negroe boy
           named Ben - negroe boy named Moses now in his
           possession - one Negroe man named Antony.
Son: James - negroe man named James - negroe boy named
           Lewis
Son: Minor Winn - one negroe man named Reuben and one
           negroe man named Solomon now in his persession,
           also my Riding horse Bridle & Saddle and all my
           wearing apparel - also my Great Bible
Son: Richard - one negroe man named Will, now in his
           possession also one negroe boy named Tom during his
           natural life and if my son Richard should die with-
           out an heir Lawfully begotten by his body then his
           part of my Estate shall be equally divided among
           my Children then a liveing.
Dau.:   Margaret Johnson - one negroe Girl named Winny now
           in her possession also one Negroe boy named Jack
           Monday
Dau.:   Mary Smith - and equal part of my Estate that is
           sold after paying my Just Debts
Dau.:   Susanna Grant - one Negroe that she had in
           persession named Dick also one negroe Girl named
           Hanner and if my Daughter Susanner Grant should
           die without an heir Lawfully begotten by her body
           then her part of my Estate shall be equally divided
           among my Children then aliving
Gr.dau.:   Martha Smith - one negroe girl named Lucy now in
           her persession
Dau.:.   Elizabeth Smith - Children forty pounds to be eq-
           ually divided among the whole after the decease of
           my wife - all the Ballance of my Estate both Royal
           & personal to be sold after the deceast of my wife
           at twelve month Credit with taking good bond &

Security and what remains after paying my Just
Debts and Funeral Charges among all my Children
then living by my said Wife Margaret Winn

Exors: Wife Margaret Winn and son Minor Winn
Signed: Minor (W) Winn
         Margaret (her M mark) Winn
Wit.:   Stephen Tolle, Thomas White, James Fleming
Codicil: 5 February 1778: Whereas I sometime ago purchased a Tract of Land of Mr. Martin Pickett
lying on the south side of Little River part
of a Tract formerly belonging to Holtzclaw and
have the said Pickett's bond for making me a
title to the same as soon as he can obtain a
Decree of the Court to put him in possession
thereof ..said Land to my son Minor Winn and
desire that Colo. Pickett may make Deeds for the
same to my said son .. And whereas I have in
partnership with my son Minor Winn, erected a
Still house on the said Minors Land & furnished
the same with Stills and the necessary Utensils
for carrying on the distilling business and have
likewise in partnership with him raised a Stock
of Hogs at the said Still House and purchased a
Sett of Blacksmiths Tools, the Profits of all
which several Articles were by bargain to be
equally divided between my said son and my self
during my life, and after my decease between my
wife Margaret Winn and my said son .. during her
life. My desire is that the said Stills, Stock,
Tools &c be kept together during the life of my
said Wife .. and the profits arising therefrom to
be equally divided between my said Wife & Son ..
after her death .. shall be appraised by persons
on Oath & my said son .. shall be at liberty to
keep the same on paying the one half of what they
shall be appraised to my Executors for the benefit
of my Estate.

Signed: Minor (his M mark) Winn
Wit.:   Peter Grant, James Winn, Hannah Winn
Proved: 23 March 1778, on o. of Stephen Tolle; Codicil
proved by o. of James Winn & Hannah Winn. Margaret
Winn and Minor Winn made o. and were granted cert.
to obtain probate. "And at a Court held for the said
County the 27th day of July 1778 this will was
proved by the Oath of Spencer Tolle a witness thereto."

<pre>
Page
347:                SARAH LEWIS (Inventory)
                    Date: 27 July 1778
App'd by: John Peake, Sen'r.   No total.
Ret.:   27 July 1778

Pages
347-348:   ELIZABETH ETHERINGTON (Inventory)
                    Court Order dated: 24 March 1778
App'd by: Thos. Bronaugh, John Wright, Henry Bramlet his
          mark +   Total eval.: L933.3.6
Ret.:   24 August 1778

Pages
348-351:   AUGUSTINE. JENNINGS "of the Parish of
                    Hamelton" (Will)
                    Date: 13 December 1776
</pre>

Wife: I lend to my wife Hannah Jennings the Plantation whereon I now live and four slaves, two of her Choice and of the Executor's hereafter named during her natural life or widowhood, not to claim any right or title to any lands hereafter

Son: William - 200 a. of Land belong to the Planatation whereon he now lives - one negroe man named Tom and L20 to be drawn out of my Estate

Son: Augustin - 200 a. of land belonging to the plantation whereon he now lives and one negroe man named Ben - one negroe Girl named Agga - if he should die without a male Heir the land and negroes to fall to my son George Jennings

Son: Berryman - that part or parcel of Land lying on the Westside of the Elk-Marsh Run, whereon he now lives and two negroes as it may fall by Lott - if the said Berryman should die without a Mail Heir to fall to my son George Jennings

Son: Baylor - the remaining part of that tract before mentioned to Berryman, lying on the Eastside of the above mentioned Run and two negroes as shall fall by Lott - if the said Baylore should die without a Mail heir then to fall to my son George. If the said Augustin, Berryman and Baylor should so die, the said Land & Negroes to be equally divided between my sons Lewis and George Jennings

Son: Lewis - the land and plantation whereon I now live after my wifes decease and two slaves as shall fall by Lott

Son: George - two slaves as shall fall by Lott and one

	more after his mothers decease
Dau.:	Betty Jennings - L40 to be paid out of my Estate after my wifes decease and if my wife should think proper to pay any part of the said Money to her the said Betty - in her lifetime it shall be good on shewing a receipt for the same.
Dau.:	Hannah Jennings - two negroes as may fall by Lott, one to be delivered on her Marriage, the other to be delivered at the discretion of my Executors who will be hereafter mentioned
Dau.:	Sally Jennings - two Negroes as may fall out by Lott (same conditions as above)
Dau.:	Jemima Hudnall - all that part of my Estate as she hath already received and L20 to be drawn out of my Estate at the discretion of my wife and Exors.
Dau.:	Fanny Obanon - one Negroe wench named Patt and all besides as she hath hitherto received and L20 to be paid to her
Dau.:	Nancy Weathers - L10 to be paid to her at the discretion of my wife and executors - one young negroe wench named Esther and all that she hath before
Dau.:	Cloe Weathers - one negroe wench named Judah - one negroe boy named Simon and all the goods & Chattels as she hath before received
Exors:	my well beloved sons William and Augustin Jennings and wife Hannah Jennings
Signed:	Augustine Jennings Hannah Jennings
Wit.:	Henry Bramlett, Benjamin Russell, Lucretia (x) Russell, Peter Barker
Proved:	24 August 1778, by o. of Benjamin Russell and Lucretia Russell. William Jennings and Augustine Jennings made o. and executed and ack. bond as the law directs, cert. granted them for obt. probate.

Pages
351-353:   MICHAEL LUTTRELL (Will)
                     Date: 16 March 1778

Dau.:	Franklin McKenzey - my large Iron Pot
Dau.:	Hannah Luttrell - one bed & furniture
Son :	Abner - my young Sorrel horse
Dau.:	Lydda - one bed and furniture
Son:	Michael - one pair of Stillards
Son:	Nathan - my Bell Metal skillet
Dau.:	Dinah - thirty weight of feathers
Son:	Richard - one hand saw
Dau.:	Sarah - one large and two small Pewter & Basons
Dau.:	Dolly - my Black walnut chest
Son:	Lot Luttrell - 120 a. of land - if he dies without Issue to my son Abner Luttrell
Dau.:	Mary Luttrell - my Sugar box
Dau.:	Betsey - my Trunk

Wife:	My loving wife Dinah Luttrell - all my moveable Estate to be by her possett and enjoyed during her natural life and after her decease to be equally divided amongst my Children
Exor.:	My loving wife Dinah Luttrell, Richard Luttrell and John Luttrell
Signed:	Michael (his ‡ mark) Luttrell
Wit.:	John Combs, Richard Coram, James Luttrell, Robert Luttrell
Proved:	24 August 1778, by o. of John Combs, James Luttrell, Robert Luttrell. Richard Luttrell and John Luttrell the Executors therein named made o. and granted cert. for obtaining a probate.

Pages
353-354:   JOHN WEBB (Inventory)
                  No date.

Details:	... we the Subscribers being convened and first sworn before Hezekiah Turner proceeded to appraise such of the Estate of John Webb Gent. dead, as was produced to our view by Mrs. Judith Webb, Adm'r.
App'd by:	John Adams, John Thos. Chunn, John Ashby
Total eval.:	L4260.4.8
Ret.:	24 August 1778

Pages
354-355:   EDWARD MOUNTJOY (Inventory)
                  Date: 14 October 1777

App'd by:	Maz'm. Berryman, John Wever, John Martin, first sworn before William Grant, a Justice of the peace for Fauquier County.
Details:	1 Servant man named Thomas Jones who has 5 years to serve - L50.
Total eval.:	L355.15.9
Ret.:	28 September 1778

Pages
355-357:   JOHN WEBB (Will)
                  Date: 7 February 1777

Wife:	Judith Webb - negroe girl Milly
Son:	John - negroe boy George
Son:	WmSon - negroe boy Ned
Dau.:	Prissilla Webb - negroe girl Alse
Wife:	my Land whereon my Mother now lives and the rite of the Land I bought of Colo. Thomas Marshall, during her widowhood and at her death or Marriage the Land whereon my Mother now lives to my Son

John .. and the Land I bought of Colo. Thomas
Marshall to my son WmSon Webb .. the Land I bought
in Northumberland of Thomas Lowther and Smith
Barret shall be sold to Discharge my debts and any
other part of my Estate .. at any time my Executors
hereafter mentioned shall think proper.
... All my Estate that is not above mentioned I
leave for the support of my wife and children during my wife's Widowhood, or til one of my Children
shall Marry or arrive at the age of 21 and at the
Marriage of my wife or one of my Children arriving
to the age of twenty-one I lend to my wife a Childs
part of all my Estate except what is above mentioned during her Life, and at her Death her part
Lent shall be equally divided among my Children.
... all the Remainder of my Estate that is not
given above I give to be equally divided between
all my children.

Exors: my loving wife & my friends WmSon Ball and William
Miskell and John Keith
Signed: Jno. Webb
Wit.: John Keith, James Key
Ret.: 25 May 1778, proved by o. of John Keith and James
Key. Judith Webb made o. and cert. is granted her
for obtaining a probate.

Pages
357-358: JOHN CHILTON (Inventory)
No date.
App'd by: George Rogers, Jas. Hathaway, Ambrose Barnett
No total. Ret.: 28 September 1778

Pages
358-361: HOWISON KENNER (Will)
Date: 9 April 1778
Elder son: Francis - the money in my son in Law's hands
William Seaton, but L40 the Ballance of Money the
said William Seaton ows me is L210 for that Tract
of Land where John Bails and John Harril now lives
which I sold to the said William Seaton for L250
and no more of my Estate I give to the above Francis
but the above sum of L210.
Dau.: Betty Seaton - L20 and no more
Dau.: Rebecca Clifton - L10 and no more
Dau.: Mary Seaton - L10 and no more
Son : George Turberville Kenner - the negroe man James he
has now in proceson and no more

Gr.Son:	Rodham Kenner, son of my son George Tur'le - parcel of land where young Moses Cumings now lives, being the Reversion of 200 a. that I bought of John Latemore and son
Dau.:	Peggy and her husband Stephen Prichard - negroe woman Lucy & her son Jacob - my old house wench Letty after the decease of my wife - L10
Gr.son:	Howson, son of my son Francis - L20
Son:	Rodham - all the Tract of Land I live on and where he now lives - 2 long tables & the great Glass - Dozen large Leather Chairs that is in my hall - L20 cash
Son:	George Turberville Kenner - 2 cows and Calves
Gr.son:	George Seaton - son of my Dau. Betty Seaton - 2 cows & Calves and his Choice of my young mares and one good bed & furniture and my wearing apparel - L10 cash
Dau.:	Catey Markham and her dau. Mary Ann - 2 negroe men, Jonathan & Abraham - 3 cows & calves - 6 head of Sheep - 2 good beds & furniture - 2 of my young mares of the youngest kind - 6 grown hogs and one Sow & pigs
Gr.son:	Samuel Eskridge Alias Kenner, son of my daughter Susannah - 2 negroes - Cate & her Increase forever negro boy Fortune - L100 cash to be applyed to Educate him, but in case the said Samuel should die before he comes of age of 18 then in that case I give the estate before given to my Grandson Samuel to the disposal of my Dau. Susannah - 2 cows & calves and the youngest of my mare Colts - Item I give to my Dau. 3 negroes - all my Cash and the rest of my Estate not before mentioned - it is my will that all my Estate be kept together for 3 years to raise cash to pay off my debts that my wife if living and my Dau. Susannah have the whole management of my Estate
Wife:	... the whole of my Estate during her natural life, then in 3 years after her decease, then my Dau. Susannah pay off every Legacy & Debts before given by me - I also desire that no appraisement be made of Estate but be divided as I have before directed
Gr.son:	Samuel Eskridge - be kept at School for 10 years and kept there after the best manner as the L100 will keep him and the over plush of my Estate if any will keep him after paying of my Just Debts
Exors:	good friend Mr. Joseph Blackwell, my wife and dau. Susannah

Signed: Howson Kenner
Codicil: (no date) - impower my good friend Mr. Joseph
            Blackwell to make such deeds to my son in law
            William Seaton of the Lands sold to him - when
            he pay off the money
Signed: H. K.
Wit.:   Original Young, William Pope
Proved: 28 September 1778, by o. of Original Young and
            William Pope. Margaret Kenner and Susannah
            Kenner, Executrixs granted cert. to obt. probate

Page
361:            JAMES HAMBRICK   (Inventory)
                No date.
App'd by: John Morehead, John Suthard, Peter Laurance
Total eval.: L215.2.6
Ret.:   23 November 1778

Pages
361-363:   JAMES STROTHER   (Inventory)
                Crt. Ord. dtd.: 28 September 1778
                Date: 23 October 1778
App'd by: John Hathaway, William Kincheloe, Hermon Hitt
Total eval.: L1899.19.6
Ret.:   23 November 1778

Pages
363-364:   MICHAEL LUTTREL   (Inventory)
                No date.
App'd by: Thomas Railey, Charles Waller, John Combs
No total. Ret.: 23 November 1778

Pages
364-367:   MAJOR AUGUSTIN JENNINGS   (Inventory)
                Crt. Ord. dtd.: August 1778
                Date: 6 November 1778
App'd by: Paul Williams, John Duncan, John Wright
Total eval.: L3527.4.6
Ret.:   28 December 1778

Pages
367-368:   JOHN BALL   (Estate Account)
Admr.:   Reginald Graham
Details: 24 January 1779: Mr. Graham's third of L1662.1.52
           By Ballance due Mr. John Ball's children -
           L55.11.22. This day the above accompt. was proved
           by Reginald Graham & settled before James Bell &

Ret.:   Edward Digges.
        25 January 1779

Page
368:          JOHN BALL (Division of Estate)

          In Obedience to the within order we have pro-
          ceeded to settle the accompt. of John Ball,
          Deceased with Riginal Graham and lay off the
          Widow's thirds, as also divided the Slaves among
          the Children, to wit, To Mrs. Graham, wife of the
          late John Ball her Negroes Castle & Adam, To
          William Ball, Peter & Hannah, & Mary Ball part
          Barsheba & Judith Ball Negroes Tim, Lettice Ball
          Negroes Lucy & Moses.
Sign ed: James Bell and Edward Digges
Ret.:   25 January 1779

Pages
368-369:   JOHN ELLIS of the Parish of Leeds and
          County of Fauquier (Will)
          Date: 3 December 1778
Dau.:   Ann Ellis - my best Bed & furniture
Son: Jonathan - Eight head of Hogs
Younest sons: Owen & William Ellis - all the rest of my
          Estate, to be equally divided between them
Exors: my well beloved son Jonathan Ellis
Signed: John Ellis
Wit.:   Benj'n. Neale, John (h. ⅃ m.) Robertson, James
          (h. ⅃ m.) Robertson
Proved: 22 February 1779, by o. of John Robertson and James
          Robertson. Jonathan Ellis granted cert. to bbtain
          probate.

Pages
369-370:   JOHN SQUIRES (Inventory)
          Date: 23 December 1778
App'd by: Wm. Murrey, Thomas Priest, Edward Turner
No total. Ret.: 22 March 1779

Pages
370-371:   HUBBARD PRINCE (Inventory)
          No date.
App'd by: James Blackwell, John Shumate, John Ashby,
          Max'm. Berryman
No total. Ret.: 26 April 1779

Pages
371-372:   JOHN BRONAUGH (Inventory)
                       No date.
App'd by: Jonathan Gibson, Thomas Railey, John Nelson
No total. Ret.: 26 April 1779

Pages
372-373:   THOMAS JAMES (Inventory)
                       Crt. Ord. dtd.: February 1776
App'd by: John James, Lott Hackley, Thomas Skinker
Total eval.: L778.15.6
Ret.:   26 April 1779

Page
374:              WILLIAM SHANK (Inventory)
                       No date.
App'd by: Edward Mountjoy, John Martin, Tilman Weaver
Total eval.: L153.14.1 Ret.: 26 April 1779

Pages
374-375:   BENJAMIN DOGGETT (Inventory)
                       Date: 26 November 1778
App'd by: William Morgan, William Jenings, John Edwards
Total eval.: L501.12.6 Ret.: 24 May 1779

Pages
375-376:   MINOR WINN (Inventory)
                       No date.
App'd by: Josiah Fishback, Joseph (x) Robertson, Thomas
         (x) Bartlett. No total.
Ret.:   24 May 1779

Pages
376-377:   JOHN ELLIS (Inventory)
                       No date.
App'd by: Benj'n. Neale, Jun'r., Thos. Harris, Wm. Strother.
No total. Ret.: 28 June 1779

Page
377:              ISAAC KING (Inventory)
                       Date: 12 June 1779
No appraisers listed. Total eval.: L175.12.0
Ret.:   28 June 1779

Pages
377-378:   TILMAN MARTIN (Will)
                       Date: 23 May 1778

Wife: Elizabeth - young bay Mare & two Cows and my land
being 70 acres which land my Wife may sell when
she thinks proper & the money arising therefrom to
be laid out in the purchase of another place which
place is to be for my Son Tilman and in case he
should die it is to revolve to my next youngest
Son

Dau.:   Elinor Martin - my young mare Colt
... the rest of my Estate be equally divided amongst
all my children

Exors: Wife Elizabeth Martin "and my Son Elijah Darnall"

Signed: Tilman Martin

Wit.:   Jeremiah Darnall, Thomas (x) Parker, John Parker

Proved: 26 July 1779, by o. of Thomas Parker and John Parker
Elizabeth Martin made o. cert. is granted her for
obtaining probate thereof.

Pages
378-379:   BENNETT PRICE of the Par. of Hamilton (Will)
Date: 9 July 1774

Wife: Judith - the use of all my Estate both real & personal during her Widowhood to be kept together for
the support of her & her children - if she should
remarry to have 1/3 part of my estate and the remainder to be equally divided amongst my children,

Dhildren: to wit: Elizabeth, Ann & Judith

Exors: loving wife Judith and Martin Pickett & William
Edmonds Gent. and Armistead Churchill, Gent.

Signed: Bennett Price

Wit.:   Martin Pickett, Joseph Blackwell, Jun'r., Samuel
Blackwell, Jun'r., Anne Pickett

Proved: 24 October 1774, by o. of Ann Pickett. Judith
Price and William Edmonds, Gent. two of the Exors.
made o. and cert. is granted them for obtaining
probate. 26 July 1779 the said Will was proved by
the o. of Martin Pickett and Joseph Blackwell.

Pages
379-380:   GEORGE SULLIVAN (Inventory)
Date: 10 November 1778
App'd by: James Lewis, Alexander Lang, Evan Griffith
Total eval.: L2677.15.9 Ret.: 23 August 1779

Pages
380-381:   NICHOLAS GEORGE (Will)
Date: 24 June 1779
Oldest son: Nicholas - one Negro man named Tom

Wife: loving wife, Margaret - all my other Estate,
             real & personable moviable and immoveable during
             her natural life and after her decease in manner
             and form following:
Son: William - one negroe Woman named Lucia and her
             child Agga - one Waggon horse, himself will make
             choice of
Son: Joseph - one Negro boy named Arch and a Negro Girl
             named Alice and the land whereon I now live and
             one riding horse such as he shall like - if either
             of these my two Sons should die without heirs the
             deceadest part shall go to the survivor
Dau.:   Elizabeth - one Negro Woman named Judah - one bed
             and furniture
Dau.:   Lydia - one Negro man named Holland also six Ewes
             with Lambs
Dau.:   Wilmouth - one Negro Man named Dick and two Heifers
Dau.:   Nanny - all my moveable Estate such as Cattle Sheep
             and hogs and horses and the rest of my household
             Goods to be equally divided among all my Children
             and as far my Negro Wench Hannah it is my desire
             she should remain among my Children where she likes
             best
Exors: my loving wife Margaret and my two Sons Joseph and
             William
Signed: Nicholas George
Wit.:   John (x) Nelson, Thos. Fidler, John Nelson
Proved: 27 September 1779, on o. of John Nelson, Thomas
             Fidler and John Nelson. Margaret George the
             Executrix made o. and cert. is granted her for
             obtaining a probate thereof

Pages
381-382:   JOHN BAILEY (Will)
                      Date: 8 September 1778
Son: Wright - the Land that I now live on and all my
             Personal Estate
Exors: Charles Morehead and Turner Morehead
Signed: John Bailey
Wit.:   Charles Morehead, Turner Morehead and Mary Morehead
Proved: 27 September 1779, by o. of Charles Morehead and
             Mary Morehead. Turner Morehead granted cert. for
             obtaining a probate thereof

Page
382:                  TILMAN MARTIN (Inventory)
                      Date: 18 September 1779

App'd by: Tilman Wever, John Wever, John Martin
No total. Ret.: 27 September 1779

Pages
383-384:   PETER BEACH (Will)
                Date: 2 April 1777

Son: John - all that Tract or parcel of land lying in the
                County of Fincastle being situate on the waters of
                Clinch River at a place called the Elk Garden
                supposed to contain 300 acres which I bought of
                Thomas Price

Gr.son: John Baker - all that Tract of land lying in the
                County of Fincastle situate on the Waters of
                Clinch River at a place called Elk Garden at the
                head or the upper part of the said Elk Garden
                supposed to contain 100 acres

4 daus: Mary, Sarah, Lettice & Ann - L30 Cash to be
                equally divided betwixt them - all my stock of
                every kind - household furniture and moveables
                of every sort to be sold and the money equally
                divided betwixt them
                ... my Will and desire is likewise that my Estate
                be not brought to an appraisement but be divided
                amicably betwixt them or if they cannot so agree
                then each side to choose two householders discreet
                men and they to divide it according to the true
                intent and meaning of this will.

Exors.:   Son-in-law Samuel Baker and William Butler
Signed: Peter (h. B m.) Beach
Wit.:   Peter Conway, Wm. (x) Butler
Proved: 25 October 1779, by o. of Peter Conway and William
                Butler. Samuel Baker granted cert. to obtain
                probate.

Pages
384-385:   FRANCIS SOUTHARD (Will)
                Date: 12 October 1779

Eldest dau.: Elizabeth - tract of land whereon she now liveth
Wife: Elizabeth - all the rest of my Tract during her
                natural life and after her death I bequeath it to
                my Son
Son: Levi - but if he die without any heirs then the land
                to be sold & equally divided amongst the other four
Son: William - a feather bed & furniture
Son: George - at the age of 21 that bay mare which he
                now owns
Dau.:   Sarah Dodd - three sheep

```
Dau.(?):  Jemima - a feather bed and furniture
Wife:     Elizabeth - after my just debts are all paid
          (during her natural life) and afterwards to be
          sold and the money to be equally divided
          amongst all my Children all my furniture and
          stock
Exors:    beloved wife Elizabeth Southard, James Duff
Signed:   Francis (X) Southard
Wit.:     Elijah Reeder, Benjamin Dodd, James Duff
Proved:   22 November 1779, by o. of Elijah Reeder and
          Benjamin Dodd. Elizabeth Southard and James
          Duff the Executors granted cert. for obtaining a
          probate thereof
```

```
Pages
385-386:      JAMES SCOTT, Jun'r. of the Parish of Leeds
              (Will)
              Date: 2 January 1779
Wife:     Elizabeth Scott - the whole of my Estate real and
          personal during her Widowhood, but upon her inter-
          marriage she have one third part and after her de-
          cease the whole of my lands except those in Prince
          William and on the Ohio, shall be advertised and
          sold to the highest bidder and likewise my Negroes
          and the money equally divided between my Children
          and that all my Stocks of every kind and household
          furniture be sold and the money be equally divided
          between my Daughters:
Daus.:    Sarah, Frances, Elizabeth and Nancy Scott .. and ..
Sons:     Alexander, James, Cuthbert and Thomas - if any of
          the above should die without issue it is my Will and
          desire that their proportion should be equally
          divided amongst the Survivors.
Sons:     James, Cuthbert and Thomas - all my lands on the
          Ohio to be equally divided between them or the
          Survivors
Exors:    Wife Elizabeth Scott, Cuthbert Bullitt and Cuthbert
          Harrison - request of them is to have my Sons well
          educated out of the profits of my Estate - but should
          my Father be inclined to undertake the care of my
          Son James's Education it is my will and desire that
          he be given up to his intire disposal.
Signed:   Jas. Scott, Jun'r.
Wit.:     Sam'l. Boyd, James Steward, Ju'r., William Stewart
Proved:   22 November 1779, by o. of James Stewart, Jun'r.
          and William Stewart. Elizabeth Scott and Cuthbert
          Bullitt made o. and granted cert. for obtaining a
          probate thereof.
```

- 104 -

Pages
386-387:   JOHN SIAS (Will)
                     Date: 6 September 1773
Dau.:   Mary Hamrick - L5
Wife: Mary Sias - a full and sufficient maintenance out
            of my Estate during her life or widowhood to be
            given her by my Executors as they shall think
            suitable for her Use.
            The Tract of land now mortgaged to William Carr
            be the same more or less to Thomas Chapman he
            paying William Carr's debt due upon the said land.
            Also I give the said Thomas Chapman my Negro Man
            Slave named Sam and all the rest of my Estate.
Exors: Thomas Chapman and William Carr
Signed: John (h. ⅹ m.) Sias
Wit.:   James Muschett, James Gwathin, John Tebbs
Proved: 22 November 1779, by o. of James Muschett and
            James Gwathin. Cert. for obtaining probate
            granted Thomas Chapman.

Page
387:   SALLY MAUZY to Thomas Conway (Guardian's Acc't.)
                     Date: 1779
Details: Signed and sworn to by Thomas Conway.
Ret.:   27 March 1780

Pages
387-388:   PETER BASHAW (Will) of the Parish of Leeds
                     Date: 6 November 1779
Wife: Celia - my whole Estate during her life but in case
            she married it is my desire she be thirded and after
            her death:
Son: Peter - all my land in Fauquier County and one
            Negro boy
Children: Molly Bashaw, Rawleigh Chinn Bashaw & Elijah
            Bashaw & Betsey Bashaw & Sukey Bashaw - all the
            remainder of my Estate that is not already
            given be equally divided between them.
Exors: my friend Charles Chilton and wife Celia Bashaw
Signed: Peter (X) Bashaw
Wit.:   John Norris, Joseph Taylor, John Coppedge
Proved: 27 March 1780, by o. of John Norris, Joseph Taylor
            and John Coppedge. Cert. to obtain probate granted
            Celia Bashaw.

Pages
388-389:   CAPT. NICHOLAS GEORGE (Inventory)
                     No date.

App'd by: Jonathan Gibson, William Conway, John Kerr
Total eval.: L8447.17
Ret.: 27 March 1780

Page
389:                RICHARD FOOTE (Will) of Stafford County
                 Date: 24 February 1779
Bro.:   William Foote - the whole of my Estate both real
                 and personal
Signed: Richard Foote
Wit.:   William Alexander, Law'r. Washington
Proved: 24 April 1780, by o. of Lawrence Washington.
                 William Foote granted Cert. for obt. probate.

Page
390:                ROGER TOLLE (Will)
                 Date: 2 February 1778
Wife: dear and loving wife Sary Tolle - full possession
                 and enjoyment of my whole Estate both real and
                 personal enduring the time of her Widowhood and the
                 determination of that time for the above mentioned
                 Estate to be disposed as followeth:
Son: Roger - L5 current money
Son: George - L5 current money
Gr.dau: Susannah Tolle, dau. of my son Jonathan Tolle -
                 L5 current money
                 ... I require and devise that my Tract of land and
                 improvements on which I now dwell shall be sold to
                 the highest bidder and the money thereof likewise
                 the rest of my Estate shall be equally divided
                 among all my children after my debts is paid ...
                 their names as follows: Jonathan, John, Ann Squires,
                 Roger, James and Stephen
Exor: loving wife Sary Tolle, son Roger Tolle and Stephen
                 Tolle
Signed: Roger Tolle
Wit.:   Edward Turner, Mary Turner, Elizabeth (x) Grogan.
                 Jonathan Tolle, D'r. to hard Cash lent April 1775 -
                 L15.0.0; James Tolle, Dr. to hard Cash lent - L6
Proved: 22 May 1780, by o. of Edward Turner and Mary Turner.
                 Sarah Tolle the Executrix made o. and executed and
                 acknowledged bond as the law directs Cert. is
                 granted her for obtaining a Probate thereof in due
                 form.

Page
391:                JOHN ARNOLD (Will)
                 Date: 7 September 1771

Son: Benjamin Arnold - 100 acres of land whereon I now
            live and after my wife's death all the stock and
            household furniture that is there and no more of
            my Estate
Wife: _____ - all my stock and household furniture during
            her natural life .. if my Son Benjamin .. should
            chance to die without lawfully begotten (heirs)
            then my two Daughters Virlinda Arnold and Margaret
            Arnold should have the said land and stock and
            household furniture before mentioned
Dau.:   Virlinda Arnold - 50 acres of land as he lives on
            now and at her disposal
Signed: John Arnold
Wit.:   Wm. Settle, John Edwards, Edward Settle
Proved: 22 May 1780 by oaths of John Edwards and Edward
            Settle, witnesses .. Benjamin Arnold granted
            Cert. for obtaining Letters of Administsation on
            the said Estate with will annexed.

Pages:
391-392:   JOHN PEAKE of County of Fauquier and Parish
            of Hamilton (Will)
            Date: 28 June 1779
Wife: Loving wife, Mary Peake - all & singular my Estate,
            real and personal, to be enjoyed possessed and
            solely disposed of by her during her natural life
            or Widowhood as her own discretion my direct and at
            her death to be again further bequeathed by her as
            her own discretion and choice may determine to be
            most proper and fit for the benefit of my several
            Children with this restriction only, that I will
Dau.:   and desire that my eldest and beloved daughter
            Sally Peake have one Negro boy called Daniel the
            son of my Negro Wench called Mill to her .. either
            at or before the decease of my loving wife .. next
Dau.:   eldest daughter .. Mary Peake Negro Girl named
Dau.:   Dinah ... youngest Daughter Elizabeth - Negro boy
            named Ben
Son: Thomas - negro Girl named Mima .. left to the dis-
            cretionary choice of my beloved Wife aforementioned
            to give said Negroes to my said Children in the
            time of her natural life or at her decease
Exor.:   Wife, Mary Peake
Signed: John Peake
Wit.:   John Cordell, Judith Cordell
Proved: 22 May 1780, by o. of John Cordell and Judith

Cordell. Mary Peake granted Cert. to obtain
probate thereof.

Page
393:
        PETER BASHAW (Inventory)
        No date. No total.
App'd by: Joseph Taylor, Jn'n. Coppedge, Wm. Norriss
Ret.: 22 May 1780

Page
393:
        JOHN BAILEY (Inventory)
        No date.
App'd by: Charles Morehead, George Carter, Moses Bailey.
Total eval.: L362
Ret.: 22 May 1780

Page
394:
        JOSEPH SMITH (Division of Dower)
Date: 1779
Details: Agreeable to an Order of Court to us directed we
the subscribers having met at the plantation of
Andrew Obanon, late the property of Joseph Smith
deceased in order to set apart the Dower of the
wife of Andrew Obanon relict to the said Joseph
Smith. And being first sworn did allott to Mary
Obanon as follows Viz: One Negro Woman named
Jemima, 1 feather bed and furniture, 4 sheep, 7
flagg chairs, a parcel of Pewter, knives and forks,
1 Chest, 1 handsaw, 4 tubs, 1 Candle stick and
snuffers, 1 mustard pott, 1 pepper box, 3 Axes, 1
spade, 1 frying pan, 1 red Cow and Calf, 1 red and
White Cow, 1 red paid yearling which being one
third of the Effects produced to us for the above
purpose Given under our hands this   day of
1779.
Signed: William Pickett, Aylett Buckner, Francis Atwell
Ret.: 22 May 1780

NOTE: Minute Book, 1773-1780, page 457: May Court,
1780: The persons appointed to set apart the Dower
of Mary Obanon late the Widow of Joseph Smith, in
the said Smith's returned an account Thereof which
was ordered to be recorded.
M.B. 1773-1780, p. 319: May Court, 1778: Order
that Aylett Buckner, William Pickett, Francis Attwell, and Moses Johnson or any three of them do

allot to Mary Obannon late Widow of Joseph
Smith her Dower in the Estate whereof the said
Smith died Possessed.

Pages
394-395:   JOHN OBANON   (Estate Account)

Exor.:   Wm. Obanon
Details: 1779 - The Estate of John Obanon dec'd Dr.
          to Wm. Obanon the Executor.
          TO: Samuel Rust, Thomas Maddux, John Elliott,
          Alexander Sanester, John Hurmons, Michael German,
          Ephraim Hubbard, To paid for a saddle devised to
          Benjamin Obanon L148, Jacob Fryer, Bryan Obanon
          L15, To the Printer, Clerk of Fauquier for 320 lb.
          Tob'o, Benjamin Elliott, Henry Asbury, Cuth't.
          Bullitt, Esq., John Morehead, Henry Berry, Capt.
          John Moffett, To part retained for a bridle for
          Ben. Obanon L30, Joseph Obanon for a ballance due
          him of his Grandfathers Legacies L40, To ballance
          due the Legatees of John Obanon, dec'd, L1428.16.7½.
          BY: John Elliott, Andrew Obanon, George Asberry,
          Daniel Flowree, Bryan Obanon, Benj. Obanon, Ben.
          Orear, Wm. Bartlett, Wm. Hutton, Joseph Nelson,
          Thomas Bartlett, William Obanon, Capt. Francis
          Triplett, Rev. John Scott, Minor Winn, Samuel
          Obanon, William Asbury, Capt. John Obanon, John
          Obanon, Jun'r., of Jno.; R. Cochran, William Elliott,
          Burr Harrison, Joseph Duncan, Thomas Maddux, Henry
          Peyton, Thomas Obanon, Samuel Grigsby, John Corn-
          well, William White, John Waddell, Patrick Hamrick,
          Thos. Watts, Michael German, Sam'l. Rust, Wm.
          Stewart, Ephraim Hubbard, Joseph Obanon, Wm.
          Courtney, George Kenard, Thomas Obanon, George
          Redman, John Waddell.

          Pursuant to an Order of the Worshipful Court oɪ
          the said County dated February Court 1780, We the
          subscribers have proceeded to settle the account of
          Administration whereof William Obanon took charge
          touching the Estate of John Obanon deceased, the
          said William produced his Vouchers as to the de-
          bited Articles, as also his book of sales on oath
          and his proven account it appears to us that the
          foregoing is a just and true state of the Admin-
          istration of the said Estate, and that there re-
          mains as Asset, in the hands of the said William

- 109 -

the sum of L1428.16s.7d. and half penny for the use of the Legatees of the said deceased. Certified under our hands this 20th day of May 1780.

Signed: J. Moffett, Hez'h. Turner
Ret.: 26 June 1780

Pages 395-397: JOHN PEAKE (Inventory)
Date: 23 June 1780
App'd by: John Cordell, Wiley Roy, Thomas Roy
Total eval.: L17731.13.4
Ret.: 26 June 1780

Pages 397-398: WILLIAM PAYNE (Inventory)
Date: 18 April 1780
App'd by: Charles Morgan, Henry Jones, Leroy Hulett
Total eval.: L21,367.2.0
Ret.: 26 June 1780

Pages 398-400: EDWARD FEAGIN (Will)
Date: 8 July 1780
Wife: dearly beloved Wife Elizabeth Feagin - the use of all and singular my Negroes, horses, Cattle and all my other moveables during her natural life and after her decease the said Negroes and other moveables to be sold and equally divided between my nine children, Viz: John, Edward, William, Elizabeth, Sarah, Susanna, Clery, Mary and Frances.
Son: John - the tract of land that I bought of John Baxter - 163 acres.
Son: Edward - the tract of land that I bought of George Grant - 277 acres
Son: William - after my Wifes decease the plantation I now live on - 150 acres.
Exors: Son Edward Feagin
Signed: Edward (x) Feagin
Wit.: Evan Griffiths, Charles Chadduck, James Thomson, Clerk.
Proved: 24 July 1780, on the o. of Evan Griffiths, Charles Chadduck and James Thomson. Edward Feagin granted cert. for obtaining a probate thereof.

**Page
400:** FRANCIS SOUTHARD (Inventory)
Date: 1 December 1779 (Court Order dated
November 1779)
App'd by: John Wright, John Duncan, Paul Williams
Total eval.: L2030.10.0
Ret.: 24 July 1780

**Pages
401-402:** CAPT. JOHN JAMES (Inventory)
No date.
App'd by: Wm. Grant, John Kerr, Nicholas George
No total. Returned: 24 July 1780.

**Pages
403-404:** AUGUSTINE SMITH (Inventory)
Date: 26 August 1780
App'd by: John Ashby, John Herndon, Tilman Weaver, being
first sworn before William Grant, Justice of
Fauquier County. No total.
Ret.: 28 August 1780

**Pages
404-407:** JAMES SCOTT, JUN'R. ESQ.
... we the subscribers have upon oath appraised
the Estate of the late .. as follows, allowing
for a depreciation from fifty to sixty for one.
App'd by: Thomas Digges, John Metcalfe, James Hathaway.
Total eval.: L58,998.
Ret.: 28 August 1780

**Page
407:** BENNETT PRICE (Division of Dower)
No date.
We the Subscribers being appointed to make a
division of the third part of the Estate of
Bennett Price, deceased, to the Widow of the
deceased having met accordingly and proceeded
to lay off her dower .. (Included: Negroes,
horses, cattle, tools, kitchen utensils, hogs,
spinning wheel, wagon, beds and furniture)
Divided by: Wm. Pickett, A. Buckner, Edward Digges
Total eval: L2526.12.0
Ret.: 28 August 1780

**Pages
408:** ROGER TOLLE (Inventory)
No date

App'd by: John French, Thomas Priest, William Murray
No total.
Ret.:   23 October 1780

Pages
409-410:   WILLIAM KIRK (Will)
                  Date: 31 May 1779
                  I give and devise the Tract of land in said
                  County whereon I now live containing about 636
                  acres to my Executors hereafter named to be by
                  them sold as soon as an intercourse may be had
                  with great Britain (in case I should die without
                  leaving a child) and the money arising from such
                  Sale to be remitted to Scotland and equally
                  divided among my four following Relations, viz:
                  John McIoar, James McIoar, Mary McIoar and
                  Elizabeth McIoar of the Stewarty of Galloway in
                  the Parish of Orr on the Water of Orr in that
                  part of great Britain called Scotland, Children
                  of John McIoar and Sarah Kirk, who once lived in
                  the mid Town of the Spots in the said Parish and
                  among the legal Representatives of such as may
                  happen to be dead.
Wife: Elizabeth - four Negro Slaves: Dembo, Moses,
                  Gudjin & Huniah .. also one half of all my per-
                  sonal Estate in lieu and full satisfaction of her
                  claim of Dower.
                  I give the rest of my Slaves to my Executors to be
                  sold and the money raised by them to be remitted
                  and applied the same manner as above ... and until
                  such remittance can be made that they be kept on
                  said plantation for the benefit of the Legatees
                  aforesaid .. Stock (excpet what is nedessary for
                  the use of the plantation) household furniture and
                  all my other personal Estate may be sold as soon as
                  may be after my death and that ½ the money .. as
                  well as one half the Cash I may have on hand be
                  laid out by my Executors to the best advantage until
                  an opportunity happens of remitting it ...
                  Item in case of my leaving a Child I give and de-
                  vise the land and Slaves hereby directed to be sold
                  and also one half my personal Estate to such Child..
                  and if more than one Child then the land to go to
                  the heir at law and the Slaves and personal Estate
                  to be equally divided among them .. provided my wife
                  should refuse to accept of the Provision hereby
                  made her and take her Dower then I direct that the

remainder of my Estate may be disposed of as
before directed in regard to the Estate not
given her.

Exors: William Allason, David Allason of Fauquier County,
Gavin Lawson of Culpeper and Adam Newall of the
Town of Falmouth and give to each that may act
L50 sterling besides the Commission.

Signed: William Kirk

Wit.: Wm. Pickett, James Bell, John Peake, Sen'r.,
Charles Morehead, Presley Morehead, William
Hunton.

Proved: 27 November 1780, by o. of James Bell and Charles
Morehead. On motion of William Allason, Gavin
Lawson and Adam Newall three of the Executors
therein named who made oath and executed and acknowledged bond as the law directs, Cert. is
granted them for obtaining a probate ...

Pages
410-412: REUBIN ELLIOTT (Will)
of the County of Fauquier and Parish of Leeds
Date: 29 July 1779
William Cundiff alias William Elliott - 100 acres
of land whereon he now lives likewise one-half of
my wearing apparel

Son: Reubin Elliott - the remainder of my land to be by
him possessed at the marriage or death of my
beloved Wife .. one half of waring Clothes, one
grey mare, one saddle which he hath now ...

Son: Thomas Elliott - one Negro girl named Alice when
he arrives at the age of 21 years, one mare colt
that came of the Mare given to my Son Reubin - one
good saddle and bridle, one feather bed & furniture

Wife: Ruth Elliott - land unto my beloved wife - after
my just debts and funeral expenses are discharged
all the remainder of my Estate for the use and
maintenance of my younger children - during her
life or Widowhood and after her marriage or decease my will and desire is that the remainder
aforesaid may be equally divided between William
Cundiff alias William Elliott and the rest of my
Sons and Daughters Viz. Reubin Elliott, Thomas
Elliott, Ann Roberson, Elizabeth Elliott, Mildred
Elliott, Jemima Elliott and Molly Elliott.

Exor.: loving wife Ruth Elliott, together with her Son
William Cundiff alias Wm. Elliott, and John Obanon

Signed: Reubin (x) Elliott
Wit.:   John Hathaway, William Peake, John Barker, Daniel
           Morrison
Proved: 27 November 1780, by o. of William Peake and Daniel
           Morrison. William Elliott one of the Executors made
           o., cert. granted him for obtaining probate thereof.

Page
412:         JOHN SQUIRES (Division of Estate)

         Pursuant to an Order of the Court of Fauquier
         County to us issued at May Court 1780 Ordering
         that we set apart the Dower of Elizabeth Squires
         Widow of John Squires deceased in the lands and
         Slaves whereof the said John Squires died possess-
         ed and also that we Share the personal Estate
         among the Widow and Children ...
Signed: Wm. Smith, Edward Turner, Thos. Priest
         The third part of the moveables amounted to
         L241.19.6 One Negro woman appraised to be L400 -
         third part L133. Division of Land. Beginning at
         a Stone and a hiccory and red oak saplin in the
         line of Edward Larrance and running with his line
         to a white stone in Thomas Priest's line thence
         with his line to his Corner joining Colo. Henry
         Lee's line thence along the said Lee's line to a
         Stone and hiccory saplin thence a straight line
         across to the Beginning being the third part of
         87 acres.
Ret.:   27 November 1780

Page
413:         REUBIN ELLIOTT (Inventory)
         No date.
App'd by: Reubin Strother, H ezekiah Shacklett, Joseph
         Robertson. No total.
Ret.:.   26 March 1781

Pages
414-415   EDWARD FEAGIN (Inventory)
         No date.
App'd by: John Hathaway, Minor Winn, Thos. Hogain
No total. Returned: 28 May 1781

Pages
415-416:   WILLIAM PRIEST of the Parish of Hamilton in
         the County of Fauquier (Will)

Date: 5 March 1781

Wife: Eneler Priest and Samuel Priest - L5 current money of Virginia to be divided between them both

Bro.:   John Priest - my bed and bedstead and furniture and all my woolen cloth and all linen cloth except 7 years of the linen I leave to my loving mother

Mother: Sary Priest

Bro.:   John - one steer

Bro.:   Thomas - a mullatter Girl

Sister: Sary Murry - one Chest, three Chairs and what Pewter I have

Bro.:   George - 34 barrels of corn except the wintering one colt to be taken out of the said Corn

Bro.:.   Richard - one cow and one heifer

Sister: Elizabeth Stark - one young horse &all the cash that I have & 541 Pounds of Tobacco that is due to me by Iphaweson

Exors: brother Thomas Priest and James Stark

Signed: William (x) Priest

Wit.:   Jas. Peters, James Dowdall, James Stark

Proved: 28 May 1781, by o. of James Peters and James Dowdall. Thomas Priest and James Stark granted cert. for obtaining a probate.

Pages
416-417·   JOHN ADAMS (Will)

Date: 14 January 1781

Son: John - all my lands lying in Maryland

Son: George - 500 acres of land whereon he now lives

Dau.:   Elizabeth - 300 a. of land to be laid off in the most convenient manner including the plantation whereon she now lives.

Dau.:   Ann - 300 acres of land to be laid off in the most convenient manner including the plantation whereon she now lives.

Dau.:   Susanna - 300 a. of land to be laid off in the most convenient manner including the plantation whereon she now lives Including the plantation whereon James Hume now lives.

Son: Josias - all that land I purchased of Capt. Turner the line to continued with the line of Capt. John Ashby untill it comes to the lowgrounds or meadow land of Kelly's branch thence to continue with the said low grounds or meadow land (though not to include any part of the same) till it comes to Kelly's spring, thence with a strait line to the old line of the land I bought of Captain Turner So as to

include all the meadow land or low grounds adjoining the said old line -

... all the remainder of my lands to be equally
divided by estimation amongst my sons Littleton,
Thomas & James ... Littleton to have the plantation whereon he now lives, and James to have
the plantation whereon I now live ..

... all the remainder of my estate of what kind
and nature soever it be or whatever it may be

Wife: found unto my well beloved wife Sarah Stacy for
and during her natural life or to be disposed of
at any time amongst my children at her discretion
and to have no appointment

Signed: John Adams

Wit.: Hez'h. Turner, John Hickman, John T. Chunn, Will.
Bailes

Proved: 28 May 1781, by o. of Hezekiah Turner, John Hickman
and John Thomas Chunn. And on the motion of Sarah
Stacy Adams who made o. and executed and acknowledged bond as the law directs cert. is granted her
for obtaining letters of administration with the
said will annexed.

**Page
418:**

JOHN COMBS, Junior (Will)
Date: 7 October 1780

"We Original Young and Enis Combs did on the
seventh of this instant attend John Combs, Jun'r.
in his sickness and at the request of the said
John Combs I the said Original Young was desired
of by the said John Combs to write his Will and
the said Enis Combs present he appeared to be in
his senses at the time and desired his Estate to
be divided as followeth, that is to say that all
his lands to be equally divided between his two
Sons Nimrod Combs alias Luttrell and John Combs
and all his other Estate to be equally divided
between his two Sons and four daughters namedly
Nimrod Combs alias Luttrell, John Combs, Hetheland
Combs alias Luttrell, Betty Combs, Heland Combs
alias Luttrell and Sarah Combs. the land to be
so divided as Nimrod Combs alias Luttrell to have
his one half, so as he to enjoy the dwelling house
of the said deceased John Combs. And that his
said Wife Sarah Combs was by his request to enjoy
all the land and Negners together with all other

of his Estate during her Widowhood or life and
then to be divided as before mentioned. And
that before I the said Original Young had wrote
the said Will the said John Combs got out of his
senses and so died.

Exors: Wife Sarah together with Joseph Combs and Enis
should be Executors

Signed: Original Young, Enis Combs. I do hereby certify
that Orginal Young and Enis Combs came personally
before me William Blackwell and made oath on thee
holy Evangelist to the above writing and that it
contained the last Will of the said John Combs,
Jun'r. who died on the 6th day October 1780.
                                        W. Blackwell

Proved: 28 May 1781 by o. of Original Young and Ennis
Combs. Sarah Combs made o. and greanted cert.
for obtaining letters of administration.

**Page
419:**   GERARD FOWKE, GENT. (Division)
                        Date: 26 July 1781
Div. by: Cuth't. Bullitt, Thomas Roy, Dan'l. Bradford
Details: ... divided the Estate .. agreeable to his last
Will with the consent of his Widow Mrs. Elizabeth
Fowke and assigned and allotted to each of the
Children their parts of the Slaves and Cattle
except to Mr. Robert Dinwiddie Fowke who had be-
fore received his full part .. and to Mrs. Sarah
Roy who had received her part of the Slaves, the
Cattle being equally allotted and divided we pro-
ceeded to allott and divide the Slaves as follows:
Miss Mary Fowke   (3 slaves)
Mr. William Fowke   (4 slaves)
Mrs. Eliz'a. Phillips   (3 slaves)
Mr. Gerard Fowke   (3 slaves)
Mr. Chandler Fowke   (4 slaves)
Mr. George Fowke   (4 slaves)
Miss Enfield Fowke   (3 slaves)
The remainder of the Slaves and five head of Cattell
being retained by the Widow Mrs. Elizabeth Fowke
for her support and to be divided at her death
among all the children except Robert & Sarah the
following Cattell Mr. Robert Fowke having already
received his full proportion ...

Retn: 28 May 1781

Pages
420-421:   SAMUEL GRIGSBY, of the County of Fauquier
           and parish of Leeds ... (Will)
           Date: 11 May 1781
Wife: beloved Wife Ann Grigsby - the whole of my Estate
           both real and personal during her Widowhood also
           that part of Mrs. Dades Estate which will belong
           to me and my heirs at her death .. after her death
           (or remarriage) I desire to will and dispose of
           as follows .. all my lands rented as well as pur-
           chased to be sold and the whole of the prices ..
           to be equally divided amongst all my Children (not
           named) .. likewise all my stock of every kind ..
           all my Negroes as well those now in my possession
           as those that may fall to me or my heirs after
           the death of my Mother or the above mentioned Mrs.
           Dade of King George County be divided into as
           many equal lots as I have Children and in this
           manner be fairly and equally shared.. Item my
           wife being now in a State of pregaancy it is my
           will and desire that any Child that she may bring
           forth within nine months after my decease be
           numbered amongst my Children
Exors: Henry Peyton, William Grigsby, and James Grigsby
Signed: Samuel Grigsby
Wit.:   John Scott, John Fishback, Peter Tait
Proved: 22 October 1781 by o. of John Fishback and Peter
           Tait. Henry Peyton granted Cert. for obtaining
           a probate

Page
422:       DIXON BROWN (Inventory)
           Date: 24 August 1781
App'd by: Charles Morgan, Andrew Hume, John Crimm
Total eval.: L98206.5.0 (Eleven books - L3000)
Details: The following articles were lent by the dec'd. to
           his son-in-law Joseph Smith which he would not
           produce nor deliver but was appraised by Mrs.
           Brown's description - Total: L101,971.1
           The above appraisement was in specie and the
           appraisers laid on 600 prices for depreciation of
           the Virginia Currency which the Securities and
           Administratrix request may be recorded.
Ret.:   22 October 1781

Pages
423-424:
JOHN PETERS (Will)
Date: 4 October 1781

Wife: (Elizabeth) - during her life or widowhood, the dwelling house and land whereon I now live ... the land to be bounded as followeth at the Begining line of John Combs deceased along the ridge road that leads to Mr. John Nelsons and the lands belonging to Luttrels Estate thence to the old Fall road thence up the road to James Peter's line thence with his lin e to Jos. Combs's thence with his line to the said ridge road .. Negroes.

Son: John - land lying over the ridge road and joining the lands of Mr. William Rousseau - 100 a. - also, one sixth part of all my lands at Caintucky .. one negro boy named Isaac - one young horse.

Sons: Nimrod and James - Land in Stafford County which I purchased of James Peters on the branch of Aquia - 413 acres - to be equally divided ...

Son: Nimrod - negroe boy named Ben - one mare colt - one sixth part of my land at Caintucky

Son: James - negro boy named George - one mare colt - sixth part of my lands at Caintucky

Son: Nathaniel - land lying on the east side of the old Fall road and bounded by the said road and Joseph Combs's line - one negro boy named Will and the sixth part of my lands in Caintucky

Son s: Lewis and William - after the death of my Wife the land and Plantation whereon I now live and which I have lent to my Wife to be equally divided between them and my Will is that my two Sons Lewis and William have one negro each paid them from the increase of my two wenches which I have lent to my wife (except the first increase be a Girl which said land and two Negroes I give to them and their heirs forever)

Dau.: Nancy - one negro girl named Winney
Dau.: Sarah - one Negro Girl named Hethey
Dau.: Betty - the first female Negro that may be born of either of my two Wenches which I have lent to my wife and in case the said Wenches should only bring male Children then my Will is that after my two sons Lewis and William have their two as before mentioned that then she have a Negro boy.

After Wife's death that the 3 Negroes which I have lent her together with all my Estate not

before bequeathed to be equally divided between
my six Sons and three daughters.

Exors:: beloved wife, John Ashby, James Peters, Joseph
Combs and Cuthbert Combs

Signed:: John Peters

Wit.: Origin al Young, Betty Young, Sarah (x) Kelley,
William Roussau.

Proved: 22 October 1781 by o. of Original Young and William
Roussau. On motion of Elizabeth Peters, John
Ashby and James Peters, the Executors therein
named .. ack. bond .. cert. is granted them for
obtaining a probat thereof.

Pages
424-425: JAMES STEWART, of the County of Fauquier and
Parish of Hamilton (Will)
Date: 26 May 1781

Son: Allen - a Negro boy named Soloman and feather bed
and furniture and one Cow and Calf

Wife: Beloved wife (Jane) - the moiety of the tract I
purchased of Richard Grubbs whereon my Son John
now lives during her natural life and after her
death to my Son John .. lend to my beloved Wife a
Negro Man - a Negro girl - two Cows and Calves, two
Ewes and Lambs, two Sows with Pigs, one Beather
bed with furniture, one pot and pan, one pewter
dish, with six plates and her choice of one of my
horses or Mares

Son: William - L14 in gold or silver

Son : James - L10 in gold or silver

Son: Charles - whereas I have before made provisions
for my son Charles it is my Will and desire that
he possess no more of my Estate
... after my death Negro Toney and Ben shall be
immediately sold and all the remainder of my
Estate except what I have lent to my beloved wife
out of which the legacies abovementioned to my
Son William and James shall be first paid off and
the remainder to be equally divided between my

Daus:. four daughters, viz: Betty, Mary, Jane and Helen
and at the death of my Wife, the articles lent
to her be also sold and equally divided between
my above daughters

Exors: beloved wife Jane, son James and James Hathaway

Signed: James Stewart

Wit: William Metcalf, Sarah (x) Elliott, Bettse (x)
Metcalf

Proved:. 22 October 1781 - by o. of William Metcalf,
Sarah Elliott and Betsy Metcalfe. Cert. granted
Jane Stewart, James Stewart and James Hathaway
who made oath and executed and ack. bond as the
law directs.

Page
426:            ELIZABETH FOWKE, of the County of Fauquier
and in Hamilton Parish (Will)
Date: 20 June 1781
Son: George Fowke - the tract of land I now live on -
in case my said Son George Fowke should die without leaving lawful issue begotten of his body -
the said land herein devised - shall go to my Son
William Fowke - but in case both my Sons George
and William Fowke shall die without leaving lawful issue - the said land shall be equally divided
betweeen my two Daughters Mary Fowke and Enfield
Fowke.
Daus:.   Mary and Enfield - shall have possession of half
the dwelling house while they continue in a single
state as also their part of the out houses and
that each shall keep a maid to wait on them
Son: George Fowke - what killable hogs there may be at
my death I give to my Son and my daus. Mary and
Enfield.
Children: ... all the slaves I have now in possession shall
be equally divided between all my Children
following Viz.: William, Mary, Chandler, Enfield,
George and Elizabeth Phillips and their heirs
forever - household furniture to be also divided
amongst the above named children.
Signed: Eliz'a. Fowke
Wit.:   Wily Roy, William Wright, Joshua (x) Butler,
Joseph Morgan
Proved: 22 October 1781, by o. of Wily Roy and Joseph
Morgan. And on the motion of William Phillips who
made oath and executed and ack. bond as the law
directs, cert. is granted to him for obt. letters
of Admin. with the said will annexed.

Page
427:            AUGUSTIN SMITH (Division of Estate)
Date: 22 October 1781
Details: Joseph Smith - Negro Sharlett - L4000 -
Bal. due L270

Thomas Smith - Reubin & Mary Jin L4200 -
Bal. due L70
Matthew Smith - Frank - 4000 - Ballance
due 270
John Smith - Cate & Harry - 4200 - Ballance
due 70
James Smith - Francis & Mary - 3800 - Ballance
due 470
William Smith - George - 5000 - pay 730
Augustin Smith - Betty - 5000 - Pay 730
Elizabeth Smith - Hannah & Ann - 4800 - Pay 530
Susanna Smith - Lid & Lewis - 4700 - Pay 430
Ann Smith - Lucy & Sharlotte - 3000 - Pay 1270
Div. made by: A. Churchill, Jeremiah Darnall, John Ashby
Ret.:   22 October 1781

Pages
427-428:   HENRY RECTOR   (Will)
              Date: 2 April 1781
Son: William - that lott of land that Capt. William
Smith now lives on, 146 a. - one negro - equal
part of my stock and stills and all my moveables
as soon as he comes of age or his mother joins
in wedlock
Son: John - one negro boy - 100 a. - joining William
Finch and an equal part of all my moveables as
soon as he comes of age or his mother joins in
wedlock
Son: Enoch - one negro boy - one lott of land that I
Henry Rector now live on containing 156 a. - and
an equal part of all my moveables when he comes
of age or his mother joins in Wedlock
        The remainder part of my negroes to be equally
divided among my daughters - likewise an equal
part of all my moveables
Exors: Brother Benjamin Rector and Frederick Rector,
Executrix and Executors (sic)
Signed: Henry Rector
Wit.:   Harman Rector, Jun'r., Harman (h. R m.) Rector,
Sen'r., Henry Utterback
Proved: 26 November 1781, by o. of Harman Rector, Jun.,
Harman Rector, Sen'r, and Henry Utterback. On
the motion of Benjamin Rector and Frederick Rector
the Executors - cert. is granted them for obtaining
a probat thereof ...

Page
428:.   WILLIAM PRIEST (Inventory)
                Order of Court dated May, 1781.
App'd by: Willi am Turley, James Murray, John French
No total.   Ret.: 26 November 1781.

Pages
428-430:.   WILLIAM SETTLE, of Hamilton Parish (Will)
                Date: 25 February 1782
Wife: Belove wife, Sarah Settle - all my Estate: real
             and personal in during her natural life, after
             her decease to be equally divided between my
             son Edward Settle, Pope William Son-in-law,
             William Freeman Son-in-law
Dau.:   Elizabeth Settle - 100 a. of land to be laid off
             next to William Morgan's - one Negro Woman named
             Dinah and her child — one boy named Tom limbrick -
             one mare called Tab and her side saddle, one bed
             and furniture, a bason dish and six plates new
             pewter, the shed room of my house with a stone
             chimney induring her natural life, if she dies
             without heir lawfully begot of her own body to be
             equally divided between Edward, Hannah and Sarah.
Son-in-law: Pope Williams - 100 a. of land adjoining
             Arnold's mill
Son-in-law: William Freeman - 100 a. of land joining that
             given Pope Williams
Son: Edward Settle - 257 a. of land with improvements
             unless its the shed room given my daughter Elizabeth
             to he and his heirs forever.
Exors.:   Son Edward Settle, son-in-law William Freeman
Signed: William Settle
Wit.:   John Spilman, Nancy (h./ m.) Settle, Henry Settle,
             Francis Suddoth, Benjamin Arnold
Proved: 25 March 1782, by o. of Henry Settle, Francis
             Suddoth and Benjamin Arnold. Edward Settle and
             William Freeman made o. and executed and ack.
             bond as the law directs, granted cert.

Pages
430-432:   THOMAS JACKMAN (Will)
                Date: 15 March 1776
Son: Thomas - 130 a. of land where he now lives and he
             is to pay Betty Hone 50 s. out of it for that is
             all I intend for her out of my Estate
Son: Richard - my Pignut ridge tract of land and he is
             to pay my daughter Sarah Nevil 50 s. out of it for
             that is all I intend for her out of my Estate
Son: Adam - my old plantation tract of land lying at
             the watry mountain and he is to pay Margaret Under-

wood 50 s. out of it for that is all I intend
for her out of my Estate

Son: William - 100 a. of land where he now lives or
less beginning at the popular spring branch and
a strait line by a great rock to the black bottom
branch then to Miller's line and thence along
and so to the beginning and if he should die without heir lawfully begotten of his body it shall
fall to my Son Joseph and likewise leave to William
Jackman my negro child Charles and he is to pay
Mary Walker 50 s. out of it for that is all I
intend for her out of my Estate as Witness my
hand Thos. Jackman, Sen'r.

Son: Joseph - the plantation where I now live which
is the remainder after my Son Thomas and William
is laid off - Negroes - my still and all my Stock
but my riding horse and Saddle that I leave to my
son John Jackman and all the rest of my stock to
my son Joseph - consisting of horses, mares and
Colts, Sheep and Cattle and hogs and all my household furniture, beds Chests chairs petter pots and
tools of all kinds and I so order it that he pay
Ann Smith 50 s. out of it for that is all I intend
for her out of it ... And I further order that he
first of all pay all my debts and take care of his
mother and never disturb her as long as she shall
live ... she shall have possession of the house
where I now live as long as she lives and nver be
mislested ... to my Son Joseph all debts due to me
from any person or persons ... if he should die
without heir lawfully betoton of his that it shall
fall to my Son Adam otherwise to my Son Joseph ..
Remember that my Son and to my Son Joseph Jackman
is interlined for I intend none of my stock for
John but my horse and saddle

Son: John - one Negro Girl — and my Rifle Gun
Dau.: Hannah Smith - one Negro Girl named Nan
Dau.: Rebecca Smith - one Negro girl named Milly
... this is my Will that my Estate shall not be
appraised nor inventoried and if any one of my
Children shall grumble or be disatisfied at this
my Will he or she I do allow but one shilling
Sterling and the part I intended for them is to
be equally divided amongst the rest of my Children

Exors: Thomas Jackman, Richard Jackman, Adam Jackman,
Joseph Jackman
Signed: Thos. Jackman

- 124 -

Wit.: Thomas James, John Johnson, Henry Moffett, Ju'r.
Proved: 25 March 1782, by o. of Thomas James and John
Johnson. Joseph Jackman made o. and was granted
cert. to obtain probate.

Page
432: BENJAMIN NEWELL, of the County of Culpeper (Will)
Date: 2 October 1780
Devisees: Ann Wheatley, Mary Wheatley, Leannah Wheatley and
Sarah Wheatley of the County of Fauquier to each of
them a gold ring of twenty shillings value in silver
Nephew: my well beloved John Newell my brother Richard's
son L400
Sister: Nancy Newell - the whole ballance of my Estate
Exor.: John Wheatley of the County of Fauquier
Wit.: Samuel Holliday, James Dobie
Proved: 25 March 1782, by o. of Samuel Holliday and James
Dobie. John Wheatley granted cert. to obtain probate.

Page
433: ALEXANDER HOLTON (Will)
Date: 5 March 1782
Wife: Elizabeth - during her natural life a full third
part of all my goods and chattels to be disposed of
by her at her pleasure so long as she lives
Son: William - all the rest of my Estate
Exor.: son William Holton
Signed: Alexander (X) Holton
Wit.: Jno. Monroe, Lewis (x) Woodyard, Henry (x) Ford
Proved: 25 March 1782, by o. of John Monroe, Lewis Woodyard,
and Henry Ford. William Holton granted cert. to
obtain probate.

Pages
433-434: WILLIAM MILLARD (Will)
Date: 4 January 1782
Wife: (not named) during her life or Widowhood the land
and plantation whereon I now live containing 100 a.
all my stocks of all kinds - household furniture
except one feather bed
... my Will is that Thomas Cummins live on the said
land and plantation without hindrance .. with my
said Wife to take care of the plantation and in
case my wife should marry again I then give all my
stocks of every kind to Thomas Cummins and his
heirs - Thomas Cummins, after the death of my Wife,

the above 100 a. which I have lent to my wife &
also all my stocks of every kind also one half of
my household furniture except one feather bed
before excepted.
    Ann Suddoth, Wife to John Suddoth, one feather
bed to her and her heirs forever - after the death
of my Wife one half of all my household furniture
Thomas Cummins have all my wearing apparel

Exors.:	beloved wife, friends James Thompson and Original Young
Signed:	William (h. VV m.) Millard
Wit.:	Richard Coram, Champ Coram, John Cummins
Proved:	25 March 1782 by o. of Richard Coram and John Cummins. On motion of Elizabeth Cummins, James Thompson & Original Young, Exors., granted cert. to obtain probate.

Pages
434-435:   MATTHEW SMITH (Will)
                Date: 25 November 1781

Son:.	Loving son William - my Gun also when of age a horse and saddle
Son:	Loving son Joseph - when of age a horse and saddle
Son:	Loving son James - a horse and saddle when of age, each horse and saddle to be valued at L10 hard money
Wife:	Loving wife Martha - the remainder of my Estate real personal during her widowhood but in case she should see cause to marry then all my Estate both real and personal except one Negro Girl named Luce to be equally divided between my three sons namely William, Joseph and James - also at her death the said Luce and her increase to be equally divided between my three Sons .. and that they may be sent to school as much as circumstances will admit
Exors:	My loving Wife Martha Smith, brother James Smith and Minor Winn
Signed:	Matthew Smith
Wit.:	Thos. Smith, Joseph Smith, James Key, Feathergill Adams
Proved:	25 March 1782, by o. of Joseph Smith and Thomas Smith. James Smith granted cert. for obtaining probate.

Page
436:           MRS. ELIZABETH FOWKE (Inventory)
              No date.

App'd by: Thomas Roy, Daniel Bradford, Jno'a. Gibson,
          Joseph Morgan. No total.
Ret.:   25 March 1782

Page
437   JAMES CHAMBERLAYNE (Division)
          Date:. 12 January 1782 - Court Order
          dated: August Court 1781
Divided by: J. Moffett, William Holton, Thomas Glascock
Estate: Nett proceeds of the personal Estate - L137.
          18s. 3½d., five Negroes: Cook, Moll, Anthony,
          Tenn and Titus
Allotment: to Mary Blackerby - Negroes Cook and Moll -
          L45.19.5 according to the appraised Articles
          as her Dower.
Ret.:   25 March 1782

Page
437:      LITTLETON COOKE, MARINER (Will)
          Date: 28 February 1782
Bro.:   Giles - my black horse, saddle, briddle, saddle
          baggs and half my Clothes
Bro.:   Thomas - all the remaining part of my Estate
          real and personal
Exor.:   Brother-in-law Rich Willis
Signed: Littleton Cooke
Wit.:   Fran's Whiting, Betty Whiting
Proved: 22 April 1782, by o. of Francis Whiting. Rich
          Willis granted cert. to obtain probate.

Pages
438-439: SAMUEL GRIGSBY (Inventory)
          Date: 18 April 1782
App'd by: John O'Bann on, Thomas Bartlett, John Hathaway
No total. Ret.: 23 April 1782

Page
440:      HENRY RECTOR (Inventory)
          Date: 15 March 1782
App'd by: (not named in Will Book) The appraisers listed on
          the original are: Capt. Dan'l. Flowree, Benj. Rust,
          Thos. Nelson
Total: L847.1.0
Ret.:   22 April 1782

Page
440:      JOHN SMITH (Inventory)

No date. No appraisers listed in Will Book, Minute Book or
original. Total eval.: L3.12.6
Ret.: 27 May 1782

Page
440:            DAVID SHARP (Inventory)
                Date: 4 June 1782
App'd by: Paul Williams, John Duncan, Peter Bowmer, John
         Wheatley.
Total eval.: L76.14
Ret.: 24 June 1782

Page
441:            WILLIAM MILLARD (Inventory)
                Court Order dated March 1782
App'd by: Champ Coram, John Cummins, William Russaw
No total. Ret.: 22 July 1782

Page
442:            JOHN COMBS, Junior (Inventory)
                Court Order dated May 1781
App'd by: Thomas Conway, James Dowdall, Original Young
No total. Ret.: 22 July 1782

Page
442:            SUSANNA SMITH (Inventory)
                No date.
App'd by: Harman Hitt, John Watts, John Utterback - being
         first sworn before William Heale, Justice of said
         County
No total. Total: L1253 in paper money
Ret.: 22 July 1782

Page
443:            CAPT. WILLIAM GRIGSBY (Inventory)
                Date: 30 May 1782
App'd by: Henry Peyton, John Obanon, John Fishback, Josiah
         Fishback.
No total. Ret.: 22 July 1782

Page
444:        JOHN RUST (Sale of Estate)
No admr. listed.
Purchasers: Betty Rust, Samuel Rust, Daniel Floweree,
            Benjamin Rector, Joshua Singleton, Benjamin Rust,
            Daniel Brown, James Barton, James Pinckard, John

Rust, Charles Rector, Henry Asberry, John Boley,
Henry Rector, Jesse Lott, Reubin Strother, James
Strother, Hezekiah Shacklett, John Cantwell, William
Pearl, John Shumate

Ret.: 22 July 1782

**Pages
445-446:** JOSEPH ROBINSON of the County of Fauquier and
parish of Leeds (Will)
Date: 21 May 1782

Wife: Martha - the use of my whole Estate both real and
personal .. during her Widowhood or natural life,
and after the day of her marriage or death .. all
my lands and other Estate whatsoever (except the
negroes and their increase that came by my beloved
Wife) to be equally divided between my loving

Children: Children to wit: Maximillian, John, William, Dorcas
Murry, Hannah Kincheloe, Nancy Robinson, Catherine
Robinson, Peggy Robinson and Molly Robinson

Gr.son: Maximillian Robinson - L10
Gr.dau: Hannah Robinson - L10
Gr.dau: Lucy Robinson - L10 ... the same being the Children
of my son Benjamin Robinson deceased
... all the negroes above mentioned that came by my
loving Wife Martha with their increase at the day
of her death or marriage should be equally divided
between my beloved Children

Exor.: Wife Martha Robinson and son John Robinson
Signed: Joseph (X) Robinson
Wit : John Barber, Joseph Robinson, Ju'r., James (x)
Whight, Jesse Robinson
Proved: 22 July 1782, by o. of John Barber, Joseph
Robinson, Jun'r., James White and Jesse Robinson.
Cert. to obtain prob ate. granted Martha Robinson,
the Executrix.

**Pages
446-447:** GEORGE LUNCEFORD (Inventory)
Date: 25 July 1781
App'd by: Charles Morehead, Turner Morehead, Moses (X)
Bailey
Total eval.: L61.14.6 Ret.: 23 September 1782

**Page
447:** LEROY HULETT (Inventory)
Date: 28 August 1782

App'd by: B. Piper, Thomas Payne, Josiah Basye, being first
sworn before Colo. Francis Triplett
Total eval.: L139.12.6   Ret.: 23 September 1782

Pages
447-448:   BENJAMIN NEWELL (Inventory)
                 Court order dated: March 1782
Details: To 1 Bond on William Freeman for 1000 lb. Tobacco
         To 1 Bond on James Freeman for 1000 lb. Tobacco
         To 1 Bond on William Jones for 1000 lb. Tobacco
         1 Note on the County for what is allowed for the
         like what is given for such being a Soldiers Note
         18 months
App'd by: Paul Williams, Charles Duncan, Cossom Day
Ret.:   24 September 1782

Page
448:             CHARLES SCOGGINS (Inventory)
                 No date.
App'd by: Reubin Wright, Peter Bowmer, Charles Martin
Total eval.: L35.0.8
Ret.:   24 September 1782

Pages
448-449:   HENRY RECTOR (Division of Dower)
                 Date: 18 July 1782
Details: Pursuant to an order of the Worshipful Court of
         Fauquier "May Court 1782" We the subscribers having
         met together in company of each other have pro-
         ceeded to set apart the dower of Mary Rector Relict
         of Henry Rector deceased being furnished with an
         Inventory of the personal Estate of the deceased
         and a Copy of the Will do allott to the said Relict
         in the following manner viz: Negro Jack L50;
         James L120; Two Stills and Utensils, L100; Choice
         bed and furniture, L12; Nine plates; 17 shillings.
         Dower of two tracts of land ... by J. Moffett,
         Hez'h. Turner, John T. Chunn. Dower consisted of
         113 2/3 acres bounded by land of Wm. Rector, Wm.
         Young and John & Enoch Rector. ... the dower in
         the lands whereof Henry Rector, Ju'r. died seised
         in fee spl. to Mary Rector, his Widow ...
         Chain carriers: Wm. Turley, Edw'd. Shacklett
         No.1 is part of 157 acres left to Wm. Rector by
         the said Henry. No. 2 is part of 257 Acres left
         to John & Enoch Rector, the Widow relinquished her

dower in part to 157 Acres, only taking 30 Acres
thereof - Registered in Book A Fauq're Surveys
folio 23.
Ret.:   23 September 1782

Pages
449-450:   MATTHEW SMITH (Inventory)
                  Date: 6 April 1782
App'd by: Feathergail Adams, John Hickman, Jno. Catlet
No total. A Continuation of the Inventory, 31 May 1782,
          by John Catlett, John Hickman, Feathergil
          Adams.
Ret.:   28 October 1782

Pages
450-451:   MARY BLAND (Will)
                   Date: 3 August 1782
Dau.:   Esther Bland (eldest dau.) - 1 shilling sterling
Dau.:   Peggey Mcaboy - 1s. sterling
Dau.:   Chloe Pilcher - 1s. sterling
Dau.:   Amelia Brady - 1s. sterling
Dau.:   Betty Bland (youngest dau.) - one feather bed and
          furniture, one loom and all belonging thereto,
          one walnut table, two spinning wheels, two pair
          of cards, my riding Beast & saddle, one cow &
          calf, two Ewes
Son: James Bland (oldest son) - one sorrell Mare
          conditionally that if he when of age agrees to
          take the mare for satisfaction of Rents due him
          according to a bargain he & I made before Wit-
          nesses but if he refuses to take her, then my
          desire is that the Executors shall sell her with
          the rest of my property & equally divided as
          hereafter directed
Son: Charles Bland - the tract of land I now dwell on,
          which I bought of William Sanford Pickett
Son: Jackey Bland (youngest son) - negro man named Will
          ... all the rest of my property that shall be
          found in the possession of any person or persons
          to be sold and equally divided among my three
          Sons and Dau., James, Charles, Jackey and Betty
          Bland.
Signed: Mary (X) Bland
Wit.:   Charles Metcalf, John Murrey
Exors.: William Sanford Pickett, son James Bland
Proved: 28 October 1782, by o. of Charles Metcalf and John
          Murry. William Sanford Pickett granted cert.
          for obtaining probate.

Pages
451-452:   LITTLETON COOKE   (Inventory)
            Date: May 1782
App'd by: John Cooke, Franc's Willis, Jurn'r, Cato
           Moore, sworn to before me this 3d day of May
           1782. W. Baker.
Total eval.: L98
Ret.:   28 October 1783 (sic)

Pages
452-453:   WILLIAM SEATON (Will) of the County of
            Fauquier and Parish of Hamilton
            Date: 8 May 1782
            ... my body to be buried after a decent and
            Christian manner at the burying place of my
            children ...
            ... at the marriage of either & each of my
            Daughters that their mother give them such part
            of each of my stock as she can conveniently spare
            with a feather bed and furniture
Sons: "Item I give and bequeath to be equally divided
            between my son James Seaton and William Seaton at
            the time when my youngest son William arrives at
            age of twenty one." (sic)
            ... residue of my estate at that time be equally
            divided between all my children, making an allow-
            ance for the girls parts which they may have al-
            ready received..
            ... in case of my wifes marriage and my my (sic)
            children , or their estates be improperly man-
Wife: aged that then my said wife Mary be put to her
            thirds
Exors: Wife Mary with my Friends Rodham Kenner and Thomas
            Conway
Signed: William Seaton
Wit.:   George Marshall, William Conway, Robert Kenner,
            Geo. Turberville, David Wickliffe
Proved: 28 October 1782, by o. of George Marshall, William
            Conway, and Robert Kenner. Mary Seaton granted
            Cert. to bbtain probate..

Pages
453-454:   MOSES KAMPER (Inventory)
            No date.
App'd by: William Jennings, Alexander Bradford, Peter Kamper
Total eval.: L38.13.4   Ret.: 25 November 1782

Page
454:.   JOHN ADAMS   (Inventory)
               No date.
No appraisers. No total.
Executrix: Sarah Adams
Ret.:   25 November 1782

Pages
454-456:   JOSEPH ROBINSON   (Inventory)
               No date.
App'd by: Minor Winn, D. Floweree, Josiah Fishback
Total eval.: L416.14.0
Ret.:   27 January 1783

Page
456:           BERRYMAN JENNINGS   (Inventory)
               No date.
App'd by: John Duncan, Charles Martain, Charles Duncan
Total eval.: L201.16.0
Ret.:   24 February 1783

Page
457:           JOHN HEATON   (Inventory)
               Court Order dated November 1782
App'd. by: Henry Peyton, John Fishback, Joseph Obannon
Total eval.: L34.15.10
Ret.:   24 March 1783

Pages
457-458:   JOHN HEATON   (Sale of Estate)
               Date: 6 December 1782
Purchasers: George Blascock, Hezekiah Bradey, John Chick,
             John Owens, John Hawkins, William Pickett, Minor
             Winn, William Owens, Thomas Nelson, Capt. Hatha-
             way.
Total eval.: L43.10.2
Signed: Jno. Hawkins
Ret.:   24 March 1783

Pages:
458-459:   DANIEL FIELD of the Parish of Hamilton   (Will)
               Date: 27 July 1777
Son s: George, Lewis, John and Fielden Field - four Negroes -
          my wife's Dower after her Decease be equally divided
          among my said Sons or the Survivors of them. I
          also desire that my Executors place the said Negroes

```
                    (except my dear wife's Dower) on some place to
                    be by him rented for that purpose and the profits
                    arising therefrom to be for my said sons main-
                    tenance & schooling
Sons:               George, Lewis, John & Fielden ...
Daus:               Hannah, Ann, Sarah, Elizabeth, Mary and Milly ...
Gr.dau.:            Charlotte Haddocks ...
                    ... all my stocks - household furniture, plan-
                    tation utensils - to be equally divided between
                    them and their heirs forever.
Exor.:              my trusty friend Mr. Daniel Field of Culpeper
                    County and to have the care of my four sons
Signed:             Daniel Field
Wit.:               Wm. Grant, Edward Turner, Lewis Field, Geo.
                    Slaughter, Benj'n. Field, Benj'n. Roberts
Proved:             24 March 1783, by o. of William Grant.  Daniel
                    Field granted cert. for obtaining a probate.
```

Page
459-460:   JOHN HITT (Inventory)
                    Date: 14 November 1782
App'd by: James Stewart, John Stewart, Thomas Porter
Total eval.: L213.8.0
Ret.:   24 March 1783

Pages
460-461:   THOMAS FURR, "allis Johnson of the County
                    of Fauquier and parish of Hamilton in the
                    Colony of Virginia" (Will)
                    Date: 5 July 1777/20 July 1777
Wife: dear & loving wife Elizabeth Furr - young Sorrell
                    mare and her saddle and bridle and the best
                    feather Bed & furniture
____: Benjamin Williams - one young mare, saddle and
                    Bridle & one feather Bed and the furniture be-
                    longing to it
Cousin: Thomas Cummins - my cousin, Ten pounds current
                    money
____: Thomas Furr, the son of Moses Furr - ten pounds
                    current money
Exors: dear and loving wife and Thomas Cummins.
                    And as for the rest of my estate that remains after
                    the death of my dear and loving wife I give the
                    one half to B enjamin Williams and the other half
                    to be at her own disposal.
Sign ed: Thomas (his X mark) Furr

Wit: Walker Conway, Anne Conway, Anne (X) McCluskey,
           Wm. Smith, Jacob Rictor, Peter Rictor, James
           Rictor
Proved: 25 March 1783, by o. of Jacob Rector & James
           Rector. Elizabeth Furr and Thomas Cummins granted
           cert. to obtain probate.

Pages
461-462:   MARY BLAND (Inventory)
                Date: 29 November 1782
App'd by: Wm. Owens, Wm. Kenton, Evan Griffiths
No total. Ret.: 26 May 1783

Page
463:            JOHN SMITH (Inventory)
                No date.
App'd by: William Barkley, Josiah Fishback, Philip Fishback
No total. Ret.: 26 May 1783

Page
464:            JOHN COMBS (Inventory)
                No date.
App'd by: Wm. Sanford Pickett, Wm. Owens, Peter OBryant
Total eval.: L178.14.0
Ret.:   26 May 1783

Page
465:            JOHN WILLOUGHBY (Inventory)
                Date: "The 29th 1782"
App'd by: Thomas Hogan, William Flowerree, Wm. Berry
Total eval.: L39.13.6
Ret.:   26 May 1783

Pages
465-467:   THOMAS FURR JOHNSTON (Inventory)
                Court Order dated: March 1783
App'd by: Daniel Floweree, Benjamin Rector, Wm. Smith
Total eval.: L62.5.8
Ret.:   26 May 1783

Pages
467-469:   CAPT. WILLIAM BALL (Estate Account)
                Admr.: John Moffett
Details: 1773: To Paid: Lewis Neale, Benjamin Elliott, To
          Waggonage of 4 hhds tobo. to Quantico in 1772, To
          a Barrell of Fish for the Servants, To ½ Barrell

Corn from Sam Pepper, Francis Cunningham, Mr.
James Gray. 1774: John Taylor, Joseph Nelson,
William Holton, To waggonage & finding for 4 hh'ds
Tobo. To Dumfries, Henry Allen & William Elliott,
Clerk of Fauquier 290 lbs Tob'o., Bryant Ganer,
Mr. James Foley, Thomas Neavill, To the Collector
of Leeds Parish for 6 levies, To the Clerk of
Prince William.
BY: Capt. Thos. Marshall, Sam'l. Pepper, Capt.
William Edmonds, Thos. Glascock, John Moffett,
Thos. Nelson, Nicholas Lawler, Wm. Holton, Wm.
Lane, Wm. Nelson, X'r. Snider, Thos. Neavil, Mr.
Armistead Churchill, Rev'd. Mr. Thomson, Doctor
Boyd, Wm. Obannon, Mr. George Pickett, Henry
Asbury, John Riley, John Shanks, Mr. Pearson
Chapman, Mr. Charles Bell, Thos. Bartlett, Mr.
Thos. Keith, Jno. Elliott, Mr. John Hathaway,
Thos. Maddux, Mr. Sam'l. Grigsby, Jos. Nelson,
Mr. Jas. Gray, Capt. Robt. Ashby, Henry Allen,
Mr. Dan'l. Floweree, James Sparum, Val. Flynn,
Jno. Ellis, Wm. Elliott, John Forrester, John
Gates, Ben Garrish, George Bennett, John Obannon,
Henry Asberry, Mrs. Sarah Ball.
Exam. by: William Pickett and Aylett Buckner, 17 May 1783.
Ret.: 26 May 1783

Pages
469-470:   JEFFRY JOHNSON (Will)
            Date: 11 June 1782
Son: Alexander - a certain parcel of land whereon he
            now lives beginning at a Rock called the chimney
            stone thence running down the chimney stone Branch
            to Carter's run strait forward across the said run
            to the Manor of Leeds and then along the said Manor
            line to the Corner adjoining the lands of Anderson
            Cockrell thence along his line to the first ...
Wife: beloved wife Sarah Johnson - all the rest of my
            estate both land and moveables during her natural
            life if she remains a widow but if she should marry
            she should have one full third part thereof & no
            more ... after the decease of my beloved wife or
            her marriage I leave & bequeath the remainder of
            my land whereon I now live to be divided between
            my two sons as followeth:
Son: Baily Johnson - all over Carters run adjoining
            Alexander Johnson & John Moffett

Son: James Johnson - the balance of my land & Plantation.

Son: Presly Johnson - a certain Tract of Land on the Rappahannock mountains now leased to William Smith containing two hundred & sixty-four acres ... It is my will if either of my two sons Presly or James die before they come of age then the surviving Brother to possess the whole left to Both & if both die before they inherit the land then the land shall be sold & the money arising from the sale equally divided among all my children

Daus: Mary Cockrell, Elizabeth Morris & Sary & Lydia Johnson - all the rest of my estate not already disposed of, after my wife's decease or marriage.

Exors: two sons, Baily Johnson & Alexander Johnson

Signed: Jeffry (his EX mark) Johnson

Wit.:   Anderson Cockrell, Jesse Moffett, William (X) Holten, Daniel Moffett, John Monroe

Proved: 26 May 1783, by o. of Anderson Cockrell, Jesse Moffett & William Holton. Cert. to obtain probate granted to Alexander Johnson the Executor.

Pages
471-473:   ROBERT STEVENS (Sale of Estate)
           Date of Sale: 1 May 1783

Adm'r.: William Barkley

Details: No purchasers listed, total L240.16.0
Richard Stevens received of his Mother to the amount of L3.0.0; William Stevens L16.17.3; Ann Adams 5s.; John Stevens L5.0.0

Ret.:   23 June 1783

Pages
473-474:   JOHN ROSSER (Will)
           Date: 6 April 1783

Wife: I lend my whole estate both real & personal during life or widowhood but in Case she marries it is then my desire she shall be thirded. (not named)

Sons: Richard & George - after wife's death my Lands lying on Rappahannock where my son Richard now lives to be equally divided but it is my desire that George shall have the part that has a mill seat on, and in case either of them shall ever offer it for Sale that it shall be forfeited and the property vested in the other son.

Sons: John & William - my Tract of Land whereon I now

	live to be equally divided but is my desire that
	William shall have the part whereon the houses &c
	are (same conditions as above)
Dau.:	Item I give to my Daughter Sukey, Violet
Dau.:	Item I give to my Daughter Letty, Winny
Son:	Richard - Yambo & Cate
Son:	George - Lucy & her son Jack & Scitter
	... And in case either of my Daughters Negroes
	should die before my wife it is then my desire
	that my son George shall give a negro Girl to the
	Daughter who has lost hers.
Son:	John - Ben
Son:	William - Jane
	... at the Death of my wife I desire that my
	whole Stock then found & furniture shall be sold
	by my sons & the monies arising from the Sale to be
	equally divided between my Daughters Mary & Hannah
	... my debts be equally paid by my Sons
Daus.:	... My Daughters Sally & Elizabeth I have already
	given their parts
Signed:	John Rosser
Wit.:	Aylett Buckner, George Rosser, Fedrick Burditt X,
	James Crockett
Proved:	23 June 1783 by o. of Aylett Buckner, Frederick
	Burditt & James Crockett. Cert. for obtaining
	letters of administration granted Mary Rosser,
	Richard Rosser & John Rosser.

Pages
474-475:   DANIEL FIELD (Inventory)
                Date: Court Order, March 1783
App'd by: Peter Grant, Max'm. Berryman, Jos: Morgan
Details: 1 large Bible 15/; Pilgrims Progress 2/6
Total eval.: L240.2.11
Ret.:   23 June 1783

Pages
475-476:   DANIEL FIELD (Allotment of Dower)
                "In obedience to an order of Fauquier Court dated
                March 1783. We have allotted to Sarah the Widow
                of Daniel Field, dec'd. her Dower in the said
                Field's Estate ..." (Books not listed in the
                property allotted her)
Div. by: Peter Grant, Max'm. Berryman, Jos: Morgan
Ret: 23 June 1783

Pages
476-477:

THOMAS MADDUX (Will) "being aged & infirm but in proper mind & senses"
Date: 15 October 1782

Wife: Margaret Maddux - a Tract of Land lying in prince William County containing two hundred & sixty four Acres, to Act, will, sell or dispose of as she thinks proper.

Dau.: Easter Sally Maddux - one horse, Bridle & saddle worth twenty five pounds Virginia currency and one Cow & Calf, one Bed & furniture

Dau.: Fanny Gausom (Garrison ?) - one bed & furniture

Dau.: Darkes Jones - one bed & furniture

Son: Thomas - one shilling and three pence

Son: Marthew - one shilling & three pence

Son: Lazarus - one shilling & three pence

Son: Schoolfield - one shilling & three pence

Son: William - one shilling & three pence

Son: Nathaniel - one shilling & three pence

Wife: Beloved wife Margaret - all my personal estate during her life

Exors: beloved wife Margaret & my Son Lazarus Maddux

Signed: Thos. Maddux

Wit.: Jeremiah Darnall, Susannah (x) Hall, James Wright

Proved: 23 June 1783, by o. of Jeremiah Darnall, Susannah Hall and James Wright. Cert. granted to Margaret Maddux for obtaining probate.

Pages
477-478:

JAMES MURRY (Will)
Date: 29 March 1783

Son: Ralph - one Negro Lad named Simon
"Secondly, My Will and desire is and, so leave it to be that my son Ralph Murry and my son in law John Seaton shall keep and be lawfully possessed of my Tract of Land they now live on, each of them possessing their part as it has been divided between them upon their paying into my Estate the just sum of money which I gave for the said Land."

Wife: Lydia - my full right and title of the Lott of Land I now dwell on during her Life and after her

Son: decease to fall to my son Reubin Murry
... my loving Wife Lydia Murry all the rest of my estate both real and personal including my Tract of Land lying on a branch of Elk run in Fauquier County during her life and at her decease then for the whole thereof including the sum of Money that

- 139 -

Ralph Murry & John Seaton is to pay shall be
equally divided between all my children
Exors: three sons Ralph Murry, John Murry and Reubin
            Murry
Signed: James Murrey
Wit.:   John Butler, Nathan Cockran, Daniel French
Proved: 28 July 1783, by o. of John Butler, Nathan
            Cockran and Daniel French. Ralph Murry &
            Reubin Murry two of the Executors therein
            named granted cert. for obtaining probate.

Pages
478-479:   THOMAS MADDUX   (Inventory)
                Date: 12 July 1783
App'd by: John Martin, John Weaver, Geo. Grant
Total eval.: L52.17.6
Ret.:   28 July 1783

Page
479:            JEFFRY JOHNSON   (Inventory)
                No date
App'd by: Benj'n. Obannon, William Holten, Andrewson
          Cockrell
Total eval.: L54.1.6
Ret.:   28 July 1783

Page
480.:   JOHN ROSSER   (Inventory)
                Court Order dated 29 June 1783
App'd by: Peter Kamper, Alexander Bradford, Wm. Jennings
Total eval.: L504.12.6
Ret.:   28 July 1783

Pages
480-481:   MARY BRADFORD "of Hamilton Parish"   (Will)
                Date: 6 July 1775
Dau.:   Sarah Rose - my riding saddle
Daus.:   three Daughters to be equally divided all my
            wearing apparel, one cotton gown only excepted
Gr.dau: which I give unto my grand Daughter Anna Fowler
Exors: my sons Alexander & Benjamin Bradford
Signed: Mary (X) Bradford
Wit.:   Charles Day, Jo's. Morgan, John (+) Mcbee
Proved: 28 July 1783, by o. of Joseph Morgan and John
            McBee. Cert. for obtaining probate granted to
            Alexander Bradford.

Page
481:                 REUBIN ELLIOTT (Division of Estate)
                        Date: 25 July 1783
Div.by: Wm. Heale, Jno. Hathaway, D. Floweree
            ... We the Subscribers have met and divided the
            estate of Reubin Elliott dec'd. agreeable to his
            will, which we find to be L76.2.0 each, after
            giving the widow of her Childs part, the Courts
            expenses unsettled because they could not be as-
            certained which they agree to settle among them-
            selves when asscertained, each bearing his part ..
Ret.:   28 July 1783

Pages
481-482:   JOHN HURMON (Estate Account)
Exor.:   John Kincheloe
Details: TO CASH PAID: (1775): Joseph Robinson, Wm. Fewell,
            Wm. Bishop, Richard Randall, Thomas Simmons,
            Benedict Spitfathom, John Barber, John Squires,
            Christian Power, Jacob Coutsman, James Tools.
            (1776): Wm. Murry, (1778): Aaron Thomas. (1775):
            To whiskey at the funeral, 8 shillings; Wm.
            Kincheloe, Cpt. Bullitt for Advice, L9; Coll'o.
            Brooke for copy of the Will, L1. (1779): Maron
            French for Schooling, L10; (1783): Powell & Harrison.
            CASH FROM: (1775): Mrs. Mary Carter's purchase at
            her Sale, formerly the Wife of Dr. John Hurmons,
            dec'd.; George Collins, Nicholas Ellzey, Thos.
            Hughs, Wm. Elliott, Wm. Turley. (1778): Mary
            Batson, Benjamin Downs, Peter Robie, Thomas West,
            James Green. (1779): Venson Tapp. (1776): James
            Toole. (1783): June 28th To 80 Gallons whiskey
            purchased at public sale L11.6.8.
Exam. by: Wm. Heale & Jno. Hathaway
Ret.:   28 July 1783

Page
483:                WILLIAM SETTLE (Inventory and Division of Estate)
                        Court Order dated March 1782.
App'd & Div. by: Wm. Pickett, Peter Kamper, John Blackwell
Details: To Edward Settle - slaves, stock and personal estate
            amounting to L360.8.0
            To John Pope Williams
            To William Freeman
Ret.:   28 July 1783

Page
483:
     BERRYMAN JENNINGS (Divison of Estate:)
     No date.
    ... We. the subscribers being first sworn have
    allotted the dower of Susanna Jennings, the
    widow of Berryman Jennings dec'd. - L73.10..0
    Berryman Jennings, son of the dec'd., his part
    L128.6
Div. by: John Duncan, Charles Duncan, Charles Martin.
Ret.: 28 July 1783

      END OF WILL BOOK ONE
       1759 - 1783

       WILL BOOK TWO
       1783 - 1796

Page
1
     MRS. MARY BRADFORD (Inventory)
     No date.
App'd by: John Ashby, Max'n. Berryman, Jos: Morgan - being
    first sworn before Wm. Grant, a Justice of the
    Peace for the said County.
Total eval.: L363.11.6
Ret.: 25 August 1783

Pages
2-3:
     WILLIAM SEATON (Inventory)
     No date.
App'd by: Jonathan Gibson, Rodham Tulloss, George Marshall
Total eval: L352.8.0
Ret.: 25 August 1783

Page
4:
     EDWIN FIELDING "of Virginia in the County of
     Fauquier Gentleman" (Will)
     Date: 11 January 1781
Wife: my dearly Beloved wife Nancy - one half of my negroes
    together with all my Stock, household goods and
    moveables
Sister: beloved sister Elizabeth Reaves - the other half
    of my Negroes to remain in my wife's hands untill
    she shall call for them.
Exors: Mr. Joseph Taylor and my wife
Signed: Ewin Fielding

- 142 -

|---|---|
| Wit.: | John James, Jeremiah Morgan, Henry Bradford, Elizabeth James. |
| Proved: | 22 September 1783, by o. of John James, Jeremiah Morgan and Henry Bradford. Nancy Fielding and Joseph Taylor granted cert. for obtaining a probate. |

Pages
6-7

CHARLES MOREHEAD of the parish of Leeds and County of Fauquire in the State of Virginia (Will) Date: 19 January 1783

Son:	Turner Morehead - all that Tract or Parcell of Land containing about 127 Acres whereon he now Resides as also Fifty Pounds Virginia Currency with one Cow and a Negro Boy named George
Dau.:	Mary Ransdell - a Negro Woman Named Jeany as also one Cow with Two Ewes & Lambs
Son:	Charles Morehead - a Tract of Land containing about 127 Acres purchased from Joseph Hudnall - one Negro Man - one grey hourse two Cows two Ewes & Lambs - Feather bed and furniture - a Iron Pot and Frying Pan, a dish and half Dozen Pewter Plates.
Dau.:	Kerenhappuch Moreh ead - L80 Virginia Currency - one Horse & side saddle two cows two Ewes & Lambs - Iron Pott and Frying Pan a Dish and Half a Dozen Pewter Plates
Sons:	James and Presley - a Tract of Land Containing about 300 Acres whereon I now live to be equally divided amongst them
Son:	Armistead - a negro man - my Still & Worm, a Horse bridle and Saddle two Cows two Ewes and Lambs One Iron Pott one Frying Pann & Dish and Half Dozen Pewter Plates
Son:	James. - One Negro Boy - my Silver Watch a Horse Bridle and Saddle two Cows, two Ewes and Lambs a Feather Bed and Furniture, a Dish and half Dozen Pewter Plates, a Iron Pott & Frying Pann
Son:	Presly - One Negro man - with half the Increase of my Negro Woman Dinah after his Mother's Decease - a Horse, saddle and briddle - two Cows two Ewes and Lambs a Feather Bed & Furniture - a Dish and half a Dozen Pewter Plates an Iron Pott and Frying Pan and my Fiddle
Dau.:	Elizabeth Morehead - one Negro Woman named Dinah with half her Increase after her Mothers Death as also a horse saddle and Bridle, two cows two Ewes & Lambs a Feather Bed and Furniture - a Dish and

Wife: Half Dozen Plates, an Iron Pott and Frying Pan
Beloved wife Mary Morehead - during her Natural
Life my Negro Man named Monday as also one N egro
Woman named Dinah and all my Personal Estate She
First Paying the Legacies as hither to mentioned
as they come of Age or Marrys.
... I do give and bequeath to Ann Butler for
Extodinary Services done Five Pounds Virginia
Currency.

Exors: Well beloved wife Mary Morehead, Charles Chilton
& my sons Turner and Charles Morehead
Signed: Charles Morehead
Wit.: George Carter, William Morehead, Rich Fisher,
John Cooke
Proved: 27 October 1783, by o. of George Carter, William
Morehead and Richard Fisher. Mary Morehead,
Turner Morehead an d Charles Chilton granted
cert. for obtaining a probate.

Page
8
JOHN KELLEY (Will)
Date: 30 September 1783
... It is my desire for this two hundred and forteen aerkers of land at joseph Kelley is returning
to be divided as joseph kelley and joseph Henery
shall agree and if joseph Kelley should not never
return that this said two hundeed and forteen
acores of land shall fall to joseph Henerys eairs ...
Signed: John Kelley
Wit.: Edmund Holmes, Thomas Kelley, Mikel Glass
Proved: 27 October 1783, by o. of Thomas Kelly and Michael
Glass. Thomas Kelly granted cert. for obtaining
letters of administration.

Page
9 :
JOHN JONES (Inventory)
No date
App'd by: Peter Grant, John Ashby, John Shumate
No total. Ret.: 28 October 1783

Page
10 :
ANN BATTALEY (Will)
Date: 12 May 1780
Dau.: Hannah Battaley and to my Son Fieldin Battaley
Son: all my Household Furniture and Stock of Horses
Cattle hogs sheep and Geas to be equally divided

between them - all my part of my fathers Estate
and L50 that Colonel Frances (sic) Talliaferro
left me in his Will

Exors: Daughter hannah Battaley, Maxmilian Berryman and
Battaley Bryan
Signed: Ann (X) Battaley
Wit.: Max'n. Berryman, Ann Berryman (X), Benjamin
Berryman
Proved: 24 November 1783, by o. of Benjamin Berryman
And on the motion of Maximilian Berryman and
John Vowls who intermarried with Hannah Battalay
an executrix therein named who made oath & exe-
cuted and acknowledged Bond as the law directs
Cert. if granted them for obtaining a Probat there-
of in due form. NOTE: I Doe Heare by Sertifie
Before the Fase of this Coart that I have no Rite
nor title to any thing mentioned in this Will as
Witness my hand and seal this 30th Day of August
1780. Max'n. Berryman.
Wit.: Joseph Morgan, Reuben Bryan, Charles (X) Berryman

Page
11 : DANIEL GARNER (Inventory)
Date: 21 November 1783
App'd by: Aaron Fletcher, James Withers, Benjamin Garner
Total eval: L15.0.6
Ret.: 24 November 1783

Pages
12-13: JAMES WITHERS (Will)
Date: 9 January 1784
Son: George Washington Withers (youngest son) - the
land whereon I now live containing 573 acres &
the following slaves, N amely: Rose, Anthony,
Sharlote & Charity - one good Feather Bed &
Furniture and one gun - but in case my son should
die leaving no chi ld lawfully Begotten then in
that case I desire that the said land & slaves and
whatever I have given him may be equally divided
among all my children.
Son: James Withers (eldest son) - slaves which he has
now in his possession namely: Robin & Sarah -
whatever else of my Estate he has now in his
possession.
Dau.: Nanny Duncan - one Slave and whatever else of my
estate which she has now in her possession
Son: John - one slave - and whatever else I have here-

- 145 -

	tofore given & which he has now in his possession.
Gr.dau:	Betty McKay - the slave which Isaac McKay & my daughter Bridget McKay parents of my s'd Grand Daughter had in possession namely Sammer & her former & future Increase
Wife:	loving Wife Jemima Withers & my Children following: James, William & John Withers, Hannah Picket, Nanny Duncan & Betty Jennings - all the remaining part of my Estate of whatever kind which I have not mentioned to be equally divided.
Exors:	Sons James & William Withers and my friend John Wigginton
Signed:	James Withers
Wit.:	William Harriss, Sabbatiah (X) Israel, John Wigginton
Proved:	26 January 1784, by o. of William Harriss, Sabbatiah Israel and John Wigginton. James Withers and William Withers two of the Executors granted cert. for obtaining a probate.

Page
13:

GREENHAM DODSON (Inventory)
Court order dated August 1777

App'd by: Nicholas George, John Nelson, Dan Bradford.
No total. Ret.: 22 March 1784

Pages
14-16:

JAMES MURREY (Inventory)
Date: 17 December 1783

App'd by: Thomas Bartlett, Wm. Sanford Pickett & Wm. Fitzjarald. Sworn before Wm. Heale.
No total. Ret.: 22 March 1784.

Page
16:

ROBERT STEPHENS (Administrator's Account)
Adm'r.: William Berkley
Details: Burial charges L1.10..0
Exam. by: Wm. Heale, John Hathaway - 15 December 1783
Ret.: 22 March 1784

Pages
16-17:

AMOS LUNSFORD (Inventory)
Court order dated March 1784

App'd by: Francis Atwell, Wm. Jones, Joseph Hudnall
Total eval.: L88.12.9
Ret.: 27 April 1784

Pages
17-18:   NATHANIEL DODD (Will)
                    Date: 9 May 1783

Dau.:   Mildred Pinkard - one Negro girl named Cathrin
Dau.:   Sarah Garner - to my Daughter Sarah Garner's
            children - L20
Son: Allen Dodd - one negro girl named Lucy
Son: Nathaniel - one negro woman named Rose and her
            increase after the fourteenth day of July 1779.
Dau.:   Hannah Hammit - L20
Son: John - one negro Woman named Phillis now in his
            possession
Dau.:   Elizabeth Williamson - L20
Son: Benjamin - one Negro Boy named William
Dau.:   Mary Wheatley - one Negro girl
Son: James - one Negro man named Moses after the de-
            cease of my beloved Wife Sarah, Also one Feather
            Bed and Furniture belonging to the same Likewise
            one Oval table two pewter Dishes and one Pewter
            Bason and one dos'n Pewter Plates
Wife: Sarah Dodd - all the Remainder of my Estate both
            Real and Personal during her Natural life and
            after her Death the Land to be Divided the Mansion
            House and Land I give to my son Nathaniel Dodd
            Excepting the Land purchased of Morgan & Waugh
            Darnall - the Land & Tenements Purchased of Morgan
Son: & Waugh Darnall his son I give to my Son James
            Dodd and the Stills I will to Nathaniel & James
            one to each, James is to have the first Choice or
            largest Still to him and his Heirs forever. The
            Remainder of my Estate not mentioned I leave to the
            Disposal of my Beloved Wife Sarah Dodd to give to
            our Children as She whall think proper.
Exors: my Beloved Wife Sarah, son Nathaniel, son James
Signed: Nathaniel Dodd
Wit.:   Daniel Marr, Martha (X) Allen, Paul Williams
Proved: 24 May 1784 by o. of Daniel Marr and Paul Williams.
            Sarah Dodd, Nathaniel Dodd & James Dodd granted
            cert. for obtaining a probate.

Pages
18-20:   JAMES WITHERS (Inventory)
                    Court order dated 26 January 1784
App'd by: William Morgan, John Mauzy, Edw. Settle, Henry
            Settle. No total listed.
Ret.:   24 May 1784

Pages
20-22:   JAMES WITHERS (Division of Estate)
                    Court Order dated 26 January 1784
                    We William Morgan, John Mauzy, Edward Settle and
                    Henry Settle (being first Sworn) have Divided
                    the Estate of James Withers Dec'd. According to
                    Will as per Lotts b elow:
                    Lott No. 1 - Sam'l. Duncan
                    Lott No. 2 - Jemima Withers Widow's Dower
                    Lott No. 3 - Wm. Withers Lott
                    Geo. W. Withers Lott
                    Lott No. 4 - Jas. Withers Lott
                    Lott No. 5 - John Pickett's Lott
                    Lott No. 6 - Wm. Jennings Lott
                    Lott No. 7 - Jno. Withers Lott
Retn: 24 May 1784

Page
24:                 JOHN PETERS (Inventory)
                    Court Order dated October 1781
App'd by: John Mauzy, Cha. Waler & Jas. Homes. *
Total evall: L537.02.09
Ret.:   28 June 1784

                    *Minute Book, 1781-84, p. 23 (October Court, 1781):
                    Order that John Mauzy, Charles Waller, James Dowdall
                    and James Hoomes or any three of them being first
                    sworn do appraise the Estate of John Peters de-
                    ceased and return the appraisement to the Court.

Page
25:                 JOHN GLAS(S)COCK of the County of Fauquier and
                    Parish of Leeds (Will)
                    Date: 9 December 1780
Exors: ... as for my burial, I desire it may be decent, at
                    the discretion of my dear wife and Son John, whom
                    I leave executors of this last will and testament.
Wife: dear wife (not named) - the Legacies shall be in
                    my dear wife's possession during her natural life,
                    or that she shall have a suffieient maintenance.
Son: Thomas - 1000 pounds of Crop Tobacco also what Land
                    and other effects I gave him before
Son: Hezekiah - Negro Harry - my black horse of that
                    name - my best feather bed and furniture and a ten
                    gallon pot, pot rack and pot-hooks
Son: George - my horse Prince

Dau.:   Mary Rictor - a pewter dish, and what else she
has had

Dau.:   Margaret Turly - my next bed and furniture with
what she has already had

Son-in-law: Francis Jackson - I desire he shall receive
what Mr. William Brent owes me

Son: John - I give the Land whereon I live, containing One hundred and Eighty eight Acres, more or
less, being bounded by the Church road of Sizas,
also all my personal estate

Exors: Son John, my dear wife

Signed: John (X) Glascock

Wit.:   James Thomson, John Fishback, Philip Fishback

Proved: 28 June 1784, by o. of John Fishback & Phillip
Fishback. John Glascock granted cert. for
obtaining probate.

Page:
27:           ELIAS EDMONDS of the County of Fauquier and
parrish of Leeds (Will)
Date: 13 October 1782

Wife: Elizabeth - to Possess and Enjoy the one moiety of
my Estate both Real and Personal During her natural
life and after her Decease to Decend to my beloved
Son Elias Edmonds

Son: Elias - the other moiety Residue and Remainder of
my Estate

Daus.:   Ann Hubbard, Judith Bucknor and Elizabeth Bruin -
shall enjoy and Possess all that part of my moveable Estate of every kind whatsoer that they and
Each of them may now have in their Possession they
and Each of their Heirs forever, Provided that
there be no Claim nor Title set up under the will
of Simon Miller Deceased, And should it happen, they
or Either of them or their Heirs Claim any Benefit
under the above mentioned will that then they or
Either of them or their Heirs Claiming such
Benefit, Shall be Excluded the Benefit of whatever
part of my Estate they may now have in their Possession, And the same to Decend to my Son Elias
Edmonds .. should my beloved Son Elias Edmonds Dye
without Lawfull Issue that then my Estate both
Real and personal may be Sold and equally divided
amongst my three Daughters.

Exors: my beloved Son Elias Edmonds

Signed: Elias Edmonds

Wit: Jacob holsclaw, William (X) Jenkins, John Barker,
             James Headley
Proved: 28 June 1784, by o. of Jacob Holtzclaw and James
             Headley. Elias Edmonds granted cert. for obtaining
             probate.

Pages
28-29:   CAPTAIN CHARLES MOREHEAD (Inventory)
               Date: 26 June 1784
App'd by: Geo. Carter, Joseph Taylor, Wm. Morris
Total eval.: L491.10.3

Pages
29-30:   EDWARD FIELDING (Inventory)
               No date.
App'd by: Ambrose Barnett, George Rogers, Jun'r.
Total eval.: L617.15.6

Pages
30-31:   DOCT'R RICH'D L. HALL (Estate Account)
Adm'r.:   Wharton Ransdell
Details: TO CASH PAID: Wharton Ransdell, Jun'r. for Build-
          ing a House L414 in Paper Money; The Rev'd. James
          Tomson for Preaching Doctr Halls Funeral Sermon
          40/; Colo. Brooke for Recording a Will. 1782:
          John Russell Proved Acct before Chas. Chilton.
          1784: To Cash paid John Russell Proved acct. before
          Colo. Arm'd. Churchill; Mr. Thomas Keith; Thomas
          Rycroft for repairing watch.
          The above acct. was Sworn to before me this 26th
          day June 1784. Thomas Digges.
          RECEIVED OF: Ariss Cox, Capt. E. Edmonds, Mr.
          John Churchill, Mr. Peter Grant for a Pair of
          Doctr. Halls Books, Henry Newby for Rent (1780).
          1783: Rec'd of the widow Newby Rent for 2 years
          1781 & 82 by the Hands of Mr. Geo. Rogers,
          Charles Chilton on acct. of Mrs. Ransdell in for
          M. M. Jones, Mrs. Eliza Scott, Joseph Baysie on
          acct of his Father John Baysie for Medicine,
          John McCormick; By a watch sold Robert Scott,
          Archibald Beshaw, Eliza Newby for Rent for the
          year 1783.
            In obedience to an Order from the Worshipfull
          Court of Fauquier County, we the Subscribers
          having Examined the Papers and Vouchers Relative
          to the Estate of Doct'r Richard Lingan Hall and

find that it appears to us that Capt. Wharton
Ransdell an Executor of the said Estate has paid
2848 lbs. of Tobo. and fourteen pounds eight
shillings eleven pence Farthing and that he has
Rec'd of the said Estate L13.18 and a Penny
Farthing and 2,000 lbs. of Tobacco so that there
appears to be a Ballance of 848 lbs of Tobo. and
Ten Shillings and Ten Pence Farthing due from the
said Estate to the said Ransdell .. 26 June 1784.
Signed: Charles Chilton, Thomas Digges
Ret.:   28 June 1784

Pages:
31-32:   Mr. JOHN GLAS(S)COCK (Inventory)
                Date: 20 July 1784. Court order dated
                June 1784
App'd by: Josiah Fishback, John Utterback, William Lake.
Total eval.: L235.5.0
Ret.:   26 July 1784

Page
32:            Mr. JOHN MITCHELL (Inventory)
                Court order dated May Court 1784
App'd by: James Crockett, Fred'k Burdett, John Kemper
No total. Ret.: 26 July 1784

Pages
32-33:   NATHANIEL DODD (Inventory)
                Court order dated May 1784
App'd by: James Wheatley, Augustine Cossom Day
Total eval.: L422.8.7
Ret.:   26 July 1784

Pages
33-35:   DUFF GREEN (Administrator's Account)
Admr.:   Col. John Green
Details: TO: Rev'd. Mr. Craig, Col'o. John Bell, Joseph
Monter, William Dale, Yelverton Peyton, John
Cook, John Matthews, Capt. Morehead, Henry String-
fellow, Green & Slaughter, William Green, William
Robinson, Mr. Gavin Lawson, Joseph Minter, John
Blackwell, John Tomlin, Mr. Wm. Rind, Colo.
Edmund Pendleton, Mr. Alex'r. Parker, John Head-
ley, William Dayle, Danl. Payne, Matthew George,
Cockrane & Co., Peter Catlett, William Carr,
Armistead Churchill, Gibson Foote, Joseph Duncan,

- 151 -

Robert Singleton, Jacob Minter, John Ayriss,
Benjamin Rice, Harslikle, Andrew Buckhannan,
Robert Gains, William Barker, John Green, Jn'r.,
John Robinson & Lewis Burwell, John Liklye.
BY: William Green, Hancock Lee, Major John Lee,
John Green, Jun'r., Rev. Mr. Craig, Colo. John
Bell, Mr. Hunton, Mrs. Ann Green, Joseph Minter,
Carr Baily, Robt. Gains, John Basy, Wm. Dale,
Yelverton Peyton, Mr. Jones, Capt. Morehead,
William White, Wm. Scoggin, Wm. Ransdell, John
Cotterel, James Taylor, Simon Morgan, Wharton
Ransdell, Will Elzey, James Buchanan, James
Hathaway.
Examin ed: 26 July 1784, by W. Grant, Jos. Blackwell,
            Jeremiah Darnall
Ret.:   26 July 1784

Pages
35-37:   CAPTAIN GEORGE NEAVILLE (Estate Account)
Exor.:   Ambrose Barnett
Details: TO PAID: 1775, Sept. 25: Doctor Samuel Boyd;
1777: James Hathaway it being the Legacy left
Jno. Rosser; Thomas Shurley; Joseph Duncan;
Martin Pickett by hands of Wm. White; Thomas
Chapman on his prov'd Acct by Maj. Ewell; Jno.
Rosser in prt. of his Legacy; Thomas Doughty;
James Barnett; John Sutton; John Blackwell for
Chair Tax; Humphrey Brooke Certificate probat;
Do. for an Order to allot Widow's Dower in
Fauq'r; Do. in Culpeper; Do. recording Inventory;
Charles Chilton & Compy; Original Graham; Martin
Pickett; Alexander Campbell; Thomas Chapman;
William Carr; John Headley; John Barnett, his
legacy; Nancy Berry, her legacy; Jno. May; Clerk
P. Wm. Court for filing Declaration agt. Campbell
BY: William Edmonds; Robert Scott; George Rogers,
Sen'r.; James Ewell; John Hutchison; William
White; the Widow;, James Hathaway; Ambrose Barnett;
Capt. Chas. Chilton; Charles Chilton; Capt. William
Carr; Robert Ashby; John Basey; Capt. James Bell;
Samuel Blackwell pr. Joseph Blackwell; James
Bogue; Peter Carter;, John Cooke; Samuel Porter;
William Suttle; Samuel Steele; George Steele;
Joseph Taylor; John Waddle; Armistead Churchill;
Will'm. Ransdell pr. Capt. Chilton; John Siddall;
John Shurley; Thomas Thornton; Jno. Minter pr.

Capt. Chilton; Alex'r. Jameson; Chas. Edmonds.
paper money; William Edmonds; Tannack George;.
Widow Lovingder; Minor Winn; Richard Shurley;
James McClanahame; John Tomlin, Aug. 1784.
Examind by: James Bell and Charles Chilton, 1 July 1784.
Ret.:   24 August 1784

Page
37:              DANIEL RICH (Inventory)
                 Date: 20 August 1784
App'd by: Thos. Porter, Josiah Holtzclaw, Joseph Martin
Total eval.: L14.19.11½ Cash and L2.9.1
Ret.:   24 August 1784

Page
38:              FRANCIS BURGESS (Administrator's Account)
Admr.:   John Suddoth
Details: TO: the legacy given to Jane Burgess paid her
          husband James Ireland; To the legacy bequeathed
          to Ruth Burgess paid her husband Brian O'bannon;
          To the legacy bequeathed to Ann Burgess paid her
          husban d Thomas Elliot; By the legacy beq. to
          Eleanor wife to William Elliot; Cuthbert Bullett;
          William Allison; James Bell Exor. of John Bell;
          John Smith; John Moffet; Nat. Moss.
Ret.:   24 August 1784

Pages
39-40:   THOMAS CONWAY (Will)
                 Date: 25 August 1784
Son: William (oldest son) - one negro Woman named Moll
          & her child named Nell
Son: Thomas - my Tract of land on Town Run being the
          same he lives on
Son: Peter - part of the Tract of land I now live on,
          beginn ing at a marked white Oak near a branch
          that run through Joseph Blackwell's old field ex-
          tending thence along a marked line to Smith's line,
          it being the part he now lives on.
Son: Joseph - the remaining part of the Tract of Land
          I live on including the land above the Road to
          the marked line above mentioned, this being the
          part my House stands on
Son: Henry - my Tract of land in Shenandoe County
Dau.:   Susanne Crosby - the sum of L5
Gr.son: James Conway, the Son of James Conway - one young

- 153 -

Gr.son:	Negro to be chosen from among my Slaves by my Executor (if he should die to go to Estate) George Crosby - a Negro boy to be chosen by my Executor out of my Slaves (if he should die to go to Estate)
_____:	Sally Mauzy, a young Woman born and raised in my House - a negro Girl named Peg

... all my Negroes, excepting those by this Will
already bequeathed, & all the rest of my moveable Estate (excepting one Bed & Furniture which
I gave to my Son Joseph Conway) shall be equally
divided among my five Sons William, Thomas, Peter,
Henry, Joseph & whereas Some of my Sons are now
in Possession of Negroes which I have formerly
lent them, but to which they have no legal Title
by Deed or otherwise my Intention is that such
Negroes so lent be still considered as part of my
Estate & subject to the General Division above
ordered.

My desire is that my Executors do commence &
prosecute a Suit against John Markham for the
recovery of two Negroe Men named Joseph & Kit
which I formerly lent to the s'd Markham & which
he has hitherto refused to redeliver to me.

Exors:	Sons William Conway, Thomas Conway & Joseph Conway
Signed:	Thos. Conway
Wit.:	Peter Grant, John Smith, Ann (X) Smith
Codicil:	I, Thomas Conway, upon more mature reflection do will & desire that the Land I live on may be de-vided into two equal parts. the one of which I hereby give to my Son Peter .. & the other to my Son Joseph .. My Son Peter having previously agreed that his Brother Joseph shall have his choice of the two parts.
Signed:	Thomas Conway (same witnesses as above)
Proved:	27 September 1784 by o. of Peter Grant & John Smith and Ann Smith. Cert. granted William Conway, Thomas Conway & Joseph Conway to obtain probate.

Pages 41-42:	JOSEPH NEALE (Will) Date: 6 November 1783
Son:	Benjamin Neale - his choice of two tracts of land located by Squire Boon of 500 acres each, on the Western Waters he making a right to the said Boon

for his part of location of said 500 acres ..
(the said Benjamin to pay all charges necessary
for obtaining a Grant in his own name) ".. a
warrent now in the hands of Jos. Nelson of about
800 acres, a rifell gun & all my wearing apparrell
& Riding Saddle" - one mare

Wife: Mary - in case my wife should be delivered of a
son, she being now in her Pregaancy that I give
and bequeath to the said Son the other 500 acres
located by Squire Boon - my Executors make a
right to the said Boon for his part of said land,
according to my agreement with him, & that they
pay out of my Estate all charges of the said
Infants land, in procuring a Grant for the same.
... during her natural life all my Negroes -
personal estate to Raise & Educate our Children
upon .. But if my said wife should marry then to
have only one third part thereof

Daus: Sarah, Anne, Mary, Judah & Joanah - the other two
thirds to be equally divided between my five
daughters - in case that the child that my wife
now carries shall be a daughter that she also
have an equal division - the one third part of my
Estate lent my said wife after her decease be
divided in the same manner as the two thirds
aforesaid.

Wife: Mary - 1/3 part of all my land not already left
away which is located by Wm. Pope .. 1000 acres ..
saving the quantity to be given the said Pope
for his trouble in locating the same .. 2/3 remaining to said five Daughters - in case either
of my said Daughters should die before they come
of age or marry that the survivor of them shall
Equally divide every part left, both real & personal - that all debts due me after paying my just
debts shall be collected & the money to be lent
out by my Executors on Interest - same to be
equally divided amongst all my sons & Daughters
at the time that anyone of the aforesaid Divisions
shall take place Except my son Benjamin & he to
receive his equal share when ever the same shall
be collected.

Exors: my loving wife Mary, my Brother Matthew Neale &
Frederick (X) Burdette

Signed: Joseph Neale

Wit: Joseph bragg, Fedreck burdette X, John burdette,

William Suttell, John Bell
Proved: 24 May 1784, by o. of Frederick Burdette & John
Burdette. Mary Neale & Matthew Neale made oath
& executed bond to obtain probate.

Page
43:                JOSEPH NEALE (Inventory)
                   Date: 24 September 1784
App'd by: Peter Kemper, Peter Kemper, Jun'r., George (X)
          Green
Total eval.: L363.19.6
Ret.:   27 September 1784

Pages
44-45:   Mr. JOHN BARKER (Inventory)
                   No date.
App'd by: William Barkley, Josiah Fishback, Thomas
          Bartlett
Total eval.: L73.4.9
Ret.:   28 September 1784

Pages
45-46:   MARY BLAND (Administrator's Account)
Exor.:   William S. Pickett
Details: TO: 1782, Esther Bland, John Owens. 1783, Wm.
          Healer Moses, John Dyer, Thomas Cater for wolf
          catching according to subscription, Jos. Fish-
          back for Do.., Hugh Nelson for Do., Manoah Stone
          for making one coffin, Charles Metcalf., John
          Murray, Hezekiah Brady, legacy left Chas. Bland,
          Elizabeth Bland & James Bland; Bal. left in my
          hands as Gdn. to John Bland, Muthy McCoy.
          BY: Hezekiah Brady, Jacob Reed, William Berry,
          Thomas Laws, William Kenton, John Willoughby,
          John Cornwell, Thomas Leachman, John Higgins,
          Johnson Owens, John Murrey, Cornelius Rains,
          William Nalls, Thos.. Fetheringston, Enoch O'Brian,
          W. Sanford Pickett, Henry Pinkstone, James
          McIntosh, John Flyn, Shadrack Pinkstone, John
          Feagan, William Ownes, Mark Kenton, Sen'r.,
          Daniel Cummins, Jno. Griffiths, Elizabeth Bland.
Examined by: Charles Chilton, Thomas Digges, 23 Aug. 1784
Ret..:   28 September 1784

Pages
46-47:   JOHN NELSON, SEN'R. of Elk Run in Fauquier

County being aged and infirm but of a
sound mind and disposing memory. (Will)
Date: 9 August 1784

Sons: Jesse and John Nelson - my Tract of land on
Dry-Run in Shanado County to be equally divided
between the said Jesse and John

Wife: Sarah - have the use of the Plantation and Tract
of Land whereon I now live together with the
Slaves and Stock of all kinds and Household
Furniture thereon during her Natural Life, provided that as any of my Children, namely Jesse,
William, Margaret, Jemima, Lettice and Sarah
Nelson's (who are n ow single) do marry that
each of them shall have Four head of Neats
Cattle, a Feather Bed and Furniture and two
Ewes - if my daus. Margaret, Jemima, Lettice
or Sarah Nelson's or any of my said four
daughters should remain single till the death
of their Mother, ... that the Hire or labor of
my two Slaves, George and Daphne, shall be
appropriated to the support and use of all or
any my aforementioned four daughters while they
remain single after the death of their mother.

Son: William - set of Smith's tools, a young Sorrel
Mare, now in his possession - (after the death
of his Mother) the Plantation whereon I now live -
Negro Boy named Lymas.
... at the death of my Wife, the whole of my
personal or moveable Estate (excepting my two
slaves George and Daphne) - shall be equally
divided between my Children Jesse, John & William
Nelsons, Lidia Morehead, Nanny Fishback, Mary
Rector, Margaret Nelson, Jemima Nelson, Lettice
Nelson and Sarah N elson or the survivor of them.

Signed: John (his X mark) Nelson, Sen'r.

Wit.: Jno. Matthews, James Gillison, James Blackwell,
Thos. Helm, Joseph George, John Thomas

Proved: 25 October 1784, by o. of John Matthews and Joseph
George. Sarah Nelson and William Nelson made
oath and were granted cert. to obtain probat.

**Pages
47-48:** JOHN SHUMATE, SEN'R. (Will)
Date: 19 May 1783

Son: Thomas - the land he now lives on after the death
of his Mother
Capt. Jonathan Gibson all that Tract or parcel of

	Land which I possess on the East side of the Branch of Elk-run which passes through between the House of Thomas Shumate & the House I now live in .. after the death of my Wife
Son:	Bailey - £15 current money of Virginia extra of his proportion of my Estate due him for the services of his Negro Nell
Sons & Daus:	William, John, Joshua, Daniel, James, Lettice & Jemima - everything I gave them after marriage (being all I ever intend for them until the death of their Mother)
Wife:	(Judith) - shall have the use of my Estate during life, & shall be at liberty (with the advice & consent of the Executors) to sell for her necessary support anything belonging to that part of my Estate not heretofore Willed to other persons - after the death of my wife the remains of my Estate shall be equally divided between my Children To wit: William, John, Joshua, Daniel, Thomas, James, Bailey, Lettice & Jemima.
Exors:	Thos. Helm, John Nelson and my wife Judah Shumate
Signed:	John (his X mark) Shumate, Sen'r.
Wit..:	Thomas Helm, William Conway (X), John Kerr (X).
Proved:	25 October 1784 by o. of William Conway and John Kerr. Judith Shumate made o. and was granted certificate to obtain probate.

Page 49:

MR. JOHN SMITH (Inventory)
"Fauquier County, to wit. This is to certify that the above named Appraisers was sworn before me to Vallue the Estate of John Smith deceased. Given from under my Hand this 20th November 1784.
Francis Triplett"

App'd by: Andrew Barbey, Garner Burges, Thomas Payne
Total eval.: L478..16s.
Ret..: 22 November 1784

Page 50:

| | MARY BROWN (Will) "of Forquia County and Hambleton Parrish" Date: 7 October 1784 |
| Bros. & Sisters: | Elizabeth Priest, Marmaduke Brown, George Brown, Jonathan Brown, Wm. Brown, Martin Brown, Frances Maddix, Sibby Brown, Rebecca Brown - my negro |

woman Dinia and her Daughter betty Shall be
sold and the money with all the money that is
Due me by Bill Bond and accnt. be equally divided between these three last mentioned shall
have five pr cent, less then the others and when
this money shall be collected before it be divided there shall be Enough taken out to Wall in
the graveyard on my father's Plantation with stone
twelve feet Square, Four feet high.

Sister: Martha - the deed of gift made to us both by Sir
Marmaduke beckwith and the first Choice of my
three gold Rings and a Ivory fan

Sister: Elizabeth Priest - my side saddle and cover and
such wareing Clothes and trunk that is at Her
house and Six Puter plates I leave to Mason
Priest my Sister son

Sister-in-law: Sary Brown my Brothers wife - six yards of
Black Dureuth and Black Silk Bonnet to peggy
Brown their Daughter.

_____: Sibby Brown & Rebecca Brown - my other two gold
rings - Sibby to have the next Choice - Remainder of my Clothes and one pair of Silver
Studs to be equally divided between all my sisters.

Bro..: Jonathan Brown - one gilt'd trunk, the first
Choice of two and the other my Brother Wm. Brown

Exors: Marmaduke Brown and Wm. Brown
Signed: Mary (her X mark) Brown
Wit.: John Starke, Rodham Kenner, Peter Hodo
Proved: 22 November 1782, by o. of John Starke, Rodham
Kenner, and Peter Hodo. Marmaduke Brown & William
Brown granted cert. to obtain probate.

Page
51: FREDERICK KEMPER (Inventory)
No date. No appraisers listed*
Total eval.: L37.17.0
Ret..: 22 November 1784
*Minute Book 1784-86, page 8: June Court 1784:
On the motion of John Peter Kamper, who made oath
& executed & acknowledged bond as the law directs,
Cert. is granted him for obtaining letters of
Administration of the Estate of Frederick Kamper,
dec'd. Ordered that Alexander Bradford, William
Jennings, George Rosser & William Pickett, or any
three of them (being first sworn) do appraise the
estate of Frederick Kamper dec'd. & return the
appraisement to the Court.

Pages
52-53:   BENJAMIN ROBINSON (Will)
                    Date: 11 January 1785

Son: Nathaniel - a Negro Girl named Vilett also a
            Negro boy named Soloman

Son: George - a N egro boy named Adam and a Negro
            Girl Named Hagga

Dau: Catharine Campbell a Negro Girl named Sisby and
            a Negro Wench named Rachel for to work for her
            the term of 5 years and then to be Returned and
            disposed of and her increase as hereafter may be
            mentioned and the said Catharine to have a small
            one of the age of ten years or forty pounds Cash

Dau.:   Elesha Robinson - Negro boy named Sam and a Negro
            boy named George

Son: Dixon - a Negro boy named Moses & a negro boy
            named James

Son: Stephen - a Negro Girl named Hannah and a Negro
            boy named Robin

Dau.:   Mary Robinson - a Negro Girl named Mymak and a
            boy named Joseph, the boy not to be delivered
            before her Mother's death

Dau.:   Lydda Robinson - a Negro Girl named Molly and a
            Negro boy named John and five pounds cash

Son: Elijah - a Negro boy named Dick and a Negro Girl
            Named Rachel also a horse ten pounds price with
            a New briddle and Saddle

Son: James - a Negro boy named Charles and a Negro
            Wench N amed luce after the death of his mother

Dau.:   Ann Masters - the sum of L500 tobo.. for her
            maintenance yearly for 12 years and that to be
            disposed of for her at the disposal of my Exors.

Son: John - a Negro Wench Named Bet and all her Increase
            also D10 cash and no more

Wife: (not named) - a Negro Wench named Pag, Moll, Jimma,
            Simon, Henry, David - also my Stafford land and
            the lease I n ow live upon with all my stock of
            Every kind, During her Natural life or Widowhood
            and at her Death or Marriage to be sold with the
            above Mentioned Negro Rachel and the money to be
            equally divided Amongst my living Children also
            all my Publick due to be paid out of the profits
            of my wifes dowry.

Exors: Son Nathaniel Robinson, Geo. Robinson, Dixon Robinson
Signed: Benj.. Robinson (also: Ely Robinson, Dixon Robinson?)
Wit.:   William (x) White, William Nalle, Robert Gibson,

Carr White

Proved: 28 February 1785, by o. of William White and Carr White. Nathaniel Robinson, George Robinson & Dixon Robinson the Executors, granted Cert. for obtaining probate.

Page
53:
JOHN SMITH (Administrator's Account)
Date: 28 April 1784

Admr.: Mary Smith

Details: TO: Richard & Wade Hamton; 10 Febr. 1773: Nathaniel Weaden who mared (married) the Widow of sd. Smith dec'd., Rich'd Smith, Peter Hutcherson for schooling of John Smith, Garland Keer for teaching Do. Bookkeeping.
BY: 16 Dec. 1784: Mary Smith, now Mary Weaden, Nathaniel Weaden.

Exam. by: Wm. Heale, John Hathaway, Josiah Fishback, 16 Dec. 1784. Sworn before Wm. Heale

Ret.: 26 April 1785

Page
54:
ANN NUGENT (Will)
Date: 14 September 1780

Nephew: Luncefield Sharpe - 4 slaves - to him & the Heirs of his Body lawfully begotten & in fault of such Heirs I desire the aforesd. Slaves with their increase may be equally divided between my Bro. Edward Nugent & my Nephew William Ballard & my niece Mary Ballard.

Niece: Mary Ballard - 1000 lbs. of crop Tobacco & cash, & one Feather Bed being the one with broad stripes.

Nephew: William Ballard - 1000 lbs. of Crop Tobacco & cast.

Nephew & Brother: Lincefield Sharpe & Edward Nugent - my Stock of Cattle - divided into three equal parts two of which I give to my nephew .. & the third to my Brother to whom I also give a Bed with Russia Drile ticking & a Green rug & Blankett.

Nephew: Lincefield Sharpe - all the Residue of my Estate to be Executor

Signed: Ann (her X mark) Nugent

Wit.: Peter Grant, Thos. Nugent, Susanna Grant

Proved: 23 May 1785, by o. of Peter Grant & Susanna Grant. Lincefield Sharpe granted cert. to obtain probate.

Page
55:                JOHN SMITH   (Allotment of Dower)
                   Date: 6 January 1785
Div. by: B.. Shackelford, Garner Burges, Fran's Triplett
Details: "Pursuant to an order of the Worshipfull
          Court of Fauquier County, We the under signers
          met at the late Dwelling house of John Smith,
          Dec'd & Assigned to Mary Smith Widow of the
          said John Smith the following Negroes to wit:
          Ben 60 pounds, George 40 pounds, & Jude 20
          pounds as her Dower in the slaves whereof the
          said John Smith died possessed."
Ret.:   27 June 1785

Pages
55-56:   ANN NUGENT   (Inventory)
                   Date: 30 June 1785
App'd by: George Eastham, John Woodside, William Woodside.
Total eval.: L353.17.9
Ret.:   25 July 1785

Pages
57-59:   ROBERT KNOX "of the State of Maryland" (WILL)
                   Date: 21 September 1781
Son: John - all that tract of land called Summer Dusk
          in the State of Virginia containing about 5,000
          acres likewise all the Negroes Horses Cattle &
          every thing that may be on said Summer Dusk
          plantation at my decease excepting what I may
          will to some of my other Children - all my Estate
          I have in Scotland
Son: Robert Dade Knox - all my lands in the State of
          Maryland
Dau.:   Eliz'h. Knox - all that tract of Land called
          Beulah in the State of Virginia containing about
          500 acres - four Negroes - two horses, four cows
          & Calves to be taken from Summer Dusk plantation.
Dau.:   Jannet Knox - all that tract of land (to be taken
          out of Summer Dusk tract) that lyes on the uper
          side of a road commonly called feilds road - four
          Negroes - two horses & four Cows & Calves to be
          taken from Summer Dusk Plantation.
Wife: Rose Townsend - whatever is customary given to
          Widows in the part of the world where my Estate.
          lyes.
          ... I desire that the Copartnership of Knox &

Baillie maybe settled & if any money or
balance coming to my share, that it may go to
the payment of my just debts
... I desire that my Executors will get my
share of my Brother John's effects from my
Brother William as I have never received any
thing & there should be a considerable ballance in my favour

Exors: wife Rose Townsend, Col. Robert Hooe of Alex'r,
Andrew Baille, Alexander Baill Martin
Signed: Robert Knox
Wit.: G. R. Brown, Verlinda Martin, Andrew Baille,
Will Millar
Codicil: Robert Knox of Charles County of the State of
Maryland ... "Whereas my beloved wife Rose
Townsend Knox is now with Child, for which there
is no provision made in my said will .. 800
pounds sterling .. be let out on bond with good
security & be paid to the sd. Child when it
shall come to age or marry - I do further cons-
titute and appoint William Allison of Fauquier
County - to be one of my Executors to this my
Codicil .. 15 February 1782.
Proved (copy): 30 October 1782, by o. of Gustavus Richard
Brown, Verlinda Martin and Andrew Baille and.
Rose Townsend Knox widow of Robert Knox late of
Charles County
Proved: In Charles County, Md., 30 October 1782, before
John Muschett, Reg'r. of Wills .. Rose Townsend
Knox granted cert.
Wit.: Walter Hanson, Gentleman, Chief Justice of the
Orphans Court of the County aforesaid .. 29 August
1783.
Fauquier County .. 25 July 1785 - Copy of the Will
& Codicil presented by Rose Townsend Knox who
made oath & granted Cert. to obtain probate.

Pages
61-62: WILLIAM PEARL (Will)
Date: 24 May 1785
Gr.son: William Pearl, son of Samuel Pearl the tract of
land whereon I now live after his Grandmothers
Martha Pearl's Decease all to fifty Acres Adjoining William Cundiff alias William Ellitt
which I lend to my Daughter Elizabeth during
her life and after her decease to fall to

Elijah her son.

Dau.: Sarah Smare - lend to .. a young Negro girl
name Nan .. at her decease to be equally
divided among her Children .. said Negro named
Nan and her increase to be delivered if living
to Sarah Smare after the decease of my beloved
wife Martha Pearl.

Dau.: Margaret Fields, wife of John Fields - 100 acres
whereon the said John Fields now lives as per
survey made by John Moffett and after her decease to be sold and equally divided among her
children.

Dau.: Martha Evins - after decease of my Beloved wife
Martha Pearl one Negro girl named Sall .. after
the decease of the said Martha Evins to be equally divided among her children.

Dau.: Mary Murry - one Negro girl named Dorcas (same
terms as above)

Gr.children: William Weadon, John Weadon, Mary Weadon,
Elizab eth Weadon and Anne Weadon - L10 each ..
to be paid after the decease of my beloved wife.

Son: Beloved son Samuel Pearl - L50 .. after decease
of wife .. and in case the said son should die
before the death of his Mother .. to be paid to
his son William Pearl.

Son: William Pearl - 1,000 lbs. of crop tobacco .. to
be paid by the hands of the Executors immediately
after my decease

Son: Richard Pearl - L100 in annual sums of L10 per
year untill the aforesaid L100 is paid off ..
after the decease of my beloved wife.

Wife: Martha Pearl - all my Estate both real and personal for and during her widowhood. And after
her decease all the Estate except the legacies
or sums before mentioned, to be sold and equally
divided among my Children William Pearl, Margaret
Fields, Sarah Smare, Elizabeth Cundiff alias
Ellitt, Martha Evins and Mary Murrey.

Exec.: Wife, Martha Pearl, Samuel Pearl and Ralph Murray

Si gned: William (his X mark) Pearl

Wit.: Reuben Strother, Daniel Brown, Benjamin Carpenter,
Benj. Strother, Reuben Ellitt

Proved: 25 July 1785, by o. of Reuben Strother and Benjamin Strother. The three executors named in will,
were granted cert. to obtain probate.

Pages
64-66:   WILLIAM KIRK (Inventory)
                  Date: 3 January 1781
App'd by: Wharton Ransdell, Presley Morehead, Charles
           Morehead.
Tot al eval: L90,686.12.6
Details:: "and b y another order of said Court have
           allotted Elizabeth Kirk her third part of the
           Lands & slaves as also her Moiety of the Per-
           sonal Estate."
Books: 10 volls. of Rollins History, 1 large book the
           works of Josephus, 2 Vol. of Sales Koran, 1
           mag'h. books, 1 novell Aescanius, Dilworth's
           spelling book, Lumber of newspapers, and 1 silver
           watch, made by W. Claten, London, No. 5586.

Page
67:              JOHN NELSON (Inventory)
               Court Order dated October 1784
App'd by: Thos. Helm, Jonathan Gibson, John Shumate,
           Thos. Shumate.
Total Eval.: L365.16.8
Ret.:   22 August 1785

Page
68:              JOHN SHUMATE (Inventory)
               Court Order dated October 1784
App'd by: Jonathan Gibson, William Conway, John Kerr,
           Tho. Helm
Total Eval: L72.4.6
Ret.:   22 August 1785

Pages
68-69:   JOSEPH MORGAN (Inventory)
                No date
App'd by: Dan. Bradford, John Ashby, John Shumate
No total. Ret.: 22 August 1785

Page
70:              DANIEL SHUMATE (Inventory)
               Court Order dated October 1784
App'd by: Thos. Helm, William Conway, John Kerr
Total Eval: L173.12.9
Ret.:   22 August 1785

- 165 -

Pages
70-71:   ROBERT KNOX (Inventory)
                Date: 17 August 1785
App'd by: Lott Hackley, Alex. McConkey, James Allen
Total Eval.: L882.10.4
Ret.:   23 August 1785

Page
72:             JOHN SHIPP (Estate Account)
                Date: 6 October 1784
Adm'r.: Richard W. Shipp
Details: Payments made to: Col. Levin Powell, Stephen
         McPherson, Jr., Edward Turner, Martin Johnson,
         Israel Janney, William Broadhusks Acₜt., Nancy
         Shipps Legacy by Consent, Cash due Richard
         Drummonds Estate, To bond and acct. of Josiah
         Settle, By ballance due from the Legatees Susanna
         Taylor excluded.
Exam'd by: Hez. Turner, Wm. Heale, John Hathaway
Ret.:   23 August 1785

Pages
73-74:   WILLIAM PEARL (Inventory)
                Dated: 26 September 1785. Court order
                dated September 1785.
App'd by: John Hathaway, Wm. Smith, Daniel Florence
No total. Retn: 26 September 1785

Page
74:             BENJAMIN ROBINSON (Inventory)
                Date: 22 October 1785
App'd by: Samuel Steele, Pharnack George, William White
No total. Ret.: 24 October 1785

Page
75:             BRYANT THORNHILL (Will)
                Date: 13 October 1785
Son: Charles Thornhill - all that came to me by his
          Mother likewise one young boy
Dau.:   Elizabeth Thornhill - one Negro girl - one feather
          bed & furniture - one beast and saddle when she
          arrives to the age of 18 years
Dau.:   Perthenia Thornhill - (same as above)
Sons: James, William and Elijah - residue of my Estate
          when the youngest son comes to the age of 21 years.
Wife: Leannah Thornhill - mother of the children

Exors:	William Hunton and Robert Sanders
Signed:	Bryant Thornhill
Wit.:	James Lawler, James Hunton
Proved:	21 October 1785, by o. of James Lawler and James Hunton. Probate and cert. obtained by exors. named.

Page
76:                    BENJAMIN NEALE   (Will)
                       Date: 23 March 1779
Sons: Jesse and Moses - all my wareing cloaths
Wife: Anstis - all the rest of my Estate, my Lease and
         plantations
Exor: Wife Anstis
Signed: Benjamin Neale
Wit.:   Christopher (his X mark) Hich, Rebechah (her X mark)
         Hich, Clement Norman
Proved: 26 September 1785, by o. of Clement Norman and
         Christopher Hitch. Anstis Neale appointed Exortx.

Page
77:                    JOSEPH SMITH   (Estate Account)
Adm'r.: Rowley Smith
Details: Payments made to: Doct'r. Dugard, Charles Adams,
         Jos. Nelson for Dugard Estate, Mr. Barker for
         Clerk's fee, Colo. Martin Pickett, George Cordell.
         Rec'd. of: Thomas Keith on acc't of Edward Riley,
         Peter Kamper, jun'r., Henry Fewel by Doctor Dugard,
         Joseph Williams, Mrs. Mary Triplett, Jesse Smith,
         Byran Gaines, Edward Ball, Smith on Acc't of Thomas
         Shaw, William Hanks, Anderson Cockrell, James
         Blyth, John Redmond, John Smith on Acc't. of
         Thomas Shaw, James McCave, Randolph Spicer,
         William Hitson, John Lathey, Peter Hord, Joseph
         Hudnall, William Smith, jun'r., Jos. Williams.
Ret.:   24 October 1785

Page
78:                    ALEXANDER PARKER   (Will)
                       Date: 9 May 1785
Wife: Amy Parker - land and plantation I now live on
         during her widowhood - Negroes - plantation horses -
         after her marriage or decease I give said land to
Sons: my two sons: Richard and William Parker
Children: Richard, William, Elizabeth Scott & Lucy Parker -
         reside of Negroes not lent to my wife. If my wife

should prove with child and if should be a
son I desire that it may be named Alexander.
If it should be a Daughter I desire that it
should be named Judy. - one equal part of
Negroes.

Exors: Wife, my Brother Richard Parker and George
          Grant
Signed: Alex (his X mark) Parker
Wit.:   Catesby Woodford, Rawly Hogain, Benjamin Neale
Proved: 28 November 1785, by o. of three witnesses.
          Richard Parker granted cert. to obtain probate.

Page
79:                 BENJAMIN NEALE   (Inventory)
                    Date: 12 October 1785
App'd by: Richard Harris, Thos. Foley, Edward Lawrence
Total eval.: L60.7.0
Ret.:   28 November 1785

Page
80:                 JOHN SMITH   (Division of Estate)
                    Date: 29 October 1785.
Div. by: Wm. Pickett, Wm. Barkley, John Fishback
Details: Divided between his sons, Richard and John Smith
Ret.:   27 February 1786

Page
81:                 ALEXANDER PARKER   (Inventory)
                    Date: Court order dated 1 November 1785
App'd by: Ambrose Barnett, Original Young and Tilman
          Weaver, being first sworn before Jeremiah Darnell,
          Gentm.
Total Eval.: L946.16.9
Ret.:   27 February 1786

Pages
82-83:   EDWARD LAURANCE, SR.   (Will)
                    of the parish of Hambleton (sic)
                    Date: 26 March 1783
Son.   John - Negroes now in his possession
Son: Peter - Negroes
Son: Edward, Jr. - Negroes
Dau.:   Sarah Priest - Negroes
Dau.:   Susanah Catlett - 5 shillings cash and no more
Dau.:   Winnefred Luttrell - Negroes
Dau.:   Jean Wicks - Negroes

Gr.Son:	Rhodam Tulloss Laurance - one feather bed and furniture - horse - Negroes
Son:	Richard - land and plantation whereon I now live .. 317 acres .. Negroes - all other estate not bequeathed
Exor:	Son Richard Laurance
Signed:	Edward (his X mark) Laurance
Wit.:	Original Young, Thomas Conway, Richard (X) Priest, William Crosby
Proved:	27 March 1786, by o. of Original Young, Thomas Conway and William Crosby. Richard Laurance granted cert. to obtain probate.

Page 84:

CHARLES MARTIN (Will)
Date: 12 January 1785

Dau.:	Catherine Baylie - feather bed & furniture, one Iron Pott & one Iron Rack, largest looking glass.
Dau.:	Susanna Allen - feather bed & furniture
	Above two daus. - my land, all my moveable Estate
Gr.Son:	Charles Allen - my gun
Dau.:	Elizabeth Edwards - 1 shilling sterling
Dau.:	_____ McCarty - 1 shilling sterling
Dau.:	Mary Pore - 1 shilling sterling
Dau.:	Frances Wall - 1 shilling sterling
Exors:	two daughters - Catherine Baylie and Susanna Allen
Signed:	Charles (his X mark) Martin
Wit.:	George Carter, William Bailey, Joseph Bailey, Samuel Hazzelrig, Marget Mason
Proved:	27 March 1786, by o. of George Carter, William Bailey and Joseph Bailey. Catherine Bailey and Susanna Allen granted cert. to obtain probate.

Page 85:

JOHN WHITING "of the County of Prince William" (Will)
Date: 20 October 1775

Sister:	Ann Brooke - after my just debts are paid I give all the rest of my Estate - to be equally divided between my nephews and nieces, Children of my Sister.
Exor.:	my Brother Francis Whiting
Signed:	John Whiting
Wit.:	Elizabeth Kemp, Betty Dodron, H. Brooke
Proved:	27 March 1786, by o. of Humphrey Brooke. Francis Whiting granted cert. to obtain probate.

Pages
86-87:   REV. JOHN SCOTT (Inventory)
                    Date: 22 June 1786
App'd by: Edward Digges, John Sinclair, W. Fitzhugh
Total eval.: L321.10.6
Details: Books: 7 vols. Sharps Sermons, Concordance to
         the Holy Scriptures, 2 vols.. Johnsons Dictionary,
         2 vols. Juds Sermons.
Ret.:   26 June 1786

Pages
87-88:   JOSEPH HOLTZCLAW (Inventory)
                    No date.
App'd by: Reuben Martin, Jacob Kamper (his X mark),
          John Kamper
Total Eval.: L372.12.2
Ret.:   26 June 1786

Pages
89-90:   STEPHEN McCORMICK of Hamilton Parish (Will)
                    Date: 3 February 1786
Wife: Margaret Macormick - all my Estate during her
         natural life and after her decease to be divided
         between Our two children John Macormick and
         Elizabeth Mtjoy Martin
Dau.:   Anne Shumate - one Cow and Calf
Exor: Wife Margaret, son John and my friend Gavin
         Lawson
Signed: Stephen (his X mark) Macormick
Wit: Paul Williams, James Haydon, William Jones
Proved: 26 June 1786, by o. of Paul Williams, James
         Hayden and William Jones. John McCormack
         granted cert. to obtain probate.

Pages
90-91:   ALEXANDER MONROE (Inventory)
                    Date: 22 April 1786
App'd by: Peter Hitt, George Green, James Penney
No total. Ret.: 26 June 1786

Pages
91-92:   EDWARD LAURANCE. (Inventory)
                    Date: 24 June 1786
App'd by: John Mauzy, Thos. Conway, Charles Waller
Total Eval.: L1072.16.3
Ret.:   26 June 1786

Page
92:             JOHN WHITING (Inventory)
                 Date: 10 April 1786
App'd by: John Wiatt, Alex. Brown, Robt. Brown
Total Eval.: L305.0.0
Ret.:   26 June 1786

Pages
93-94:   WHARTON RANSDELL of the County of Fauquier
            and Parish of Leeds (Will)
            Date: 27 January 1786
Children: William Ransdell, Anne Morehead, Margaret Ransdell
       and Sarah Ransdell - equally share in ½ of the
       proceeds from the sale of a Tract purchased of
       Archibald Allen and Two Tracts more I purchased
       of John Debutts, 1,000 acres.
Son: Thomas - to receive the other half of the pro-
       ceeds arising from sale of above lands - reser-
       ving L20 currant money for the education of my
       Grandson Charles Morehead Ransdell and Wharton
       Ransdell.
Son-in-law: Cadwallader Slaughter - Negroes
Son: Edward - Negro
Son: John - Negroes
Son: William - Negroes, smith tools, one feather bed
       and furniture
Dau.:   Anne Morehead - Negroes
Dau.:   Margaret Ransdell - Negroes
Son: Thomas - Negroes, wearing appareel, bigg still,
       silver watch, one best Bed and furniture.
Dau.:   Sarah Ransdell - Negroes, one best bed & furniture
Son: Wharton - Negro, a cow and calf, bed & furniture,
       set of Joiners tools and a table
Gr.sons: Charles Morehead Ransdell and Wharton Ransdell -
       a Tract of land in Jefferson County that I pur-
       chased of Cadwallader Slaughter - 500 acres.
       "... if either my sons William Ransdell or Thomas
       Ransdell or my Dau. Sarah Ransdell should Die
       without lawful issue their Estate be equally
       divided between the surviving Heirs of William,
       Thomas, Anne Morehead and Margaret Ransdell."
Exors: Charles Chilton, Elias Edmonds, Thomas Ransdell,
       Sr., William Ransdell, Jr., and Thomas Ransdell, Jr.
Signed: Wharton Ransdell
Wit.:   Nathaniel Gray, John Green, Jr., Dan'l. Gray,
       Wharton Ransdell, Enoch K. Withers.

Proved: 26 June 1786, by o. of Daniel Gray, Wharton
Ransdell, and Enoch K. Withers. Three exors.
named granted certificate to obtain probate.

Page
95:               AMY PARKER (Renunciation of Will)

           "Know all men by these presents, that I Amy
Parker, widow and relict of Alexander Parker
of the County of Fauquier, dec'd., do by
these presents renounce all the benefit & advantage that I might claim under the will of
the said Alexander Parker as witness my hand
and seal this 17th day of January 1786."
Signed: Amy (her X mark) Parker
Wit: Catesby Woodford, Original Young, Jeremiah
Darnall, Tilman Weaver.
Ret.:   24 July 1786, proved by o. of Catesby Woodford,
and Jeremiah Darnall.

Pages
95-96:   WILLIAM BRADFORD (Estate Account)
            No date
Admrx: Mary Nash, executrix
Details: Payments made to: Jacob Minter; W. Buchan-
non; John Rector; Samuel Earl; Bacon Obanion;
George Green; W. Marley, saddler; Wm. Robin-
son; Thomas Grubbs; quit-rents; Richard Gra-
ham; William Hambleton, schooling 2 children,
2 years each at 20 shillings; Ephriam Hubbard;
W. Churchill, by a Negro woman Nan delivered
William Fowler who married Anne Bradford.
Ret.:   24 July 1786 and examined by Charles Chilton,
Alfred Buckner and Hezk. Turner.

Pages
96-97:   CAPT. WILLIAM BLACKWELL (Inventory)
            No date
App'd by: Jeremiah Darnall, Jon' Gibson, Original Young
Total evall.: L1173.18.0. (Virginia Laws, one vol.
                fol. - 10s.)
Ret.:   25 September 1786

Pages
98-99:   MRS. CELIA FOOTE (Dower Allotment)
            Date: 1 February 1779

Divided by: William Grant, Jeremiah Darnall, Original
           Young.
Note ed.: <u>Minute Book, 1775-83</u>, 24 August 1778: "Ord.
           William Grant, Jeremiah Darnall & Original
           Young do allot to Celia, the widow of George
           Foote & now the wife of Wm. Blackwell her
           dower in the said George Foote's Est. &
           also settle her acct. of the Admor. of the
           sd. Foote's Est."
Details: Allotment of slaves, livestock, household
           utensils, amounting to L2457.15. "We then
           proceeded to allot her Dower of the Land
           in presence of Capt. John Mofett, Surveyor
           of the County which amounted to 476½ acres.
           (Plat included) Notes from plat and descrip-
           tion: Dowells Run, Mr. Wm. Coppage, Mr. John
           Wood, Town Run, Mr. Rich'd. Foote, Mr. Bullett,
           Cedar Run, Mr. Richard Foote, dec'd., Col.
           Harrison's Old Mill Dam. "The above is a plot
           of 1430 Acres of Land belonging to the Estate
           of Mr. George Foote Deceased & Divided as
           above agreeable to the will of Mr. Rich'd.
           Foote, Sn. Deceased & an Order From the
           Worshipfull Court of Fauquier County Between
           Capt. William Blackwell, Miss Betty Foote &
           the Orphans of the said George." John Wood
           and Bailey Wood, chain-carriers, J. Moffett,
           S.F.C. Anthony Jett and Andrew Flowers.
Ret.: 25 September 1786.

Pages
99-102:   JOHN SCOTT "of the Parish of Dettingen
           and County of Prince William Clerk" (Will)
           Date: 9 February 1783
Children: All my Estate real and personal that I have
           either in possession or reversion in America
           or Great Britain equally to be divided bet-
           ween them share and share alike
Wife: Elizabeth - during her widowhood one half of
           all my Estate above mentioned on Condition she
           accept the same in lieu of all marriage settle-
           ments and dower .. (with the hope she should
           not remarry) .. share of each child to be paid
           at the age of 21 or in case of dau. at marri-
           age if made with Consent of their Guardian.
Aunt: Elizabeth Innes of the Kingdom of Great
           Britain - any estate to be repaid to my Exe-

cutrix or Executors to the use of this my
will

Son: Robert - all my Estate real and personal be
sold .. at such time when my eldest son
Robert shall attain his full age of 21.

Wife: Elizabeth - a Mulatto woman named Aminta -
that she may never sell or hire her out
during her life time and that if the said
slave should survive her she may be left
free, her children shall be free also -
direct that L5 sterling be paid out of my
Estate to the said Mulatto.
... to be sole guardian of children as long
as she remains single, in case of death or
marriage, appoint my much esteemed and sin-
cere friends Thomas Blackburn and William
Alexander, Esq'r. Guardians.

Exor.: Wife - during her life and widowhood, otherwise, son Robert and above friends.

Wit: Cuthbert Bullitt, Alexander Scott, Thomas
Fitzhugh - signed 29 April 1784.

Signed: John Scott Clerk

Codicil: Date: 29 April 1784. Land recently purchased
from Alexander Scott Bullitt, Esqr. and
Negroes sold - to be a part of estate and
treated as above .. "that any provision made
by my Aunt Elizabeth Innes should not be
equal to what my other children will enjoy and
have under my said will and Codicil that in
that case the child or children so provided
for shall have such Provision made equal to
their other Brothers and Sisters out of my
Estate." "... desire that my Children with all
Convenient speed be carried to and Educated in
Scotland untill they arrive to the age of 21
years." After paying all just debts from
sale of real estate, the remainder to be
rented "untill my youngest son John arrives
to the age of twenty-one." "... in case of
my wife's marriage I add to my other Executors
my Friend William Fitzhugh, Esqr. of Fauquier
and my kinsman the Rev. Mr. Robert Patterson
of Scotland, the latter only to be considered
as Executor within the Kingdom of Great Britain ..."

Proved: 27 April 1785 by o. of Cuthbert Bullitt.
Elizabeth Scott made oath and granted certi-

ficate to obtain probate. Proved also on
25 September 1786 by o. of Thomas Fitzhugh,
another witness.

**Pages
104-105:**   JOHN HATHAWAY (Will)
                       Date: 13 April 1786

Dau.: Elizabeth - in lieu of a bond of mine given
to my Brother James Hathaway which he
assigned to her - one Negro Girl.

Wife: Sarah - the tract of land whereon I now live
all Negroes, horses, cattle & household
furniture during her natural life.

**Sons &
Daus.:** It is my Will and desire that if my wife
Sarah Hathaway should die before my Sons
Henry Lawson Hathaway & Francis Hathaway
& Dau. Sarepta receives their Education that
they shall be educated: Lawson 3 years more
than he has received; Francis five and
Sarepta two - at the expense of my Estate.

Children: After decease of wife, real and personal
property sold and equally divided between
all my Children Viz. Juday Kamper, Sarah
Bartlett, Elizabeth, John, Nancy, Susannah,
Molly, Dolly, Peggy Lawson, Sarepta &
Francis. Juday Kamper and Sarah Bartlett to
have L12 less than the others.

Son: John - the land which Simon Kenton was to
locate for me which is 1100 acres lying near
Big Sandy River.

Sons: Lawson and Francis - the Tract of Land I
bought of Powers and Davison lying on Tyger
River in Harrison County - 561 acres - if
my son John should not get the Land above
mentioned that then he shall have an equal
part of the tract of Land I willed to my
sons Lawson & Francis.

Exors Wife Sarah, Executrix & son John Hathaway
Signed: John Hathaway
Wit: Josiah Fishback, Philip Fishback, William
Metcalf
Proved: 25 September 1786 by o. of above witnesses.
Sarah Hathaway and John Hathaway granted
certificate to obtain probate.

- 175 -

Page
106:                STEPHEN McCORMACK (Inventory)
                   No date
App'd by: Chas.Duncan, James Dobie, Daniel Marr,
          Cossom Day
Total eval.: L922.6.0
Ret.:   23 October 1786

Pages
107-108:   CAPT. JOHN HATHAWAY (Inventory)
                   No date.
App'd by: Josiah Fishback, John Fishback, Thomas
          Glascock, William Metcalf.
Total eval.: L428.19.6
Ret.:   23 October 1786

Page
109:                WHARTON RANSDELL, JR. (Inventory)
                   No date.
App'd by: Wm. Norris, Geo. Carter, Turner Morehead
Total eval.: L240.7.0 (1 violin - 10s.)
Ret.:   23 October 1786

Page
110:                MARY BROWN (Inventory)
                   No date.
App'd by: Geo. Crump, Wm. Conway, Thos. Conway, Thomas
          Brooks.
Total eval.: L97.16.9
Ret.:   23 October 1786

Page
110:                CHARLES MARTIN (Inventory)
                   Date: 14 April 1786
App'd by: Turner Morehead, George Carter, John Tomlin,
          Jr.
Total eval.: L14.8.3
Ret.:   23 October 1786

Page
111:                DAVID DARNELL "of Parish of Leeds" (Will)
                   Date: 22 March 1785
Son: John - Lot of land lying on Lord Fairfaxes
          Mannor of Leads (sic)
Gr.dau.: Molly Leer - one cow and calf
Gr.son: John Shaver - be educated with one years
          schooling by my Executors.

Wife:	Mary - all my estate for her natural life - at her death my son John should have all and singular of my estate.
Exors:	Wife Mary and son John
Signed:	David (his D mark) Darnall
Wit.:	William Pickett, Edward (h. X m.) Riley, Eave (her X mark) Riley.
Proved:	23 October 1786 by o. of three witnesses. John Darnall granted cert. to obtain probate.

Pages
112-114: GEORGE WILLIAMS, SEN'R. (Will)
Date: 13 November 1786

Wife:	Ann Williams - lend ½ of the land and plantation whereon I now live
Son:	Elijah - the other half of the land if he chooses not to continue on the land to go to son George Williams, as long as his wife possesses her half. ... after the expiration of the Term mentioned to be sold at Publick Sale to the Highest Bidder on 12 month credit - the Money arising from the sale to be divided into four Equal Parts and divided as follows: ¼ to each of the following: Son William Williams, son George Williams, son Elijah Williams, and one fourth to be divided equally between sons of son John Williams: Richardson and George Williams.
Son:	William - 100 acres of Leased Land (being a Lease formerly given by Peter Hedgman, Gent., to Thomas Davis)
Son:	John - all that part he hath already received and 25 s. to be paid out of my estate.
Dau.:	Elizabeth Butler - all that part she hath already received and 25s.
Dau.:	Ann Butler - all that part she hath already received and 25s. All the rest of my Estate be it Real or Personal I leave to be sold Immediately after my Decease at Publich Sale and divided as follows:
Gr.son:	Benjamin Butler, Jun'r. - if living, L7
Gr.son:	George Butler (son of John) - L7
Son:	William - L30 to be used for the support and maintenance of my Dau. Catherine Williams during her life.
Wife:	1/6 part of the residue of money arising

	from above sale
Son:	William - 1/6 part
Son:	George - 1/6 part
Son:	Elijah - 1/6 part
Dau:	Margaret Freeman - 1/6 part
Gr.Children:	James, George & Ann Collins (heirs of dec'd. dau. Mary Collins) - 1/6 part to be equally divided.
Exors:	William Williams & George Williams
Signed:	George (his X mark) Williams
Wit:	James Routt, Augustine Jennings, Joseph Selman
Proved:	25 December 1786 by o. of above witnesses. Cert. granted William Williams and George Williams to obtain probate.

Pages
115-116:   GEORGE WILLIAMS   (Inventory)
                          No date.
App'd by: Hancock Lee, Augustine Jennings, James Routt.
Total eval.: L487.10.6
Ret.:   26 February 1787

Pages
116-117:   JOSEPH BLACKWELL, SENIOR   (Will)
                    Date: 26 April 1787

Wife:	(not named) - the use of my whole estate both real and personal except the land I purchased of Thomas Barby which I give and bequeath unto John Lee Beale, his father having paid me for the said land.
Son:	Joseph - after decease of wife, land purchased of Charles Gaines.
Son:	Samuel - all the land I hold on the North East side of Jeffries Branch - also 30 a. of land including the Mill to be laid off adjoining to the land he purchased of William Butler.
Son:	John - all the land I now live on, and the land I purchased of Thomas Watts, of Edward Carter and Jeremiah Darnall lying on Carters Run - after the decease of my beloved wife.
Sons:	Joseph, John & George Steptoe - all the remainder of the Negroes, as well those in their possession.
Dau.:	Judith Keith - Negro
Son:	Joseph - two ninths of what I have in trade

with my Son-in-law Martin Pickett the rest
of the said money, goods & Debts, etc. in
the said trade I give to be equally divided
between my two sons John & George Steptoe and
my Daughters Anne, Betty, Lucy, Judah and one
equal share to the Representatives of my Deceased Daughter Lettace Chilton.

Son: Joseph - 8 large silver spoons
Son: John - desk & bookcase
Son: George Steptoe - my desk
Sons: Joseph, John & George Steptoe - all the rest
of my household goods - stocks of horses,
cattle, sheep and hogs, after death of wife.
Estate not to be appraised.
Exors: Wife and four sons.
Signed: Jos. Blackwell
Wit.:   Peter Grant, Peter Conway, Jas. Thompson
Proved: 25 June 1787 by o. of Peter Grant, James
Thompson, witnesses. Joseph Blackwell and
John Blackwell granted cert. to obtain probate.

Page
118:         CAPT. WHARTON RANSDELL (Inventory)
Date: 14 September 1786
App'd by: Ambrose Barnett, James Hathaway, Geo. Carter
Total eval.: L891.8.11
Ret.:   25 June 1787

Page
119:         ISHAM KEITH (Will)
Date: 13 March 1787
Wife: Charlotte - one third of estate during her natural life and a grey Horse for Ever.
Son: John - all my lands in Fauquier County & the
land that was allowed me for my Service as an
oficer in the Continental Army, when he Comes
to the age of 21 years.
Dau: Betty Keith - Negro boy James when she marries
or becomes 21 years of age
Dau: Mary Isham Keith - Negro boy - when she marries or becomes 21 years of age.
Dau: Charlotte Ashmore Keith - Negro boy - when
she marries or becomes 21 years of age.
Dau: Caty Gallahue Keith - Negro girl when she
marries or becomes 21 years of age.
Children: John, Betty, Mary Isham, Charlotte Ashmore,
and Caty Gallahue Keith - have an equal portion of all Negroes that I have not willed
when they become 21 years of age.

- 179 -

Exors:	Wife Charlotte, Brother Thomas Keith and Charles Marshall
Signed:	Isham Keith
Witnesses:	William Hunton, Jr., William (his X mark) White, George (his X mark) Roach
Proved:	24 September 1787 by o. of William Hunton, Jr., William White and George Roach. Cert. granted to Charlotte Keith and Charles Marshall to obtain probate.

Page
120:
WM. WAITE (Inventory)
Date: 30 June 1787
App'd by: Samuel Blackwell, Jonathan Gibson, James Markham.
Total eval: L210.5.9
Ret.: 24 September 1787

Page
122:
JOHN HEALY (Will)
Date: 2 April 1787
Son: William Healey - after paying L14.4 current money of Virginia - have Negro boy.
Dau.: Febea Healy - one feather bed & furniture
Son: Anthony Healy - L35 lawful money of Virginia
Wife: Mary Healy - all the remainder of my goods, lands, Negroes, etc. as long as she remains a widow but if she should marry then my will and desire is that she have but what the law allows her. ... after the death of my wife .. that my said Estate that is in her care be equally divided among all my children except Anthony.
Exors: friends John Dareing and John Morehead
Signed: John Healy
Wit: James Genn, James Ball, Celia (her X mark) Green
Proved: 22 October 1787 by o. of James Genn and James Ball. Cert. granted John Dearing to obt. probate.

Page
123:
CHAMP CORUM (or Corham) (Inventory)
Court Order dated: July, 1787
App'd by: William Roussau, Thom Bailey, John Cummings
Total eval: L112.15.6
Ret: 28 January 1788

Page
124:
FRANCIS WATTS (Inventory)
Date: 19 October 1787

- 180 -

App'd by: (from: <u>Minute</u> <u>Book</u> <u>1786-88</u>, p. 348, September Court 1787): Ordered that Daniel Shu-
mate, Moses Johnson, John Owens and Andrew
O'Bannion or any three of them being first
sworn do appraise the Estate of Francis Watts,
deceased ...

Pages
125-126:   CHARLES CHINN (Will)
                      Date: 13 May 1787
Son: Charles - my silver watch, one feather bed &
            furniture, one cow, six new pewter plates, one
            pewter dish, one case knives & Forks and L50
            current money
Sons & daus: Rawleigh, John, William Ball, Joseph, Mar-
            garet, Betty, Suckey, Nancy - each one fea-
            ther bed and furniture, one Cow, six new pew-
            ter plates, one pewter dish, one case knives
            & forks & L50 ... and to the after said William,
            Joseph, Margaret, Betty, Suckey and Nancy
            each one horse of the value of L10.
Son: Elijah - 500 acres of land lying in the County
            of Nelson and district of Kentucky, adjoining
            lands of Samuel & William Pearles & Cuthbert
            Harrison & Joseph Hutchison.
Sons: Charles, Rawleigh, John, William Ball & Joseph -
            all the residue of my lands in the District of
            Kentucky to be equally divided - son Charles
            have first choice
Wife: Seth Chinn - during her natural life the use
            of one third of all my Estate or in lieu of one
            third of my Loudoun & Fauquier Lands I give
            her the use of the following Negroes ... also
            one Horse saddle & Bridle, two Cows, one fea=
            ther bed & furniture, 6 pewter plates, two
            pewter dishes, 2 pewter Basons, one case of
            Knives & Forks, one frying pan, 2 Iron pots,
            half a nest of wooden ware as she may chuse.
            I direct that all my lands in the Counties
            of Loudoun and Fauquier be sold for Cash
            Tobacco or Slaves - be divided into twelve
            equal parts, and that my Children ... receive
            each one of those parts & that the Executors
            lay out the other part in the purchase of
            Slave or slaves, which I direct my son Elijah
            Chinn to hire outand that he lay out the
            money for the support of my daughter Mary
            Reno & her children until the death of Lila
            Reno her husband, when the same are to be

given up to her if living, or if otherwise to
be equally divided among her children. At
death of wife, allestate left her I give & be-
queath to be equally divided among my children
excepted out of this clause so much as shall
Son: hereafter be bequeathed to my son Christopher
Chinn.
Son: Christopher - Negroes and 25 shillings
Exors: sons Charles, Rawleigh & John Chinn and my
friend Rawleigh Chinn,Sen'r.
Wit: Ralph Murray, John French x, Daniel French x
Signed: Charles Chinn
Proved: 25 February 1788 by o. of Ralph Murray, Daniel
French. Charles, Rawleigh and John Chinn
granted cert. to obtain probate.

Page
127:              GAYTON SETTLE (Will)
                Date: 9 July 1787
Wife: Mary - during her life three beds with furniture & all other my household furniture whatsoever - my stock of horses, namely 2 mares,
2 Colts being Horse Colts one black horse &c -
One cow and my stock of hogs, &c.
Son: William - after the death of my beloved wife -
have the whole of my Estate
Exors: Son William Settle & Mary Settle my beloved
wife.
Signed: Gayton (his X mark) Settle
Wit: John (his X mark) Askins, Edward Settle
Proved: 25 February 1788 by o. of John Askins and Edward Settle. William Settle granted cert. to
obtain probate.

Page
128:              ISHAM KEITH (Inventory)
                No date.
App'd by: John O'Bannon, William Hunton, Wm. Hampton
No total. Returned: 28 April 1788.

Page
130:              GEORGE CRISWELL (Inventory)
                Date: 27 February 1788
App'd by: Lewis Ferguson, Jas. Withers, Dickerson Wood.
Total eval: L25.16.6
Ret: 28 April 1788 (also spelled: George Chriswell)

Page
131:                    WILLIAM RANSDELL   (Inventory)
                         Date: 10 March 1788
App'd by: Ambrose Barnett, David McNish, Thos. Saunders,
           being first sworn before Charles Chilton
Total eval.: L168.18.0
Ret: 29 April 1788

Page
132:                    GAYTON SETTLE   (Inventory)
                         No date.
App'd by: Edward Settle, Geo. (his X mark) Tracey,
           John Askins. No total.
Ret.:   29 April 1788

Page
133:                    THOMAS MACKIE   (Will)
                         Date: 19 May 1786
           I desire that Mrs. Elizabeth Scott widow of my
           Late Worthy Friend James Scott, Esq. may be
           Paid the annuity left me by my Friend The
           Reverend Mr. James Scott from the Death of
           his Widow Mrs. Sarah Scott Deceased untill
           my Death and also all the Rest of my Estate.
Extrix: Mrs. Elizabeth Scott
Signed: Thomas (his X mark) Mackie
Wit: Charles Chilton, William Stewart
Proved: 29 April 1788 by o. of witnesses. Elizabeth
           Scott granted cert. to obtain probate.

Pages
133-134:   WILLIAM HAMILTON   (Will)
                         Date: 17 August 1784
Bro.:   Henry Hamilton - all my land and Negroes during
           his life, after his decease the Negroes to be
           equally divided amongst his children, the land
           to his Eldest son, the Negro Girl, Jenny to
           William Barker and his wife, after their De-
           cease to return to my Brother Henry Hamilton.
Sister: Rebecca Thrift - L10
Nephew: Hamilton Thrift (son of Rebecca) - L10 and a
           silver watch
           William Waddle - one bay mare Colt three years
           old neither docked nor branded
           Thomas Skinker - one sorrell mare near 11
           years old
           Thomas Keith - one sorrell mare 5 years old
Brother: Henry - all the remainder of my stock of Cattle

except one horse.
John Ridley - one roan horse.
Exors: Thomas Keith and Isham Keith
Wit: John Ridley, William Waddell
Signed: William Hamilton
Proved: 23 June 1788, by o. of John Ridley and
           William Waddell

Page
134:                  JOHN WADDELL "of the parish of leads
                      in the County of Fauquire" (Will)
                      Date: 21 April 1788
Dau.:   Teny Murphy - 1 shilling
Son: John - one Negro Girl
           ... the remainder of my Estate to be equally
           divided between Matthew Waddell and all my
           Children after the death of my Loving wife
Wife: Elizabeth Waddell; William, James, George,
           Margaret, Elizabeth, Poley, John, Frances.
Exors: Wife Elizabeth, son William and my old friend
           Matthew Waddell.
Wit: Joseph Taylor, John Coppadge, James May
Signed: John (his X mark) Waddell
Proved: 23 June 1788 by oaths of Joseph Taylor, John
           Coppage, James May. Elizabeth Waddell the
           Executrix named granted cert. to obtain probate.

Page
135:                  JOHN PETER KEMPER (Inventory)
                      Date: 5 July 1788
App'd by: Alexander Bradford, Issachar Pawling, Edward
           Settle.
Total Eval.: L163.3.6
Details: "a Large dutch Bible and parcel of other books"
Ret.:   28 July 1788

Pages
136-137:   THOMAS BLAND (Will)
                      Date: 1 April 1788
Son: Thomas - all my Tract of Land lieing and
           being in Prince William County on the Waters
           of Powels Run .. except the Lot of Land where-
           on William Cornell now lives, containing 130
           acres.
Son: youngest son James Bland - all that lot of
           Land lieing on the Waters of Powels Run in
           Prince William County whereon William Cornell
           now lives, 130 acres - all My Right and Title

to the Land whereon I now live which said
land I leased of Benjamin Harrison and lies
in Fauquier County - the Colt that my Bay
riding Horse is now with foal with.

Daus.: Catherine and Mary Bland - two Negroes

Dau.: Mary - one feather bed and furniture

Son: Thomas - one Negro woman

Son: James - the rents of the two Plantations
whereon Humphrey Colvert and William Cornell
now lives for six years next ensuing the

= date of my decease - my Exors. shall apply
(rents) to the education of my son James and
to no other use.

Exors: wife Jane Bland, Thomas Bland and Benjamin
Harrison

Wit.: John (his X mark) Lansdoun, Phillip (his X
mark) Spiller, William Threlkeld.

Proved: 22 September 1788 by o. of Philip Spiller,
and John Lansdoun. Jean Bland and Thomas
Bland granted cert. to obtain probate.

Page
137: JOHN BALL (Division of Estate)
Date: 14 March 1788

Div. by: Alexander Lithgow, James Reid, Alexander Bruce.

Details: Div. of estate consisting of Negroes, to:
Widow and children: Widow, one-third; Miss
Molly Ball; Mrs. Judith Blackburn, Miss Letty
Ball; Mr. William Ball.

Ret.: 23 September 1788

Page
138: WILLIAM BARKER of the Parish of Leeds
(Will)
Date: 27 May 1788

Wife: Susannah - my whole Estate as long as she lives
a widow and after her death (or Marriage):

Son: Charles - one feather bed & furniture and a
horse, saddle & bridle

Dau.: Nanny Barker - one feather bed & furniture &
one maple oval table

Dau.: Mary Barker - one Feather Bed

Sons: William and James - all my land & Negro man -
all the remainder of my Estate - if either
should be deceased that portion to go to son
Charles Barker
... remainder of my loving Children who is
married they have got their parts already but
it is my desire that one shilling may be
given unto each of them.

```
Exors:      sons William and Richard
Wit:        Hugh Bradley, Matthew Waddell, Jeremiah Morgan
Signed:     William Barker
Proved:     27 October 1788 by o. of Hugh Bradley, Matthew
            Waddell, Wm. Barker granted cert. to obtain
            probate.
```

Page
139:

JOHN BLAND (Guardian Account)
Date: 7 August 1788
We the subscribers have met and examined the
account between Wm S. Pickett and John Bland
and we find that there is due from the sd.
Pickett as Guardian to the sd. Bland the sum
of L27.4s.11d.

```
Signed:     John Craine, Minor Winn, Wm. Hale, H. Neilson
Ret.:       22 September 1788
```

Page
139:

CHARLES DUNCAN, GUARDIAN TO THE ORPHANS
OF DAVID SHARPE, DEC'D. (Account)
Date: 20 March 1789
We the subscribers being appointed to settle
the Account of the Guardianship of Charles
Duncan .. with the Executors of George Williams,
Dec'd; .. we find that there is L20.11d. due
from the Estate of said George Williams, Dec'd.
to the said Orphans. (not named)

```
Signed:     John Blackwell, Augustine Jennings, James Routt
Ret.:       29 April 1789
```

Page
140:

JOHN HALEY (Inventory)
Date: 13 March 1789

```
App'd by:   Richard Rixey, Joseph Barbee, James Foley
Total eval: L273.16.0
Ret.:       28 April 1789
```

Pages
141-142:

REV. JOHN SCOTT (Adm'rx. Account)
Date: 23 May 1789

```
Adm'rx.:    Mrs. Eliza Scott
Examined by: John O'Bannon, Henry Peyton, John Sinclair
Details:    PAID TO: Funeral expenses paid General Wood,
            L4.11s.; Enoch Withers, Sheriff; Sarah O'Reer;
            John White; Col. Blackburn per George Smith's
            order; Richards & Co. printers per Coll.
            Blackburn; Clerks note H. Brooke; James Hed-
```

ley; Wm. Scott per Robert Scott; Ephriam
Hubbard acct. per Robert Scott; Mr. John
Craine; Mr. John Sinclairs acct.; Mr. Ludwell
Lee attorney for the estate; Mrs. Scott 1
steer purchased att the sale proved to be the
property of Thomas Keithly Brown; Thomas
Glascock Crier at the sale; 2 gallons West
India Rum used at the sale; Peter Grant's
acc't.; Cuthbert Bullett in discharge of
mortgage; for rent of 1 Tract land at Bren-
town for 5 years; Mrs. Anne Grigsby 4 busels
rye for Mr. Sinclair; James Muschett Mercht.;
John Edmonds pd. Richard Grahame; Richard
Grahame paid W. G. Scott; Bruice & Murrays
acct. for Ronand pd. Jas. Muschett; Mr. Chas.
Lee protested Bill of Exchange on Eden & Co.;
Mr. William Hartes home acct.; To Bond George
Wilson; paid George Smith tax on the Fairfax
Land; paid Mr. Bullett Taxes; Levies on Ditto;
Richard Grahames acct. per Mr. Sinclair;
Sheriffs fees for Gilchrist.
ACCOUNTS REC'D BY: sale of the personal
estate; 1113 acres of land in Fairfx sold to
Mr. Gustavus Scott; judgement against Eden &
Co.; sale of Gilchrist's effects.

Ret.:   22 June 1789

The will of John Ashby "of the county of
Fauquier" was recorded "At a District Court
held at the Town (of) Dumfries the 13th day
of May 1789." No copy of the will is on record
in the Clerk's Office of Fauquier County,
although the extant copy bears the signature
of H. Brooke who was the Clerk of the Fauquier
County Court. This copy was published in:
THE VIRGINIA GENEALOGIST, Vol. 9, pp. 147-153.
(1965), with notes by George Harrison Sanford
King.

Page
142:      WILLIAM HAMBLETON (Hamilton?) (Inventory)
          Date: 23 May 1789
App'd by: Joseph Taylor, William Barker, Richard Keeble
Total eval.: L370.15.6
Ret.:   22 June 1789

Page
143:
JOHN FISHBACK   (Inventory)
No date
App'd by: Henry Peyton, Joseph O'Bannon, John O'Bannon
Total eval: L325.0.3
Ret.:   22 June 1789

Page
144:
GEORGE CRUMP   (Inventory)
No date. Court order dated April 1789.
App'd by: Dan'l. Bradford, Jno. Shumate, Peter Grant
Total eval.: L373.5.7
Ret.:   22 June 1789

Page
146:
JOHN GRIGSBY   (Will)
Date: 29 December 1788
Dau.:   Fanny Rout - all the Negroes and other articles
of my Estate that she and her Husband (Richard
Rout) are at Present possessed of.
Gr.dau.: Jane Rout - L20
Dau.:   Winnefred - 3 negroes, one bed & furniture, 2
cows & calfs, 5 sheep & L12
Dau.:   Eadey - 2 Negroes, one bed & furniture, 2 cows
& calves, 6 sheep & L15
Son: Lewis - 2 Negroes
Son: Bayliss - 2 Negroes
Son: Nathaniel - 4 Negroes, one bay colt & smith gun
Sons: Lewis, Bayliss and Nathaniel - estate not other-
wise mentioned.
Exor: Son Lewis and Richard Rout
Wit.:   Hez'k. Turner, John White, John Catlett
Signed: John (his X mark) Grigsby
Proved: 22 June 1789 by o. of John Catlett and on 28
September 1789 by oaths of Hezekiah Turner and
John White. Richard Routt granted cert. to
obtain probate. H. Brooke, C. C.

Page
147:
HARMON RECTOR   (Will)
Date: 23 September 1782
Son: Harmon - 100 acres lying in the German Town
joining Agness Utterback's land - one Negro -
Sons: (not named) - my household furniture and stock
to be equally divided among my three sons.
Exors: Capt. Tilman Weaver and John Martin
Wit.:   Henry Utterback, William Nelson, Charles
Utterback
Signed: Harmon (his X mark) Rector
Proved: 28 September 1789 by o. of William Nelson and
Charles Utterback. Tilman Weaver and John

- 188 -

Martin granted cert. to obtain probate.

147:

FRANCIS CORTNEY   (Inventory)
Date: 11 March 1789
App'd by: Thomas Foley, Thos. Harris, Christopher Hitch
Total Eval.: L6.8.2
Ret.:   28 September 1789

Page
148:

JOHN CRUMP of Parish of Hamilton   (Will)
Date: 5 February 1789

Son: George - 5 shillings
Daus.: Elizabeth Utterback, Mary Waugh, Hannah Branan, Ann Lewis - 5 shillings each
Sons: William and Daniel - one feather bed & furniture each
Son: John - the land whereon I now live and all the lands I am possessed with during his life if he don't take up with or marry a Certain Woman by name of Mary Westall - at his death to go and belong to my son Daniel Crump .. to go immediately to Daniel if the said John breaks the will and marries Mary Westall
Daus.: Sarah & Catherine - to have the use of chamber room so long as they shall live single and that my said son John is to pay of(f) creditors and receive by debts and to live and do for them as in my lifetime
Exors: Brothers George and Benjamin Crump, William Eustace Junior and John James
Signed: John Crump
Wit.: John James, John Shumate, Mason Shumate
Proved: 28 September 1789 by o. of John James and John Shumate.

Page
149:

JEMIMA HARRIS   (Allotment of Dower)
Date: 27 July 1789. Court Order dated June Court 1789. "... allotted to Jemima Harrys late wife of James Withers Dec'd her dower in thesaid Withers land Except the land lately recovered by John Withers."
Details: Road in William Gibson's line & corner to the land that John Withers lately recovered of ye said Estate ... mouth of the Great branch then up Great Run ... 120 acres ... leaving 240 acres on the West side for the Orphans part..."

Signed: Peter Routt, Edward Newgent, James Routt
Ret.:   28 September 1789

Page
150:           GEORGE JENNINGS (Inventory)
             Date: 26 September 1789
App'd by: Chas. Duncan, Wm. Brent, James Routt
Total Eval.: L84.5
Ret.:   28 September 1789

Pages
150-151:   HARMON RECTOR, SEN'R. (Inventory)
             Date: 22 October 1789
App'd by: John Herndon, John Wever, John Mizner
Total Eval.: L71.11.7
Ret.:   26 October 1789

Page
152:           BENJAMIN ROBINSON (Estate Account)
             Dates: 21 February 1785 - 26 April 1787
Admr.:   Dixon Robinson
Details: TO: Humphrey Brooke; Thos. Doughty on arbi-
          tration; Ambrose Barnett; Robt. Gibson; Alex.
          Lithgow; Parnick George; Geo. Robinson;
          Jeremiah Foster; Wm. Melton; Wm. Pickett;
          John Sutton; Wm. Carr & Chapman; Henry Hampton;
          Wm. White; Jas. Bly; John Headly; Travers Nash;
          Isaach Ustice; taxes on Stafford land; Geo.
          Wm. Stewart; Peter Byram; Ann Masterson Legacy
          due 1785; Natha'l. Robinson; Bruce and Murray;
          Doctor Horner; John Robinson Legacy; Martin
          Pickett; Elijah Robinson Legacy; Alvin George
          Legacy; Doctor Norris; Alex'r. Campbell, Benj'n.
          Thos.; Henry Hope; White Nesbitt.
Examined by: W. Edmonds, Jas. Bell, Thos. Digges, 22
          August 1789
          REC'D. BY: Margit Oglisby; Epha Night; Peter
          Byram; Charles Modesett; Wm. Roach; John
          Minter; Thos. Thornton; John Anderson
Ret.:   26 October 1789

Pages
153-154:   JAMES STINSON (Will)
             Date: 17 October 1789
Wife: Elizabeth - the hole of my Estate Duering hir
          life
Children: John Stinson, Mary Stinson, Sarah Stinson,
       · Elizaboth & Leannah Stinson - estate to be

sold to highest bidder after decease of wife and money divided among children.

Exors: Friend James Wright and Peter Hitt
Signed: James (his X mark) Stinson
Wit: John McQuown, Mary (her x mark) McQuown, Jeremiah Darnall
Proved: 28 December 1789 by o. of John McQuoun, Mary McQuoun and Jeremiah Darnall. James Wright and Peter Hitt granted cert. to obtain probate.

Pages 154-155: DANIEL MONROE (Inventory)
Date: 25 August 1789
App'd by: Dan'l. Floweree, Harmon Hitt (signed: Martin Hitt), Thomas Fitzhugh
Total Eval.: L45.11.11
Ret.: 28 December 1789

Pages 155-156: HONOUR HALEY (Will) "parish of Leeds Planter"
Date: 22 February 1787
Son: Michael Cavanaugh - all the money arising from my Estate if he comes in the space of one year, after my death if not in that time the said Estate to go as hereafter mentioned.
____: Mary Johnston, dau. of Henry Peyton, - that still in my possession
____: Sarah Fishback, dau. of Josiah Fishback - one guinea
____: John Morcy - L5
____: Honour O'Neal, the dau. of Christopher O'Neal - the money that the said Christopher O'Neal is indebited to me
Exors: Josiah Fishback, Henry Peyton
Signed: Honour (her X mark) Haley
Wit: George Leach, James Fishback, George (his X mark) Leach, Sr.
Proved: 25 January 1790 by o. of George Leach, Sr. and James Fishback. Josiah Fishback granted cert. to obtain probate.

Pages 156-157: JOHN HAILEY (or HEALY*) (Adm'r. Account)
Dates: 4 May 1787 - 23 November 1788
*See Will, dated 2 April 1787, page 179

Adm'r.: John Dearing
Details: TO: James Bawl; Joseph Donephan; Mary Haley;
Joseph Smith; Smith Johnson; Wm. Lane for
making a coffin, L1; Harmon Cuin; Leonard
Smoote; E. Edmonds; Charles Marshall; J. L.
Barba; John Maddux; John Laramon; James
Mashett; Horney Dinnason; Joseph Withers;
S. Strother; William Carr; Neamiah Dowell;
Clemm Norman; For 19 days expenses at Dumfries
for attending on the estate of the John Hailey.
BY: Wm. Hamlet; William Pickett; James Ginn;
James Hey; Mary Haley; Wm. Jett; Joseph Barba
Examined by: Francis Triplett, B. Shackelford, 31 December
1789
Retn: 25 December 1790

Page
157:           ROBERT EMBREY (Will)
              Date: 26 October 1784
Gr. son: Robert Embrey, son of Charles Embrey Deceased -
82 acres lying between Carter's line and Summerduck Run including the plantation whereon his
father lived.
Sons: Thomas and Robert Embrey - remainder of my
land to be equally divided .. the plantation
whereon Thomas Embrey lives to be included in
his part and the plantation whereon I lived to
be in my son Robert Embrey's part
Wife: Ann - all my stock and other effects
Exors: Sons Thomas and Robert
Signed: Robert (his X mark) Embrey
Wit: Lincfield Sharpe, Swanson Brown, John (his X
mark) Brown
Proved: 25 January 1790 by o. of Swanson Brown and
John Brown. Robert Embrey granted cert. to
obtain probate.

Pages
158-159:   HARMON BUTTON (Will)
              Date: 25 December 1789
Wife: Catherine - all my Estate, during her life
Son: Jacob - all Estate now in his possession ex-
cept the land whereon he lives, which is
to hold until the Death of his Mother
Dau.: Anne Hockman - Estate now in her possession -
L20 from estate after death of her mother
Dau.: Sarah Sinsel - (same as Jacob)
Daus.: Susanna, Catherine, Rebekah - all the movable

property remaining after the Death of their
Mother.
All land to be equally divided amongst the
whole of my children except Anne Hockman who
is to have no share in the Land.

Exors: John Kemper, Sen'r., Jacob Kemper, Sen'r.
Signed: Harmon Button
Wit.:   Robert (his x mark) Turnbull, Randolph Smith,
         Charles Kemper
Proved: 25 January 1790 by o. of Randolph Smith and
         Charles Kemper. John Kemper, Sen'r. and Jacob
         Kemper, Sen'r. granted cert. to obtain probate.

Pages
160-161:   THOMAS NUGENT (or NEWGENT) (Will)
                Date: 11 September 1789
Nephew: Lincefield Sharpe - all lands whereon I now
         live, purchased of John & Dixon Brown and of
         Mr. Wm. Skinker - also tract where Lincefield
         Sharpe now lives purchased of Joseph James, to
         him and his heirs. If he should leave no
         heirs to be sold and divided among the children
Brother: of my Brother Edward Nugent - slaves - live-
         stock - plantation tools and equipment.
Children of brother: Edward Nugent - slaves - Lincefield
         Sharpe to supply each Negroe a sufficient
         sute of warm clotheing.
Nephew: Thomas Nugent - Negro girl
Brother: Edward Nugent - title to land he lives on -
         two feather beds, all the chairs, excepting
         one arm chair, a cross-cut saw, pewter and
         one half plantation tools.
Niece's children: Niece Mary Hampton's two daughters -
         Frances and Susanna - Negroes.
         Ann Nugent Sharpe, dau. of nephew Lincefield
         Sharpe - Negro girl
Nephew: William Ballard - L10
Nephew: Lincefield Sharpe - residue
Exors: Lincefield Sharpe and bro. Edward Nugent (in
         case of his death, his son Thomas Nugent to
         be exor. in his place)
Signed: Thos. Newgent
Wit.:   Peter Grant, George S. Blackwell, William
         Woodside
Proved: 22 February 1790 by o. of Peter Grant and
         George S. Blackwell. Edward Nugent and Lince-
         field Sharpe granted cert. to obtain probate.
         with Jeremiah Darnall, Thomas Keith and Peter

Grant to act as their securities.

Page
162:
     PETER CARTER (Inventory)
     No date
App'd by: Wm. Hunton, George Rogers, Jun'r., Thomas
    Sanders.
Total Eval.: L100.3.0
Retn.: 22 February 1790

Page
163:
     JAMES STEPHENSON (Inventory)
     Date: 10 February 1790. Court Order
     dated December 1789
App'd by: William Sinclor, Will Bradford, John Martin
Total Eval.: L82.11.0
Ret.: 22 February 1790

Page
164:
     HUMPHREY ARNOLD (Inventory)
     Date: 1 January 1790
App'd by: Thomas Porter, James Stewart, Wily Roy
Total Eval: L336.19.2
Details: 1 Large Bible, 12s.; 1 hymn Book, 1s.
Ret.: 22 February 1790

Page
165;
     MRS. ELIZABETH SETTLE (Division)
     Date: 27 February 1790
Legatees: Edward Settle, John Pope Williamson,
    William Freeman - 78½ acres of land to be
    equally divided among the three legatees.
Divided by: John Ball, Peter Kemper, C. Kemper
Ret.: 22 February 1790

Page
166:
     HONOUR HALEY (Inventory)
     No date.
App'd by: William Nalle, Jr., Thomas Glascock, Andrew
    McClannahan.
Total Eval: L13.11.0
Ret.: 26 April 1790

Page
166:
     BENJAMIN GARNER (Will)
     5 September 1789
Wife: Diannah Garner - all estate during her natural
    life or Widowhood, if she should marry then

my whole estate to be equally divided between all my Children.

Exors: loving wife, Brother Vincent Garner & James
Withers

Signed: Benjamin (his X mark) Garner

Wit.: James Withers, John Withers, James (his X
mark) Garner.

Proved: 26 April 1790, by o. of James Withers and
John Withers. Cert. granted Diannah Garner
executrix with Vincent Garner and John Garner,
her securities.

**Page
167:**
ANN EMBREY (Nuncupative Will)
Date: 9 February 1790

Son: Robert Embrey - one mare and one horse, one
big coat, saddle, one bed and furniture, one
stear, yearling, one pot & baker, one dish and
chest.

____: Elizabeth Taylor - one bed & furniture, one
flax wheel.

Dau.: Nancy Butler - my saddle

Wit.: William Snelling, Alexander Brown, Sarah (her
X mark) Benjey. Oath made by William Snelling
and Sarah Benjey that the "instrument of
writing was drawn up at the request of Ann
Embrey.." Signed: Thom Keith.

Proved: 27 April 1790 by o. of Thomas Keith, Gent.,
"Thomas Embrey the next of kin having been
summoned to contest the validity thereof and
failing to do so, and on the motion of Robt.
Embrey who made oath together with Jeremiah
Brown his security .. granted cert. to obtain
probate."

Note: 22 February 1790, Thomas Embrey "summoned to
appear at April Court next to contest the nuncupative will of Ann Embrey deceased if he
shall think fit."

**Pages
167-168:**
JOSEPH SMITH (Division of Estate)
Date: 30 April 1790. Court Order dated
October 1789.

Div. by: W. Edmonds, Edward Digges, John Obannon

Details: Children: TO: Ruth Smith - one Negro woman;
Abner Smith - to pay Ruth Smith L2.6.8;
TO: Wilhilmina Smith - one Negro woman, Abner
Smith to pay L2.6.8; TO: Abner Smith, two

Negroes. "It likewise appearing to us by
an Inventory produced that there is L35.4.3
half penny due from the estate to the above
Children, Andrew Obannion Father in law to the
above children presented his act. for their
bord, etc. We the Subscribers are of opinion
that the above negroes work were a sufficient
satisfaction."
Ret.:   28 June 1790

Pages
168-169:   THOMAS BLAND, SEN'R. (Adm'r. Account)
Executrix: Mrs. Jean Bland
Details: TO: 1789, Jan.: David W. Scott; Thomas Harrison;
Enoch Oscar Smith; John William Smith; Joseph
Blackwell; Bronaugh; Capt. Ben Harrison for rent
dues for 1788; Daniel Coal for making Wm.
Bland's coffin; David Jameison for plank;
Tho. Bland, Jr.; Wm. Alex'r. Sithgow; Samuel
Byrne; Campbell, sheriff Pr. Wm. for tax in
Byrnes by Sithgow fortunes, etc.; Capt. William
Carr.
BY: Capt. Ben Harrison; Hum Colvert for his
rent Due for 1788 due Bland; Eb Ethis for his
rent due for 1788; William Cornwell; John
Woods; Jos. Brady; Wm. Ficklen; Sam'l. Buniss;
Sam'l. Byrnes; William Coppage; George Hardin;
Alex. Wilson; Roby Haley; Original Young;
Thomas Cox; Thomas Harrison, Gent.; Thos.
Bland, Jr.; John Wilson; Brawner Dowdall;
Sinicah Chizeldene; Lewis Oliver; Ben Harrison;
Hiss Oliver; Alexander Sithgow; Charles Craw-
ford; David Jamieson; Joseph Jordin.
Examined by: Joseph Blackwell and Original Young
Ret.:   28 June 1790

Page
169:        PETER PIERCE (Division of Estate)
            Date: 15 February 1789
Divided by: J. Blackwell and John Blackwell
Details: Benjamin Pettitt, gdn. of orphans of Peter
Pierce, due L3.17s.
Children: Rosanna Pierce - one Negro woman
          John Pierce - one Negro woman
          Susanna Pierce - One Negro woman
Ret.:   28 June 1790

**Page
170:**   JOHN GRIGSBY (Inventory)
          Date: 26 December 1787
App'd by: John Keith, George Adams, Littleton Adams
Total Eval: ₤1018.5.6
Ret.:   28 June 1790

**Page
171:**   JOHN LUTTRELL (Inventory)
          No date
App'd by: Thos. Harris, John Barber, Rich'd. Harris
Total Eval: L140.16.0
Ret.:   28 June 1790

**Page
172:**   THOMAS NEWGENT (Inventory)
          No date
App'd by: William Grant, John Woodside, William Woodside
Total Eval: L1644.7.0
Ret.:   28 June 1790

**Pages
173-174:**   JOHN BARKER (Adm'r. Account)
              Date: 26 March 1790
Adm'r.:   Joseph Doniphan
Details: TO: 1784: Capt. John Moffett; Col. H. Brooke;
          Wm. Helms. 1790: Samuel Rust, Simon Morgan,
          Sen'r. 1784: BY: Simon Morgan, Sen'r.; Capt.
          Wm. Helms; Mrs. Barker.
Exm'd by: John Edmonds, John Thos. Chunn, John Ashby.
Ret.:   26 July 1790

**Page
174:**   FRANCES THROCKMORTON (Will)
          Date: 2 May 1790
Brother: William Throckmorton - money due from him on
          father's estate.
Sisters: Mary and Ann - rest of estate
Exor: Friend Morgan Tomkies of the County of Glou-
          cester.
Signed: Frances (her T mark) Throckmorton
Wit.:   H. Brooke and Francis Brooke
Ret.:   27 September 1790 by o. of Humphrey Brooke
          and Francis Brooke

**Page
175:**   ROBERT SANDERS (Will)
          Date: 27 May 1790

___:	William Sanders - the Tract of land I bought of Nathan Matthews, no more of my Estate
Wife:	Anne Sanders - lend to her the rest of estate during her widowhood and if she should marry she shall possess no more of my estate but a Negro woman.
Sons:	James, Britain, Gabriel, Thomas, Lewis and Larking - estate after death of wife.
Son:	James - first volume of Dr. John Gill on the New Testament
Son:	Britain - the second volume
Son:	Gabriel - the third volume
Son:	Thomas - the fourth volume
Son:	Lewis - the fifth volume
Son:	Larking - Doctor Gill's Exposition on the Songs of Soloman
Exors:	James Sanders, William Hunton, James Hunton, Thomas Sanders
Signed:	Robert Sanders
Wit.:	Charles Chilton, Wm. Hunton, Jr., Elizabeth Sanders.
Proved:	27 September 1790 by o. of Elizabeth Sanders and William Hunton, Jr. James Sanders and Thomas Sanders with Joseph Blackwell and Peter Grant as securities, granted cert. to obtain probate.

Page
176:      HENRY HAMILTON   (Inventory)
            No date
App'd by: Simon Morgan, Wm. Barker, Harmon Utterback
Total Eval: L39.13.6
Ret.:   27 September 1790

Page
177-178:   WILLIAM STEVENSON   (Inventory)
            Date: 30 July 1790
App'd by: Wm. Smith, John Ashby, Sam'l. Butcher
Total Eval: L137.18.3
Ret.:   2 September 1790

Page
179:      RICHARD LANCELOT LEE   (Will)
            Date: 24 September 1790

Sister:	Priscilla Lee - L200 Virginia currency, riding horse and a genteel woman's saddle
Brother:	Arthur - my bay horse, saddle & bridle
Bros. & Sisters:	William, George, Kendall, Hancock, Arthur, Betty Edwards, Judith Pierce - all the re-

mainder of my estate, after my own and my
proportion of my father's debts are paid.

Exors: Mr. Thomas Edwards and Bro. George Lee
Signed: Rich'd. L. Lee
Wit: Wm. Bronaugh, Jr., Wm. Hale, Solomon Ewell,
        Joseph Hale
Proved: 25 October 1790, by o. of William Bronaugh, Jr.,
        and Solomon Ewell. Thomas Edwards and George
        Lee, with Edward Digges their security, granted
        cert. to obtain probate.

Page
180:       GARNER BURGES of Parish of Leeds (Will)
        Date: 19 April 1790
Wife: Anne Burges - during her life or widowhood all
        my whole Estate
Dau.:   Susanna Burges and James Burges - the planta-
        tion whereon I live - one cow and Calf and one
        Bed and furniture to each of them
Dau.:   Susanna - Dutch over, pewter dish, and two plates
Dau.:   Peggy Burges - one Bed and furniture, one Cow
        and calf, 2 pewter dishes
Son: John - one Bed and furniture, one cow and calf
Dau.:   Nancy - one Bed and furniture, one Cow and
        calf, 2 pewter plates, one iron skillet
Children: Mary Neal, Susanna Burges, Sarah Settle, Peggy
        Burges, Edward Burges, Jno. Burges, James
        Burges and Nancy Burges - all the rest of my
        estate.
Exors: wife Anne Burges, son Edward Burges and
        Matthew Neal
Signed: Garner Burges
Wit: B. Shackleford, Matthew Neal, Isaac Arnold
Proved: 25 October 1790, by o. of Matthew Neal and
        Isaac Arnold. Anne Burges, Edward Burges and
        Matthew Neal, with Dickinson Wood and Isaac
        Arnold as their securities, granted cert. to
        obtain probate.

Pages
181-182:   JOHN ELLIOTT (Inventory)
        Date: 16 October 1790
App'd by: William Pepper, James Barton (X his mark),
        and Sal. Pepper.
Total Eval.: L164.18.2. Widows L54.19.4½. Remains
        L109.18.9½.
Ret.:   25 October 1790

Page
183:
CHARLES JONES (Administrator's Account)
Date: 4 November 1790
Ex'md. by: B. Shackelford, Dickerson Wood, Francis
Payne
Details: Inventory was produced by the Adm'r. and a
balance of L30.13.1 farthng due Elijah and
Elisha Jones, orphs. of said Charles Jones,
dec'd.
Ret.: 24 January 1791
Court order dated: September 1790 - that
Benjamin Shackelford, Henry Clarkson, Dickerson
Wood and Francis Payne or any three settle
the Account of the Admr. of Charles Jones, dec'd.

Page
183:
WILLIAM HARRISON, JR. (Division of Estate)
Date: 1 January 1791
Div. by: John Thos. Chunn, Robert Allison, Wm. Edmonds,
Jr.
Details: Jane Mallory, the decedent's Mother - Negroes
Burr Harrison, "   "   Brother - Negroes
Lucy Mallory, "   "   Sister - Negroes
"... Whereas it appears from the Settlement of
the Guardianship of William Harrison dec'd
with Phillip Mallory that there is a Ballance
due the said Mallory from sd. Estate of
L38.8.3.3 and we divided the Estate Gross
which occasions Burr Harrison and William
Mallory each to stand indebted to Phillip
Mallory L12.16.2.3.
Ret.: 24 January 1791

Page
184:
WILLIAM ROBINSON Parish of Leeds (Will)
Date: 18 March 1790
Wife: my Lawful weded wife Elizabeth - my lot of
land and all my hole Estate during her life
and after her deceas to bee Equelly devided
amunkst all my Children.
Dau.:= Mary - excepted to above - 5 shillings
Signed: Wm. Robinson
Wit.: John Robinson, Joshua Luttrell, Nathan (his X
mark) Ellis
Proved: 24 January 1791 by o. of John Robertson and
Joshua Luttrell. Elizabeth Robertson, with
Richard Harris and Joshua Luttrell as securities
granted cert. to obtain probate.

Page
185:   SANFORD CARROLL (Adm'r. Acc't. and Division)
                    Date: 27 January 1791
Admr.:   Col. John O'Bannon
Details: due estate by O'Bannon from Dec. 1787, L17.6.
                10.3 Three legatees: David Prunty, who married
                Anna Carrol, L5.15.7½, also Negroes Harry &
                Alley with L8.6.8 which he obtained by Lott.
                (no other legatees named)
Div. by: Henry Peyton, Law. Ashton, Wm. Metcalf
Ret.:   28 February 1791

Pages
185-186:   WILLIAM HAMILTON (Adm'r. Account)
                    Date: 28 February 1791
Admr.:   Thomas Keith
Details: TO: Thomas Keith; Thomas Nelson, dec'd.; Swan-
                son Brown; Doctor Horner; Stuart & Marshall;
                Daniel Gray & Co.; William Waddle; Charles
                Marshall; To 20 lb. Tobacco pd. Clk. of Fauquier.
                BY: Chas. Marshall; Gray's Acc't.
Ex'md. by: Charles Marshall, William Barker, Simeon
                Morgan
Ret.:   28 February 1791

Pages
186-188:   WILLIAM HARRISON, JR. (Gdn. Account)
                    Date: 16 April 1791
Guardian: Philip Mallory
Details: TO: Thomas Nelson; William Withers; Rich'd.
                Boyce; Enoch Withers; Suddoth; William Haner;
                John Austin; Estate of Thos. Chinn; McKittrick;
                Edward Humston; Waggonage Tob'o to Dumfries;
                William Fishback for 2 years Schooling; Colo.
                Powell; I. Sudduth for Overseeing; Keeport for
                clothing; Bennet Wats; McMahon; Anthony
                McKittrick; Fosher for schooling 2 years 6
                mos.; Charles Tyler; Yates & Lovel; John Clark
                for Mdze; John Matthews for Schooling; Andrew
                Francis; Doctor Walterhouse; Charles Day; M.
                Pickett; John Thompson for Coffin, 20/;
                Doctor Savage; To 6 years Board L60; Zapha-
                niah Legg. BY: Alex'r. Francis.
Ex'md. by: John Thos. Chunn, Robert Allison, Wm. Edmonds,
                Jr., Joseph Smith, Thos. Smith.
Ret.:   25 April 1791

- 201 -

Pages
188-189:   ROBERT EMBREY   (Inventory)
                No date
App'd by: Linsfield Sharpe, John Brown, Swanson Brown
Total Eval.:   L25
Ret.:   25 April 1791

Pages
189-190:   BENJAMIN GARNER   (Inventory)
                Court Order dated: 26 April 1790
App'd by: John Mauzy, James Withers, James Parr
Total Eval.:   L171.3.6
Ret.:   27 June 1791

Pages
190-191:   HUMPHREY ARNOLD   (Executor's Account)
                Date: 1790
Exor.:   Benjamin Arnold
Details: TO: James Barnett; Richard Fisher; William
            Pinkard; Peter Kamper; John Turner; Capt.
            Jennings; Sam'l. Fisher; To plank & making a
            Coffin for Negro; Johnson for Rum; Martin
            Pickett & Co.; Wm. Brian; Doctor Horner;
            Isaac Arnold; Bought by Mrs. Arnold at sale
            which she is to keep as long as she lives -
            L28.13.7; Mrs. Arnold is to have all the Land
            her lifetime except some that George Arnold
            is to have & some that John West has a deed
            for; George Arnold. BY: George Gordon; John
            Hitt; Sam Blackwell; Solomon Kamper; Charles
            Kamper; Jno. Kamper; John Withers; Jesse
            Withers; John Turner; Ambrose Barnett; Wm.
            Bragg. Balance to be divided between Isaac
            Arnold, Sam. Arnold, Benj'n. Arnold; Geo.
            Arnold, Seymour Arnold, John Arnold and John
            West.
Ex'md. by: Joseph Blackwell, Wily Roy, Thomas Roy
Ret.:   27 June 1791

Pages
192-194:   ROBERT SANDERS   (Inventory)
                Date: 15 October 1790
App'd by: Parnack George, Wm. Hampton, Wm. Hunton, Sen'r.
Details: Books: Gill on the New Testament & Song of
            Solomon - L10; 5 Vollumes of Sermon Books by -
            15s.; 1 Dictionary 3/; To sundry other Books -
            L2.15.0

Total Eval.: L495.3.8
Ret.:   25 July 1791

Pages
194-196:   BRYANT THORNHILL (Invantory)
                Date: 1 December 1785
App'd by: James Lawler, Benjamin Thomas, Parnack George
Total Eval.: L272.14.0
Ret.:   25 July 1791

Page
197:            WILLIAM ROBERTSON (Inventory)
                Date: 25 February 1791
App'd by: John Barbee, Nathan Ellis, Rich'd. Harris,
          Joshua Luttrell
Total Eval.: L76.1.10
Ret.:   25 July 1791

Pages:
198-199:   BRYANT THORNHILL (Administrator's Acc't.)
                Date: 24 May 1790
Admr.:   William Hunton
Details: TO: (1785) - Wm. Mason; 1786, Dec. 21: Benj'n.
          Thomas; Wm. Sanders. To bording & schooling
          4 Scholars L36; Robert Sanders for bording
          and schooling 1 scholar L9.10.0; Parnack George;
          James Primm; Dale Carter; Geo. Rogers; Wm.
          Suttle; Sol'o. Ewell; Sam'l. Watson; Mr. Law-
          son; Mr. Lithgow. 1788, Dec.: James Lawler;
          Colo. John Blackwell; Colo. Powell; John
          Blackwell; Mr. Murray, merchant; Doctor Graham;
          Thomas Cave; Colo. Pickett; Dan'l. Gray; Capt.
          Cave; Sheriff Enoch Weathers; John Morgan;
          Doctor Norris for attending the sick; Capt.
          Carr; Joseph Thomas; James Muschett; Valentine
          Peyton. BY: Thomas Legg; John Hopper; Thomas
          Sanders; John Nash; Benj. Thomas; David Brent;
          Dale Carter; Joseph Thomas; Daniel Donaldson;
          John Sutton; Parnack George; James Lewis; Wm.
          White, Jr.; Mr. Ransdell; Wm. Creel; Alexander
          Keith; Doctor Norris; Wm. Sanders; Robert
          Sanders; Joseph Bailey; Wm. Bailey; Simeon
          Bailey.
Ex'md. by: Charles Chilton, James Bell, Thomas Digges.
Ret.:   25 July 1791

Page
200:               JOHN MINTER (Division of Estate)
                   Date: 1791
Divided by: Parnack George, Wm. Hunton, Samuel Steele
Details: William Minter - Negro girl
          William Bailey - Negro boy
          Jacob Minter - Negro boy; to give Wm. Bailey
          L10 "to make their Negroes equal."
Ret.:   25 July 1791

Pages
200-201:   GARNER BURGES (Inventory)
                  Date: 31 January 1791
App'd by: B. Shackleford, Henry Clarkson, Aquila Davis,
          James Foley
Total Eval.: L456.3.6
Ret.:   25 July 1791

Page
201:              CALEB BROWNING (Inventory)
                  Date: 14 November 1787
App'd by: Henry Clarkson, James Foley, Christopher Hitch.
Total Eval.: L148.16.6
Ret.:   25 July 1791

Page
202:              JAMES WITHERS (Will)
                  Date: 4 May 1791
Wife: Elizabeth - all estate during her lifetime or
          widowhood.
Children: Thomas, John, Elizabeth, Hannah, Cain, Lucy,
          Centhy, Enoch, William, Sithey, Sally and Pattey .
          all property at death or marriage of wife.
Exors: Wife Elizabeth, son John
Signed: James Withers
Wit.:   Aquilla Davis, Samuel Nichols, Elizabeth (X)
          Nichols
Proved: 25 July 1791 by o. of Aquilla Davis and Samuel
          Nichols. Elizabeth Withers and John Withers
          granted cert. to obtain probate.

Pages
203-204:   EDWARD NEWGENT (Inventory)
                  No date.
App'd by: James Withers, William Withers, James Dodd
Total Eval.: L198.11.6
Ret.:   25 July 1791

<u>Pages</u>
204-205:   JONATHAN GIBSON (Will)
                  Date: 2 July 1788

Children: Three youngest children: Jonathan Catlett,
           Susanna Grayson and Mary Gibson - L40 to be
           equally divided among them, from the sale of
           household furniture.
Son: Thomas - balance of residue, if any, from sale
           of household estate - Negroes
Son: John - Negroes
Son: Jonathan Catlett Gibson - Negroes
Dau.:   Ann Grayson Blackwell - Negroes
Dau.:   Susanna Grayson Gibson - Negroes
Dau.:   Mary Gibson - Negroes
Niece: Margret Adie - Negroes
Gr. dau.: Margret Catlett Gibson - Negro
Gr. dau.: the child (not named) of dau., Ann Grayson
           Blackwell - Negro
Exors: Benjamin Harrison, sons Thomas, John & Jonathan
Signed: Jonathan Gibson
Wit.:   John Mauzy, Matthew Harrison, Jun'r.
Proved: 26 September 1791, by o. of John Mauzy. Benjamin
           Harrison granted cert. to obtain probate, with
           Joseph Blackwell, his security.

<u>Page</u>
206:         AARON GEORGE (Inventory)
                  Date: 1791
App'd by: Rob't. Hunton, Jas. Hunton, Wm. Hunton, Jun'r.
Total Eval.: L111.15.6
Ret.:   26 September 1791

<u>Pages</u>
207-208:   JOSEPH BARBEE (Inventory)
                Court order dated: September 1790, we
          have met on the premises of Ann Barbee's,
          present Benj'n. Shackelford, Gent.
App'd by: Aquilla Davis, Dickerson Wood, Matthew Davis
Total Eval.: L121.8.11
Ret.:   26 September 1791

<u>Page</u>
209:         AARON GEORGE (Administrator's Account)
                  Date: 10 October 1791
Admr.:   Parnack George
Details: TO: Colo. Powell; Doct'r. Horner, Colo. Pic-
           kett; William Carrs Estate; Humphrey Brooke

for Clerks fees. BY: Robt. Brown; Wm.
Hampton for Rice's bond; Bailey Rice; Thomas
Bailey.

Ex'md. by: Martin Pickett, Joseph Blackwell
Ret.:   24 October 1791

Page
210:          JOHN NELSON, SENIOR (Will)
                Date: 22 March 1791
Wife: Mary - all estate during her life, to be sold
        after her decease and divided into five equal
        parts, one-fifth part to each of the following
        heirs: Catherine Horton and Elizabeth Green;
        Hannah James, wife of Thomas James; Mary Nelson,
        widow of John Nelson, Jr., dec'd.; Thomas
        Nelson and Joseph Nelson (sons).
Exors: Wife Mary Nelson, William Phillips of Stafford
        County and Garrart Gray, Jun'r.
Signed: John Nelson, Sen'r.
Wit: Original Young, John Green, Elizabeth (X) James
Proved: 26 December 1791, by o. of Original Young, John
        Green and Elizabeth Green. Garrett Gray and
        Mary Nelson granted cert. to obtain probate.

Page:
211:         EDWARD NEWGENT (Division of Estate)
               Date: 19 October 1791
Divided by: John Blackwell, John Bronaugh, Hancock Lee
Details: Thomas Newgent - Negroes, cash
        Frances Williams (dau.) - Negroes, cash Which
        sums the younger children of Edward Newgent
        deceased are indebted to the above mentioned
        persons.
Ret.:   26 December 1791

Page
212:         JOHN MINTER (Administrator's Account)
Admr.:   Joseph Minter
Details: 25 April 1778, To articles bought at your
        Brothers Sale; TO: (1781): James Gafney, James
        Barimore, William Mullekin; John Tomlin. BY
        CASH PAID: (1779): John Barker Sheriff, for
        taxes; Daniel Brown Collector for quit rents;
        James Barrimore, for the bord of Jacob Minter;
        By the Boarding Anthony & William Minter;
        Charles Chilton. (1787): William Carr. (1786):
        By Articles got of Gray for Children; Mr.

George Rogers, Jr. (1788), John Tomlin,
Thomas Evans, Thomas Watts. (1782), By
Cash paid Wm. Metcalf for schooling Anthony,
Jacob and Betsy Minter; John Metcalf for
Bord of Schoolmaster & two spelling books;
James Muschett. "By cash paid Wm. Lowry
for schooling Anthony, Jacob and Betsey
Minter for time Wm. Metcalf was in the
Melitia" (1782). (1786), Martin Pickett acc't.
by Chas. Chilton; Clarks notes; Wm. Metcalf
for schooling; Enoch Withers for taxes; Elias
Edmonds for serving Execution; Alexander
Keith for taxes; Nathaniel Gray for Taxes.

Ex'md by: Ambrose Barnett, Samuel Steele, Thos. Ransdell.
Ret.: 26 December 1791

Pages
214-215:   WILLIAM YOUNG (Will)
           Date: 20 December 1790

Almighty God: soul
Son: Bryan - slave
Son: William - slave
Dau.:   Mary Jeffries - slave
Dau.:   Hannah Owsley - L20 current money of Virginia
Dau.:   "Sukey or Susanna" Smithey - L20 current money
           of Virginia
Wife: Patience Young - all property not above devised
           to be "enjoyed during her natural life or
           widowhood" - at death or marriage all the Es-
           tate both real and personal be sold at pub-
           lick auction and proceeds to be divided am-
           ongst all Children or their representatives.
Exors: Joseph Jeffries, Thomas Fitzhugh
Signed: William Young
Wit.:   J. Moffett, Menoah (X) Stone, Edward Feagan,
           Benj'n. Carpenter
Proved: 27 February 1792 by o. of Edward Feagan, John
           Moffett and Benjamin Carpenter. Joseph Jeffries,
           Junior, the executor, made o. and together
           with Joseph Jeffries, Sen'r., his Security,
           granted cert. to obtain probate.

Pages
216-217:   ROBERT ASHBY (Will)
           Date: 2 June 1790
Son: Benjamin - one tract of land on "Shanandoah
           River being the Land whereon my said son

	now lives - slave.
Gr.son:	William Ashby - son of Benjamin - slave when he becomes 21 years of age
Son:	Enoch - for and during his natural life the tract of land whereon I now live and after his Decease, to:
Gr.sons:	Robert and Alexander - sons of Enoch - to be divided by a branch known by the name of Ann Churchill's Spring branch and empties into the Deep branch near George Ashes Meadow .. southside to Robert Ashby and the remainder or **Manner** plantation (sic: Manor) to Alexander Ashby.
Dau.-in-law:	Sally Ashby - wife of Enoch - ½ of slaves after decease of husband, during her natural life or widowhood -
Gr.children:	Children of Enoch - ½ slaves above
Dau.:	Ann Farrow - L10 and no more
Gr.son:	Bayles Ashby - one feather bed and no furniture
Gr.dau.:	Molley Fargarson - slave
Dau.:	Winifred Piper - one cow & no more
Gr.sons:	Martin & Thomas Ashby (sons of Nimrod) - 1 slave each and no more
Dau.:	Molley Athel - one gown and no more
Son:	John - slaves, to purchase a slave for grand-dau. Lucinda Ashby to be paid for by Exor. five years after testator's death - one tract of land lying in Fauquier County joining George Ash and a part of Ewells tract which I purchased of Martin Ashby - 100 acres.
Gr.son:	Benjamin Farrow - slave
Gr.son:	Nimrod Ashby - any furture children of Negroe Rachel
Sons:	John & Enoch - remainder of Estate equally divided, but that the said Enoch shall have no right to Dispose of any of the aforementioned Legacies which is bequesthed him as it is Intended purely for the benefit of his Children.
Exor.:	Son, John Ashby
Signed:	Robert (his X mark) Ashby
Wit.:	Wm. Withers X, John Fishback, Jno. Clark X
Proved:	27 February 1792, by o. of John Clarke and William Withers. John Ashby made o. and with Charles Marshall and William Withers as securities, granted cert. to obtain probate.

**Pages
219-220:**   JOHN WRIGHT   of the Parish of Hamilton   (Will)
                Date: 1 June 1785

Son: James - my land lying on the east side of the
               run, being part of the tract of land whereon
               I now live in the County of Fauquier - slaves

Gr.dau.:   Betsey Wright (dau. of James) - slave

Daus.:   Mary and Rosamond Wright - the plantation
               whereon I now live and all the land I hold
               lying on the West side of the side run above
               mentioned - to be divided between the two as
               they can agree. In case of their death, with-

Son: out heirs, to go to son James - slaves - house-
               hold furniture and livestock.

Sons: William and John - 20 shillings - the reason
               why I have left my two sons no more is that I
               gave them both land which they sold.

Dau.:   Elizabeth Parlow - should she ever apply that
               then my executors pay her L15 out of my estate.

Wife: Elizabeth - to have all estate above mentioned
               during her life and then divided as directed.

Exors: Son James and daus. Mary and Rosamond

Signed: John Wright

Wit: George Maddox, John Nelson, Francis (X) Latham,
               Wm. Kernes.

Proved: 27 February 1792, by o. of George Maddux and
               William Kerns. James Wright made o. and with
               Thomas Keith as his security, granted cert. to
               obtain probate.

**Page
221:**   ANDERSON COCKRELL (Will)
                Date: 7 September 1791

Dau.:   Rosana - one young dark bay mair

Son: William - one bald face horse and colt - the
               rest of my estate - should be kept together

Dau.:   untill my youngest daughter Sally Cockrell
               shall arrive to the age of Eighteen or marys
               and then to be equally divided among my
               surviving children.

Exor: "my brother Jesse Moffett" and son William

Signed: Anderson (his X mark) Cockrell

Wit.:   John Cooke, John Porter, Augustin Banister

Proved: 27 February 1792 by o. of John Cooke and John
               Porter. Jesse Moffett and William Cockrell
               made oaths, and with John Cooke and Simon
               Cornwell as securities, granted cert. to
               obtain probate.

Page
222:                    JOHN GILLISON (Division of Estate)
                       Date: 31 December 1791
Div.by: Peter Grant, John Blackwell, Jr., John James,
            Thos. Shumate
Details: TO: John Gillison - negroes and L1 to be paid
            by James Gillison; Thomas Helm - negroes and
            L1 to be paid by James Gillison. To: William
            Eustace for his dau. Mary - negroes. To: James
            Gillison - negroes. To: Samuel Blackwell -
            Negroes, L4 to be paid by William Eustace for
            his dau. Mary and L2 to be paid by James
            Gillison.
Ret.:   23 April 1792

Pages
223-224:   ROBERT ASHBY (Inventory)
                       No date.
App'd by: Francis Ash, George Ash, Thomas Adams.
Total Eval.: L434.9.6½
Ret.:   23 April 1792

Pages
224-225:   JAMES WITHERS (Inventory)
                       Court order dated July 1791.
App'd by: Dickerson Wood, Sen'r., Jno. Smoot, Sr.,
            Aquilla Davis, with Capt. Benj'm. Shackel-
            ford, Esq. present, met on the premises of
            Elizabeth Withers.
Total Eval.: L420.18.8
Ret.:   25 June 1792

Pages
226-228:   JAMES FREEMAN, SENIOR (Will)
                       Date: 8 May 1792
Dau.:   Salley Freeman (youngest dau.) - one feather
            bed & furniture, one small square walnut table,
            one mare, one cow & calf, full benefits of the
            profits of all that part of her Grandfather
            George Williams's Estate which was by him Be-
            queathed to her Mother, all which estate so
            Bequeathed it is my will and desire shall be
            considered as distinct from my estate, and to
            descend to my youngest Daughter aforesaid at
            her Mother's decease.
Wife: Margaret Freeman - 1/3 of all lands, and use
            of personal estate during her life
Gr.son: Gollop Freeman (Alias Duncan) - one feather

- 210 -

	bed and furniture
Son:	Garrett - one feather bed and furniture - slave
Son:	Nathaniel - slave and estate he has been given already
Dau.:	Mary Hackley, wife of James Hackley - 30 s. together with estate she has received already
Dau.;	Eleanor Silman, wife of Joseph Silman, L10 which shall arise from the sale of that part of my lands not lent to my wife, "to be deposited in the hands of son William Freeman and by him contributed to her use as he shall think most convenient."
Sons:	William and James - equally divide 1/3 of proceeds from public auction of land not lent wife above.
Sons:	Garrett and Nathaniel - 1/6 of monies arising from the sale of the lands above mentioned
Gr.son:	Gollop Freeman (alias Duncan) - 1/6 part of monies mentioned above
Dau.:	Elizabeth Fletcher, wife of John Fletcher - 1/3 part of monies mentioned above, except L10 to be deducted for Eleanor Silman as bequeathed above.

Estate "lent" to wife should be disposed of in the following manner after her death: 1/7th part divided equally between all the surviving children of daughter Mary Hackley and residue to be equally divided between

Sons:	four sons: William, James, Garrett and Nathaniel and two daughters: Elizabeth Fletcher and Eleanor Silman.

Residue of estate not bequeathed to be divided as follows: 1/7th part to surviving Children of dau. Mary Hackley and remainder between four sons and two other daughters.

Exors:	Sons, William and James and wife Margaret
Signed:	James Freeman, Sen'r.
Wit.:	James Routt, William Williams, Sam'll. Wharton, Jun'r.
Proved:	25 June 1792, by o. of James Routt, William Williams and Samuel Wharton, Jun'r. William Freeman, James Freeman and Margaret Freeman made oath and with John Blackwell, Samuel Wharton and William Williams as securities granted certificate to obtain probate.

<u>Page</u>
230:                 JOHN WRIGHT (Inventory)
                 Court order dated February 1792
App'd by: W. M. Bradford, John Weaver, Tilman Weaver
No total.
Ret.:   25 June 1792

<u>Page</u>
231:                 STEPHEN TOLLE (nuncupative Will)
                 Made: 12 October 1791
Told to: Sam'l. Pearle, George (X) Tolle, Francis
         Murray - 9 October 1791.
Wife: Anne Tolle - all estate until "son George
         come of age, at whch time, a Horse, Saddle
         & Bridle .. be given him. Also he expected
         his Wife was with Child, which Child should
         have a Horse, Saddle and Bridle of the same
         Value. Negroes. He also appointed George
         Tolle & Enoch Murray to conduct her affairs
         in here, & Uriall Crosby & George Crosby,
         in case she removed to Nolachucky or jointly
         together with herself, with Privilege to sell
         the Waggon to purchase Land for his Wife Anne
         Tolle, to settle upon with such other property
         as they think best, for her Removal & settle-
         ment in that Country."
Wit.:   Wm. Hale
Proved: 25 June 1792 by o. of Samuel Pearle, Frances
         Murry. Anna Tolle, George Tolle and Enoch
         Murray, who made oath, with Samuel Pearle and
         Hugh Chinn, their securities, were granted
         certificate to obtain probate.

<u>Page</u>
232:                 WILLIAM YOUNG (Inventory)
                 Date: 21 March 1792
App'd by: D. Floweree, Sen'r., John Barker, Geo. Glascock.
No total.
Ret.:   25 June 1792

<u>Pages</u>
233-236:   ROBERT EMBREY (Division of Estate)
                 Date: 12 April 1792
Div. by: John James, Joseph Blackwell, Jr., John Shumate
Details: Divided between sons: Robert and Thomas Em-
         brey and grandson Robert (son of Charles,
         dec'd.). The division contains a plat by
         James Routt, deputy surveyor of Fauquier
         County. The land divided was on Summer
         Duck Run and where it divided to become the
         Horsepen Run and Hudnall Branch. Corner
         b

boundaries were: "Carters now Capt. Peter
Grant's." Chain carriers: Thomas Embry, Jun'r.
and William Embry.

Ret.:   25 June 1792

Pages
238-239:   WILLIAM STEVENSON (Administrator's Account)
                  Date: 24 September 1791
Adm'rs.: James Stevenson and Marthy Stevenson
Details: TO CASH PAID: (1791): Dr. Charles Waterhose
          for medesens (sic - medicines ?) & attendance;
          Jacob Hunt; Joseph Shipp, Sen'r.; Bayly
          Johnson; Peter Hansbrough for schooling;
          Land lord for rent; the Reven'd John Monroe
          for preaching the funerall sermon - 6 shillings;
          John Hickman; John Haus; John Shipp; Exekill
          Norman; Mr. Pickett & Co.
          BY CASH OF: Capt. John Ashby.
Ex'md. by: John Thos. Chunn, Wm. Smith, Thos. Massie,
          16 June 1792
Ret.:   23 July 1792

Pages
239-240:   JAMES FREEMAN, SENIOR (Inventory)
                  Court order dated 25 June 1792
App'd by: Peter Bowmer, Charles Duncan, James Routt.
Total Eval.: L242.10.0
Ret.:   23 July 1792

Pages
241-242:   EDWARD NEWGENT (Administrator's Account)
Admrx.:   Elizabeth Newgent
Details: TO: Gavin Lawson; Lawson & Dunbar; James Withers;
          Charles Garner; James Sharpe; James Dodd;
          Robert Henson; George Kemper for making Coffin,
          15 shillings; Funeral expense, 1 gallon Whis-
          key; Presley Garner; Joseph Sylman; Robert
          English; James Routt; Augustine Jennings; Sher.
          for taxes; John Withers; Joel Bruce; William
          Bradford; Col. John Blackwell.
Ex'md. by: John Blackwell, Thos. Bronaugh, Sr., 6 August
          1792
Ret.:   29 August 1792

Pages
242-243:   CATESBY WOODFORD (Will)
                  Date: 8 September 1791
Wife: Mary Woodford - all estate during her widow-

hood - to be sold after her decease and
divided among children.

Sons: "educated according to the circumstances of
my Estate & bound to some trade as they
arrive at sixteen or sooner if their Guardians
think proper."
   "Whereas I have acted as Exor. to the Will
of John Carter, dec'd. If my accounts with
that Estate & the estate of Chas. Carter of
Cleve, for whose Exor. I have been Agent for
many years, are not settled at the time of
my death, I desire that my Friend George
Buckner, Jr. do under take the settlement of
the same .. & to charge 10 per ct. for my
transacting the business, observing that the
Legacy left me by John Carter did not oblige
me in any wise to undertake the Execution of
his Will."

Exor.: Wife Mary Woodford, son Mark Woodford (when of
age), my friends Geo. Buckner, Jr., John and
William Woodford, Wm. Fitzhugh and Thos. Buckner, also guardians to children.

Signed: Catesby Woodford
Wit.:   Thos. Montgomerie, Yr. Johnson.
Proved: 24 September 1792. Thomas Montgomerie was
dead at this time and Younger Johnson was unable to attend, oaths were made by John Blackwell, Sen'r., Robert Randolph and Humphrey
Brooke. George Buckner, Jr. and John Woodford
refused to act as executors, "and the other
executors not appearing, on the motion of the
said George Buckner, Junior who made oath and
with Francis Whiting his security," cert.
granted him for obtaining letters of administration.

Page
244:    GEORGE ROGERS (Will)
        Date: 4 May 1792
Wife: Betty Rogers - all real and personal estate
during her natural life
Son: George - slave
Sons: George and Edward - the land I now live on -
1/5th part each of estate
Dau.:   Betty Newby - 1/5 part after her death "her
proportion of Negroes be sold and equally
divided among all my other children."
Dau.:   Mary Sanders - 1/5th part
Dau.:   Sally Matthews - 1/5th part of estate in trust

to "my Trust friends Ambrose Barnett, George
Rogers and Edward Rogers" for her and her
children during her natural life, the 1/5th
part shall be equally divided by the said
Barnett, George and Edward Rogers among the
children of my said daughter.

Exors.:	Sons George and Edward
Signed:	George Rogers
Wit.:	Samuel Steele, Henry Steele, Robert Gibson
Proved:	24 September 1792 by o. of Samuel Steele, Henry Steele, Robert Gibson. George Rogers and Edward Rogers made oath and with Martin Pickett as security, were granted certificate to obtain probate.

Page 245:

   HENRY TAYLOR (Inventory)
    Date: 8 September 1792

App'd by:	James Bailey, Wm. White, Dixon Robinson
Total Eval.:	L31.18.2
Ret.:	24 September 1792

Page 246:

   GEORGE CRUMP (Account of Sale)
    Date: 8 May 1789

Details:	The Moveables - L66.7.6
	The Negroes - L218.16.1
Ret.:	24 September 1792

Page 246:

   WILLIAM HARRISON (Division of Estate and
   allotment of Widow's Dower)
    Date: 29 August 1792

Div. by:	John Monroe, Joseph Chilton, Laur. Ashton
Details:	"... met at the dwelling house of Philip Mallory on Tuesday the 6 September 1792 and proceeded to allot to Jane Mallory, late Jane Harrison, her dower in the negroes recovered by Burr Harrison .. to Jane Mallory .. to Burr Harrison .. to Lucy Mallory late Lucy Mallory .. We then allotted to Jane Mallory as her part of her son William, Deceased .. (Negroes) .. on her paying the sum of L6.12.4, the one half to Burr Harrison the other Lucy Mallory."
Ret.:	24 September 1792

- 215 -

Pages
247-248:   CATESBY WOODWARD (or WOODFORD) (Inventory)
                    Date: 26 September 1792
App'd by: Robt. Randolph, Thomas Fitzhugh, Thos. Porter
Total Eval.: L477.11.7
Ret.:   22 October 1792 - This inventory and appraise-
          ment of the estate of Catesby Woodford ..."

Pages
248-249:   JAMES NELSON (Administrator's Account)
                    Date: 15 October 1792
Admr'x.: Betty Asberry
Exam'd by: Laur. Ashton, Jno. Monroe, Thos. Smith, who
          reported they find her indebted to the said
          Estate L116.4.7 which sum, upon closing the
          Ledger and other open Books appears to have
          been rec'd. and not accounted for...
Ret.:   22 October 1792

Pages
249-250:   JOSEPH BULLETT (Will)
                    Date: 17 November 1792
          Susannah Redd - five Negroes - during her life
          and afterwards to be equally divided between
          her children.
          Joseph Bullett Redd, son to Susannah, 7 Negroes,
          if he should die without heirs to go to his
          brother, Permercis Redd.
          Mary Steatad - 4 Negroes - during her life and
          afterwards to her children.
          Joseph Bullett Steatard, son to Mary, one
          Negroe, if he should die without heirs to go
          to his brothers and sisters.
          Priscilla Redd - 4 Negroes during her life and
          then to her children.
          Joseph Bullett Redd, son to Pricilla Redd, -
          3 Negroes, if he should die without heirs to
          go to his brothers and sisters.
Wife: Barshaba Norman, now Bullett, - 3 Negroes and
          after her death to go to Joseph Bullett Redd,
          son of Susanna, and Pricilla Redd.
          Negro John shall have liberty to stay on the
          plantation whereon I now live untill he
          arrives to the age of 18 and afterwards to be
          free.
Wife: All personal property for life, afterwards to
          go to Susannah Redd, Mary Stealard and Pris-
          cilla Redd. One third part of my land and

- 216 -

plantation. Joseph Bullett Redd, son to
Susannah Redd, to have remaining part of
plantation and wife's one third at her death.
Until he arrives at age of 18 the slaves and
land to be in the care of Thos. Conway and
Original Young.

Exors: Joseph Blackwell, Thomas Conway, Original
Young, John Young.

Signed: Joseph (his X mark) Bullett

Wit.: Peter Conway, Charles Coppedge, William Young,
O. Young

Proved: 24 December 1792 by o. of Original Young,
Peter Conway and William Young. Joseph Blackwell, Thomas Conway, Original Young refused
to take up execution and other executor not
appearing, Baersheba Bullitt made oath with
Philip Redd, Allen Redd & Randolph Stalliard
as securities, for L5,000, granted certificate
to obtain probate.

Pages
252-253: RODHAM KENNER (Will)
Date: 5 June 1792

Dau.: Lucy - when she comes of age, 200 acres of land
whereon I now live, which I purchased of James
Markham.

Dau.: Judith - the ballance of the land whereon I
now live and as much of my other tract of
land left me by my father whereon Moses Harrill
now lives as will make her up 200 acres.

Son: Lawrence - all the rest of my land, that I have
not already given to him. And with dau. Judith
to have their estate when they marry or come
of age.

Children: Lucy, Lawrence and Judith - when they come of
age - all my Negroes and movable estate to be
equally divided between them. It is my desire
that my son Lawrence at ten years old shall be
given up to his uncle Rodham Kenner if he in-
clines to take him, to be put by him to a well
Instructed Seminary of learning where he may
be well Ingrafted in the french language only
and the principles of the Mathematicks ...

Exors: Rodham Kenner, Sam'l. Blackwell and Judith
Kenner.

Signed: R. Kenner

Wit.: Sam'l. Blackwell, James Seaton, Jonathan Brown

- 217 -

Proved: 28 January 1793 by o. of Jonathan Brown and
James Seaton. Judith Kenner, the Executrix
therein named, made oath, and with Rodham
Kenner and Wily Roy her security, granted
certificate to obtain probate.

Page
254:
JAMES HEADLEY (Will)
Date: 11 December 1792
Wife: Lucy Headley - all my estate during her natural
life or widowhood but if she remarries to have
1/3 and the rest tobe equally divided between
my children.
Father and mother: not to be interrupted during both
their lives, to live in quiet possession at the
place they now live.
Exors: friends Eppa Timberlake, William Day and John
Cooke
Signed: James Headley
Wit.: John Cooke, James Ready, William Day
Proved: 28 January 1793, by o. of John Cooke, James
Ready and William Day. John Cooke and William
Day. John Cooke and William Day, with Joseph
Blackwell their security, granted certificate
to obtain probate.

Page
255:
STEPHEN TOLLE (Inventory)
Date: 29 September 1792. Court order
dated June 1792
App'd by: Thomas Priest, Uriah Byrne (or Burns), William
Thomas, Edward Turner
Total Eval.: L172.5.1
Returned: 28 January 1793

Page
256:
GEORGE ROGERS, SENIOR (Inventory)
Date: 10 January 1793
App'd by: Samuel Steele, Thos. Ransdell, James Hath-
away.
Total Eval.: L564.1.0
Returned: 28 January 1793

Page
257:
GEORGE WASHINGTON WITHERS (Guardian Account
Date: 27 July 1791 (Court Order dated June
Court 1791)

Gdn.:   William Harris
Details: "... up to the end of the Year 1790, there
        is due to George Washington Withers, L45.14.4½"
Signed: John Blackwell, Thomas Bronaugh, Aug.
        Jennings, James Routt.
Ret.:   28 January 1793

**Pages
258-259:**   JOHN NELSON, SENIOR (Inventory)
            Date: 8 January 1793. Court order dated
            December 1791.
App'd by: Original Young, John Mauzy and Banj'm. Payne
No total. Sworn as true statement before John Blackwell,
        Jr., by Original Young, 27 January 1793.
Ret.:   28 January 1793

**Pages
260-261:**   SIMEON MORGAN (Will)
            Date: 10 November 1792
Son: Joseph - 162 acres being the plantation where-
        on I now live and part of a larger Tract of
        486 acres, to be taken off of the South end
        in such a manner as to include the House and
        improvements by a line running parallel to the
        south end line according to the desire of his
        Mother and my late wife whose the property of
        the aforesaid land was. A small Tract, 77½
        acres, in Fauquier County which I purchased
        from Mr. Joseph Blackwell. A tract, 200 acres,
        on the Pignut Ridge and adjoining the tract
        of 77½ acres.
Son: Charles - 1/3rd part of tract whereon I now
        live to adjoin his brother Joseph's on the
        North end, and to be laid off by a line runn-
        ing parallel to the end line according to the
        desire of his Mother and my late wife whose
        property it was. One featherbed and furniture.
Son: Simeon - the remainder of theabove tract. One
        cow and calf.
Son: Jeremiah - one feather bed and furniture - one
        cow and calf.
Dau.:   Sucky Clark - one cow and calf
Dau.:   Caty Bradford - one cow and calf
Gr.son: William Cockrum, son of dau. Rosey Cockrum -
        L10 cash.
Dau.:   Rosey Cockrum - 1 shilling cash
Son: Joseph - Negroes, one still and utensils, all

livestock, household and farming furniture
and utensils. If he should die without
heirs, Negro to go to son Charles and Simeon
to have all the rest of the property both
real and personal.

Exors.: Sons Simeon and Joseph
Signed: Simeon Morgan
Wit.: Hugh Bradley, Geo. Carter, Wm. Carter
Proved: 25 February 1793, by o. of Hugh Bradley and
William Carter. Simeon Morgan, Jr., with
Charles Marshall as security, granted cert.
to obtain probate.

Pages
263-264:   JOSEPH SMITH (Will) of Parish of Leeds
            Date: 6 January 1793
Son: William - 200 acres of the tract I now live on,
at the upper end of the said tract.
Dau.: Mary Burdett - Negroes
Dau.: Hannah Ball - Negroes
Son: John - Negroes, wearing apparel, saddle & bridle,
one chest that was my Father's
Son: Rowley - Negroes
Son: Enoch - Negroes
Dau.: Jane Porter - Negroes
Dau.: Lucy Pepper - Negroes
Gr.son: Abner Smith - Negro, horse, bridle and saddle,
gun that was my Father's and one rasor that
was his father's, colt that my Black mare is
now with fold by Mr. Gray's horse, son John
Smith to take care of Grandson and keep him
and all that is herein given him until he
shall arrive to the age of 21 years.
Sister: Jean Owings - L10 and released from all debts
due devisor
Gr.dau: Ruth Smith - Negro and colt
Gr.dau: Wilhalmina Smith - Negro and colt
All remainder of propety to be equally divided
between following children: Mary Burditt,
Hannah Ball, John Smith, Rowley Smith, Enoch
Smith, Jean Porter and Lucy Pepper.
Exors: Sons Rowley Smith, John Smith and son-in-law
John Porter
Signed: Joseph Smith
Wit: William Dulin, David Ball, Wiiliam D. Darnall,
Benjamin Ball, Wm. (X) Ridding.
Proved: 25 February 1793 by o. of William Dulin, David

Ball and William D. Darnall. Rowley Smith
and John Porter, with William Pickett,
Joseph Taylor, Thomas Porter, William Ball
and John Smith their securities, granted
certificate to obtain probate.

Page
266:

FRANCIS MANUEL (Will)
Date: 6 September 1792

Dau.:   Abbe Manuel - all my Stock, personal property
Exors: daughter and her son, Zachariah Manuel
Signed: Francis (his X mark) Manuel
Wit.:   Wm. Stuart, Wm. Horton
Proved: 25 February 1793 by o. of William Stuart and
          William Horton. Abbey Manuel, with William
          Horton her security, granted certificate
          to obtain probate.

Pages
267-268:

ANDERSON COCKRELL (Inventory)
No date. Court order dated: February 1792

App'd by: William Ball, John Cooke, John Porter
Total Eval.: L46.7.6
Ret.:   25 February 1793

Page
268:

WILLIAM BROADHURST (Inventory)
Date: 21 May 1792

App'd by: John Edmonds, Kimble Hicks, Hezekiah Shacklett
Total Eval.: L67.2.7
Ret.:   25 February 1793

Pages
269-270:

JAMES HEADLEY (Inventory)
No date. Court order date: January 1793

App'd by: Daniel Shumate, John Smith, Enoch Smith
Details: 1 Englis Dictionary; 1 Docter's Book; 4 old
          Books; A percell of old Books.
Total Eval: L95.8.0
Ret.:   25 February 1793

Pages
270-271:

SMITH JOHNSON (Inventory)
Date: 16 February 1793

App'd by: John Dearing, Joseph Smith, John Morehead, Sen'r.
Total Eval.: L263.5.0
Ret.:   25 February 1793

Page
272:
          CHARLES WATERHOUSE (Administrator's Bond)
          Date: 27 March 1793
Admr.:   Joseph Chilton
Bondsman: Thomas Keith
Justices: William Pickett, Edward Digges, William Hale
         and Samuel Blackwell, Gent., Justices of the
         County of Fauquier.
Ret.:   27 March 1793

Page
273:
          CHAMP CORAM (Administrator's Account)
          Date: 12 March 1793
Admr.:   Richard Coram
Details: Balance of L28.4s.8d. to be divided in ten
         parts - TO: Richard Coram, Champ Coram, Sarah
         Coram, Elizabeth Coram, Catharine Coram, Sen'r.
         Mary Coram, Catharine Coram, Jun'r., Jane
         Coram, Auster Coram Elias Patton, William Coram -
         each L2.16.5½, except the last two, who received
         L2.16.6.
Signed: Sam'l. Blackwell, John Goldsmith
Ret.:   22 April 1793

Pages
274-275:
          GAYTON SETTLE (Administrator's Account)
          Date: 14 March 1793
Adm'r.: William Settle
Exm'd. by: Joseph Blackwell, Wm. Edmonds, Jr., Wm.
         Horner. Sworn to before Martin Pickett.
Details: TO: (10 Jan. 1786) Colo. John Blackwell, Doctor
         Horner, Thos. Keith, Kemper, Geo. Jennings,
         Wm. Bryan.
Ret.:   23 April 1793

Pages
275-276:
          WILLIAM YOUNG (Administrator's Account)
          Date: 10 April 1793
Adm'r.: Joseph Jeffries
Details: TO: (August 1792) Anthony Owsly his wife's
         Legacy; Sept. 1792 - Anthy Owsly per Order
         of Thomas Smith his Legacy; ferry'g to George
         Town & inspection 2 hhd. Tobo.; Benjamin
         Bronaugh. 9 Nov. 1792 - John Bronaugh Shff.;
         Joseph Withers Shff., Charles Marshall.
         BY: 1793 - Aaron Grigsby, Hezekiah Rutter;
         Isaac Cundiff; Aquilla Davis; William Ellett;

- 222 -

Edward Shacklett, James White; John Robinson;
John Feagen; David Scofield; Edwin Furr; Benj.
Carpenter; Rodham Kenner.
Em'd by: Wm. Hale, Jno. P. Harrison
Ret.: 23 April 1793

Pages
277-278:   RODHAM KENNER (Inventory)
               Date: April 1793
App'd by: John Blackwell, Jun'r., Thomas Raley
Total eval.: L499.5.0
Ret.:   24 June 1793

Page
279:           FRANCIS MANUEL (Inventory)
               Date: 20 March 1793
App'd by: Wm. Foote, Henry D. Hooe, John Hogain; sworn
          before Wm. Stuart.
Total eval.: L40.10.0
Ret.:   24 June 1793

Page
280:           IGNATIUS WEST "of the County of Spotsyl-
               vania" (Will)
               Date: 16 September 1791
Dau.:   Mary Hanor - L17.2 in the hands of Mr. Harmon
          Hanor (her father-in-law) which is justly due
          me, in part of per portion with the rest of my
          children.
Children: (not named) - residue of estate to be equally
          divided, except --
Dau.:   Elizabeth Bolling - I desire she may have her
          proportion in Clothing, etc.
Exor.:   son, Benjamin West
Signed: Ignatius West
Wit.:   P. Grant, Lott Hackley, Robt. Stringfellow
Proved: 22 July 1793, by o. of Peter Grant, Lott
          Hackley and Robt. Stringfellow. Benjamin West,
          with Peter Grant and John Blackwell, Jun., his
          securities, granted cert. to obtain probate.

Page
281:           JOSEPH MARTIN, SEN'R. (Will)
               Date: 4 November 1791
Son: youngest son, Benjamin - 72 acres of land I
          now live on.
Son: eldest son, "John Martin deceased Heir Enoch

& all my sons & daughters" - livestock and personal property.

Wife: (not named) - all property, real and personal during her life, except she marry.

Exors: friends Katharine Martin, wife, and Charles Martin.

Signed: Joseph (his X mark) Martin

Wit.: Jno. Fletcher, Joseph Martin, Hosea Martin

Proved: 22 July 1793, by o. of John Fletcher, Joseph Martin, Hosea Martin. Catherine Martin and Charles Martin, with John Martin their security granted cert. to obtain probate.

Page 283:

THOMAS FLETCHER (Will)
Date: 3 November 1792

Son: John - all and every of the effects belonging to me, conditionally, that is to take care of his Mother, brothers & sisters, and to act and do for them in every respect as if I myself were present, and if anything should remain to be equally divided amongst my children.

Exors: Richard Fletcher, John Fletcher and Thomas Fletcher

Signed: Thos. (his X mark) Fletcher

Wit.: John Dawson, Thos. Ball, Rich. Fisher, Wm. Pinchard.

Codicil: That nothing is to be bothered during Wife's life.

Wit.: Samuel Blackwell, Peter Kemper, Edward Morrison, R. Fisher.

Proved: 22 July 1793, by o. of John Lawson and Richard Fisher and Codicil by o. of Samuel Blackwell and Richard Fisher. John Fletcher, with Benjamin Holtzclaw, his security, granted cert. to obtain probate.

Pages 284-285:

JOSEPH DUNCAN (Will)
Date: 13 February 1792

Wife: Lydia - Negroes, plantation whereon I now live during her natural life, and no longer - 328 acres - all estate, real and personal.

Children: Joseph, Myrna Mauzy, Rose Withers, Hannah Porter, Housen, Mary Wright, dec'd. - Negroes, heretofore given them.

Son: Housen - after death of wife - plantation
of 328 acres - remainder to be sold and
money equally divided between dau. Lydia
Obannon, son Joseph Duncan, dau. Myma
Mauzy, dau. Rose Withers, dau. Hannah Porter,
and son Housen Duncan.

Exors: Sons, Joseph and Housen Duncan, sons-in-law
John Obannon and John Mauzy.

Signed: Joseph (his X mark) Duncan

Wit.:   John Kerr (x), Peter Kemper, James (x) Parr,
John Downing.

Proved: 23 September 1793 by o. of John Kerr and James
Parr. Howsen Duncan and John Obannon, with
Eppa Timberlake and John P. Harrison their
securities, granted cert. to obtain probate.

Page
286:          THOMAS FLETCHER, SEN'R. (Inventory)
               Date: 21 September 1793

App'd by: Aaron Fletcher, Benj'n. Holtzclaw, Rich'd.
Fisher.

Total Eval.: L57.4

Ret.:   23 September 1793

Page
287:        _____ ASBERRY (Dower)
          No date.
Allottment made by John O'Bannon, George
Glascock, Joseph O'Bannon, Charles Metcalf.

Details: "... allotted to Jane Asberry her Dower of
Lands as follows begining at William Leaks
Corner in Reuben Triplett's line running
with said line as many poles as will include
the Dwelling House and 75 acres of Land by
running a straight line to Scott's line."

Ret.:   23 September 1793

Page
287:        BENJAMIN NELSON (Guardianship Account)
           Date: 3 August 1793

Gdn.:   John O'Bannon

Exm'd by: Joseph Blackwell, Septimus Norris, William
Ball, Jr.

Ret.:   23 September 1793

Page
288:        LOTT LUTTRELL (Guardianship Account)
           Date: 20 September 1793

Gdn.:   Original Young, gdn. of Lott Luttrell, orph.
            of Michael Luttrell, dec'd.
Exm'd by: Samuel Blackwell, John Blackwell, Jr.
Details: TO: (1787) "Cuth. Bullett for his Oppinion
            on yr. Fathers will by myself Robt. & John
            Luttrell," Diniah Luttrell yr. Mother for
            your support; Mr. Henderson's store; Hen.
            Lee yr. tenant. (1793) Mr. Jas. Smiths
            store Dumfries; paid you at Fauq. Court
            House to carie you out to Patrick County.
            BY: (1784) Robt. Luttrell; (1788-91) by
            O. Young of Hen. Lee.
Ret.:   23 September 1793

Page
289:                    WILLIAM CHILTON (Division)
                        Date: 2 January 1792
Divided by: Ambrose Barnett, Thos. Ransdell, George
             Rogers, Jun.
Details: TO: Orrick Chilton - Negroes
             Susanna Chilton - Negroes
             William Chilton - Negroes
Ret.:   23 September 1793

Pages
290-291:   CHARLES CHILTON (Inventory)
                        No date.
App'd by: Ambrose Barnett, George Rogers
Total eval.: L1014.0.0
Ret.:   23 September 1793

Pages
291-292:   JOHN CHILTON (Division)
                        Date: 12 December 1788
Div. by: Ambrose Barnett, George Rogers, Thos. Sanders
Details: TO: Thomas Chilton - Negroes
             Joseph Chilton - Negroes
             Lucy Chilton - Negroes
             George Chilton - Negroes
             Nancy Chilton - Negroes
Ret.:   23 September 1793

Pages
292-293:   THOMAS GLASCOCK (Will)
                        Date: 1 July 1793
Wife: Agatha - all estate during her natural life
Signed: Thomas Glascock
Wit.:   Charles Dulany, Lucey Fishback, Elizabeth

Cunningham
Proved: 23 September 1793 by o. of Charles Dulany,
            Lucy Fishback and Elisabeth Cunningham.
            George Glasscock, with John Obannon his
            security, granted cert. to obtain probate.

Pages
293-294:   JOSEPH MARTIN (Inventory)
                    No date.
App'd by: Thos. Porter, Samuel Porter, Samuel Fisher
Total eval.: L137.6.1
Ret.:   23 September 1793

Page
294:            JOHN HATHAWAY (Administrator's Account)
                    Date: 19 September 1793
Admr'x.:   Mrs. Sarah Hathaway
Details: TO: 1786 - Colo. Chilton. BY: (1786-1793)
            Enoch Withers for taxes; H. Brooke; Doctr.
            Horner; Jno. Lathy; Wm. Elliott for making
            coffin - L1; Jno. Obannon; Jno. Dyer; Thos.
            Glasscock; Martin Pickett; Aaron Drummond;
            Jno. Sinclair; Charles Dulany; Jno. Blackwell;
            Benj'n. Hannibal; Geo. Glasscock.
Exm'd. by: Jno. P. Harrison, Laur. Ashton
Ret.:   23 September 1793

PAGES
295-296:   IGNATIUS WEST (Inventory)
                    Date: 12 August 1793
App'd by: Lott Hackley, Robt. Stringfellow, William
            Jones.
Total eval.: L181.3.0
Ret.:   23 September 1793

Pages
296-297:   URSULA ALLEN (Will)
                    Date: 12 August 1789
Father: James Withers of Stafford County - slaves
            "from him to deceased" to be joined with
            those of her late husband and to be equally
Sons: divided between sons: William, James, Joseph
Dau.:   Allen and dau. Ann Bradford - according to
            her husband's will.
Dau.:   Ann Bradford - all my Wearing apparel - side
            saddle
Gr.son: Baldwin Bradford - colt 2 years old
Sons: Thomas, Joseph, James Allen and dau. Ann

Bradford - personal estate to be equally
divided.

Daus.-in-law
and gr.son: Widows of late sons, John and William
Allen, Armistead Minor - 40 shillings each
and proceeds from sale of land in Culpeper
County at the Great mountains.

Sons & dau.: to have residue from above sale
Son: Thomas Allen - whatever money or Tobacco
"due me at my decease for the hire of Negroes."

Exors: Sons, Thomas, James & Joseph Allen
Signed: Ursula (her X mark) Allen
Wit.: Wm. Grant, Major (his M mark) Dillard, Wm.
Grant, Jun'r.

Proved: 23 September 1793 by o. of William Grant, Jun.
Thomas Allen made oath and together with
Joseph Allen his security, entered into bond
for $2,000, cert. granted him for obtaining
a probate.

Pages
298-302: JAMES NELSON (Estate Account)
No date

Admr.: Mrs. Elizabeth Asberry
Exm'd. by: Laur. Ashton, Thos. Smith, Robert Allison,
Joseph Chilton.

Details: TO CASH REC'D. OF: Moses Cummins, Jno. Moffett,
Jno. Sharham's yearly wages; Wm. Body's wages
for year; Sam'l. Grigsby; Jno. Obannion; Jno.
Grigsby's order on Mr. Nelson Merch; Wm.
Grigsby by Jos. Nelson; Wm. Phillips; Isaac
Cundiff; Dan'l. Floweree; Jas. Magraw; Thos.
Watts; Wm. Obanion; Wm. Norris; Henry Parker;
Jno. Eliott; Jno. Waver; Daniel Brown; Wm.
Hotton; Bryant Obanion; Honor Haley; Minor
Winn; Jno. Keith; Mary Eliott; Jno. Stewart;
Peter Cornhill; Wm Harrison; Standley Single-
ton's note of hand payable the 15th April 1772;
Glasscock; Wm. Ford; Wm. Ball; Jno. Nevil; Jno.
Rust; Lewis Eliott; Lewis Woodyard; Jno.
Barker; Jos. Obannion; Jas. Nevil; Anderson
Cockrel; Wm. Bullett for so much of S. Bullett;
George Gibson; Thos. Ransdell; Archibald Allen;
Jas. Wright; Wm. Kenton's order on Montgomerie;
Wm. Eliott; Jno. Duncan; Wm. White; Wm.
Barbee; Chas. Taylor; Mark Kenton's order on
Mr. Neldon; Wm. White; Wm. Hawkins; Joseph

Bailey for so much pd. John Likely. Total:
L407.8.6¼.
BALANCES DUE FROM: Thos. McCoy; Burr Harrison;
Jno. Cummins; Jno. Moffett; Jno. Davis; Thos.
Keith;; Sam'l. Obanion; William Lane; Jas.
Duncan; Wm. Hambrick; Thos. Obanion; Henry
Dawson; Wm. Grigsby; Wm. Philips; James
Magraw; Jno. Fishback; Thos. Watts; Jno.
Waddle; Henry Allen; George Glasscock;
Humphrey Brooke; Henry Peyton; Thos. Marshall;
Martin Pickett; Daniel Brown; George Canard;
David Barton; Jeremiah Redman; Mark Kenton,
Sen'r.; Wm. Pickett; Richard Oldham, Jr.;
Murtley McCoy; John Keith; James Siers; Charles
Rector; Jos. Taylor; Wm. Ball; Joseph Evins;
Thos. Mackey; Sam'l. Blackwell; Jno. Rilay;
James Wright; Jno. Pepper; Lewis Eliott; Robt.
Ashby; Jno. Williby, Jun.; George Oldham;
Thos. Eliott; Uriah Squiers; Thos. Harrison;
Moses Morgan; Wm. Ransdell; James Cummins;
Wm. Bullett; Peter Glasscock; Henry Moffett;
George Bennett; Stephen Conner; George Ford;
William Blackwell; William Brown; William
Hutchison; Rich'd. Rixey; James Gray; James
Wright; Alexander Mcpherson; Wm. Nelson; Wm.
Strawther; George Farrow; Simon Cornwell;
Dan'l. Rector; Thos. Nelson; Edward Fielding;
Wm. Morgan; Jno. Harmons; Charles Taylor;
Robert Hall; Wm. Lake; Jno. Eliott; George
Howell; Peter Cornhill; Jno. Parker; Jno.
Siers, Jr.; Wm. Hawkins; Thos. Hughes; Joseph
Baisey; Vincent Lake. Total: L227.8.2½

Ret.: 23 September 1793

Pages
303: ROSANNAH HURST (Will)
Date: 17 October 1793
Son: Henry - lot and plantation where I now live
Dau.: Elisabeth Thompson (husband, Jesse Thompson) -
1 shilling sterling.
Dau.: Mildread Markwell (husband, William Markwell) -
1 shilling sterling
Dau.: Nancey Hefferling (husband, Augustin Hefferling)
1 shilling sterling
Dau.: Delila Crim (husband, Joseph Crim) - 1
shilling, sterling

Dau.:   Jane Hurst - two feather beds and furniture,
               household goods, livestock, grain "and
               provision on Everything belonging to me
               that can be found after my Death."
Signed: Rosannah (her X mark) Hurst
Wit.:   John H. Ferguson, Gracy Quesenberry, Salley
               (her x mark) Thompson
Proved: 28 October 1793, by o. of John H. Ferguson and
               Grace Quisenbury, witnesses. Henry Hurst, with
               John Gaunt as security, upon bond of $100,
               granted certificate to obtain probate.

Page
304:          GEORGE SULLIVAN (Division of Estate)
               No date.
Divided by: Wm. Sanford Pickett, Charles Metcalf, John
               Pickett.
Details: TO: Owen Sullivan - 2 slaves - other property
               valued to L45.14.5 and L10 cash.
               John Sullivan - 2 slaves, propety valued at
               L31.7.10 and L10 cash.
               Elizabeth Sullivan - 2 slaves, bonds to amount
               of L38.4.5 and L10 cash.
               Anne Sullivan - 2 slaves, bonds to the amount
               of L38.4.5 and L10 cash.
Ret.:   28 October 1793

Pages
305-306:   JOSEPH DUNCAN (Inventory)
               Date: 10 October 1793
App'd by: Thos. Bronaugh, John Kerr, Enoch K. Withers
Total Eval.: L728.3.8
Ret.:   28 October 1793

Pages
306-309:   WILLIAM BLACKWELL (Inventory & Division)
               Court Order dated - 25 September 1786
App'd. by: Jeremiah Darnell, Original Young, Ben Harrison
Details: A Parcel of Books, L3; Virginia Laws, 1 vol.,
               10 shillings.
Allotment: "To Celia Graham late the widow William Black-
               well, deceased, but now the wife of George
               Graham her dower": cash, plus "all that tract ..
               purchased by the said William Blackwell from
               John Wood, by deed bearing date the 16th
               September 1779 containing 130 acres on Town Run

adjoining the lands of George Crosby and
George Foote deceased. We allot this tract
of land for the Dower of Celia Graham in
lieu of her Dower in all the Lands of the
said Wm. Blackwell deceased and also in lieu
of 111 acres of Land decreed to her by the
High Court of Chancery dated 16th May 1791
as by deed of relinquishment hereunto annexed
will more fully appear."
Ret.:   28 October 1793

Page
310:            WILLIAM HEATON   (Inventory)
                No date.
App'd by: John Barbee, Nathan Ellis, John Smoot.
Total Eval.: L48.10.8
Ret.:   23 December 1793

Page
310:            ROSANNA HURST (Inventory)
                Date: 30 November 1793
App'd by: Nathan Warden, John Gaunt, John H. Ferguson,
          Elisha Warden.
Total Eval.: L33.11.8
Ret.:   23 December 1793

Page
311:            SPENCER RECTOR (Inventory)
                Date: 18 November 1793
No appraisers listed.
Total Evall: L142.5.1
Ret.:   23 December 1793

Pages
312-313:   JOHN DUNCAN (Will)
                Date: 4 April 1788
Son: John - 10 shillings sterling
Son-in-law: Benjamin Grigsby - 5 shillings sterling
Son: Williss - when he arrives to the age of 20
         years - all estate, real and personal, to be
         sold and equally divided "amongst my six
         children .. and my beloved wife Wilkey Duncan"
Sons &   Moses, Elias, Enoch, Williss, Milley,
Daus.:   Lucinda Duncan.
Exors: Son Mosses Duncan and Charles Duncan
Signed: John (his X mark) Duncan

Wit.: Charles (x) Duncan, Cossom Day, Margett (X) Williams

Proved: 23 December 1793, by o. of Cossom Day and Charles Duncan. Moses Duncan, with John Blackwell, Sen., his security, under bond of $6,000, granted cert. to obtain probate. Wilky Duncan, the widow, refused to take anything but one third.

Pages
313-314: JOHN RILEY "of Parish of Leeds" (Will)
Date: 21 January 1791
"... land purchased of Charles Williams and lately
Recovered of the said Williams and William
Alason in a suit in the County Court of Fauquier
be sold at the Discretion of my Executors ..
and the money arising .. to be applyed as
followeth ..:"

Son: Thomas - L50
Son: Hugh - L50
Son: Edward - L70
Son: John - L10
Son: George - L10
Son: Charles - 5 s.
Dau.: Catharine Darnal - L10
Dau.: Elizabeth Grear - L10 - cow & calf - one feather bed
Dau.: Letice Fennen - L10
Dau.: Mary Hill - L10
Gr.Son: Charles Riley (son of Charles) - L5
Gr. dau: Catharine Riley - L5
Gr. dau: Susannah Riley -(dau. of Edward) - L10, cow and calf now in her father's possession
Son: Thomas - "one half of my lot of Land (100 a.) whereon he is now living being Part of the Lot I am now Living one .."
Son: Edward Riley - "residue of my said lot"
Exors: Sons, Edward, Thos. and Hugh Riley
Signed: John (his X mark) Riley
Wit.: William Pickett, Francis Triplett, Reuben Bramlett, John (X) Riley, son to Thomas
Proved: 23 December 1793 by o. of William Pickett and Reuben Bramlett. Charles Marshall, with Simon Morgan and Aylett Buckner, his securities, in bond of $5,000, granted cert. to obtain probate.

Page
315:                    IGNATIUS WEST (Sale of Estate)
                          Date: 27 January 1794
Exor.:   Benj'n. West
Total Eval.: L200.16.2
Ret.:   27 January 1794

Page
316:                    HUMPHREY ARNOLD (Administrator's Account)
                          Date: 20 March 1792
Admr.:   Benjamin Arnold
Exm'd by: Joseph Blackwell, Thomas Roy, Wily Roy, James
           Stewart
Details: Clerks fee, L1.11.3; rum at sale, 2s.o.; Lawyer
           for advise, 6s.0.; Isaac Arnold, cost of 2
           suits pr. agreement of Heirs, L1.10.0
Ret.:   27 January 1794

Page
317:                    THOMAS GLASCOCK (Inventory)
                          No date.
App'd by: William Metcalf, Josiah Fishback, Philip Fishback
Total Eval.: L369.3.11½
Ret.:   27 January 1794

Pages
318-319:   BENJAMIN NEWHOUSE (Inventory)
                          Date: 14 November 1793
App'd by: William Hunton, Jr., Wm. Bradford, James Hunton
Total Eval.: L73.13.0
Ret.:   24 February 1794

Page
319:                   JOHN PETER KEMPER (Administrator's Account)
                          Date: 8 February 1794
Admr.:   Charles Kemper (also spelled 'Kamper')
Settled by: Martin Pickett, Joseph Blackwell
Details: TO: Lux, Boley & Russell; Neale Jameson &
           Co.; Peter Bowers; Thos. Lee rent; John
           Moffett; James Burdett; John Kerr; Jacob Button;
           John Mauzy; John Bradford; Benjamin Morgan;
           Ashton & Horner; Doctor Horner; Eppa Timber-
           lake; Josiah Fishback; Joseph Hawkins.
Ret.:   24 February 1794

Page
320:
          THOMAS RANSDELL (Inventory)
           Date: 8 January 1794
App'd by: David McNish, William Hunton, Jr., Thomas
        Hunton, Daniel Gray
Admr.:   Mr. William Ball
Total Eval.: L237.7.9
Ret.:   24 February 1794

Pages
321-322:
          JOSEPH SMITH (Inventory)
           Date: 25 February 1794
App'd by: John Cooke, John Taylor, Eppa Timberlake
No total.
Ret.:   25 February 1794

Pages
322-323:
          JOHN GRIGSBY (Division of Estate)
          Court Order dated: October 1792
Div. by: Little'n Adams, Jno. Edmonds, Geo. Adams
Details: Divided according to the deceased will with
        the residue divided between his three sons:
        Lewis, Bayles, Nath'a.
Ret.:   28 April 1794

Pages
323-324:
          JOSEPH HOLTZCLAW (Division of Estate)
          Date: 29 March 1794
Div. by: Charles Kemper, Nath'l. (X) Rector, Benjamin
        Ball, John Kemper, Jun.
Details: Catharine Holtzclaw, widow; Archibald Holtz-
        claw; Elizabeth Jeffries; Stephen Holtzclaw;
        Eli Holtzalaw; Agnes Payne; Frankey Hitt;
        Salley Holtzclaw.
Ret.:   28 April 1794

Pages
324-325:
          JOHN RECTOR (Division of Estate)
          Court Order dated: March 1794
Div. by: George Grey, Hez. Glasscock. (Plat on p. 325
        by French Flowerree)
Details: (1) "Courses of the widow's thirds ..." 20 a.
        houses and part of orchard. Marked "Quain-
        tance" on plat.
        (2) "Courses of Peter Lukins lot .. bounded
        by Quaintance and Ringo .. Hez. Glasscock ..
        57 acres.

(3) Courses of Bertice Ringo's lot ...
corner to Lukins and Quaintance .. 40 acres
(4) Courses of Sarah Rector's lot ..
corner to Ringo .. 60 acres.

Ret.:   23 June 1794

———————

The above was the result of the following suit in
Chancery, styled "Quaintance vs. Rector", dated 1793.
The Bill and Answer consists of one folded page and
the following is an exact copy:

"To the Worshipful Court of Fauquier in Chancery
now sitting Humbly complaining sheweth unto your
Worships your Orators, William Quaintance & Grace
Quaintance, that John Rector now deceased was siezed
at his death of a Tract of Land lying in Fauquier, but
died intestate leaving three children, Viz. Hannah who
has since intermarried with Burtis Ringo, Manna who has
since intermarried with Peter Lukins, & Sarah who is
an Infant under the age of 21 years who has since appointed Burtis Ringo her Guardian all of whom your
Orators pray may be made a Def't. that your Orator
William Intermarried with Grace the Widow & relict of
the said John Rector, & after the Defend'rs. had
intermarried all parties became anxious for a partition
of the land but was advised that Sarah being under age
no division could be legally made but by order of the
Court. The parties in conformity to this opinion came
to the Court House at the last Court the Defendant Sarah
in order for a division appointed Burtis Ringo her
Guardian, application was then made for an order of
Court for a division, which was rejected, they being of
opinion a suit in Chancery ought to be brought to
affect the same. To the end therefore that a Division
of the said Tract of Land may legally be made as all
parties are consenting to the same, may it please your
Worships &dc -- & to make such further or other order
& decree in the premises as is just & equitable.

"The Answer in Chancery of Burtis Ringo and
Hannah his Wife, Peter Lukins & Manna his Wife, &
Sarah Rector by Burtis Ringo her guardian -

"The Defendants admit that John Rector was at

the time of his death siezed of the Land in the bill
mentioned, that he died intestate & that the Comp't.
William has since intermarried with the Widow, &
consequently entitled to her Dower in the said Land.
They also admit that they were all anxious for a
division but was informed it could not legally be made
but by order of Court, they admit application was made
to Fauquier Court for that purpose which was rejected
the Court being of opinion a suit in Chancery should
have been brought for that purpose & Burtis Ringo was
then appointed Guardian for the Def'd. Sarah in order
to affect the division - These Defendants & therefore
perfectly willing that Com'r. should be appointed by
your Worships, for the division of the said Land
agreeable to Law & will ever pray &c.

Commissioners, George Glascock, Hezekiah & Gregory
Glascock."

Pages
325-326:   DORCUS HAMBLETON   (Will)
                  Date: 6 March 1794
Brother: Presley Hambleton - all property except L3
            cash owned by Henery Southard - to him "in
            consideration of his services to me in my
            present illiness."
Signed: Darkis (her X mark) Hambleton
Wit.:   Mary Sudduth (X), Leanner Sudduth, Seley
            Whit (X).
Proved: 23 June 1794, by o. of Mary Suddoth and
            Celia White. Presley Hamilton, with Edward
            Burgess as security in bond of $300, granted
            certificate to obtain probate.

Pages
326-327:   SIMON MORGAN   (Inventory)
                  No date.
App'd by: Turner Morehead, Wily Roy, William Barker
Total Eval.: L451.14.0
Ret.:   24 June 1794

Pages
327-328:   RUTH SMITH   (Guardianship Account)
                  Date: 19 July 1794
Gdn.:   Account of Ruitt Smith, orphan of Joseph
            Smith, Jun'r., with John Porter, her Gdn.

- 236 -

Details: (John Carter is named her guardian in the June 1790 account) Clothes, shoes, etc. 1790-1793. TO: Andrew Obanion for the estate; Jos. Smith, lawyers fee in suit against William Dulin; cash from Abner Smith in division of Negroes; John Dawkins for hire of slave; John Kemper for same; by Jos. Hudnald; John Turner; Jas. Barton.
Ex'md by: Joseph Blackwell and Charles Marshall
Ret.: 28 July 1794

Pages 328-329: JAMES BALL (Will)
Date: 20 February 1794
Wife: Nancy Ball - plantation, personal & real estate, during her life or widowhood
Children: Peggy Stevinson; Judy Ball; Lucy Ball; Shealtial Ball; Taliaferrow Ball; Elizabeth Ball; James Ball; John Ball; Nancy Ball and "the one that my dear wife is pregnant with."
Exors: Benjamin Stephinson and John Singleton
Signed: James Ball
Wit.: Joshua Singleton, Jesse Thompson, Jason Thompson, John (X) Rily
Proved: 22 September 1794, by o. of Joshua Singleton Jason Thompson, John Riley. Benjamin Stevenson, with Joshua Singleton and John Riley his securities in bond for $1,500, granted cert. to obtain probate.

Pages 329-330: WILLIAM ASBERRY (Inventory)
No date.
App'd by: John O'Bannon, Charles Metcalf, Joseph O'Bannon, George Glascock.
Total Eval.: L354.14
Ret.: 22 September 1794

Pages 330=331: WILLIAM ASBERRY (Allotment of Dower)
Date: 29 October 1793
Widow: Jane Asberry - personal estate
Allotted by: John O'Bannon, Chas. Metcalf, Joseph O'Bannon, George Glascock
Ret.: 22 September 1794

- 237 -

Pages
331-332:
JOHN BARKER (Administrator's Account)
Date: 4 June 1794. Court Order dated:
February 1788.
Admr.: Minor Winn
Details: 15 April 1784: 2 gallons Whiskey for the use
of the sale, 8 s.; John Brown as Cryer; pd.
Thos. Keith on Capt. Moffetts order; Col.
Elias Edmonds for Capt. Moffett; Nathan
Cochram; Maj. Floweree for Capt. Moffett;
Clerk's notes from Frederick Cty.; for
Lawyers fee at suit of Stuart; p. Samuel
Rust; By Wm. S. Pickett; by Jos. Jeffries
by Mcsamilliam Roberson; by John Mason for
rent; by Minor Winn.
Ex'md. by: John Thos. Chunn, John Ashby, John Edmonds
Ret.: 22 September 1794

Page
332:
JOHN BARKER (Administrator's Account)
Court Order dated: February 1788
Admr.: Joseph Donaphan
Details: "Acc't. of John Barker Dec'd. and John Moffett
with Joseph Donaphan, one of the admrs. of
John Barker, Dec'd."
Exm'd by: John Edmonds, John Thos. Chunn, John Ashby
Ret.: 22 September 1794

Pages
332-333:
JOHN BARKER (Will)
Date: 25 September 1794
Children: Eldest children, Elizabeth, Mary, Chloe -
slaves - when Chloe "arrives at the age of
18 years of Age" - feather bed and furniture
and horse.
Dau.: Elizabeth - side saddle
Daus.: Mary & Chloe - a new side saddle each
Dau.: Ann - Negro boy
Dau.: Milly - Negro girl
Dau.: Sarah - Negro girl
Wife: Sarah - all remainder of estate
Exors: John Glasscock and George Adams
Signed: John Barker
Wit.: John Monroe and Jno. (X) Rawlins
Proved: 27 October 1794, by o. of John Monroe and
John Rawlins. John Glasscock, with John
Monroe and John Rawlins as securities under

- 238 -

bond of $3,000, granted certificate for
obtaining probate.

<u>Page</u>
333:          ABNER SMITH (Guardianship Account)
            Dates: 1790-1794
Gdn.:   John Smith
Details: 1791: Cash to M. Pickett & Co.; John Porter;
        Enock Smith; Taylor.
Retn.: 27 October 1794

<u>Page</u>
334:          WILHELMINO SMITH (Guardianship Account)
            Date: 1791-1794
Gdn.:   Enock Smith
Details: 1791: To: William Horner; Andrew Obannon;
        Pickett & Blackwell
Ret.:   27 October 1794

<u>Pages</u>
334-335:   CAPT. JOHN ALLEN (Division)
           No date
Div. by: Peter Grant, George S. Blackwell, Lincfield
        Sharpe
Details: William Allen's estate - slaves
        James Allen's lot - slaves
        Benjamin Bradford's lot - slaves
        Joseph Allen's lot - slaves
Ret.:   27 October 1794

<u>Pages</u>
335-336:   URSULA ALLEN (Inventory)
           No date
App'd by: P. Grant, Lin Sharpe, G. S. Blackwell
Details: Some of the items were "sold at the Quarter
        in Culpeper & not seen by us, but an acct.
        of the sale returned us by the Executors."
Total eval.: L184.6.1½
Ret.:   27 October 1794

<u>Pages</u>
336-337:   JOSEPH SMITH (Executor's Account)
           Dates: 27 May 1793 - 1794
Exors.: Rowley Smith and John Porter
Details: TO: Lawyer Marshall - L6; John Bronaugh,
        Sheriff; to the Minister his yearly fee,
        L1.5.0; for funeral by consent of parties, L1;

- 239 -

William Pepper; James Lamkin; Enoch Smith;
Jane Owens her Legacy; William Reading,
Overseer; John Porter; Wm. Suddoth; Thornton
Buckner for Sarah Mann; Francis Brook, Clerk
of Court; William Ball; Wm. Smith; Frederick
Burditt; William Ball, Sen'r.; John Smith his
full proportion; Rowley Smith his full pro-
portion; Enoch Smith his full proportion;
John Porter his full proportion; William
Pepper his full proportion.
Settled by: Martin Pickett, Joseph Blackwell, Charles
Marshall.
Ret.:   27 October 1794

Pages
338-341:   JAMES D. SMITH (Inventory)
                Date: 20 October 1794
App'd by: Tilman Weaver, John Martin, John Herndon
Total eval.: L291.3.6 Note: From the list this was
            probably the contents of a store.
Ret.:   20 October 1794

Page
343:            WILLIAM WAITE (Administrators Account)
                Date: 15 December 1794
                Dates of Account: Sept. 1787-1791
Admr.:   Wily Roy
Details: TO: Cuthbert Bullett for advise; Ludwell
         Lee, suit of Bronaugh vs. Waite.
Exm'd. by: Joseph Blackwell, Thos. Digges, Charles
          Marshall
Ret.:   22 December 1794

PAGE
344:            JAMES BALL (Inventory)
                Date: 21 November 1794
App'd by: Joel Settle, John Rily, Joshua Singleton
Total eval.: L460.10.6
Ret.:   22 December 1794

Page
345:            JOHN LYNN (Will)
                Date: 18 August 1794
Sons: John and Lewis - tract of land I now live
         on .. John to have upper and including the
         dwelling house and the other buildings.

Son: Francis - L20
Children: Fielding, Thompson and Sukey Thomas - all rest
            of estate
Gr.dau.:   Jane West - L5 "to Buy her a suit of Clothes"
Exors.:   Sons Fielding, Thompson and Lewis
Signed: John (his X mark) Lynn
Wit.:   Charles Metcalf (X), James (X) Lawson, thomas
            Lawson.
Proved: 22 December 1794, by o. of James Lawson and
            Charles Metcalf. On 23 APril 1795 Peter Grant,
            with Charles Marshall and Joseph Chilton his
            securities, under bond for $2,000, granted
            cert. to obtain a letter of administration.

Pages
346-347:   JANE WAITE (Will)
                    Date: 1 April 1794
_____: Mr. Richard Eustace Beale - part of my Tract
            of Land, on which at present he resides -
            250 acres - bounded agreeable to the courses
            mentioned in a Deed of Lease for it formerly
            made and given to Mr. John Bronaugh dec'd.
Nephew: William Bronaugh, son of my brother William,
            and Mr. Willy Roy - remainder of ?my said
            Tract of Land (to wit) The part that I now
            live on.."
Slaves: "All the Slaves belonging to me (four) at my
            death, be liberated and forever hereafter
            free." Bob and Lucy - "the tenement now
            occupied by Mrs. Purciful, with 20 acres of
            Land adjoining .. for their life time ..
            then to go to Mr. Willy Roy and William
            Bronaugh - also one cow and calf and one bed.
_____: Eustace Beale - to pay debts and take all my
            stock & Household furniture
_____: Mrs. Margarett Beale - "my Shag cream case,
            with Six Tea Spoons, Tongs and Strainer."
Exor.:   friend, Capt. Thomas Gibson
Signed: Jane Waite
Wit.:   Jno. Fox, William Eustace, Jun'r., Igns.
            Luckett
Proved: 22 December 1794, by oaths of John Fox, William
            Eustace, Jr. and Ignatius Luckett. On 23
            February 1795, Thomas Gibson, with Richard E.
            Beale his security under bond of $1,000,
            granted cert. for obtaining probate.

Pages
347-349:   FRANCIS TRIPLETT (Will)
                     Date: 24 September 1794

Children: William, Hedgman, Robert, Betty Hedgman Triplett, Benedicte, Anne, Francis Amelia - 20,000 acres of Land which I am entitled to in the State of Kentucky, lying on the North fork of Licking .. to be equally divided.

Son: Robert - 1,600 acres in Kentucky "lying on the Ohio River."

Daus.:   Betty Hedgman Triplett & Benedite - 1,400 acres in Bourbon County, Ky.

Wife: Benedicte and two youngest daus.: Anne and Francis Amelia - 5,000 acres in Kentucky upon Cabbin Creek

Wife &
Children: dispose of 2,000 acres in Kentucky on Clear Creek - "also all my moveable estate of every Kind, which I may die possessed of except two Negroes to wit Cate & James and twelve silver tablespoons marked thus $_F^T_B$ THE said Slaves .. and the silver spoons I give and bequeath to my beloved Wife Benedicte .. and the money arising from the sale of moveable estate it is my desire shall be appropriated towards defraying the expense which may attend removing my family to the State of Kentucky."

Wife: Benedicte Triplett - money due from Joseph Smith for the sale of the Lease whereon I now live ..

Son: Robert - and daus.: Anne and Francis Amelia - 7,000 acres on Licking Creek in Kentucky.

Exors: Sons, William and Robert

Signed: Francis Triplett

Wit: Jos. Withers, Wm. Clarkson, James W. Wallace, John Gaunt, Charles Marshall

Proved: 26 January 1795, by o. of Charles Marshall and James W. Wallace. On 23 February 1795, Robert Triplett, one of the executors named .. who had been summoned to appear, and shew cause why he would not qualify, failed to enter into bond with security according to law, and upon the motion of Francis Payne who appeared to be a Creditor, and who together with Thomas Jett, Thomas Payne, Isaac Arnold, James Devers & William Payne, his securities .. bond of $2,500 cert. granted him to obtain letters of administration.

**Pages
349-351:**

THOMAS WITHERS (Will)
Date: 5 November 1794

Son: John - Negro, property in his possession,
"money due to me on Bond from my son,
Enoch Withers."

Sons: Matthew Keen Withers - Negroes, "beds with
the Furniuture belonging to it, " - residue
of stock after dau. Susanna Chinn take out
horse, 2 cows and their calves. Furniture,
after son, Joseph, takes his choice of
beds and furniture belonging thereto, to
be equally divided between Matthew Keen
Withers and Joseph Withers.

Son: William - Negroes, money he owes me

Son: Enoch - Negroes, sundry articles amounting
to L80.

Son: Benjamin - Negroes, also his Wife's share of
her Father's Estate which I purchased of him.

Son: Joseph - Negroes and his first choice of my
beds & the half of my Stock & Furniture

Dau.: Hannah Winn - Negro, L100 out of the Sale of
the Land which I am now at law with my Brother
William Withers for if the same shall be recovered.

Dau.: Betty Winn - Negroes - my warming pan - what
ever Money Capt. Minor Winn her Husband may
= owe me at my Death.

Dau.: Nancy Jordan - Negroes

Dau.: Sally West - Negroes

Dau.: Susanna Chinn - Negroes and roan horse, 2 cows
and calves, above mentioned

Gr.dau.: Hannah Winn (dau. of Betty Winn) - Negro girl
to be under the Direction of Capt. Minor Winn
till my said grand Daughter marries or comes
of age.

Servant: "my Mulatto Boy Roger alias Martin be bound to
a Shoemaker for the term of two years, or To
any other Trade at the Discretion of my
Executors .. after which he is to serve my
executors till he comes to the Age of 31 years
when I hereby declare him to be free for the
Rest of his life."

Servant: "my old Negro Woman Bess shall go to which ever
of my Children she shall Chuse.."

Children: to have money arising from sale of land "now
at Law with my Brother William Withers." First
offering it to him at 40 shillings per acre

and "the Mill at fifty pounds," deducting
the L100 to dau. Hannah Winn. Also money I
may recover of Mr. Isaac Hite Adm'r. of Mr.
James Buchanan dec'd.

Exors: Son William Withers and Capt. Minor Winn
Signed: Thos. Withers
Wit.: P. Grant, Benj. Bronaugh, Weathers Smith
Proved: 22 December 1794, by o. of Weathers Smith
and 26 January 1795 by o. of Benjamin Bro-
naugh. William Withers and Minor Winn, with
Thomas Keith, Charles Marshall, John Withers,
James Withers, their sec. on bond of $20,000,
granted cert. for obtaining probate.

Page
353: JAMES JOHNSON (Inventory)
Date: 11 October 1794
App'd by: James Wright, Tilman Weaver, John Herndon
Total eval.: L8.3.3
Ret.: 23 February 1795

Page
353-354: BENJAMIN ROBINSON (or ROBESON) (Admr. Acct.)
Date: 10 February 1795
Dates of Account: 22 Feb. 1785 - 21 June 1790
Exor: Dixon Robinson
Details: TO: Enoch Weathers; James Prim for your Stafford
Land; Thomas Anderson; Ann Masterson; William
White; Caty Campbells Legacy; William Roach;
Ann Mastersons Legacy; Nath'l. Robeson; Mr.
Murchett; Mrs. Nancy Martin.
Admr.: Nathaniel Robeson; Dixon Robeson, George
Robeson.
Exm'd by: Thomas Chilton, Ambrose Barnett, Wily Roy
Ret.: 23 February 1795

Pages
354-355: JOHN ROGERS (Will)
Date: 8 August 1794
Son: Henry - my lot and Lease of Land that I now
live on in during his life and to his wife
Sarah Rogers in during hir widowhood .. after
their death .. to my grandson John Rogers
ye son of Henry Rogers .. also 2 pewter dishes
and eight pewter plates and one pair iron
wedges.
Gr.son: John Rogers, ye son of Henry, - one small Cow
& calf and one Green Rugg.

Children: All ye rest of my Estate both within and
without doors I give .. to my four children,
to wit, Stephen Rogers, John Rogers, Mary
Rogers and Margarett Mason.
Exor: Son, Henry Rogers
Signed: John (his X mark) Rogers
Wit: Dan'l. Greenwood, James Dennis, Matthew Neale
Proved: 22 December 1794, by o. of Matthew Neale;
23 February 1795, proved by o. of James Dennis
and Daniel Greenwood. Henry Rogers, executor,
made oath with Augustine Jennings, his sec.,
with bond of $1,000 granted cert. to obtain
probate.

Page
356: SANFORD CARROL (Estate Account)
Admr.: John Obannon
Details: 28 January 1791 - pd. David Prunty his legacy
L14.0.4; 3 March 1795 - pd. Doc'r. Horner for
Physic, 6/0.
Exm'd: 4 March 1795 by John Monroe, L. Ashton, Wm.
Metcalfe.
Ret.: 27 April 1795

Page
357-358: JAMES WHEATLEY (Inventory)
No date.
App'd by: George S. Blackwell, Lincefield Sharpe, Charles
Martin
Total eval: L1788.12.4
Details: ½ doz. books - 15/0.
Ret.: 27 April 1795

Pages
358-359: JAMES WHEATLEY (Division of Estate)
No date.
Div. by: George S. Blackwell, Linsfield Sharpe, Charles
Martin
Details: For each child - L108, Widows dower, William
Wheatley, James Wheatley, Heathey Wheatley,
George Wheatley, Elizabeth Wheatley, Landon
Wheatley, John Wheatley, Mary Wheatley, Lawson
Wheatley, Lucy Crumps lot, Sukey Wheatley.
Ret.: 27 April 1795

Pages
359-360: JOHN ROGERS (Inventory)
Date: 13 March 1795

- 245 -

App'd by: John Dearing, Clement Norman, Joseph Morgan
No total
Ret.:   27 April 1795

Page
360:              ABRAM OLDAKER (Will)
                 Date: 10 December 1794
Wife: Hester - the Lot of land whereon I live, one
         sorrel horse & saddle, 2 cows, 5 sheep, one
         bed and furniture, one chest, 2 puter dishes
         and 6 plates
Children: All the rest of my property I give and be-
         queath to my eight children (not named)
Exor.:   wife Hester
Wit.:   Joseph Shultz, Samuel Taylor, Benjamin (X)
         Shultz.
Signed: Abram (his X mark) Oldakers
Proved: 27 April 1795, by o. of above witnesses.
         Hester Oldacre made oath and with Daniel Harris,
         her sec., granted cert. to obtain probate.

Pages
361-362:   JOHN BARKER (Inventory)
                 Date: 25 April 1795
App'd by: Thos. Adams, Josiah Adams, John Rawlings
Exor.:   John Glasscock
Total eval.: L683.1.0
Ret.:   27 April 1795

Page
363:              FRANCIS TRIPLETT (Inventory)
                 Date: 14 March 1795. Court Order
                 dated: February 1795.
App'd by: Rich'd Rixey, Henry Clarkson, Dickerson Wood
Details: One bond on Capt. Joseph Smith
Total: L154.70.4½
Ret.:   27 May 1795

Page
364:              FRANCIS TRIPLETT (Sale of Estate)
                 No date.
Details: Purchasers: Henry Clarkson, Joseph Withers,
         Thomas Triplett, John Smith, Robert Humes,
         Nicholas Lawler, Jesse Payne, Clem Billings-
         by, Francis Payne, Cr. Mr. Triplett by A.
         Ford To a Cryer, 12s., to 3½ gals. Whiskey
         15 s.

Signed: Francis Payne
Ret.:   28 May 1795

Page
365:          FRANCIS TRIPLETT (Administrator's Account)
Admr.:   Francis Paine (Payne)
Details: TO: 1795, Thomas Triplett for making coffin,
           L1.4.0; expenses to Prince William Court and
           Lawyers fee 4; lawyers fees at suit of
           Slaughter and one of Pritchett, Simon Fraysers
           Judgment.
Date: 28 May 1795
Exm'd by: Joseph Blackwell, Wm. Horner, Geo. Bastable
Ret.:   28 May 1795

Page
366:          JOHN McKENNEY (Will)
           Date: 24 January 1795
Son: Francis - one shilling sterling
Wife: Mary - one shilling sterling
Son: John - 200 a. land which is from the Date of
           the Lease Ninety nine years - 7 head of cattle -
           1 horse - 20 hogs - 4 sheep - all the household
           furniture.
____: Mary Cain - one shilling sterling
____: Elizabeth McKenney - one shilling sterling
____: Alice McKenney - one shilling sterling
____: Susanna McKenney - dau. of John McKenney, Jr. -
           one Negro wench Named Milly
Signed: John McKenney
Wit.:   Nimrod Utterback (x); Ezekial Davis, Daniel
           Carter (X).
Codicil: 24 January 1795 - named son, John McKenny,
           Executor.
Wit.:   Wm. Smoot
Signed: John (his X mark) McKenny, Sen'r.
Proved: 22 June 1795 by o. of Nimrod Utterback and
           Daniel Carter. John McKenney made o. with
           Aquilla Davis and Matthew Neale his securities,
           granted cert. to obtain probate.

Page
367:          WILLIAM SUDDUTH (Will)
           Date: 10 November 1785
Wife: Alse Sudduth - during her life the Tract of
           land plantation and house whare I now live -

stock of horses, stock of cattle, hogs,
household furniture and after her death -
"be sold and Eaqually divided Amongst the
whole of my Children now living or their
Representatives Except my Cubbart which I
give to Daughter Mary Sudduth after the death
of her Mother."

Exor: Son Francis Sudduth and George Sudduth
Signed: William (his X mark) Sudduth
Wit.:   Edward Settle, Benjamin Arnold, John (X)
           Forrister.
           N.B. The pewter my son Francis Sudduth &
           George has lent them ust come to appraisement.
Proved: 22 June 1795 by o. of Benjamin Arnold and
           John Forrister (they) also made o. that they
           saw Edward Settle (who is since dead) subs-
           cribe his name as a Witness. Francis Suddoth
           and George Suddoth, the Exors., made oath
           with Martin Porter their security and cert.
           granted them for obtaining a probate.

PAGES
368-369:   JEREMIAH DARNALL (Will)
                Date: 10 April 1795
Wife: Catherine - all my Estate both "rale and
           personal during her life"
Dau.:   Elizabeth Sinclor - tract of land whereon she
           now lives, 130 acres and 49 acres "joining
           the same whereon my son Joseph Darnall formerly
           lived" to her and her heirs forever.
Dau.:   Ann Weaver - L50
Son: Joseph - 300 a. "of my Kentucky land to be
           laid of in any convenient manner joining
           any two of the outlines."
Dau.:   Mary Russell - 300 acres "of Kentucky land
           joining the land given to my son Joseph"
Dau.:   Margaret Sinclor - 300 a. of my Kentucy land
           joining the land given to Mary Russell
Dau.:   Susannah Smith - 20 s. "the reason why I give
           her no more is because she is already pro-
           vided for."
Dau.:   Leannah Ashbey - 215½ a. "being part of the
           tract I sold to Josiah Fishback."
Dau.:   Caty Darnall - "all myland lying on the South
           west side of licking run it being part of the

tract of land whereon I now live" also
"the Tavern with five acres of land to be
laid of in such manner as to include all
the houses and gardin and join Colo'l.
Randolph line."

Dau.:   Rosamond Darnall - the house wherein I now
live and all the land lying on the North
East side of licking run except the five
acres given to my dau. Caty.

Daus.:   Rosamond and Caty - after the decease of my
wife that my daus. have full possession of
the lands devised to them. Also all "Negroes
stock of all kinds and household furniture
to be equally divided, except one negor Garl
named Silvey which I give to my grand dau.
Lucy Luess Ashby.."

Exor.:   friend James Wright - to sell "balance of my
Kentucky land and 100 acres of land lying in
Fauquier County and onthe Broad run Mountain."

Signed: Jeremiah Darnall

Wit.:   Tilman Weaver, John Martin, Henry Kerns

Proved: 22 June 1795, by o. of Henry Kerns, Tilman
Weaver, John Martin. James Wright made o.
with Tilman Weaver, John Martin and John Mauzy
his securities under bond of $10,000, and
granted cert. to obtain probate.

**Pages
370-371:**   ABRAHAM OLDACRES (Inventory)
           Date: 6 June 1795

Details: To account with Thomas McNutt

App'd by: John Dearing, James Foley, Joel Settle,
William Whitley

Total eval.: L130.13.3

Ret.:   22 June 1795

**Pages
371-372:**   ROBERT BERRYMAN (Inventory)
           Date: 2 April 1777

App'd by: Edward Humston, Augustin Smith, Edward
Mountjoy

No total.

Ret.:   22 June 1795

**Pages
372-373:**   JOHN WALLER (Inventory)
           Date: 2 May 1795

App'd by: George Lowry, Henry Lewis, Aaron Grigsby
Total eval.: L49.9.1
Ret.:   22 June 1795

Page
373:
                    JOHN WITHERS, SEN'R. (Division of Real Estat
                    Date: 25 February 1795
Div. by: Hancock Lee, Peter Routt, Augustine Jennings,
         Commissioners.
Details: ... appointed .. to lay off and divide a
          certain Tract or parcel of Land whereof John
          Withers, Senr. late of Stafford County died
          seized of. We the subscribers being first
          sworn in pursuance of the Will of the said
          John Withers proceeded .. in presence of
          George Withers one of the Exeros. named by
          the said John Withers, and John Mauzy the
          Surveyor of Fauquier to allot and lay off the
          aforesaid Tract of Land, or that part .. de-
          vised to William Withers .. described in the
          plat & survey .. hereto annexed .. 27 April 1795.
Desc. of Land: "Beg. at A, a Box Oak on the East side
          of Gibsons Road Corner to Bronaughs former
          purchase .. crossing the Walnut Branch .. White
          oak corner to James Parrs Land .. crossing
          Blackwells road .. Garners line by J. Kerrs
          fence, thence with Garners Patent lines ..
          488¼ acres & 12 poles .. agreeable to Welsh's
          Deed making a difference of 7 acres from this
          Survey.
Ret.:   22 June 1795

Page
374:
                    EDWARD NUGENT (Division)
                    Date: 21 November 1794
Div. by: Hancock Lee, Fauntleroy Dye, John Bronaugh
Details: "Agreeable to an order of Court to us directed
         we have Lotted to Edward Nugent his proportion
         of the Estate left by Thomas Nugent (sic)
         agreeable to his will & have given him Mingo &
         L21.17.6d. .. to be paid him out of the
         higher of the other Negroes."
Ret.:   28 September 1795. "This Division of the Estate
         of Edward Nugent deceased was returned and
         ordered to be recorded."

Pages
374-375: JEREMIAH DARNALL (Inventory)
          Date: 23 July 1795
App'd by: Tilman Weaver, John Martin, John Herndon
Details: Books L1.10.0
Total: L1099.3.0
Ret.:   28 September 1795

Pages
375-376: ROBERT ROGERS (Inventory)
          Date: 23 July 1795
App'd by: Wm. Clarkson, Aquila Davis, Matt Neale
Details: a small parcell of books - 10s.
Total eval.: L90.1.6
Ret.:   28 September 1795

Page
377:      JOHN PETERS (Inventory)
          Date: 29 July 1795
App'd by: James Wright, John Herndon, John Martin
Total eval.: L30.4.0
Ret.:   28 September 1795

Pages
377-378: JAMES ROUTT (Inventory)
          No date.
M. B. 1793-1795, p. 228, September Court, 1794: "Ordered
          that Charles Duncan, Cossum Day, Daniel Marr
          and James Withers or any three of them being
          first sworn do appraise the estate of James
          Routt, deceased and return the appraisement
          to the Court."
No total.
App'd by: Chas. Duncan, Daniel Marr, Cossam Day.
Ret.:   28 September 1795

Pages
378-379: THOMAS PRIEST (Will)
          Date: 15 February 1790
Wife: Sarah - use of all my Negroes and Moveables
          During the term of her Natural life and at
          her Decease to be disposed of as hereafter
          mentioned.
Son & Dau: Peter and Mary - the same part that the rest
          of my Children had when they left me before
          my Estate is divided any my Desire is that
          after they have got that part .. that my
          Estate shall be equally divided amoanghts

Item: all my Chrildren after the Decease of my wife.
            My desire is that my Negro Will and Negro
            Sarah shall not be parted if it can Possible
            be hoped.
Exors: wife Sarah Priest, son Thomas Priest
Signed: Thomas (his P mark) Priest
Wit.:   Richard Larrance, William Coppedge, Edward
            Larrance
Proved: 28 September 1795, by o. of Edward Laurence
            and William Coppedge. Sarah Priest and
            Thomas Priest, together with Joseph Blackwell
            and Ralph Murray, their securities in bond
            of $3,000, granted cert. to obtain probate.

Pages
379-380:   MARY KIDWELL (Will) of Parish of Leeds
                Date: 18 March 1795
Son: James Kidwell - one White face Cow call Joe
Son: William - one Negro Fellow call'd Peter
            Three Years to Commence from and after 1
            January 179six .. sold to the highest bidder
            & the money equally divided between the said
Dau.:   William Kidwell and my Daughter Dorcus Kidwell.
Item: after Geo. Thompson takes his part out of the
            present Crop the Balance to pay the rent &
            my Debts, the Rem'dr if any to be equally
            divided between the said William and Dorcus
Son-in-law: Geo. Thompson, Joshua Drummond and Noth
            Snape - the Remdr. of my Estate
Exors: Henry Peyton, Sen'r. and Henry Peyton, Jun'r.
Signed: Mary (her X mark) Kidwell
Wit.:   Wm. Fishback, Hezekiah Glasco
Proved: 28 September 1795 by o. of William Fishback
            and Hezekiah Glascock. Henry Peyton, Jr.,
            with Joseph Obannon his security in bond for
            $1,000, granted cert. for obtaining probate.

Page
380:            WINNIFRED BERRY (Inventory)
                Date: February Court 1795 - "Ordered
            that William Flowrence, Bartlett Leach,
            Thomas Leach, and James Pilcher .. appraise
            the estate of Winnifred Berry, deceased .."
            (Minute Book 1793-95, p. 274)
App'd by: Bartlett Leach, James Pilcher, Thos. Leach
Admr.:   Thomas Whiting

- 252 -

Details: John Griffiths bond for L8.17
              Mason Owens bond for L20
App'd by: Bartlett Leach, James Pilcher, Thos. Leach
Ret.:   26 October 1795

Pages
381-382:   THOMAS BROOKS (Will)
                    Date: 20 January 1792
Wife: Elizabeth Brooks - the whole of my Tract of
              Land Whereon I now live during her life or
              Widowhood and after her decease .. to be
              equally divided Betwixt my Three Sons:
Sons: Thomas, William & John - as follows: The 100
              acres I purchased of Joseph Conway shall be
              in a lot to itself, the other 200 acres be-
              longing to my old Tract shall be equally divided
              by a line extending across from Conways line
              to Blackwells formerly Browns .. son Thomas
              shall have his first choice.
Son: Thomas - horse called Britain - choice of
              bridle and saddle
Son: William - at his Mothers decease or when he
              comes of age, a Horse Bridle and saddle (to
              the amount of L10 cash)
Son: John - (same as above)
Daus.:   Mary and Dorcas - shall have an equal pro-
              portion out of my Estate at the day of Their
              Marriage or when they come of age, as my other
              daughters had at the time of their marriage.
Sons: Thomas, William and John - (same as above)
Wife: Elizabeth - all my Household Furniture and
              stock of every kind except such Legacies as
              before mentioned - after her decease to be
              equally divided among all my Children their
              Heirs and my three sons Thomas, William and
Daurs: John and my Six daughters: Elizabeth, Nancy
              Fox, Sally Linn, Winny Northcut, Mary Brooks
              and Dorcas Brooks.
Exors: Wife Elizabeth Brooks, friends Colonel John
              Blackwell and Peter Conway
Signed: Thos. (his TB mark) Brooks
Wit.:   Peter Conway, Joshua Tulloss, Rodham Tulloss
Proved: 26 October 1795 by o. of Peter Conway and Joshua
              Tulloss. Peter Conway and Elizabeth Brooks,
              with Thomas Keith and Thomas Brooks as securities,
              in bond of $3,000, granted cert. to obt. probate.

- 253 -

Pages
382-383:   JACOB RECTOR (Inventory)
                  Date: "Order dated June Court 1795.
                  William Turley, Joseph Jefferies, Henry
                  Rector and John Glascock .. appraise the
                  estate of Jacob Rector deceased .."
(Minute Book, 1793-1795, page 392)
Details: Parcel of old books, L0.10.0
App'd by: William Turley, Joseph Jeffirs, Henery Rector.
Total eval.: L101.8.1
Ret.:   26 October 1795

Page
384:              HUGH BRADLEY (Will)
                  Date: 21 October 1795
                  "Thisbeing my desire before witnesses that
                  my wife should hold in possession all my
                  Estate only that Richard my son is to stand
                  its Agent under her when he becomes of full
                  age .."
Signed: Hugh Bradley
Wit.:   Benjamin Arnold, James Sudduth, Peter Bashaw
Proved: 26 October 1795, by o. of Benjamin Arnold,
           James Suddoth, and Peter Bashaw. 25 January
           1796 - Celia Bradley, with Turner Morehead
           her security, in bond of $1,000 granted cert.
           to obtain probate.

Pages
384-385:   BRERETON JONES (Will) of the parish of
           Hamilton
                  Date: 9 August 1795
Friend: Sam Blackwell - 100 acres, the land he formerly
           bought of me beginning at corner of Hackley
           & Allen - strait line to Wm. Prims line - for
           him to dispose of to pay a debt due to Cunning-
           ham & Company which is by Replevy bond
Sons: Robert and Daniel - all the ballance of my
           land .. to begin the dividing line at ..
           town run in the line of Hackley & Allen ..
           strait line to Wm. Prims
Son: John Warner Jones - L40 - ballance of my
           Personal Estate except one cow and calf each
           to sons, Robt. and Dan'l.
Gr.Children: Daughter Molly Shumate's children - to be
           paid to them when they arrive to the age of
           18 years, after death of wife estate to be

- 254 -

```
              sold and put out at interest for them till
              they arrive at the age mentioned.
Sons:         Henry and William - land and personal estate
              formerly given them
Son-in-law:   Wm. Primm - land and personal estate formerly
              given him
Wife:         Lettice - land given Sam'l. Blackwell above,
              during her widowhood
Exors:        Wife Lettice and friend Sam'l. Blackwell
Signed:       Brereton (his X mark) Jones
Wit.:         Francis Simms, Thomas Chancellor, Presley Gill,
              John (X) Prim
Proved:       26 October 1795, by o. of Francis Simms, Presley
              Gill and John Primm.
```

```
Pages
387-388:           ANDREW BARBEE  (Will) "of Parish of Leeds"
                   Date: 28 December 1790
Son:          Andrew Barbee - Lott of land whereon he now
              lives - Negro girl Hannah - Negro child peuler -
              one gun - after death of wife, 2 more Negroes
Son:          John - Negro girl Lisa - one cow & calf - after
              death of wife 2 more Negroes
Dau.:         Mary Foley - Negro boy Jesse - after death of
              wife, 2 more Negroes
Dau.:         Elizabeth - Negro Girl Rose
Dau.:         Sarah Bradford - Negro girl Eve - one cow &
              calf - after death of wife, 2 more Negroes
Wife:         Jane Barbee - during her natural life the
              Lott of Land whereon I now live - 12 Negroes
Gr. son:      Abijah Withers, son of my dau. Elizabeth - Negro
Gr. son:      Thomas Barbee, son of my son Joseph - Negro
              (which is in lieu of that part of my Estate
              that I intended to give unto my said Son Joseph)
Children:     Andrew, John, Mary, Sarah & my Grandson Andrew
              Russel Barbee, son of my son Joseph - to share
              in remainder of estate after payment of debts.
Exors:        Sons: Andrew and John Barbee
Signed:       Andrew Barbey
Wit.:         B. Shackelford, Thos. Harris, Cristefore (X)
              Hych, Aquilla Davis
Ret.:         28 December 1795, by o. of Aquilla Davis and
              Thomas Harris. Andrew and John Barbee obt.
              cert. of probate with Aquila Davis and Thomas
              Harris their securities in bond of $7,000.
```

Page
389:
                      FRANCES BELL   (Will)
                      Date: 14 December 1795
Gr.son: William Bell - the whole of my household and
                      Kitchen furniture - Stock of Horses, Cattle,
                      Sheep and hogs - Negro
Exors: friends, Elias Edmonds, Sen'r., William Edmonds,
                      Jun'r. and Eppa Timberlake
Signed: Frances (her X mark) Bell
Wit.:   John Edmonds, James Edmonds, Sarah Timberlake
Proved: 28 December 1795 by o. of John Edmonds and
                      James Edmonds. Exors. refused to take on
                      execution. William Bell, with William Edmonds,
                      Jun'r. and Eppa Timberlake as securities in
                      bond of $2,000, made oath and obt. cert. of
                      probate.

Page
390:
                      JOHN McKENNEY, SEN'R.   (Inventory)
                      Date: 7 December 1795
App'd by: Thos. Hand, Lewis Withers, William Smoot
Total Eval.: L60.18.3
Ret.:   28 December 1795, "estate of John McKennie
                      deceased."

Page
391:
                      ROBERT BERRYMAN   (Administrator's Account)
Admr.:   Maximilion Berryman
Details: First entry dated: 10 June 1776; 4 January
                      1777: To Cash paid, Sarah Berryman, Thos.
                      Lawson, Corbins Negro.
Ex'md by: Jas. Wright, Wm. Smith, Joseph Blackwell,
                      15 September 1795
Ret.:   28 December 1795

Pages
392-393:
                      JOSEPH WHEATLEY   (Inventory)
                      Date: 21 January 1796 (Court Order dated:
          December 1795)
App'd by: Peter Conway, Jas. Thompson, James Wright
Total eval.: L423.8.3
Ret.:   25 January 1796

Pages
394-395:
                      THOMAS BROOKS   (Inventory)
                      Date: 20 February 1796
App'd by: Samuel Blackwell, John James, Joshua Tulloss

- 256 -

Details: Books of several kinds, $1.00
Total Eval.: $1,056.05
Ret.:   22 February 1796

Pages
395-396:   ANDREW BARBEE (Inventory)
                Date: 9 January 1796 (Court order dated:
                December Court, 1795)
App'd by: Aquilla Davis, Thos. Harris, Ben Bradford
Details: "parcel of old Books 7/6"
Total eval.: L244.10.3
Ret.:   22 February 1796

Pages
396-399:   JONATHAN GIBSON (Administrator's Account)
Admr.:   Benjamin Harrison
Details: TO PAID: Edward Marsh; F. Brooke, Clerk Fauquier
Court for fees 1791, 1792, 1793, 1794; Thomas
Riley for making a Coffin 15 shillings; Robert
Dunbar; Lawson & Dunbar; James & Thos. Dowdalls
bond and Wm. Green & Jos. Blackwell bond;
Robert Dunbar for several bonds; Wm. Malory;
John Gibson; Jos. Blackwell; O. Young; Gavin
Adams; Thos. Keith; Isaac & Wm. Eustace;
Augustine Smith; Samuel Baker; Short and
Richards Acct.; Henderson & Gibson for two
bonds; James, John & Wm. Woods; Peter & John
Woods; Susanna H. Gibson's Act.; Stuart &
Muschett; for 3 dutch Blanketts; Negro Women;
Gillison & Adie; H. F. & Gibson for Goods for
S. Gibson; Guss Smith for Clothes for Davy,
Davy & Whisky; John Shumate; Thos. Keith
Sheriffs Fees; Clerks Fees in Stafford Court;
Lawyer & Sheriffs fees in Stafford; H. F. &
Gibson Goods for Sara Gibson; Samuel Blackwell;
Jos. Blackwell Land & Property tax; Clerks
note in Fauq'r. 20 w. Tobacco; Francis Boyle
Acct. Mary Gibson; Langhorn Dade Esq'r.; Clerk
District Court; Jonathan Gibson 546 w. tobo.;
Adams the Cryer of the Sale; funeral expenses
attending the interment of Jonathan Gibson,
Dec'd. L2.10.0; To Feeding, Cloathing &c two
old Negroes who were unable to work; Gowen
Adams; Captain Thomas Gibson; Wm. Richards for
Goods furnished Miss Molly Gibson; Jos. Black-
well Fauq'r. Clerks fees; Wm. Woods; James

Murchett; A. Blackwell; Pickett & Co.; Doct'r.
Horner; Morrison, his Acct. for schooling
Miss Gibson; Isaac Eustace; Samuel Blackwell;
Sam'l. & B. Gordon; Wm. Gunyon; John Gibson
for goods furnished Miss Susa Gibson; James
Thompson; Mr. Boyles; 1 looking glass sold
Miss Beale & claimed by Thos. Gibson as
annexed to the freehold; waggoning of 6 hogs-
heads tobacco to Dumfries belonging to the
estate.
BY: Tobacco on hand at the death of Capt. Gibson

Ex'md. by: James Wright, William Foote, John James,
             Chilton Ransdell
Ret.:   22 February 1796

Pages
400-401:   EDWARD NUGENT (Dower)
                Date: 5 February 1796
Comm'rs.: Hancock Lee, Charles Duncan, Aug't. Jennings
Details: "to allott and lay off to James Robbin and
          Elizabeth his Wife late Elizabeth Nugent, the
          widow and relict of Edward Nugent, deceased"
          ... land on Great Run.
Other distributees: Thomas Williams in right of his Wife
          Francis (sic); Thomas Nugent and Edward Nugent -
          John Bronaugh had purchased the several
          proportions of the said Land to which they were
          legally entitled, .. fifty acres we reserved
          for Charles Nugent, Polly Nugent and Jale Nugent.
Survey: Page 401, by John Mauzy, S. F. C., dated
          4 February 1796
Ret.:   22 February 1796.

END OF WILL BOOK NO. 2

WILL BOOK NO. 3

Pages
1-2:   EVAN GRIFFITH "of Parish of Leeds" (Will)
                Date: 10 September 1795
Son: John - all my wearing apparrel
Son: Elijah - land and plantation whereon he now
          lives - 60 acres.
Son: Willoughby - one bed & furniture, one cow and

calf - 500 a. in the State of Kentucky - having the first choice in one piece out of 2050 acres

Son: John - 500 acres of land in Kentucky, adjoining to the lands of his brother Willoughby.

Daus.: Amelia Owens, Rachael Creel, Peggy Griffith and Susanna Griffith - the remainder of said land in Ky. - 1050 acres.

Dau.: Peggy Griffith - one bed and furniture, one cow, one ewe and lamb, 6 pewter plates

Dau.: Saraianne - one bed & furniture, one cow, one ewe and lamb, 6 pewter plates

Son: Dennis Griffith - horse called his, one cow one ewe and lamb, one bed & furniture - after his mother's death the plantation whereon I now live and land adjoining, 163 acres, if he should die in the lifetime of his mother without heirs, plantation to be sold and money equally divided among my then surviving children.

Wife: Sarah - plantation whereon I now live - the remainder of my moveable estate.

Exor.: son Elijah Griffith and wife
Signed: Evan Griffith
Wit.: Benjamin (X) Goldsmith, Rachel (X) Flynn, William (X) Flynn

Proved: 25 April 1796 by o. of witnesses. Executors made oath and granted cert. to obtain probate. (27 June 1796).

Page 3

MOLLY BROWN (Wife of Robert Brown) (Nuncupative Will)

Date: 28 February 1796

___: George Brooke - my land - equal proportion of my Negroes to him George Brooke, Francis Brooke, Matthew Brooke, Anne Brooke, Kitty Powell, Elizabeth Digges, Lucy Brooke - the Negroes equally to be divided among seven.

___@ Lucy Brooke - furniture and books, my dressing table, a small table with one drawer, both of which are of Walnut and what Books I have. "This Day William Chilton and Samuel Chilton appeared personally before me and made oath that Molly Brown, the wife of Robert Brown Gentleman in her last sickness at the House of Thomas Digges Gentleman where they believe

she had resided ten Days preceeding her death,
did pronounce the above writing to contain
the perport of her last will and testament
and that she called on the said William Chilton
for that purpose and was of sound mind.
That this was declared on the night of the
28th February 1796 and that some time in the
course of that night she departed this life.
Given under my hand this second day of March
1796."

Signed: Aylett Buckner
            Doctor Samuel Chilton swears to all of the
            above Summary to the best of his knowledge
            except the memorandrum mentioning the furni-
            ture and Books.

Ret.:   26 April 1796, proved by o. of William Chilton.
            Charles Marshall and Francis Brooke made
            oath, with John Thomas Chunn and William
            Stanton their securities, for bond $3,000,
            cert. granted for obtaining probate.

Pages
4-5:   THOMAS PRIEST   (Inventory)
                Date: 25 _____ 1796
App'd by: Charles Waller, George Crosby, John Fox.
Total eval.: L396.1.3
Ret.:   25 April 1796

Pages
5-6:   BENJAMIN NEWHOUSE   (Administrator's Account)
                No date or administrator.
Ex'md. by: Martin Pickett, Joseph Blackwell, Wm. Horner
Details: REC'D OF: Joseph Morgan, William White, Thomas
            Chilton, Polly Newhouse. DUE: Parnack George.
            PAID TO: doctor Horner; William Ball; James
            Kibble; Nimrod Johnston; Francis Brooke.
Rec.:   25 April 1796

Pages
6-7:   WILLIAM SEATON   (Division of Real Estate)
                Date: 25 March 1796
Div. by: Thomas Gibson, Joseph Blackwell
Details: Plat and description of land made and recorded
            by Peter Conway, D. S. F. C., 2 October 1795.
            298 acres divided into 3 equal portions between
            Mary Brown the widow of William Seaton, dec'd.
            and his two sons: James Seaton and William Seaton.

Desc.:   .. on Furrs run Corner to George Brown .. a
hiccory in Captain Gibson's line .. a white
oak by Cummingses spring branch .. to Furrs
run .. Other estate: son James Seaton -
Negroes; George Seaton, to be paid L20 by
James; William Seaton, to be paid L20 by James;
David Wickliff "who married one of the heirs" -
Negroes; George Seaton "who married another
of said heirs" - Negroes. William Seaton,
his lot of Negroes. William Seaton the
lower lot of Land joining George Brown.
James Seaton, the upper lot joining Captain
John James. Widow, the middle lot.

Ret.:   25 April 1796.

Page
7:
          WILLIAM SEATON (Widow's Dower)
          Date: 25 March 1796
Div. by: Thomas Gibson, Joseph Blackwell.
Details: .. the middle lot containing 93 1/3 acres ..
whereon the mantion house stands on ..
Negro .. 1/3 of stock, household furniture and
plantation utensils.

Ret.:   25 April 1796

Pages
8-9:
          SIMEON HAINES (Inventory)
          Date: 2 March 1796
App'd by: William Daniel, Richard Thatcher, James Dillon.
No total.
Details: Benjamin Scott's note; a book account against
Josiah Dillon; note on Charles Metcalf & Joseph
Hampton; note on John Wilabe and Thomas
Clark; a note on Withers Smith; bond on John
Peyton Harrison.

Ret.:   27 June 1796

Pages
9-10:
          MOLLY BROWN (Inventory)
          Date: 18 June 1796
App'd by: Thomas Chilton, Ambrose Barnett, Wm. Hunton
Total eval.: L600
Ret.:   27 June 1796

Pages
10-11:
          JOHN WHEATLEY (Inventory)
          No date.

App'd by: Peter Bowmer, George Bowmer, John Ficklin
Total eval.: L423.7.9
Ret.:   27 June 1796

**Pages
11-12:**   JAMES WHEATLEY (Sale)
               No date, no administrator.
Purchasers: George Wheatley, Lucretia Wheatley, Robert
     B. Voss, Richard Hudson, Thomas Oliver, Daniel
     Canady, Charles Arnold, John Slaughter, John
     Allen, Lucy Wheatley, John W. Smith, Charles
     Martin, Joseph Wheatley, James Wheatley,
     Robert Pendleton, Selah Shackelford, Joseph
     Oliver, Fielding Ficklin.
Total eval.: L211.2.6
Ret.:   27 June 1796

**Pages
12-15:**   JAMES D. SMITH (Sale)
               Date: 1 September 1794
               No buyers listed. Seems to have been the
               contents of a store.
Total: L272.0.6
Ret.:   27 June 1796

**Pages
15-16:**   JAMES D. SMITH (Administrator's Account)
               Date examined: 8 February 1796
Ex'md by: John Blackwell, Samuel Blackwell, Thos. Keith
     "Dr. the Estate of James D. Smith, Deceased,
     to the Estate of Jeremiah Darnall, dec'd. Cr."
     1793 - to boarding your two younger men 15
     days. 5 July 1794 - To coffin and burial -
     L1.10. TO; Doctor Kincade; John Matthews for
     acting as Clark 2 days at the sale of the
     estate; John Herndon for 3 days Crier of the
     sale; James Wright for settling the books;
     James Brown of Richmond in part of a bond
     granted by said Smith pr said Brown; James
     Wright for his expenses in going to Dumfries;
     Robert Grayham, C. Pr. Wm. Court for Fees.
     BY: Merchandize and Tavern account; sale of
     house and lot to the highest bidder until the
     first of January 1795 - L6; by 6 gallons W.
     Rum and 5 quarts Whiskey - L2.1.
Ret.:   27 June 1796

**Pages
16-17:**   FRANCIS BELL   (Inventory)
                      Date: 21 April 1796
App'd by: Edward Digges, Wm. Edmonds, Jr., Eppa Timberlake
Total eval.: L419.10.10
Ret.:   27 June 1796

**Pages
17-18:**   VINCENT GARNER   (Will)
                      Date: 28 August 1795
Son: Benjamin Garner - whatever I have heretofore
          put unto his possession also ten shillings
Son: James - (as above) also the tract of land
          whereon he now lives, as follows: .. James
          Wither's line formerly purchased of Jonas
          Garner .. to James Pares line - 50 acres
Son: Jonas Garner - whatever I have put him in
          possession of, also 10 shillings
Dau.:   Heirs of my Daughter Sarah Suttel, wife of
          William Suttel - Negro girl after death of
          my wife.
Gr.son: James Withers Garner - one horse colt & 20L
          cash, after the Death of his Grandmother.
Wife: Jemimah Garner - during her natural life or
          Widowhood all the rest of my estate real and
          personal - after her death to be equally
          divided among my five children, viz: Vincent,
          William, Jesse, Elizabeth Garner and Jemimah
          Harris wife of William Harris.
Exors: sons Vincent and William W. Garner
Signed: Vincent (his X mark) Garner
Wit.:   Enoch K. Withers, James Withers, Aaron Fletcher,
          John (X) Kines.
Proved: 27 June 1796, by o. of James Withers, John
          Kines, Enoch Withers. Vincent Garner, with
          James Withers and Jesse Garner his securities
          in bond of $3,000, made o. and obtained cert.
          for probate.

**Pages
19-22:**   JOHN CHURCHILL   (Inventory)
                      Date: 23 July 1796
App'd by: Thos. Digges, James Stewart, Turner Morehead,
          Bn'rd. Duffey
Details: 33 volumes Books - L5
Total eval.: L2890.0.0
Ret.:   25 July 1796

Page
23: JOHN REDMON(D) (Inventory)
          No date
App'd by: Wm. Barker, Edward Burgess, Mark Shumate
Total eval.: L189.15.3
Ret.: 25 July 1796

Pages
24-25: WILLIAM HUME (Inventory)
          No date
App'd by: Benjamin Rector, T. Mallory, Thos. Smith
Total eval.: L90.15.4
Ret.: 25 July 1796

Pages
26-27: JOHN DUNCAN, SEN'R. (Division of Estate)
          Date: 13 October 1795
Admr.: Moses Duncan
Div. by: John Bronaugh, Augustine Jennings, Peter Routt
Details: Widow - dower - 55 acres of land, Negroes, one
          feather bed and furniture, livestock, farm
          equipment, cash, etc.
Son-in-law: Pierce Henderson Bailey, husband of Milly
          Duncan, dau. of John, - one Negro woman.
            In the latter end of December, 1795 the said
          Moses Duncan proceeded to sell the residue of
          the aforesaid Estate both real and personal:
          land purchased by Moses Duncan; Negro man Tom
          purchased by Moses Duncan for his Brother Elias
          Duncan; Negro man purchased by Moses Duncan for
          his Brother Willis Duncan; Negroes .. purchased
          by Lucinda Duncan in part of her Legacy.
Total: L477.17.3 - after debts the remainder was di-
          vided between five children: Moses, Elias,
          Enoch, Willis and Lucinda.
Ret.: 25 July 1796

Pages
27-28: WILLIAM EMMONS (Will)
          Date: 5 February 1795
Wife: (not named) - all estate during her life except
          as follows:
Dau.: Agatha Emmons - bed and furniture, cow & calf,
          ewe and lamb.
            After death of wife, all estate tobe sold
          and equally divided among all children or their
          children.
Exor.: son Joseph Emmons and son-in-law William Jones

Signed: William (his X mark) Emmons
Wit.:   Peter Grant, Thos. Keith, John Weedon
Ret.:   25 July 1796, proved by o. of Thomas Keith,
            Joseph Emmons and William Jones, with Thomas
            Keith their security for bond of $500, made
            o. and granted cert. to obtain probate.

Pages
28-29:   EZEKIEL HADDUX   (Inventory)
                   Date: 24 December 1795
App'd by: Lewis Withers, James Genn, Samuel Stinson
Total eval.: L43.15.3
Ret.:   26 September 1796

Pages
29-30:   MINOR WINN   (Administrator's Account)
Admr.:   Minor Winn
Details: TO: 1778 - Leven Powell, John Metcalf. 1779 -
          Martin Pickett. 1782 - Aaron Thomas. 1783 -
          Thomas Nelson; Eli Thompson; Cain Withers.
          1784 - Leven Powell; Ambrose Barnett Execution
          Geo. Nelson Dec'd. 1785 - Samuel Love, Junior.
          1786 - To my Ordinary Expenses tending Loudoun
          Court at the suit of Ashby v. Hambleton res-
          pecting a suit of land the said Deceased sold
          said Ashby; Ludwell Lee Attorney; Thompson
          Mason Attorney. 1787 - Colo. Clapham. 1788 -
          Enoch Withers; A. Barnett Execution of Geo.
          Nevel Dec'd; J. Gibson; H. Stewart; John Barker;
          Alexandria Gazette for advertising; Leith for
          Crying Sale; 6½ Gallons whiskey for said Sale;
          Margaret Young; William Metcalf for Surveying;
          Margaret Winn Deceased. BY: Deduction of Geo.
          Nevels Acct. Deceased; Ballance of Margaret
          Winn's Acct. Deceased.
Exam'd by: Hugh Neilson, Wm. Hale, John P. Harrison,
           1 May 1788.
Memo: I have paid James Johnson for James Ritchie &
            Co., L27.14.9½. /s/ Minor Winn.
Ret.:   26 September 1796

Pages
31-32:   WILLIAM EMMONS   (Inventory)
                   Date: 7 August 1796
App'd by: Joseph Oder, John Weedon, Benjamin West
Total eval.: L111.5.0
Ret.:   24 October 1796

- 265 -

Pages
32-33: CLEMENT BILLINGSBY (Inventory)
No date
App'd by: Matthew Neale, Joseph Smith, P. (or T.) Mallory.
Total eval.: L601.3.6
Ret.: 24 October 1796

Pages
33-34: MAJOR THOMAS RANSDELL (Inventory)
Date: 21 October 1796
App'd by: Samuel Steele, George Rogers, Joseph Hale
Total eval.: L669.4.6
Ret.: 24 October 1796

Pages
34-35: EVAN GRIFFITH (Inventory)
Date: 25 August 1796
App'd by: William Sinklair, William Flourance, James Leach
Total eval.: L370.8.0
Ret.: 24 October 1796

Pages
35-36: JOHN TALBERT (TALBUT) (Will)
Date: 12 April 1796
Wife: Ann Talbert - Negroes
Son: Paul Talbert - Negroes
Dau: Ann Talbert - Negroes
Son: John Talbert - Negroes, also my tract of land in
Maryland in Prince George County
Wife & children: all estate to be sold for cash and equally
divided.
Exors: Wife Ann Talbert and son Benjamin Talbert
Signed: John Taulbert
Wit.: John Wren, Samuel Dennis, Isaac Wren
Proved: 24 October 1796, by o. of John Wren and Samuel
Dennis. Ann Talbut and Benjamin Talbut, with
William Debell and John Wren their securities
in bond for $8,000, made o. and granted cert.
to obtain probate.

Pages
36-38: JOHN KERR, SEN'R. (Will)
Date: 8 November 1796
Dau.: Margaret Bronaugh - L5
Dau.: Mary Peters - Negro girl
Dau.: Betty Kerr - Negroes, also L36.5.0; one saddle
and one grey mare colt; Negroes to be owned
jointly by daus. Mary Peters and Betty Kerr.

I do not wish that the children of the
present wife to have any claim to the bequeath given to my first wife's children nor
the first wife's children to have any to those
of the present wifes.

Son: John Kerr, Junr.: Negro, horse
Son: William Kerr - Negro
Wife: Sarah Kerr - residue of estate during her life
        or widowhood, in order that she may be Inabled
        to raise the young children that I have by her.
Son: John Kerr, Jun'r. - land whereon I now live.
Son: William Kerr - to Inherit the land bequeathed
        to my son John Kerr, Jun'r. if he should die
        before he arrives to the age of twenty-one
        years of age.
        All Estate, land excepted, lent to my wife
        to be equally divided at the death or marriage
        of wife between my children Sarah Crosby Kerr;
        William Kerr, Darcus Kerr, Lucy Kerr, Peggy
        Smith Kerr and Asenoth Kerr.
Exors: Wife Sarah Kerr, John Withers "son of old field"
        and John James.
Signed: John Kerr
Wit.:   Benjamin Bronaugh, Garrott Freeman, James Fox,
        Alexander Cresenberry.
Proved: 26 December 1796, by o. of Garrett Freeman and
        Benjamin Bronaugh. Sarah Kerr, with John James
        and John Bronaugh her securities in bond of
        L4,000, made oath and granted cert. to obt. probate

Pages
38-39:   JOHN TOMLIN, SEN'R. (Inventory)
            Date: 9 November 1796
App'd by: James McClanaham, George Rogers, Thomas Chilton,
          Ambrose Barnett
Total eval.: L759.5.11
Ret.:   26 December 1796

Pages
39-40:   JOHN KERR (Inventory)
            Date: 10 January 1797
App'd by: James Withers, Howsen Duncan, James (X) Parr
Total eval.: L1146.14.6

Pages
40-41:   GEORGE EMBRY (Inventory)
            Date: 20 January 1797
App'd by: Sanders Mortis, Robt. Stringfellow, Thos. Keith.

Total eval.: L35.19.0
Ret.:   23 January 1797

Page
41:                    WILLIAM ALLEN (Division of Estate)
                       Date: Court order dated October 1796
Details: Widow's Dower - L465.3.3; Six children - L917.18.'
Div. by: Linefield Sharpe, Chilton Ransdell, Austin Brad-
          ford, George Eastham.
Ret.:   27 February 1797

Pages
41-42:   JOHN TOMLIN (Division of Estate)
                       Date: 27 January 1797
Details: Joseph Minter, John Tomlin, William Tomlin,
          Samuel Tomlin
Div. by: Thomas Chilton, Ambrose Barnett, James McClanahan,
          George Rogers.
Ret.:   27 February 1797

Pages
42-43:   JOHN JOHNSON (Inventory)
                       Date: 25 February 1797
App'd by: William Wood, James Wood, John Hogain, first
          sworn before William Stewart.
Total eval.: L390.18.10
Ret.:   27 February 1797

Page
44:                    MARY HUNTON (Sale of Estate)
                       Date: 24 February 1797
Adm'r.:   Robert Hunton
Details: Sale of slave
Ret.:   27 February 1797

Pages
44-45:   MARY HUNTON (Account of Estate)
                       Date: 1 February 1797
Adm'r.:   Robert Hunton
Details: 1795, 4 May: To moving you from Richmond County,
          120 miles; 1796, 23 Jan.: To going and bringing
          up your Negro fellow; To 1 year and six months
          board and cloathing and attendance.
Ex'md by: John Bronaugh, Enock K. Withers
Ret.:   27 February 1797

Pages
45-46:   WILLIAM EMMONS (Account of Sales)
              Date: 10 November 1796
Exors: William Jones, Joseph Emmons
Details: SOLD TO: William Emmons; Martin Hefferlin;
              John Wills; Willis Freeman; William Jones,
              Sen'r.; Embry, William, Sen'r.; Joseph Oder;
              Alexander McConky; George Henry; Reason Olliver;
              Joseph Olliver; Joseph Anderson; Robert Emry;
              George Freeman; James Keith; Bennett Freeman;
              Thomas Keith; James Emmons; Christopher Black-
              burn; Thomas Humphries; William Jacobs; William
              Young; Anthony Marcus; Jacob Branson; Jesse
              Brown; William Emry; William Huffman; James
              Owens; William Pool.
Ret.:   27 February 1797

Pages
47-48:   SAMUEL MOREHEAD (Will)
              Date: 16 December 1796
Dau.:   Sarah Jennings - Deep Run tract adjoining the
              land of Joshua Tullos
Gr.son: Baylor Jennings - Negro
Dau.:   Lydia Morehead - Negro
Dau.:   Mary Morehead - Negro
Dau.:   Elizabeth Morehead - Negro
Dau.:   Peggy Morehead - Negro
Son: Charles Morehead - Negro
Son: Samuel B. Morehead - Negro
Wife: Wilmouth Morehead - all my estate .. during her
              widowhood but in case of marriage only her thirds.
Exor.:   Wife Wilmoth, Thomas Helm and Charles Morehead
Signed: Samuel Morehead
Wit.:   Thomas Humston, Isaac Eustace, Alexander Morehead,
              John Morehead.
Proved: 26 December 1796, by o. of Thomas Humston.
              27 February 1797, by o. of Isaac Eustace and John
              Morehead. Wilmoth Morehead, with Joseph George
              and George Lawry her securities in bond for
              $6,000, made oath and granted cert. to obtain
              probate.

Pages
48-50:   PARNACH GEORGE (Inventory)
              Date: 24-25 February 1797
App'd by: William Bradford, James Hunton, George Rogers,
              William Hunton, Jr.

Total eval.: L1045.12.0
Ret.:   24 April 1797

Page
50:              CHARLES THORNTON   (Division of Estate)
                 Date: 30 June 1796
Details: TO: Thomas Thornton, Jr.; children of Charlotte
           Curtice, Dec'd.; Lettice Thornton.
Div. by: James Hunton, William Hunton, Thomas Hunton.
Ret.:   24 April 1797

Page
51:              JAMES FOLEY   (Will)
                 Date: 14 October 1793
Wife: Elizabeth - 2 Negroes - one-half land on which I
           now live, "to Begin at William Smith's line and
           Running towards my Present Dwelling House for and
           During the Natural life of the said Elizabeth and
           after her Decease to be Equally divided Between
           my Children by the said Elizabeth (to wit):
Children: Susanna Foley Oglevie, Presly Foley Oglevie, Leah
           Foley Oglevie, Lettuce Foley and Molley Foley.
Wife: two horses - one-half of my Waggon and gear - one
           good Feather Bed and furniture - one large Iron
           Pot - 2 pewter dishes - ½ doz. pewter plates -
           ½ of all cattle, sheep and hogs - 1/3 part of my
           Plantation utensils - all the meat and crop - all
           the fowls and bees.
Dau.:   Susanna Foley Oglevie - Negro girl
Son: Presley Foley Oglevie - Negro boy
Dau.:   Leah Foley Oglevie - Negro girl
Dau.:   Lettice Foley - Negro boy - feather bed & furniture
Dau.:   Molley Foley - Negro boy - one feather bed and
           furniture
Son: Enoch Foley - the other half of my land, to Include
           the Dwelling house - 2 horses - remaining half of
           my Waggon & Gear
Children: Residue to be equally divided Between my Children:
           (to wit): John, James, Thomas, William, Bryant,
           Sarah Watts and Enoch Foley.
Exor.:   Wife Elizabeth Foley and son Enoch Foley and
           William Smith.
Signed: James (his + mark) Foley
Wit.:   Alexander Keith, Henry Harris, William Keith,
           Lettice Thornton, Catty Keith.
Proved: 24 April 1797, by oaths of Alexander Keith,
           William Keith and Caty Keith. Enoch Foley, made

oath and together with James Foley and James
O'Bannon, his securities, acknowledged bond in
the penalty of $10,000, cert. granted for ob-
taining probate.

Pages
52-56:

Wife:

Son:

Dau.:
Son:

Dau.:
Son:

Son:

Son:

Son:

JOHN O'BANNON (Will)
Date: 21 February 1797
Lydda - the plantation whereon I now live during
her life - Negroes - stock of horses, cattle,
hogs and sheep - 2 feather beds - $\frac{1}{2}$ of all household furniture - plantation utensils, wagon and
gear for each horse.
Joseph - Negro boy - horse - 1/3 part of all my
Lands being in the State of Kentucky
Elizabeth Smith - Negro boy
James - 1/3 part of all my Lands lying in Fauquier
County after the Death of my wife which said Lands
are to be equally Divided in quantity and my said
son James is to have his choice of said Lands and
may proceed after my decease immediately to make
the Division but is not to prevent his Mother
from clearing or cultivating any part during her
life - one Negro boy - one Negro girl - one feather
bed - stud horse - L300 cash, to be collected out
of a Bond due me from John Love
Jemima Johnston - Negro boy
Isham - Negro man - one feather bed and furniture -
a yearling colt - $\frac{1}{2}$ part of land at Kentucky -
L40 cash as soon as money can be collected from the
sale of my present crop of wheat.
Elias - 1/3 part of all my lands lying in the State
of Kentucky - one feather bed and furniture - one
bay colt - L40 cash from debts due me.
John - 1/3 part of all my land lying in Fauquier
County - Viz, the second part to be laid on the
lower part of the Land so as to include the quarter
Negro boy and woman - one bay Horse he now uses -
a sorrel Colt at the quarter - one feather bed and
furniture - L40 cash out of debts due me.
William - all the residue of my Land lying in this
County - one Negro man and woman - one feather bed
and furniture - a Horse call'd Doncarless - a Colt
L40 cash from debts due me.
... it is my desire that the Negro Woman call'd
Jude shall be continued under the care of my Wife
during her life.

```
                    ... it is my desire that the whole expense of
                    clearing out Securing my Kentucky Lands should
                    be paid out of my Estate.
Exors:              Wife Lydda, sons Joseph, James and Isham
Signed:             John O'Bannon
Wit.:               William Metcalf, Alexander Keith, Richard Parker
Codicil:            21 February 1797 - that all slaves be kept on the
                    plantation until "the present crop is furnished"
                    also that the securing of the Kentucky lands not
                    exceeds L80.  (same witnesses as above)
Proved:             24 April 1797 by o. of Richard Parker and Alexande:
                    Keith.  Joseph O'Bannon, James O'Bannon and Isham
                    O'Bannon, the exors. named, made oath, with
                    William Smith, Alexander Scott and William Chilton,
                    their securities on bond of $10,000, granted
                    cert. to obtain probate.  On 26 June 1797 William
                    Metcalf, another witness, made oath.

Pages
56-57:                       BENJAMIN CLARK  (Will)
                             Date: 27 November 1794
Wife:               Mary Clark - lend all estate during life - after
                    death to be divided amongst my children and
                    grandchildren
Son:                Thomas - one Negro man - 1/6 part of the rest of
                    my Estate after the death of Mary Clark
Dau.:               Anne Crupper - 1/6 part of estate after decease
                    of wife
Dau.:               Elizabeth Clark - 1/6 part of estate after de-
                    cease of wife
Dau.:               Mary Clark - 2/6 of estate after decease of
                    wife
Gr.children:        Children of my dau. Cloe Crupper - 1/6 part
                    of my Estate
Exor.:              Wife Mary Clark and son Thos. Clark
Signed:             Benjamin (his X mark) Clark
Wit.:               Sam'l. Pearle, Nathan Moore, Henry Downs
Proved:             26 June 1797, by o. of Nathan Moore and Henry
                    Downs.  Thomas Clark, together with Henry Downs
                    his security, under bond of $2,000, made oath
                    as Exor. and granted cert. to obtain probate.

Pages
58-59:                       JOHN SMOOT  (Will)
                             Date: 5 September 1796
Wife:               Tomsen - right and title of the lott of Land I
```

	now possess - household goods.
Son:	Leonard - one shilling
Son:	John - one shilling
Dau.:	Mary - one shilling
Dau.:	Betsy - one shilling
Son:	James - one shilling
Son:	Barton - one shilling
Son:	William - one shilling
Son:	Clabourn - one shilling
Dau.:	Charity - one shilling
Son:	Lewis - one shilling
Son:	Enoch - one shilling
Dau.:	Frances - one shilling
Exor.:	Wife Tomsen
Signed:	John (his X mark) Smoot
Wit.:	Aquila Davis, De Wood, William Wood
Proved:	26 June 1797, by o. of Dickason Wood and William Wood. Tomsen Smoot made oath as Executrix and with Matthew Neale and Dickasen Wood as securities in bond of $1,000, granted cert. to obtain probate.

Pages 59-60: SAMUEL MOREHEAD (Inventory)
Date: 25 April 1797
App'd by: John Shumate, Thomas Shumate and Isaac Eustace
Total eval.: L795.13.2
Ret.: 26 June 1797

Page 61: JAMES BALL (Administrator's Account)
Date: 12 December 1796
Ret. by: Richard Rixey, Wm. Withers, John Ashby
Details: TO: 22 Dec. 1794 - Pickett, Blackwell & Co.; James Stinson; 1795 - Thomas Drake; James Channel for medicine; 2 May - Arch'd. Duncan; 5 Oct. - Eli Thompson; 1796 - Joseph Chilton for medicine; 27 Jan. - William Edmonds, Pickett, Blackwell and Co.
Ret.: 26 June 1797

Pages 62-63: JOHN TALBART (Talbert) (Inventory)
Date: 10 November 1796
App'd by: Uriah Byrne, Thomas Priest, John Bishop
No total
Ret.: 24 July 1797

Pages
63-64:
                SMITH GARNER (Inventory)
                Date: 20 July 1797
App'd by: Eppa Timberlake, John Smith, Enoch Smith
No total.
Ret.:   24 July 1797

Pages
64-65:
            CAPTAIN THOMAS SMITH (Inventory)
            No date.
App'd by: John H. Clarke, Benjamin Rector, Charles C.
         Chunn.
Total eval.: L784.3.9
Ret.:   24 July 1797

Pages
66-67:
            LYDDIA DUNCAN (Will)
            Date: 2 October 1795
Dau.: Lyddia O'Bannon, wife of John O'Bannon - Negro
     Boy
Son: Joseph Duncan - Negro boy
Son: Howsen Duncan - Negro boy
Dau.: Jemimah Mauzy, wife of John Mauzy - Negro woman
Dau.: Hannah Porter, wife of Ebenezer Porter - Negro
    boy
Exors: Sons Joseph and Howsen Duncan
Signed: Lyddia (her X mark) Duncan
Wit.: Enoch K. Withers, Moses Duncan, John Kerr
Proved: 24 July 1797, by o. of Enoch K. Withers and Moses
Duncan. Howsen Duncan made o. and with James
Withers and John Withers, his securities under
bond of $3,000, granted cert. to obtain probate.

Pages
67-69:
          THOMAS CAVE (Will)
          Date: 26 July 1797
Children: Rhody Cave, John Cave, Sarah Cave, Samuel Cave -
to receive estate, equally divided at the age of
seventeen
Dau.: Rody Cave - two Negroes
Exor: Dear and well beloved friend John Roylands
Signed: Thomas (his X mark) Cave
Wit.: James Drummond, Philip Cooksey, Joseph Hickman
Proved: 25 September 1797, by o. of Philip Cooksey and
Joseph Hickman. John Rollins, the Exor. named,
made o. and with John Rector and James McFarland
as securities in bond of $2,500, granted cert.
to obtain probate.

Pages
69-70:   LIDIA DUNCAN (Inventory)
                    Date: 5 August 1797
App'd by: John Withers, Vincent Garner, Robt. Henson
Total eval.: L267.18.6¼
Ret.:   25 September 1797

Pages
70-71:   BENJAMIN CLARKE (Inventory)
                    Date: 21 July 1797
App'd by: John P. Harrison, Sam'l. Pearle, Wm Hale,
        Nathan Moore
Total eval.: L69.13.0
Ret.:   25 September 1797

Pages
71-73:   JEREMIAH DARNALL (Administrator's Acct.)
                    Date: 25 September 1797
Adm'r.: James Wright
Exam'd by: Wm. Edmonds, Jun'r., Jo. Blackwell, Joseph
        Blackwell, Jun'r.
Details: TO: Kine, for a Coffin, L2.10; Mr. Robert Dunbar;
        George Gordin; Doctor Horner; Wm. Horner; Samuel
        Porter; George Lowry; Bowse the tanner for leather;
        Lawyer Harrison in suit against said estate with
        Augustine Smith; Jas. Weaver balance due him for
        paying tax of the Kentucky land belonging to said
        Estate; Bastable; James Brown of Richmond as
        Admr. on the Estate of James D. Smith; Elizabeth
        Bray; Samuel Horton; Edward Godley for casting
        plats for Estate; F. Brooke; Wm. Smith; Benjamin
        Taylor, for Kentucky land tax; advertising Negro
        Kitt Winchester papers; Expense of Negro Kitt
        belonging to said Estate which ran away; William
        Drummon. BY: 1795-Kine for Tavern rent; Robert
        Dunbar; James Hopwood; Elijah Griffith who bought
        100 acres of land belonging to Estate; John Clarke.
Ret.:   25 September 1797

Pages
73-80:   CHARLES CHILTON (Guardianship Account)
                    Date: 2 August 1794
Exam'd by: Ambrose Barnett, William Metcalf, Charles
        Marshall
Adm'r.: William Chilton
Details: TO: Board of Orrick and Wm. Chilton; Board of
        Sucky Chilton; William Metcalf for Teaching O.

and Wm. Chilton; Eliz'a. Methcalf for making a
Coat and jack Coat; 1784, 16 Aug.: Mrs. Ransdell's
for making 7 shirts; John Kincheloe admr. of
John Hermmond for medicine; Thomas Renno for
schooling Orrick Chilton; Presley Morehead for
pork; Turner Morehead; William Asbury; Dale Carter
Thomas Ervins; Thomas Nelson for blacksmith work;
Mrs. Taylor for lay in Negro Lucy; Joseph H.
Jones for schooling William Chilton; Hudson and
Daniel Muse; John Hopper; Mrs. Taylor for weaving;
M. Pickett and Co. for Bond givn when went to
Kentucky; Maj'r. Thomas Ransdell; Nathaniel Gray;
Expenses to Dumfries to Inspect Tobacco; Peggy
Mayson; Thomas Maddux; James Hedley; Robert Sander
for his sons Teaching William Chilton; board for
Sucky Chilton since she came from Westmoreland
(1789); William Horner; Daniel Donaldson for
Taylors account; Samuel Watson; James Campbell
for teaching Orrick and William Chilton, Jonathan
Newhouse; Robert Gibson for making shoes; Doctor
Samuel Boyd. BY: John Tomblin; John Shurley
hire of Prince; Turner Morehead; Samuel Boyd;
William Duglass; John Metcalf; John Cooke;
William Edmonds; Thomas Ransdell; George Kendall;
Capt. Hugh Duglass; Capt. Turner Morehead; Wm.
Emmons; Jonathan Newhouse; Thomas Keith; John
Hooper.

Then follows an explanation of the account,
especially an account due by William Douglass for
the hire of slaves. He married the widow of
William Chilton and then died insolvent.
Ret.:   25 September 1797.

Pages
81-85:   JOHN O'BANNON (Inventory)
                Date: 22 September 1797
App'd by: William Metcalf, William Smith, Minor Winn
Details: Consists of Slaves, livestock, plantation utensils
          household furniture, and account of bonds from:
          Samuel Jackson, John Love, Metcalf and Johnston,
          Burwell Bullett and Daneil Gray, Richard Gregory,
          Alexander Keith, Thomas Brady, Joseph Brady,
          Richard Keeble, Samuel Turner, Cumberland Wilson.
Total eval.: L3710.6.9$\frac{1}{2}$
Ret.   23 October 1797

- 276 -

Pages
85-85b: JONATHAN GIBSON   (Inventory)
                   No date.
App'd by: Wm. Foote, John James, Isaac Eustace
Total eval.: $6,200.00
Ret.:   23 October 1797

Pages
85b-86:   THOMAS CAVE   (Inventory)
                   Court Order dated September 1797
App'd by: John Ashby, Lyttleton Adams, Thomas Adams, as
          shown by John Adams Rawlings, Executor.
Total eval.:   L479.17.9
Ret.:   23 October 1797

Pages
86-87:   WILLIAM EMMON(S) (Adm'r. Account)
                   Date: 10 October 1797
Exam'd by: Sam'l. Blackwell, John Blackwell, Jun'r.
Details: Amount of Sales L189.3.10. TO: Joseph Emmons,
           William Jones, William Powle, James Emmons,
           Robert Stingfellow, Robert Dunbar, Thomas Keith,
           Joseph Oder for Crying the property. Dividend
           the Legatees: Mary Emry, Betty Henry, Joseph
           Emmons, Sarah Jones, William Emmons, Anne
           Husk, James Emmons, Agathor Heflin.
Ret.:   23 October 1797

Pages
87-89:   SAMUEL THORNBERRY   (Inventory)
                   No date.
App'd by: James Bates, George Lowry, Joseph Hale
Total eval.:   L175.4.0
Details: Consists of slaves, household furniture, etc.
           and livestock. Also the following receipts:
           One waggon and one cart Load (wheat) to Cedar
           Run Mills, one sent Bernard Galligher at
           Dumfries.
Ret.:   25 December 1797

Pages
89-90:   EDWARD FEAGAN   (Inventory)
                   Date: 1 November 1797
App'd by: Phillip Fishback, Aaron Thomas, James McClanahan.
Total eval: L464.4.0
Ret.:   22 January 1798

Pages
90-92:   BENJAMIN HARRISON   (Will)
                        Date: 2 January 1798
Dau.:   Margaret Short Wagener - L10 Virginia Currency
___ :   David Arragon - L10 Virginia Currency to be paid
                   him annually during his natural life - all
                   wearing aparel - this for his faithful services.
                   Negro Man Samuel be emancipated with L10
                   annually during his life for his maintenance
                   and support.
Gr.son: Benjamin Harrison Wagener - all the remaining
                   estate
Exors.:   Colonel Peter Wagener of the County of Fairfax
                   and Benjamin Botts attorney at Law in Dumfries
Signed: Ben Harrison
Wit.:   Philip (X) Spillar, James Lloyd, Charles Waller.
Codicil: Date: 2 January 1798. Same witnesses.
Details: That the executors retain the inheritance of
                   Benjamin Harrison Wagener until he comes of age.
                   Until that time the profits be used for his
                   maintenance and education.
Proved: 22 January 1798, by o. of Charles Waller, Philip
                   Spillar and James Lloyd. Benjamin Botts, with
                   Matthew Harrison, Robert Henning and William
                   Chilton as securities in bond of $10,000, made
                   oath and was granted cert. to obtain probate.

Pages·
92-93:   JOHN LAWSON   (Will)
                        Date: "This being the beginning of a new
                        year .." (1 January 1798 ?)
Details: Capt. Hancock Lee has a land warrant of mine for
           840½ acres which I wish to be located and disposed
           of for the benefit of my creditors
              .. wish Mr. Joseph Blackwell merchant to take
           possession of what little I am in possession for
           the benefit of my Creditors.
              "True there is part mortgaged to Kendall Lee,
           which mortgage may be easily got from Thomas
           Edwards of Northumberland Clerk of that District
           Court - I would wish Edward Digges Junior to
           inherit this lot of land after my wifes decease
           on condition that he will advance L50 to my
           Creditors, the lot has cost me six times as
           much, and more, ..."
              "Mrs. Lawson thinks after my decease to hire
           her negroes out and board herself with some of

her friends. Should that be the case, Mr.
Digges will allow her while she lives her
third part of the profits ..."
  "... should I live I am in debted to General
John Blackwell which is the oldest account, to
Pickett and Blackwell the next oldest, to Docter
Horner about eleven dollars, to Doctor Chilton
I do not know what, also to Wm. Horner nine of
ten pounds, Gedion Johnston something, John
Turner something, Geo: Bastable about 50 shillings.
However, should I live to get some money from
Northumberland shall discharge what I can of
them."

Signed:	John Lawson
Codicil:	No date. "Should Mr. Blackwell's business be

such that he cannot attend to the above should
wish that Mr. Edward Digges would undertake it."
  "I also owe George Kemper about 18 shillings,
he is to take the cot back as it is; Geo.
Robinson has some leather of mine to tan, for
which there is receipt in one of my draws. The
Winchester printer I am in arrears to about five
dollars which hope may be paid out of the money
Edward Digges brings from Northumberland.
Pickett & Blackwell has not given me sufficient
credit for two loads of wheat delivered them
in the fall 1793, they have given me credit for
another load of the same crop delivered in June
1794 for 5/6 which is not enough according to
their writing with me, which writing is in my
desk."

Wit.:	Wily Roy, Edward Digges, Jun'r.
Proved:	22 January 1798, will presented in the Ledger

of John Lawson .. proved by o. of Wily Roy
and ordered that it be removed from the ledger
and recorded. Joseph Blackwell, with John
Blackwell, Jr. his security in bond of $1,500,
made oath and granted cert. for obtaining a
probate.

Pages 93-95:	PARNACK GEORGE (Division of Personal Estate) Date: 10 July 1797
Div. by:	William Hunton, Jr., James Hunton, George Rogers.
Details:	Wilmoth George - widow - dower - L419.7.6 (one Book, Titlers Geographa)

```
         Diannah Robinson - L94.5.7 3/4
         Peggy George      - L94.5.7 1/2
         Gabriel George    - L94.5.7 3/4
         Presley George's part Son of Aron - L94.5.7 3/4
         Lucy Cleveland    - L94.5.7 3/4
         Reubin George     - L94.5.7 3/4
         Polly Newhouse    - L94.5.7 3/4
         Abner George      - L94.5.7 3/4
         Fanny George      - L94.5.7 3/4
Ret.:    22 January 1798
```

Pages
96-97:   JAMES FOLEY   (Inventory)
                Date: 29 June 1797
App'd by: Joseph O'Bannon, Isham O'Bannon, Alexander Keith
Total eval.: L1308.9.6
Ret.:   22 January 1798

Page
97:             JOHN FISHBACK   (Divison of Dower)
                Date: 3 November 1797
Div.by: William Metcalf, Minor Winn, J. Wake
Details: Sarah Fishback, widow - "Beginning at a Chesnut
          Oak on a hill side corner of the original Tract ..
          to a mark'd white oat and three stumps at the
          fork of the Road that leads to Ashby's Gap and
          to Fauquier Court House thence with the main
          road that leads to said Gab .. to a small hicory
          sapling in the dividing line between Philip
          Fishback and the tract of John Fishback deceased..
          corner to Philip Fishback .. 83 a. 3r. 8p.
Ret.:   22 January 1798

Pages
98-99:   JAMES WHEATLEY   (Administrator's Account)
Adm'r.:   James Wheatley
Details: TO: 1794 - George Johnson; John Minor (lawyer
          fee); Robert Bates. 1795 - Charles Duncan;
          Benjamin Pettit; Landon Carter for rent due;
          John West for repaining a still; Thomas Collins
          for Opening Tobacco; Samuel Johnson for smith's
          work; William Kernes; John Turner; John Brown
          Schoolmaster; Griffin Landman; Archibal McColley;
          Richard Hudson; Doctor Horner; Septimus Norris;
          Martin Pickett; Robert Love for John Strode;
          Evern Brown; Thomas L. Allarson; Robert Dunbar;

John Thornton; Richard Williamson; Nathaniel
Dodd; Toughler Williams. 1796 - Henry Field.
BY: 1794 - Alten Johnson. 1795 - Joseph
Oliver; Selah Shackleford; George Eastham;
Rec'd. of John Wheatley's Estate; Benjamin
Norman; John Crestenbury; Aiana Garner;
James Wheatley.

Exm'd by: John Hooe, Chilton Ransdell; William Skinker,
20 January 1798.
Ret.: 22 January 1798.

Pages
99-101:   BENJAMIN HARRISON (Inventory)
        No date.
App'd by: Ennis Combs, Joseph George, Philip (X) Spiller
Total eval.: L676.13.0
Ret.: 26 February 1798

Pages
102-103:   WILLIAM SANFORD PICKETT (Will)
        Date: 10 February 1798
Wife: Martha - one bedstead now at Rices and one pair
fire dogs
Son: William S. Pickett - young black Mare, colt of
my riding mare - one feather bed, bedstead and
furniture - one cow and calf.
Son: James S. Pickett - feather bed, bedstead and
furniture
Dau.: Anna Pickett - a negro man named Daniel - one
bed and furniture which she now claims
Dau.: Sukey Brady - one young bay mare colt - freely
enjoy and possess all the property she had in
possession when she came here to live - $256 in
lieu of a Certificate I received from her of
L128 which I sold for $2 per pound.
Children: .. all the rest of my Estate both real and
Personal after my Decease it is my desire should
be sold at publick Sale to the highest bidder
and the money arising therefrom to be equally
divided between my ten children, Viz. John S.
Pickett, Sanford Pickett, William Pickett,
James Pickett, Patty Fishback, Sukey Brady,
Molly Jackson, Sally Metcalf, Anna Pickett and
_____ Smith.
Exors.: Sons William S. Pickett, James S. Pickett
Signed: William Sanford Pickett
Wit.: William Metcalf, Joseph Smith

Proved: 26 February 1798, by o. of witnesses. William
Pickett and James Pickett, with Martin
Pickett, William Metcalf, John Craine and
John Wake their securities in bond of $10,000,
granted certificate for obtaining probate.

Pages
103-104:   PARNACK GEORGE (Administrator's Acct.)
Court Order dated January 1798
No admr. listed.
Exm'd by: James Hunton, George Rogers, William Hunton, Jr.
Details: Received from the Sale: Carr Bailey; Henry
Steele; Thomas Roach; Joseph Pierson; James
White; Dennis Hudson; Thomas James; Rec'd John
Kemper's bond; James Hunton; William Hunton;
Reubin George. PAID: Taxes; Francis Brooke;
Polly Newhous; Elias Edmonds; Richard Fisher;
Richard Gill.
Ret.:   26 February 1798

Page
104:           WILLIAM SMITH of Parish of Hamilton (Will)
Date: 15 October 1789
Son: William - Negroes
Dau.:   Mary Soddust - Negroes (after decease of dau. the
Negroes and their increase to be divided between
her children)
Son: Andrew - Negroes, land and stock
Exors: Son Andrew and Cousin James Withers
Signed: William Smith
Wit.:   Thomas Withers, John Withers, Hannah (X) Smith
Proved: 26 February 1798, by o. of Thomas Withers and
John Withers. Andrew Smith, with John Gaunt,
Francis Payne, Thomas Withers and John Withers
his securities in bond of $6,000, granted cert.
for obtaining probate.

Pages
105-106:   EDWARD SETTLE (Inventory)
No date.
App'd by: George Settle, John Edwards, Henry Carter
Total eval.: L10,941.3.5
Ret.:   26 February 1798

Pages
106-108:   EDWARD SETTLE (Settlement of Estate)
             Dates: 1793 - 1798
Adm'rx: Rozanna Settle
Details: TO: Gavin Lawson; S. Garner; Walter Colquhonn;
             William Cunningham and Company; Jonas Garner;
             Daniel Morgan; Samuel and B. Gordon; Alexander
             Marson of Falmouth; Estate of William Settle,
             dec'd.; Frances Settle; George Settle's Saw
             Mill; Francis Brooke; Charles Marshall.
Exm'd. by: Fauntleroy Dye, James Withers, George Settle
Date: 28 November 1797.
Teste: William Morgan
Ret.:   26 February 1798

Page
109:                 BENJAMIN HARRISON (Relinqishment of
                                           Executorship)
                     Date: 29 January 1798
Exor. & Details: Whereas the subscriber was appointed in
             and by the last will and Testament of Benjamin
             Harrisons Dec. - as one of the Testators Exe-
             cutors and the Subscriber living at a con-
             siderable distance from the Decedents Estate
             also being very infirm do hereby renounce and
             relinquish my Executorship in all and every-
             thing appertaining to the said Decedents Estate.
Signed: Peter Wagener
Wit.:   Thomas Gibson, John P. Williams, Beverly R.
             Wagoner
Ret.:   26 February 1798

Page
109:                 BENJAMIN HARRISON (Renounciation of Will)
                     Date: 30 January 1798
Details: "I Mary Harrison Widow of Benjamin Harrison do
             hereby declare that I will not take or accept
             any provision made me by my said husbands will
             if such there is or any part thereof and that I
             do renounce any benefit which I might claim under
             same, and that I will not abide by said will ..."
Signed: Mary Harrison
Wit.:   Thomas Gibson, Joseph George, Ennis Combs
Ret.:   26 February 1798

Page
110:                 WILLIAM SEATON (Administrator's Account)
                     Dates: 1796 - 1797
Exm'd by: Joseph Blackwell, Samuel Blackwell, George
             Marshall

Ret.: 26 February 1798

Pages
110-111:
                JOHN SMITH   (Guardian Account)
                Dates: 1795 - 1796
Guardian: John Smith
Orphan: Abner Smith
Details: TO: William Day, William Tancil,
Wit.:   T. Taylor
Ret.:   26 February 1798

Pages
111-112:
                WILLIAM SMITH   (Inventory)
                Date: 22 March 1798
App'd by: Aquilla Davis, Thomas Foley, Thomas Withers
Total eval.:   L378.10.0
Ret.:   23 April 1798

Pages
112-113:
                PETER MASON   (Inventory)
                No date
App'd by: Joseph Green, William Turley, John Bishop
Total eval.:   L233.6.3
Ret.:   23 April 1798

Page
114:
                JOHN BRAY   (Inventory)
                Date: 15 March 1798
App'd by: John Payne, John Chadelle, Allen Guttridge
Total eval.:   L43.17.0
Ret.:   23 April 1798

Pages
115-116:
                JOHN BRAY   (Sale of Estate)
                No date.
Adm'r.: Charles Marshall
Purchasers: Jinny Bray, John Lawson, James Vowels, Reuben
             Goutrich, George Kendall, Allen Gutrich, Joseph
             Warder, Thomas Sympson, Sally Dennis, Henry Ford,
             William Payne, John Gaunt, Archibald Campbell,
             John Payne, Lewis Strawther, Elias Little, Franci:
             Payne, Betsey M. Kinsy, Elijah Arnold, Samuel
             Aylett, Hugh Monroe, John Warder, Charles C.
             Chun, John Withers, Jr., Augustin Payne.
Am't of Sale: L66.8.0
Ret.:   23 April 1798

- 284 -

Pages
117-118:   JOHN BARKER (Administrator's Account)
               Dates: 1795 - 1797
Adm'r.:   Mr. John Glascock
Details: BY: Josiah Adams; John Herringdon, Thomas Simpson,
            Thomas Smith, John Glascock, Charles Chunn,
            Benjamin Rector, George McCabe, Sarah Barker,
            S. Ruth, William Lake, John A. Rollins, Charles
            C. Chunn.
Exm'd by: Joseph Chilton, John Ashby, James Adams, 25 October
          1797
Ret.:   23 April 1798

Pages
118-120:   BENJAMIN HARRISON (Inventory)
               Date: 19 March 1798
Adm'r.:   Benjamin Botts
Details: BY: George Lane, Deputy Sheriff of Pr. Wm. Co.;
            Simon Luttrill; Henderson, Fergerson & Gibson;
            John Cannon; Catesby Graham; Mary Harrison;
            Beverly Wagener; Gowin Adams; Thomas A. Smith;
            William Ross; Stephen Francis; John Brumback;
            Alexander Ross; Charles Cook; John Wilson; James
            Smith; Thomas Jones; Henry Bethel; Richard Foot;
            Thomas Homes; Hez'k. Oliver; Presley Bredwell;
            Zelah Williams; Nimrod Combs; Zachy Comyus; Wml.
            Cloe; V. Peyton; Benjamin Botts; John Tuttle;
            John McClanaham; William Green; John Gibson.
Total eval.: L739.13.3½
Ret.:   25 June 1798

Pages
120-121:   JOHN SMOOT (Inventory)
               No date.
App'd by: Matthew Neal, Dickerson Wood, William Wood
Total eval.: L83.19.6
Ret.:   25 June 1798

Pages
121-122:   JOHN PETERS (Administrator's Account)
               Date: 17 February 1798. Court Order dated
               September Court 1797.
Exm'd by: James Weaver, James Wright, John Martin, Charles
          Utterback.
Details: BY CASH PAID: Benjamin Payne; Doctor Horner;
            Cornelius Hall; William Jones; Samuel Neill;
            William Mountjoy; Augustine Smith; John Martin;
            James Thompson; Owen Woodruff; James Peters.
Ret.:   25 June 1798

- 285 -

Pages
122-123:   SMITH JOHNSON (Administrator's Account)
                Date: 24 June 1798
Adm'r.:   William Payne
Details: TO: Joseph Chilton; Bidy Johnson; Philip
            Mallory, Sen'r.; James Edmonds Sheriff in full
            of an Account Pickett & Co. against the Estate;
            Daniel Flowerrie, Jun'r.; James Billingsly;
            Matthew Harris deceased; on account of Executor
            C. Johnson ag't. the Estate; Pratt; Reubin Gutt-
            ridge.
Exm'd by: Richard Rixey; Joseph Chilton, Joseph Smith
Ret.:   25 June 1798

Page
124:            JAMES STEWART (Sale of Estate)
                Date: 3 April 1798
Exors: James Hathaway, sen'r., James Stewart, sen'r.
Purchasers: Elizabeth Stewart, Helen Griffin, Edward
            Norman
Ret.:   25 June 1798

Pages
125-127:   CHARLES GARNER (Inventory)
                Date: 28 February 1798
App'd by: Howsen Duncan, James (X) Pau, Joseph Parker
Total eval.: L324.12.0
Ret.:   23 July 1798

Pages
127:            EDWARD MATTHEWS (Inventory)
                Date: 12 May 1798
            No appraisers listed.
Total eval.: L106.10.0
Ret.:   23 July 1798

Pages
128-129:   JOHN MATTHEWS, of the County of Fauquier
                School Master being aged and infirm .. (Will
Beq.:   Date: 24 February 1798
            Mary, the dau. of Josiah Fishback and Ann his
            wife of Little River in the County of Fauquier,
            a Tract of Land .. 500 acres .. lying .. in the
            County of Lincoln in the State of Kentucke ..
            William Blackwell, son of Colo. John Blackwell of
            Tinpot in the County of Fauquier, my horse,

- 286 -

saddle, Bridle and saddle bags.
Sarah Battaille Fitzhugh, Dudley Fitzhugh, the
children of William Fitzhugh of Prospect Hill
in the Cjounty of Fauquier; Mary Fitzhugh, the
dau. of George Fitzhugh of Turkey Run the said
County of Fauquier - all remainder of estate
to be sold and together with cash on hand to be
equally divided among the above.

Exors: worthy Friend Colo. John Blackwell of Tinpot,
William Fitzhugh of Prospect Hill and George
Fitzhugh of Turkey Run.
Signed: John Matthews
No witnesses.
Ret. & Proved: 23 July 1798. Handwriting sworn to by George
Lowry, James Neale and Whiting Digges.

Pages
129-130:   ISAAC JOHNSON (Will)
                Date: 9 June 1798
Wife: Lydia - the Lease of Land whereon I now live -
200 acres - two Negroes - livestock and personal
estate during her widowhood.
Bro.:   Baldwin Johnson - after decease of wife, shall
possess all my Estate.
Exors: John Smith and his son Thomas.
Signed: Isaac (his X mark) Johnson
Wit.:   Jacob (X) Neigh, Ann (X) Neigh, Dosha (her X mark)
Crim, William (X) Griffin.
Proved: 23 July 1798, by o. of Jacob Neigh, Ann Neigh and
William Griffin. ".. and the Executors appearing
refused to qualify and on the motion of Thomas
Smith who made oath and together with John Smith
his security," acknowledged bond of $5,000 and
received letters of administration.

Pages
130-133:   WILLIAM ROUSSAU (Will)
                Date: 19 July 1792
Wife: Prissilla - Tract of Land whereon I now live
during her natural life - Negroes - Household
furniture.
Children: Henry, Margrit Combs, Nancy Peters - after decease of wife, land to be sold and money to be
equally divided among the three ..
Son: John - "Negro Man named Peter which I lent to
him to take to Georgia" - Negro named Anthony
Gr.son: William, son of John - Negro Peter after decease of father.

Gr.dau.: Margret, dau. of John - Negro Anthony after
         decease of father.
Son: William - and his wife Lydda - Negroes - after
         their death to go to their sons: John and
         William.
Son: Henry, and his wife Sarah - Negroes - after
         Henry's death to be divided among their
         children (not named)
Dau.:   Margret Combs, and her husband Ennice Combs -
         Negroes - to go to their children after their
         deaths
Son-in-law: Benjamin Payne, and wife Susanna - Negro
         woman Hannah - "provided he does not marr the
         said Negro nor suffer her to be removed out of
         the County of Fauquier and if he should atempt
         so to do my will is that my Exors. shall take
         possession of the said wench with her increase ..'
         After years the increase of said Negro woman
         to be equally divided among the children of
         Benjamin and Susanna Payne. At the decease of
         Benjamin Payne the Negro woman and her future
         increase to be equally divided among the following
         grandchildren: Henry Payne, Priscilla Payne,
         Sarah Payne and James Payne.
Dau.:   Nancy Peters and her husband John Peters - Negroes
         and after their deaths to be divided among their
         children.
Gr.dau.: Betsey Karr - Negro - one bed and furniture
Children: Henry, Margret Combs and Nancy Peters - after
         death of wife, to equally divide all stock and
         household furniture.
Exer.:   Wife Priscilla, son Henry, sons-inlaw Ennice Combs
         and John Peters.
Signed: William Roussau
Wit.:   Ignatius Luckett, James Cox, Susanna (X) Jenkins
Proved: 23 July 1798, by o. of Ignatius Luckett and James
         Cox and Susanna Jenkins. Priscilla Roussau, with
         John Peters her security in bond of $6,000,
         granted certificate for obtaining probate.

Pages
133-136:   GEORGE WHEATLEY (Inventory & Div. of Dower)
             Date: November 1796
App'd by: John Hooe, Jr., Linefield Sharp, William Woodside
Total eval.: L344.16.0
Details: The "widow's dower" was allotted, but there is
         no name mentioned. Also, an entry entitled,

"The Child's part."
Ret.: 23 July 1798

Pages
136-137:   JAMES BLYTHE   (Administrator's Account)
                Date: 13 July 1798
Adm'r.: William Nalls, Sen'r.
Exm'd by: L. Ashton, Wm. Hampton
Details: "To Mary Nalls for sundry sums paid by her during
          her widowhood for the above Estate in the year
          1792 as pr. proved account;" TO: Mr. Wake;
          William Nalls; James Lawler; Mary Nalls. BY:
          Nathan Matthew; Anthany Minter; William Hampton;
          Thomas Doughty; Thomas Thornton; William Nalls,
          Sen'r.; William Nalls, Jr.; Dennis Hudson; William
          Blythe.
Ret.:   23 July 1798

Page
137:            JOHN RUST   (Inventory)
                No date
App'd by: Benjamin Rector, George Glascock, Joseph Jeffries.
Total eval.:   One Negro - L38
Ret.:   23 October 1797

Pages
137-138:   WILLIAM SINKLAIR   (Will)
                Date: 24 January 1798
Wife: Lydda - all property, real and personal, except
         one acre.
Dau.:   Mary Feagans - to have the annual rent of $20
         for the one acre and house "to be laid off in a
         square .. to include the spring called Berrys
         Spring and the Building already built there .."
         The rent to be paid to Mary "during her life to
         be paid her only and not to her Husband Edward
         Feagans." If there should be other buildings
         constructed on the property, to cause the rent
         to be higher, the balance "to be equally divided
         among the whole of my Children."
Children: James, John, Isaac, Archibald, William Middleton,
         Horatio, Elizabeth Jones and Nancy - all slaves
         to be sold, including one loaned to George Jones,
         to the highest bidder - money to be equally
         divided. Personal property and real estate to
         be sold in like manner.

```
Exors:      Wife Lydda, sons James and John
Signed:     William Sinklair
Wit.:       William Metcalf, Charles Barnett, George Payne,
            Joshua Kenard.
Proved:     23 April 1798, by o. of Joshua Keneard and on
            24 September 1798, by o. of William Metcalf and
            Charles Barnett. John Sinklair made oath and
            with Walter Graham, his security in bond for
            $10,000, granted cert. for obtaining probate.
```

Pages
139-140:   JOHN LAWSON (Inventory)
                  Date: 24 January 1798
App'd by: Wily Roy, Thomas Roy, John Ball
Total Eval.: L647.5.0
Ret.:   24 September 1798

Pages
140-141:   CHARLES DAVIS (Will)
                  Date: 16 May 1796
Wife: Lydia - all property, real and personal, during
            her life
Gr.daus.:   Elizabeth and Lydia Davis - each one featherbed
            and furniture
Daus.:   Lucy Wheat and Lydia Davis - Negroes to the value
            of those received by their three brothers:
Sons: Griffith, Charles, William
Sons: The remaining 1/5 to be divided amongst Levi,
            Richard and John Davis.
Exors: Griffith, Charles and William Davis
Signed: Charles Davis
Wit.:   James Highlington Beckham, Gerrard Keating,
            Jemima Keating
Proved: 24 September 1798, by o. of Gerrard Keating and
            Jemimah Keating. On motion of William F. R.
            Davis,who made o. with Joseph Chilton and Nimrod
            Farrow his securities in bond of $10,000, granted
            certificate for obtaining probate.

Pages
141-142:   WILLIAM SETTLE (Administrator's Account)
                  Dates: 1781 - 1792
Adm'r.:   Edward Settle
Details: TO: Thomas James; William Southard; Joseph Ander-
            son; James Withers; Reuben Bramblet; Samuel
            Bronaugh; Ambrose Barnett for A. Leach and for

G. Nevile; John Kincheloe for Stermons
receipt; James Mushitt for John Scott; Edward
Baysie; Mr. William Norris; Robert Henson;
Edward Settle; James Spenney; Payne, Moore &
Co.; Martin Pickett; Francis Triplett; James
Forrister; John Headley; Benjamin Settle; James
Jett for James Craig; William Allason; Gavin
Lawson; James Truman; Joseph Anderson; Junis
Johnson; James Huffman; William Suddoth; Robert
Lawson; George Turbervill for 2 years rent.
BY: Wm. Jefferson; E. Settle; Wm. Willis; George
Turberville.
Exm'd by: Robert Rose, James Withers, Fauntleroy Dye
Ret.:   24 September 1798

Pages
143-144:   WILLIAM SINKLAIR (Inventory)
                Date: 4 October 1798
App'd by: Joshua Owens, Joshua Kennerd, Thomas Whiting
Total Eval.: L733.13.0
Ret.:   22 October 1798

Page
145:            GEORGE HARRIS (Inventory)
                Date: 8 October 1798
App'd by: John Norris, William Barker, Harmon Utterback
Total eval.: L15.19.8½
Ret.:   22 October 1798

Pages
145-146:   RICHARD SANFORD (Will)
                Date: 22 September 1798
Wife: Betty - all estate for life or widowhood, after
           her death, to be sold and equally divided amongst
           my children.
Children: Robert, John, William Bennet
Exors: Wife Betty, son Robert, friends Mr. James Hunton
           and Mr. Richard Baker
Signed: Richard Sanford
Wit.:   Hannah Hunton, Bernard Duffey, Owen Thomas,
           Thomas Hunton
Proved: 22 October 1798, by o. of Owen Thomas, Bernard
           Duffey and Thomas Hunton.

Pages
146-150:   WILLIAM SANFORD PICKETT (Inventory)
                Date: 30 August 1798

Details: 1 Baileys Dictionary; 1 Large Bible; 1 History
Joesphus; 1 Mouses Geography; Several Old Books.
App'd by: William Metcalf, Philip Fishback, Thos. Clark.
25 January 1799
Total eval.: L1340.0.1½
Certified by James Pickett and William Pickett,
the Executors - January, 1799
Ret.: 28 January 1799

Pages
150-151:   JOHN MATTHEWS   (Inventory)
               No date.
App'd by: George Lowry, Thos. Fitzhugh, Ambrose Barnett
Details: 1 Book Case and Library, L12; John Blackwell's
Note; Mr. William Fitzhugh, Prince William County
Total eval.: L187.16.8
Ret.: 28 January 1799

Pages
151-152:   WILLIAM ROUSSAU   (Inventory)
               Date: 13 October 1798
App'd by: Charles Waller, James Starks, James Cowles
Total eval.: L538.14.3
Ret.: 25 February 1799

Pages
153-154:   JOHN KEMPER   (Will)
               Date: 2 February 1796
Son: Peter - 100 acres in Culpeper County, horse,
bridle, saddle, cow and calf, "Phether" bed &
furniture, Sow & pigs, etc.
Son: Moses - one horse, bridle, saddle, cow & calf,
Ewe & lamb, 1 dish, one bason, three plates.
Dau.:   Susannah, now the wife of Henndry Hardistree -
L5
Son: John - 100 acres in Culpeper County, one horse,
bridle, saddle, one cow & calf, one ewe & lamb,
one Phether bed, 3 plates, one dish, one bason,
one sow & pigs.
Son: Tilman - Negro, one cow and calf, one horse,
bridle & saddle, one ewe and lamb, one dish, one
bason, 3 plaits, one sow & pigs.
Son: Charles - one horse, bridle, Saddle, phether bed
& furniture, one dish, one bason, 3 plaits.
Son: Joseph - one horse, bridle, saddle, one phether
bed, one cow & calf, one Ewe and lamb, one dish,
one bason, 3 plaits.

Son: Elias - one horse, saddle and bridle, one cow and calf, one ewe and lamb, one dish, one bason, 3 plaits.

Wife: Ann - land where I now live one - Negroes - 2 beds, 2 cows, one horse and saddle, Sow and pigs, and Milk and Bread for one year, two dishes, fore Basons, twelve plaits, Six spoons, six chairs, one ovill tabill and Table Clouth.

Daus.:   Caty, Elizabeth, Susannah, Mary, Anney - rest of my estate to be equally divided among my Daughters

Sons: Charles, Joseph and Elias - to receive the same amount as sons Peter and John - judged to be L123 each - each child to be equal with Peter and John

Exors: Peter Kemper, John Kemper, Charles and Joseph Kemper

Signed: John Kemper

Wit.:   Jacob Kemper, Sen'r., Jacob Kemper, Jun'r.

Proved: 25 February 1799, by o. of witnesses. Charles, John and Joseph Kemper qualified as Exors.and with Francis Payne, Jacob Kemper, Sen'r. and Jacob Burger, Sen'r. their securities on bond for $5,000, were granted cert. for obtaining probate.

Pages 154-155:   JOSEPH DUNCAN (Sale & Adm'r. Account)
                Date: 30 November 1797

Purchasers: Howson Duncan, Sarah Kerr, Joseph Duncan, John Mauzy, Lydia O'Bannon, Ebbin Porter, John Withers, William Withers, Sen'r., Lewis Withers, John O'Bannon, Nathaniel Rector, William Pickett, Enoch K. Withers, Armisted Holder, Archibald Duncan, James Edmonds, Walter Adams.
           PAID TO: Charles Marshall's fees in the Suit Henderson & Co.; Daniel Greenwood; Timothy Green; Jno. Mauzy; Frances Suddith; Jno. Withers; Howson Duncan; Gawin Lawson.

Signed: John Withers, Clk.

Settled by: Peter Lucas, James Withers, John Bronaugh - 23 February 1799.

Exors: Howson and John Duncan

Pages 156-157:   LYDIA DUNCAN (Sale of Estate)
                Date: 30 November - 1 December 1797

Purchasers: James Withers, Nath'l. Johnston, Garret
Freeman, Wm. Duncan, Joseph Duncan, Moses
Duncan, Thos. Brent, Wm. Pickett, Walter
Adams, Ebbin Porter & wife; John Parker,
Joseph Parker, George Gordon, Armisted Holder,
John Kemper, James Right, Benj'n. Bronaugh,
John Mauzy, James Routt, Presley Garner, Howson
Duncan, Cash due from Dunbar & Vass.
Account: TO: Benj. Bronaugh, Sarah Kerr, G. B. Horner,
Moses Duncan, Edward Digges, Diana Garner,
Jale Garner, Martin Pickett, Wm Duncan,
Overall & Bronaugh, Howson Duncan, Francis
Sudith, John Withers Clerk one days writing,
Timothy Green for Gazetting Sale, Francis
Brooke, Rich'd. Rixey Sheriff for Taxes.
Exm'd by: Peter Lucas, James Withers, John Bronaugh.

Pages
157-158:   JOSEPH DUNCAN (Account of Sale)
Date: 18 July 1797
Clerk: Daniel Greenwood, Clk of the Withers
Purchasers: Mr. Joseph English, Mr. Enoch Withers,
Mr. Tunis Johnston, Mr. John Craig, Mr.
Joseph Parker, Mr. George Deanny, Mr. Daniel
Greenwood, Mr. Nathaniel Johnston, Mr. Howson
Duncan, Mr. Benjamin Mathews, John Maddux,
Mr. Elijah Withers, Galvain Debbins, William
Junyon, Presley Garner, Enoch Smith, George
Robinson, William Pritchett, Robert Rose,
Joseph Duncan, John O'bannon, Lydia Obannon,
Nimrod Greenwood, Nath'l. Dodd, Jno. Mauzy,
Garrett Freeman, James Parr, Col. John Black-
well.
Ret.:   25 February 1799. This Account of the sales
and administration of Joseph and Lydia Duncan
Deceased ...

Page
160:    MISS SARAH SCOTT (Inventory)
Date: 21 February 1799
App'd by: Thomas Chilton, Presley Morehead, Wm. Hampton
Total Eval.: L458.7.6
Ret.:   25 February 1799
Note: The property (slaves and personal) was at the
house of L. Ashton.

Pages
160-161:   WILLIAM ALLEN (Division of Estate)
               Date: 4 February 1799
Div. by: Chilton Ransdell, George Eastham
Children: William Woodside, Charles Allen, Dan'l. Allen,
           Alice Allen, Joanna Allen.
Ret.:   25 February 1799

Page
161:          JAMES BURGESS (Inventory)
               No date.
App'd by: James Foley, Christopher Hitch, Thomas Foley
Total eval: L179.7.0
Ret.:   25 February 1799

Pages
161-162:   SAMUEL GRIGSBY (Division)
               Date: 26 October 1798
Div. by: Joseph Chilton, John O'Bannon, Laur. Ashton,
           "met at the House of William Tuttle (it being
           the place appointed by the Legatees).."
Details: The division does not mention whose estate it
           was, nor the legatees. In the Margin of the
           will book is a note: "Grigsby's division" and
           the MINUTE BOOK, 1798-99, page 216, has the
           following entry: "Ordered that Alexander Scott,
           Joseph Chilton, John Thomas Chunn and Thomas
           Chilton or any three of them divide the Slaves
           of Samuel Grigsby Deceased among his Representa-
           tives agreeable to his will." The slaves were
           divided into seven lots, but no mame of the
           legatee is mentioned in the recorded division.
           MINUTE BOOK, 1798-99, page 245: "Joseph O'Bannon
           and Larrence Ashton are added to the Commissioners
           appointed to divide the estate of Samuel
           Grigsby deceased."

Page
163:         ^   JOHN LAWSON (Administrator's Account)
               Dates: January 1798 - 28 January 1799
Adm'r.:   Joseph Blackwell
Details: TO: Richard Fisher; Lamkin, for rent; William
           Morgan; G. Lawson; John Blackwell; Matthew
           Hawson; Pickett & Blackwell.
Exm'd. by: Thad's. Norris, Charles Marshall
Ret.:   25 February 1799

Pages
164-165:   JAMES YOUNG (Inventory)
              Date: 5 April 1799
App'd by: George Lowry, George Grant, James McClanaham.
No total.
Ret.:   22 April 1799

Pages
165-172:   WILLIAM SANFORD PICKETT (Acc't. of Sales)
              Date: 12 September 1798
Purchasers: James Bland, Aaron Thomas, Gerard McClanaham,
         John Wilson, Thomas O'Bannon, Thomas Whiting,
         Thomas H. Brown, John Turner, James Smith,
         Benjamin O'Bannon, Hugh Rogers, John Crupper,
         Cuthbert Harrison, John Barlis, James Pickett,
         Catesby Graham, Sampson Leakman, Withers Smith,
         Joseph O'Bannon, William Brook, Sandford Pickett,
         Valentine Flint, Joseph Randall, Henson Barrott,
         John Jones, John Bowyce, Sarah Griffith, Joseph
         Hampton, Charles Metcalf, Ann Pickett (Josephus'
         History), John Wake, 1 Book titled Morses Geo.;
         Micajah Crupper, David Hopkins, Baileys Dictionary
         Susanna Brady, Joseph Randall; James Smith,
         Joshua Owens, Thomas Clark, William Leonard,
         Mason French, Elijah Griffith, 1 still; Minor
         Winn, mash tubs; Wm. Tuttle, James Hamilton,
         Wm. Pickett, Benjamin Downs, Samuel Rust, Philip
         Langfit, James Channel, Enoch Grigsby, Thomas
         O'Bannon, Philip Fishback, Robert Pierce, John
         Hathaway, John Thomas, Alexander Foster, Wm.
         Pilcher, Andrew Smarr, Stephen Pilcher, Thomas
         Brent, Joseph Smith, Joseph Hampton, Nancy
         McIntush, Henry Wey (also Way); Charles Barker;
         George Harper, Roger Tolle, Samuel Henderson,
         John Lynn, Wm. Canstable, Negro John, 1 walnut
         table.
Total: L1629.6.0½
Ret.:   22 April 1799

Pages
172-173:   JOHN KEMPER, SEN'R. (Inventory)
              Date: Tuesday, 26 February 1799
App'd by: George Settle, John Fishback, Francis Suddoth
No total
Ret.:   22 April 1799

Pages
174-175:   RICHARD SANFORD (Inventory)
                     Date: 5 April 1799
App'd by: David McNish, Owen Thomas, William Hunton, Jr.
Total eval.: L396.17.6
Ret.:   22 April 1799

Pages
176-177:   WILLIAM THOMAS (Will)
                    Date: 14 November 1798
Wife: Allenner - whole estate, except below:
Son: Daniel - two Negroes
Son: Erasmus - Negro - feather bed and furniture
Son: John - two Negro girls - horse - feather bed
            and furniture.
Son: William - two Negroes - black mare - one
            feather bed and furniture
Sons: Youngest sons: John and William - all my lands
            after decease of wife.
Dau.:   Rebekah - two Negroes - L50 cash to be divided
            among her children.
Dau.:   Precious - three Negroes - one feather bed and
            furniture - "and a Riding Beast."
Children: Daniel, Erasimus and Precious - to equally divide
            all that remains after wife's death.
Exors: wife, son Daniel and son William
Signed: William Thomas
Wit.:   Reuben Strother, Richard Turner, Jas. Channel
Proved: 22 April 1799, by o. of Robert Strother and
            Edward Turner (sic). Eleanon Thomas and Daniel
            Thomas made oath and with Edward Turner,
            Reuben Strother and William Thomas their
            securities in bond of $6,000, granted certificate
            to obtain probate.

Pages
177-178:   HONER WINKFIELD (Will)
                    Date: 24 November 1798
           "... I give to Ben a Negroe man Slave belonging
           to James Gillison, Sen'r. whom I Claim as my
           Husband all my Estate..."
Exors: my friend John Gillison and Lewis Shumate
Signed: Honer (her X mark) Winkfield
Wit.:   Elizabeth Shumate, Betty (X) Corum, Jane (X)
            John.
Proved: 22 April 1799, by o. of Betty Coram and Jane

John. John Gillison made oath and with
Joseph Blackwell his security in bond of
$100, granted certificate for obtaining a
probate.

Pages
178-179:   ISAAC JOHNSON (Inventory)
                    Date: 24 July 1798
App'd by: Aquilla Davis, Dickerson Wood, Jun'r., James
          Payne
Total eval.: L167.4.9
Ret.:   24 June 1799

Pages
179-180:   CHARLES DAVIS (Inventory)
                    Date: 20 October 1798
App'd by: Edward Shacklett, John Cooke, Benjamin Rector.
Total Eval.: L769.11.9
Ret.:   24 June 1799

Page
181:                MICHAEL BUCHANAN (Will)
                    Date: 15 January 1799
Bro.:   John - 1,000 acres "lying on the waters of Paint
          Creek, in the Northwestern Territory, which I
          purchased of Doctor Seldon with this reserve,
          That he give my two nieces, Mary and Hannah
          Buchanan, of Pensilvania, Daughters of my Bro-
          ther Thomas, dec'd, each one hundred acres of
          said land, or else, pay them the sum of $200
          each in 18 months after my decease."
Friend: Aquilla Janny - 100 acres or $200 from said
          land, as bro. John thinks best.
Bro.:   John - all debts due me
Exors: Brother John and Aquilla Janny of Berkley
          County
Signed: Michael Buchanan
Wit.:   Joseph Lloyd, Hezekiah Glasscock, William
          McEndree.
Proved: 24 June 1799, by o. of Hezekiah Glasscock and
          William McEndree. John Buchanan made o. and
          with Daniel Flowerree, Jun'r. and Hezekiah
          Glascock his securities in bond for $2,000,
          granted cert. for obtaining a probate.

Pages
182-184:   HENRY RECTOR   (Will)
                Date: 8 January 1799
Wife: (not mentioned) - all property, real (150 a.)
          and personal, for her life and at her decease
          to be divided in the following manner:
Son: Elijah - L30 Virginia money, second choice
          of Feather bed and furniture, a man's saddle,
          colt, plantatinn utensils.
Dau.:   Caty - L12, first choice of feather bed & furni-
          ture, colt, woman's saddle, the loom with the
          gear belonging thereto, should she die before
          her mother this bequeath shall be null and void,
          except for the bed which shall be her daughter
          Polley's.
Children: After death of wife all property to be sold and
          divided between all my children then living
          respecting the Hundred acres of land, that my
          son Spencer lived on, in consequence of a pro-
          mise made to him I leave it to his children:
          Edward, John, Henry, Mary Ann and Pencey to be
          equally divided between them, on condition that
          they pay my Children one thousand weight Crop
          Tobacco (which I lent their father to pay for
          some land he bought) at 14 s. pr. Hundred with
          interest from Eleven years back from the Date
          of these presents, and in case they refuse to do
          so they forfeit all claim to the land which
          shall then be sold with the rest of my property.
No executors named.
Signed: Henry (his X mark) Rector
Wit.:   Joseph Lloyd, Hezekiah Glasscock, William Finch.
Proved: 24 June 1799 by o. of Hezekiah Glasscock and
          William Finch. Nancy Rector, made o. and with
          George Glascock, Joseph Jeffries and Eli Rector
          her securities, on bond of $2,000, granted
          cert. for obtaining a probate.

Pages
184-185:   THOMAS PORTER   (Will)
                "of Parish of Hamilton"
                Date: 10 May 1799
Son: Eli - 150 acres, part of the Tract whereon I
          now live - one feather bed & furniture - live-
          stock - ½ pewter and ½ pot iron.
Dau.:   Betty Porter - 100 acres, the remainder of the

Tract whereon I now live - Negro - Livestock

Married
Children: Hannah Jackman, Sarah Scott, John Porter, William
          Thomas, Charles and Edwin - to have what has
          been given them already.
Children: Hannah Jackman, Sarah Scott, William, Thomas,
          Charles, Betty, Eli and John Porter deceased,
          his heirs - remainder of estate, up to L100,
          if there is more "Edwin shall come in for a
          proportion of that balance."
Servants: Jack, Will and Sam - my wearing clothes
Exors: Sons, William, Thomas and Edwin
Signed: Thomas Porter
Wit.:   Wily Roy
Proved: 24 June 1799, by o. of Wiley Roy. William,
          Thomas and Edwin Porter made o. and with Samuel
          Porter and Martin Porter their security in bond
          for $10,000, granted cert. for obtaining a
          probate.

Pages
186-188:   JOSIAH FISHBACK (Inventory)
               Date: 11 February 1799
App'd by: Minor Winn, Thomas Clark, William Elliott
Total Eval.: L1,484.17.8¼
Note: Jesse Fishback and Charles Monday, Adm'rs. of
          .the Estate of Josiah Fishback made o. that the
          Inventory was correct - 17 July 1799.
Ret.:   22 July 1799

Pages
188-189:   JONATHAN BROWN (Will)
               Date: 19 May 1799
Wife: Mary - the whole of my property for her use and
          to be at her disposal forever.
No executor named.
Signed: Jonathan Brown
Wit.:   Samuel Chilton, William Brown, James Seaton,
          Betty Kennor
Proved: 22 July 1799, by o. of Samuel Chilton and James
          Seaton. Mary Brown made oath and with James
          Seaton her sec. in bond for $500, granted cert.
          for obtaining a probate.

Pages
189-190:   THOMAS ROOKARD (Will)
               Date: 8 August 1798

Wife: (not named) to have all estate for life or widowhood
Dau.:   Nancy Rookard and her son Robert Carter Rookard -
        one half of my estate - after daughter's death
        what has been given her, together with the lease
        I now live on, to go to her son.
Dau.:   Lydia Oden - 1 s. sterling
Gr.children: Hiram, Elizabeth Rookard - other half of
        estate.
Exor.:   wife and George Calvert
Signed: Thomas Rookard
Wit.:   Joseph Blackwell, James Weeks, George Walker,
        Richard Cockran
Proved: 22 July 1799, by o. of Joseph Blackwell. Sarah
        Rookard and George Calvert made o., and with
        James Weeks and Robert Combs their security in
        bond for $10,000, granted cert. for obtaining
        probate.

Pages
191-192:   DUNCAN GRAHAM (Administrator's Account)
             Date: 29 December 1798
Exm'd by: William Ash, Joseph Chilton and Richard Rixey
        who found Thomas Massie's (Guardian) account for
        the "guardianship of Graham's orphans" correct.
Dates: 1795 - 1798
Details: TO: Wm. Ash; Wm. Hambrick; "Cash for Wm's Hatt;
        Joseph Chilton; Paid for various items for:
        Joseph, Nancy, Polley, Wm.; James Fulton.
Ret.:   22 July 1799

Pages
193-196:   JOHN EDMONDS (Inventory)
             Date: 23 January 1799
App'd by: Hezekiah Shacklett, John Ashby, Joseph Chilton
Total eval.: L1,499.15.1
Ret.:   25 February 1799

Pages
196-198:   JOHN THORNBURY (Will)
             Date: 23 November 1795
Wife: Elizabeth - 486 a. as long as she lives or re-
        mains a widow. If she remarries, the property
        to be disposed of as follows:
Son: William - possession of the lplantation whereon
        I now live and half of the 486 a. above.
Son: Thomas - the other half of the above

```
Son:        Henry - the plantation he now lives on - 186 a.
Son:        Samuel - the plantation he now lives on - 150 a.
Son:        Francis - the plantation he now lives on - 238 a.
Children:   Peggy Myres, Mary Wigginton - slaves - "I have
            a patent for one thousand and seven hundred and
            three acres of Land in the state of Kentucky .."
            to be sold by son Thomas and money to be equally
            divided among ten (10) children.
Exors:      Sons Samuel, Francis, William
Signed:     John Thornbury
Wit.:       Henry Dade Hooes, Moses Moss, Thomas Green
Proved:     23 September 1799, by o. of Henry Dade Hooe,
            Moses Moss and Thomas Green. William Thornbury
            made o. and with Thomas Green and James
            McClanaham his securities in bond for $18,000,
            granted cert. for obtaining probate.
```

Pages
199-201:   WILLIAM THOMAS (Inventory)
                    No date.
App'd by: Reuben Strother, William Elliott, Edward Turner,
            Thomas Priest.
Total Eval.: L1,286.17.9
Ret.:   23 September 1799

Pages
202-203:   CLEMENT BILLINGSBY (Adm'r. Acct. & Inventory)
                    Date: 15 February 1799
Exm'd by: Joshua Singleton, William Watkins, John Warder
Details: TO: William Hunt, James Strother, Joseph Morgan,
            Joseph Smith, John Payne, James Edmonds, Reuben
            Guthridge, William Gibson, John Monroe, Augustine
            Payne, John Warder, Archibald Cammel, Daniel
            Bradford, John Morehead, Joseph Chilton, William
            Payne, Joseph Warder, Elijah Arnold, James
            Billingsby.
Total Eval: L193.16.6
Ret.:   23 September 1799

Pages
203-206:   GEORGE CROSBY (Inventory)
                    Nodate.
App'd by: John Mauzy, Ennis Combs, Daniel Orear
Total Eval: L501.13.5
Ret.:   23 September 1799

- 302 -

PAGE
206:                    JAMES HATHAWAY (Inventory)
                        Date: 28 June 1799
App'd by: Thomas Chilton, Ambrose Barnett, George Rogers
Total eval: L1,793.15.0
Ret.:   23 September 1799

Pages
207-210:   SEPTIMUS NORRIS (Inventory)
                        Date: 19 September 1799
Adm'r.:   Thaddeus Norris
App'd by: William Horner, Joseph Blackwell, Thomas Hunton
Details: Books: 4 vol. Goldsmith's Animated Nature; 4
           Pemilia; 1 Bible Testament and Spelling; 4 vol.
           Evalina; 1 Housewife; 1 Henry's Meditation; 1
           Invincible Rambler; 1 Family & School New
           Testament; 1 Geography & Testament; 1 Pockett
           Dictionary; 1 small History.
Total Eval: L559.1.4½
Ret.:   23 September 1799

Pages
210-212:   JOSEPH WHEATLEY (Administrator's Account)
                        Date: 4 June 1799
Adm'rx.:   Mary Wheatley
Dates: 1795 - 1797
Details: TO: Waggonage of wheat to Falmouth; Lawyer Chilton;
           Hopwood for crying sale (1796); Baylor Jennings;
           F. Ficklin; George Suddoth; Daniel McClaren;
           B. Bryan; Peter Conway; James Wheatley; Lawyer
           Marshall in suit against Kerns; Gillison;
           Whitton; S. Fox; Simon Boling; Samuel Snelling;
           G. Glendenny; Batly Bryant. BY: Lawson & Morson;
           James Wheatley; George Maddon, Jun'r.; John Oliver;
           William Oliver; Dunbar; Shumate; William Brown.
Exam'd by: Peter Conway and James Wright
Ret.:   23 September 1799

Pages
212-213:   JAMES STEWART (Administrator's Account)
                        Date: 2 March 1798
Adm'r.:   James Stewart
Details: TO: Joseph Blackwell, John Stewart, James Steward,
           Joseph Nelson, William Stewart, Allen Steward,
           Elizabeth Stewart for her proportion of sale in
           full, 8815 lbs. Tobol, L14.15.6½; Thomas Nevill

in full for Mary Stewart part of sale; Helen
Stewart, 'do'; Edward Norman for Jane's part
of 'do'; BY: (1781) - Charles Chilton, Colonel
William Edmonds.
Exm'd by: Charles Marshall, Thomas Diggs, Wily Roy,
B. Duffy.
Ret.: 23 September 1799

Page
214: THOMAS PORTER (Inventory)
No date.
App'd by: Enoch K. Withers, John Ball, Samuel Fisher
Total eval: $3,152.33
Ret.: 28 October 1799

Pages
215-216: BERNARD DUFFY (Inventory)
Date: 4 October 1799
App'd by: John White, John Tomblin, Joseph Bailey
Total Eval.: L213.2.9
Ret.: 28 October 1799

Page
216: JAMES SEATON (Guardianship Account)
Date: 16 October 1799
Dates: March 1798 - October 1799
Orphan: William Seaton
Details: Cash Received of: William Brown, Jonathan Brown.
Ret.: 28 October 1799

Page
217: HENRY RECTOR (Inventory)
Court order dated: June 1799
App'd by: Hezekiah Glasscock, William Finch, William Rector
Total eval: L103.3.0
Ret.: 28 October 1799

Pages
218-219: MR. THOMAS ROOKARD (Inventory)
Date: 20 December 1799
App'd by: James Weeks, John Monday, Joseph Hampton
Total eval: $939.1
Ret.: 23 December 1799

- - -

INDEX

ADAM: Jacob, 24
ADAMS: Absalom, 47; Ann, 114,
136; Charles, 166; Enoch, 63;
Feathergill, 125, 130; George,
114, 196, 233, 237; Elizabeth,
114; Gavin, 256; Gowen, 256,
284; James, 115; John, 50, 63,
69, 76, 94, 114w, 115, 132i;
Josias, 114, 245, 284 (Josiah);
Littleton, 115, 196, 233, 276;
Sarah, 132; Sarah Stacy, 115;
Susanna, 114; Thomas, 115; 209,
245, 276; Walter, 292, 293.

ADIE: Margaret, 204.

ALGIERS: Heronomos, 61.

ALLAN (See also Allen): Henry,
58; Robert, Jr., 61; William,
61.

ALLEN: Alice, 294; Ann, 12;
Archibald, 19, 21, 48, 170,
227; Betty, 71, 84; Charles,
168, 294; Dan'l., 294; Henry,
71i, 135, 228; James, 12, 19,
78, 165, 226, 227, 238; Joanna,
294; John, 11w, 16i, 71i, 227,
238d, 261; Joseph, 12, 226,
227, 238; Martha, 146; Susanna,
168; Thomas, 11, 227; Ursilla,
12, 226w, 227, 238i; William,
12, 70, 226, 227, 238, 267d,
294d; _____, 253;

ALLISON (Allason, Alason,
Allarson): David, 112; John,
24; Robert, 199, 200, 227;
Thomas L., 279; William, 112,
152, 162, 231, 290.

AMBROSE: Elizabeth, 15.

ANDERSON: Andrew, 50; John,
61, 189; Joseph, 268, 289,
290; Samuel, 24; Thomas, 243.

Ann Churchill's Spring Branch,
207.

ARNOLD: Benjamin, 105, 122,
201, 232, 247, 253; Charles,
261; Elijah, 283, 301; George,
60, 201; Humphrey, 193i, 201a,
232a; Isaac, 198, 201, 232,

Sam, 201; Seymour, 201.

Arnold's Mill, 122.

ASBERRY-ASBURY: Betty, 215;
Elizabeth, 227; George, 108;
Henry, 108,128,135; Jane, 224,
236; William, 108,236i, 275.

ASH: Elizabeth, 62,63; Elon,
62,63; Frances,62; Francis,
62w,63,69,209; George, 62,207,
209; James, 62,63; Littleton,
62,63; Molly, 62,63; Uriel,
62,63; William, 62,63,300.

ASHBY: Alexander,207; Bayles,
207; Benjamin, 20,62,74,206,
207; David, 61,62; Enoch, 207;
John, 4,16,24,35,41,46,71,94,
98,110,114,118,121,141,143,164,
196,197,186w,207,212,237,272,
284,300; John, Jr., 82;Leannah,
247; Lucinda, 247; Lucy Luess,
248; Martin, 207; Nathaniel, 77,
Nimrod, 24,60i-a,61,207; Robert,
35,38,40,44,60,62,63,135,151,206
207,209i,228; Sally, 207; Thomas, 207; William, 62,207.

Ashby vs. Hambleton, 264.

Ashby's Gap, 56, 279.

ASHTON: Laur., 200,214,215,226,
227,244,293,294 (Larrence).

Ashton & Horner, 232.

ATHEL: Molley, 207.

Augusta County, Va., 7.

ALEXANDER: William, 41,54,72,
105,173.

Alexandria Gazette, 264.

Alexandria, Va., 162.

ALSUP: Dorothy (Ash), 62, 63.

Aquia Creek, 118.

ARRAGON: David, 277.

ASKINS: John, 181.

ATWELL-ATTWELL: Francis, 33,51,69,72,107,145; Thomas, 61.

ATWOOD-ATTWOOD: Gilbert, 76; John, 77.

AUSTIN: John, 200.

AYLETT: Samuel, 283.

AYRES: Thomas, 34,51.

AYRISS: John, 151.

- B -

BAILEY: Carr, 281; Milly (Duncan), 263; Joseph, 303; Pierce Henderson, 263.

BAKER: John, 102; Richard, 290; Samuel, 102,256; W., 131.

BALDWIN: _____,64.

BALL: Benjamin, 219; David, 219; Edward, 14,40,45,81, 166; Elizabeth, 236; Hannah, 219; Judith, 98,236 (Judy); Lettice, 98; Letty, 184; Lucy, 236; Mary, 52,98; Molly, 184; James, 179,236w,239i, 272a; John, 51i,52i,97,98, 184,193,236,289,303; Nancy, 236; Sarah,135; Shealtial, 236; Taliaferro, 236; Thomas, 223; William, 40,58i,98,134, 184,220,224 (Jr.), 227,233,

239,259; Williamson, 95.

BALLARD: Mary, 160; William, 160,192.

BANKS: G., 61; Gerard, 78.

BANNISTER-BANESTER-BANISTER: Augustin, 208; Frances, 31; Mary, 31; William, 41.

BARBEE-BARBY-BARBA: Ann, 204; Andrew, 157,254w,256i; Andrew Russell, 254; Elizabeth, 254; J.L., 191; Jane, 254; John, 202, 230,254; Joseph, 185,191,204, 254; Mary, 254; Sarah, 254; Thomas, 177, 78, 254; William, 227, 228.

BARBER: Charles, 61; John, 18, 71,73,128,140,196; Thomas, 48; William, 151.

BARKER: Ann, 237; Charles, 184, 295; Chloe, 237; Elizabeth, 237; James, 184; John, 149, 155i,237a, 196a, 205,211,227,284a,264; Mary, 184,237; Milly, 237; Nanny, 184; Peter, 93; Richard, 185; Sarah, 237,284; Susannah, 184; William, 182,184w,185,186,197,200,235,263, 290.

BARKLEY-BERKLEY: William, 134, 136,144,155,167.

BARLIS: John, 295.

BARNETT: Ambrose, 63,64,68,74, 95,149,151,167,178,182,189,214, 225,206,243,260,264,266,267,274, 289,291,302; Charles, 289; James, 61,62,64,151,201; John, 64; Judith, 63,64; Milly, 64.

BARRET: Smith, 95.

BARRIMORE: James, 205.

BARROTT: Henson, 295; Mary,32.

BARTLETT: James, 79;
Sarah (Hathaway), 174;
Thomas, 36,79,99,108,126,
135,145,155; Wm.,52,108.

BARTLEY: William, 87.

BARTON: David, 60,61,228;
James, 127,198,236; Thomas,
5.

BARWICK: Edward, 39.

BASHAW-BESHAW: Archibald,
149; Betsey, 104; Celia,
104; Elijah, 104; Molly,
104; Peter, 104w,107i,253;
Rawleigh W. Chinn, 104;
Sukey, 104.

BASTABLE: ____,274;
George, 246,278.

BASYE-BAYSIE-BAISEY:
Edmund, 4,30; Edward,290;
John, 44,149; Joseph, 149,
228; Josiah, 129.

BATES: James, 276; Robert,
279.

BATSON: Mary, 140.

BATTALEY: Ann, 143w,144;
Fieldin, 143; Hannah, 143,
144.

BAWL: James, 191.

BAYLES-BAILES-BAILS:
John, 95; William, 61,115.

BAYLIS: John, 24; Samuel,
23.

BAXTER: John, 109.

BAYLEY-BALEY-BAILEY:
Andrew, 162; Betty, 43;
Carr, 14,43w,45,151;
Catherine, 9,168; James,
30,43,45i,81i,214; John,43,
101w,107i; Joseph, 43,202,
228,168; Mary, 43,83;

BAYLEY-BAILLE-BAILLIE-BAYLIE:
(con't.) Minter,43; Moses, 107,
128; Simeon, 202; Thom, 179;
Thomas, 205; William, 43,202,
203,168; Wright, 101.

BEACH-BEECH: Alexander, 17,18;
Ann, 102; John,102; Lettice,102;
Margaret, 18; Mary, 17,102;
Peter, 17,102w; Sarah, 18,102;
William, 17.

BEALE: Eustace, 240; John Lee,
177; Margarett, 240; Miss ____,
257; Richard Eustace, 240.

BECKHAM: James Highlington, 289.

BECKWITH: Sir Marmaduke, 158.

BELL: Charles, 69,135; Frances,
255w, 262i; James, 97,112,151,
152,189,202; John, 11,24,26,28,
30,35,150,151,152,154; William,
255.

BENJEY: Sarah, 194.

BENNETT-BENNITT: George, 38,40,
44,61,71,135,228; John 34.

Berkeley County, Va., 297.

BERRY: Enoch, 60; George, 19,
20,47,69; Henry, 21,108; Joseph,
61; Nancy, 151; Reuben, 24;
William, 67,155; Winnifred, 251i

BERRYMAN: Ann, 144; Benj., 144;
Charles, 144; Maximillian, 16,
18,48,94,98,137,141,144,255;
Robert,248i,255a; Sarah,255.

BETHEL: Henry, 284.

BEWLEY: Nathan, 51.

Big Sandy River, Kentucky, 174.

BILLINGS: Clem, 245.

BILLINGSBY: Clement,265i,
301a; James,285,301.

BIRURAM: Conney, 44.

BISHOP: John, 272,283;
William, 140.

BLACKBURN: Christopher,
268; Col., 185; Edward,
61;Judith, 184; Thomas,
173.

BLACKERBY: Joseph, 71;
Mary, 126.

BLACKMORE: Ann, 64; John,
61; Joseph, 60.

BLACKWELL: _____,252; A.,
256; Ann Grayson, 204;
Anne, 178; Betty, 178;
Ceclia, 229; Elizabeth,
68; George Steptoe, 177,
178, 192; George S.,238,
Hannah, 67,68; James,51,
98,156; John,33,67,68,76,77,
140,150,151,177,178,185,
195,202,205,210,212,221,
222,226,252,261,278,285,
286,291,293,294; John,Jr.
82,209,218,225,276; John
Sen'r.,209,213,231;Joseph,
34,67,68,69,97,100,151,
152,117,178,195,197,201,204
216,217,218,221,224,232,
236,246,251,255,256,259,
260,274,277,278,282,300,
302; Joseph,Jr.: 82,211,
274,294,297; Joseph,Sr.,
177w,178; Judy,69; Judah,
178; Lucy, 67,68,69,178;
Sarah, 67,68; Samuel, 67,
68,100,151,177,179,201,
209,216,221,223,225,228,
253,254,255,256,257,261,
276,282; William,14,30,
40,67w,68,76,77,116,171i,
172,228,229i-d,239,285.

Blackwells Road, 249.

BLAIN: Thomas, 66.

BLAND: Benj., 44; Betty, 130;
Catherine, 184; Charles, 130,
155; Elizabeth, 155; Esther,
130, 155; Jackey, 130; James,
130, 155,183,184,295; Jean,184,
195; John, 155,185; Mary, 130w,
134i, 155, 184; Thomas, 183w,
184; Thomas, Sr., 195a, Thomas,
Jr., 195; William, 195.

BLANSET: John, 83; William 83.

BLY: James, 189.

BLYTH(E): James, 166,288a;
William, 288.

BODES: Tolliver, 33.

BODY: William, 227.

BOGGESS: Hannah,47; Jeremiah,47
Richard, 47; Thomas, 47w,48i.

BOGUE: James, 151.

BOLEY: John, 128.

BOLLING-BOLING: Elizabeth,222;
Simon, 302.

BOLT: Thomas, 58i.

Books: 201,220,253,256,258,262,
278,291,295,302.

BOON(E): Squire, 153.

BOSWELL: William, 51i.

BOTTS: Benjamin, 277,284.

BOWERS: Peter, 232.

BOWMAN: Jacob, 62.

BOWMER: George, 261; Peter, 127,
129,212,261.

BOWSE: _____ (the tanner), 274.

BOWYCE: John, 295.

BOYCE: Rich'd., 200.

BOYD: Dr. _____, 135.
Samuel, 82,103,151,275.

BOYLE: Francis,256; Mr.,
257.

BRADFORD: Ann,5,171,226;
Alexander, 5,10,11,14,16,
24,31,35,42,65,131,139,158,
183; Austin,267; Baldwin,
226; Benj.,139,256; Caty,
218; Daniel,29,42,65,5,10,
11,16,17,24,116,126,145,
164,187,301; Henry,5,142;
John,232; W.M., 211;
William, 4,5w,10i,

BRADLEY: Celia, 253; Hugh,
185,219,253w; Richard,253.

BRADY: Amelia,130; Heze-
kiah, 132,155; Jos.,195;
Joseph, 275; Sukey, 280;
Susanna, 295; Thomas,275.

BRAGG: Joseph, 72,154;
Wm, 201.

BRAHAN-BRAHAWN: James,
72; John, 41,72w,74i,
Lettice, 72,73; Thomas,
72,73; Wm.,72.

BRAMLETT-BRAMBLET:
Henry (Harry),84,92,93;
Reuben, 231,289.

BRANAN: Hannah (Crump),
188.

BRANSON: Jacob, 268.

BRAY: Elizabeth, 274;
Jinny, 283; John,283i-s.·

BREDWELL: Presley, 284.

BRENT: David, 202; Robert,
24; Thomas, 293,295; W.,41;
William, 148,189; _____, 22.

Brent Town: 186.

BRIGHAM: Elizabeth, 34.

BRINKER: Henry, 17,61.

Broad Run Mountain, 248.

BROADHURST-BROADHUSKS: William,
165, 220i.

BRONAUGH: Benjamin, 221,243,
266,293; Francis, 25,33,34,50;
John, 86w,99i,205,221,238,240,
249,257,263,267,293,292; Margaret,
86,265; Martha,82;Mary Ann,86;
Mary Mason,86; Samuel,289; Sarah,
82; Sympha Roseinfield, 86;
Thomas, 33,92,218,229; Thos.,Sr.,
212; William, 86,240; Wm.Jr., 198;
_____,195;249.

Bronaugh vs. White, 239.

BROOK: William, 295.

BROOKE: Ann,168,258; Francis,
196,239,256,258,259,281,274,282,
293; George, 258;H. 196,226;
Humphrey, 2,10,13,17,20,43,140,
149,151,168,185,186,187,189,196,
204,213,228; John, 26,68; Lucy,
258; Matthew,258; Mr.,40.

BROOKS: _____,34; Ann,1; Daucher (or)
Danckus),1; Dorcus,252; Elizabeth,
1,252; Hannah,1; John, 252;
Mary, 1,252; Nancy, 252; Sally,
252; Sarah, 1; Thomas, 1,175,
252w,255i; Wm., 1,252.

BROWN: _____ 252;Alex.,170,194;
Bennitt,33; Daniel,127,163,205,
227,228; Dixon,11,117i,192; Evern,
279;George, .33,157,260;

BROWN (con't.)
Gustavus Richard,162;
James, 261,274; Jeremiah,
194; John, 11w,141,237,
191,192,201; Jonathan,
157,158,216,217,299w,303;
Marmaduke,88,157;Martha,
158; Martin, 157; Mary,
157w,1751,259,299; Molly,
258w,2601; Peggy, 158;
Rebecca, 157,158; Robert,
170,205,258; Sary, 158;
Sibby, 157,158; Swanson,
191,200,201; Thomas H.,
295; Thomas Keithly, 186;
Wm., 157,158,228,299,302,
303;

Brown's Run, 11.

BROWNING: Caleb, 203;
Nicholas, 691.

BRUCE: Alexander, 184;
Charles, 78; Joel, 212.

Bruce and Murray, 186,189.

BRUIN: Bryan, 24; Eliza-
beth, 148.

BRUMBACK: John, 284.

BRUTON: Mary, 54,55.

BRYAN-BRYANT-BRIAN-BRIEN:
B.,302; Battaley,144;
Batly, 302; Bryant, 61;
Reuben, 144; Wm., 201,221.

BUCHANAN-BUCHANNON-BUCK-
HANNAN: Andrew,151;
Arthur, 61; Hannah,297;
James, 243; John,32,297;
Mary, 297; Michael, 297w,
Thomas, 297; W., 171.

BUCKNER: Alfred, 171;
Aylett, 107,110,137,231,
259; George,Jr.,213;
Judith, 148; Thomas,213;
Thornton, 239.

BULL: William, 40.

Bull Run Mountains, 63.

BULLITT-BULLETT: Alexander
Scott, 173; Barshaba Norman,215;
Benj., 2,8,27w; Benoni,28; Bur-
well,28,275; Cuthbert, 27,37,60,
83,103,108,116,152,173,186,225,
239; Capt.,140; Elizabeth, 28;
George, 28,228; John, 28; Joseph,
27,82,215w,216; Parmanus,28;
Sarah,28; Thomas,27,28,82w,83;
S.,227; William,28,227.

BUNISS: Sam'l., 195.

BURDETT(E)-BURDITT: Frederick,
137,150,154,155,239; James, 232;
John, 3,4,55,154,155; Mary,219;
William (alias Bullitt),28.

BURGER: Jacob,Sr., 292.

BURGES(S): Anne, 38,40,152,198;
Edward, 198,235,263; Francis, 20,
38w,401,44,152; Dawson, 39,40;
Garner, 78,157,161,198w,2031.;
James, 198,2941, Jane,38,40,152;
John,198; Susanna, 198.

BURWELL: Lewis, 151.

BUSSELL-BUSSLE: George, 3,4,33.

BUTCHER: Samuel, 197.

BUTLER: Ann, 143,176; Benj.,Jr.,
176; Elizabeth, 9,17,176; Gedvge,
176; John, 14,139,176; Joshua,120;
Nancy, 194; William, 48,102,177.

BUTTON: Catherine, 191; Harmon,
5,191w,192; Jacob, 191,232;
Rebekah, 191; Susanna, 191.

BYRAM: Peter, 189.

BYRNE: Samuel, 195; Uriah,217,
272.

- C -

Cacaphon River, 22.

CAIN: Mary, 246

CALMES: Lucy, 64.

CALVERT: George, 300.

CAMPBELL: Alex'r., 189, 151; Archibald, 283; Catharine, 159; Caty, 243; James, 275; ____, Sheriff, Prince William Co., 195.

CANADY: Daniel, 261.

CANARD: (See also, Kenard-Kennard) George, 228.

CANNON: John, 284.

CAMMEL: Archibald, 301.

CANSTABLE: Wm., 295.

CANTWELL: John, 128.

CAPPER: John, 25.

CARLE: Elizabeth, 79.

Caroline County, Va., 28, 29.

CARPENTER: Benjamin, 163, 206,222; Sarah, 51.

CARR: ____, 70; Mr., 77; Capt., 41,202; Darkey, 76; William, 32,33,41,104, 150,151,189,191,195,204, 205.

Carr and Chapman, 40,41, 189.

CARROLL-CARRELL: Anna, 79, 200 (Anna Carrol Prunty); Demsey Porter, 79; Elizabeth, 79; Sanford, 79w,81i, 200d,244a.

CARTER: ____, 64,191,212; Charles of Cleve, 213; Dale, 202,275; Daniel, 246; Edward, 177; George, 6,107,143,149,168,175, 178,219; Henry, 281; John, 213,235; Landon, 279; Mrs. Mary, 140; Peter, 151,193i, William, 219.

Carter's Run, 135.

CARVER: Thomas, 55,76.

CATER: Thomas, 155.

CATLETT: A., 76; Alexander, 85; Ann, 41; Elizabeth, 85; James, 60; John, 8,20,26,51,76,85,130,187; John, Sr., 85w,89i; Peter, 61,150; Susanah, 167; William, 85.

CAVANAUGH: Michael, 190.

CAVE: John, 273; Rhody, 273; Samuel, 273; Sarah, 273; Thomas, 202,273w,276i.

Cedar Run, 3,57,63,64,172.

Cedar Run Mills, 276.

CHADDUCK: Charles, 109.

CHAMBLING: Aron, 61.

Champes Run, 3.

CHANCELLOR: Thomas, 254.

CHANNEL: James, 272,295,296.

CHAPMAN: John, 21; Mr., 76,77; Pearson, 135; Thomas, 54,55,104, 151.

Charles County, Maryland, 162.

Cherry's Branch, 22.

CHICHESTER: Richard, 64,46,68; Sarah, 64.

CHICK: John, 132.

CHILTON: Capt., 152; Col.,
226; Dr., 278; Betty, 69;
Charles, 67,82,83,104,143,149,
150,152,155,170,171,182,202,
205,206,225i,274a,303 - & Co.,
151; George, 225,82; John, 65,
66,67,82w,95i,225d; Joseph,
82,214,221,225,227,240,272,284,
285,289,294,300,301; Lucy, 82,
225; Nancy, 82,225; Orrick,
225,274,275; Samuel, 258,259,
299; Sucky, 274,275; Susanna,
225; Thomas, 82,225,243,259,
260,266,267,293,294,302;
William, 65,74i,79,225d,258,
259,271,274,275,277. _____,
(Lawyer) 302.

Chimney Stone Branch, 135.

CHINN: Betty, 180; Charles,
180w; Christopher, 181; Elijah,
180; Hugh, 211; John, 180; Joseph, 180; Margaret, 180; Rawleigh,
180, Sr., 181; Suckey, 180; Susanna (Withers), 242; Thomas, 200;
Seth, 180; Wm. Ball, 180.

CHIZELDENE: Sinicah, 195.

CHOWNING: Wm., 52.

CHUNN: Charles C., 273,283,284;
John Thomas, 69,71,76,94,115,129,
196,199,200,212,237,259,294.

CHURCHILL: Armistead, 17,100,121,
135,149,150,151; Henry, 171;
John, 10,17,61,149,262i; W., 171.

Churchills Oat Patch, 64.

CLAPHAM: Colo., 264.

CLARK(E): Benjamin, 271w, 274i;
Elizabeth, 271; John, 200,207,
274; John H., 273; Mary, 271;
Sucky, 218; Thomas, 260,271,291,
295,299.

CLARKSON: Henry, 199,203,
245; Wm., 241,250.

CLATEN: W., 164.

CLAY: Henry, 76,77.

CLAYTOR: John, 52i.

Clear Creek, Kentucky, 241.

CLEMENT: Alexander, 67.

CLEVELAND: Lucy, 279.

CLIFTON: Rebecca, 95.

Clinch River, 102.

CLOE: William, 284.

CLUG: Parson, 17. (Rev.
John Klug, see Meade, Vol.
I, p. 361.)

COAL: Daniel, 195.

COCHRAN-COCKRANE-COCHRAM:
_____ & Co., 150; Andrew, 60;
Nathan, 139, 237; Richard, 300;
William, 60,108.

COCKRELL-COCKRILL-COCKRILLE:
Anderson, 135,139,166,208w,
220i,227; Anne, 75; Joseph,
47i; Mary, 136; Rosana, 208;
Sally, 208.

COCKRUM: Rosey, 218; William,
218.

COLLIERS: John, 25.

COLLINS: Ann, 177; George, 177,
77, 140; James, 177; Mary, 177;
Thomas, 279.

COLQUHONN: Walter, 282.

COLSON: Thomas, 60.

COLVERT: Humphrey, 184,195.

COLVIN: John, 31.

COLYER-COLLAR: Richard, 25, 28.

COMBS: Betty, 115; Cuthbert, 82,83,119; Ennis, 115,116,280, 282,287,301; Heland (alias Luttrell), 115; James, 291; John, 25,27,76,94,97; John,Jr., 115w,116,118,127i,134i; Joseph, 41,116,119; Margrit, 286, 287; Nimrod, 115, (Alias Luttrell), 284; Robert, 300; Sarah, 115,116; Seth, 27,82.

COMING: Margaret, 24.

COMYUS: Zachy, 284.

CONGROVE: Moses, 39.

CONNER: Rose, 62; Stephen, 228; Thomas, 60.

CONWAY: Anne, 133; Henry, 152, 153; James, 152; Joseph, 153, 252; Mary, 88; Peter, 1,41, 102,152,153,178,216,252,255, 259,302; Thomas, 1,2,22,37, 41,44,60,78,104,127,131,152w, 153,168,169,175,216; Walker, 133; William, 28,41,105,131, 152,153,157,164,175.

CORBIN: Elisha Hall, 66; Hannah, 65,66; Martha, 66.

CONRAD: Frederick, 60.

COOKE: Charles, 284; Giles, 126; John, 10w,11i,45,67,68, 131,150,151,208,217,220,233, 275,297; Littleton, 126w, 131i; Mrs._____, 55; Sarah, 10; Thomas, 126.

COOKSEY: Philip, 273.

COPPEDGE-COPPADGE-COPPAGE: Charles, 216; Elizabeth,20;

Jane (Catlett),85; John, 20, 53,58,104,107,183; Moses, 85, 86; Sally, 20; Wm., 20,53,76, 172,195,251.

CORDELL: George, 166; John, 79,106,109; Judith, 106.

CORDER: John, 11i,11,13; Patience, 13.

CORNELIUS: Absalom, 34.

CORNELL: William, 183,184.

CORNHILL: Peter, 227,228.

CORNWELL: Daniel, 75; Jacob,75; Jarvice, 75; John, 21,108,155; Mary, 75; Peter, 75w,89i; Sarah Ann, 75; Simon, 75,208,228; William, 195.

CORUM-CORAM-CORHAM: Auster, 221; Betty, 296; Catharine, 221,25; Champ, 81,125,127,179i,221a; Elizabeth, 221; Jane, 221; Mary, 26, 221; Richard, 94, 125, 221; Sarah, 221; William, 221.

COTTEREL: John, 151.

COURTNEY-CORTNEY: Francis, 188i; William, 108.

COUTSMAN: Jacob, 140.

COVINGTON: Richard, 34.

COX: Ariss, 149; James, 287; Thomas, 195.

CRAIG: James, 32,38,290; John, 293; Rev. Mr., 150.

CRAINE: John, 185, 186, 281.

CRAMP: Benjamin, 78.

CRAP: James, 48; James, Jr., 78

Craven County, S. C., 39.

CRAWFORD: Charles, 195; Peter, 76.

CREEL: Rachael, 258; William, 202.

CRESENBERRY: Alexander, 266.

CRESTENBURY: John, 280.

CRIM(M): Delila (Hurst), 228; Dosha, 286; John, 48i, 60, 117; Joseph, 228.

CRISWELL-CHRISWELL: George, 181i.

CROCKETT: James, 137,150.

CROSBY: George, 4, 153, 211, 230, 259, 79, 301i; Susanne, 152; Urial, 81, 211; William, 168.

Crummie's Run (also known as Cromwell's Run), 8,49.

CRUMP: Benjamin, 11, 188; Catherine, 188; Daniel, 188; George, 11, 16,17,25,29,88, 175,187i,188,214a; John, 67, 88, 188w; Lucy, 244; Sarah, 188; William, 188.

CRUPPER: Anne, 271; Cloe, 271; John, 295; Micajah, 295.

CUIN: Harmon, 191.

CULLIN: ____,3; James,33.

Culpeper County, Va., 238, 227, 291.

CUMMINGS-CUMMINS: Alexander, 43,44,60; Daniel, 155; James, 228; John, 44, 125,127,179, 228; Moses, 96; Thomas, 124, 125,133,134.

Cummings Spring Branch, 260.

CUMMINGS: Elizabeth, 44,126; Malachi, 36; Peter, 44; Simon, 43w, 53i.

CUNDIFF: Elizabeth (alias Ellitt), 163; Isaac, 221,227; Richard, 23; William (alias Elliott), 112,162.

CUNNINGHAM: Alex., 21,24; Elizabeth, 226; Francis, 135; William, 20,40; ____ & Co., 253,282.

CURTICE: Charlotte, 269.

- D -

DADE: Francis, 62; Langhorn, 256; Mrs. ____, 117.

DALE: William, 150,151.

DANIEL: William, 260.

Daniel's Branch (Maryland), 27.

DARNALL-DARNELL: Catherine, 247, 231; Caty, 247,248; David, 11, 175w,176; Elijah, 100; Elizabeth, 26; Isaac, 26; Jean (or Jane), 26; Jeremiah, 6,7,16, 20,37,38,78,84,100,121,138,151, 167,171,172,190,192,229,247w, 248,250i,261,274a; John, 26, 175,176; Joseph, 6,247; Katharine, 6,7; Mary, 176; Mr., 20; Morgan, 146; Morgan, Jr., 26w, 271; Morgan, Sr., 26,27; Rosamond, 248; Waugh, 26,146; William, 45w,46i; William D., 219,220.

Darrell's Run, 57.

DAVIS: Aquilla, 203,204,209, 221,246,250,254,256,272,283, 297; Charles, 289w,297i; Elizabeth, 289; Ezekial, 246; Griffith, 289; James, 62; John, 228; Levi, 289; Lydia,289;

DAVIS (con't.) Matthew,204;
Richard, 289; Samuel, 58;
Thomas, 176; William, 86,289;
William F. R., 289.

DAVISON: _____, 174.

DAWKINS: John, 236.

DAWSON: Henry, 228; John,
223.

DAY: Augustine Cossom, 150;
Charles, 139, 200; Cossom,
129, 175,231,250; Tran's, 10;
William, 217, 283.

DEALL: Mr., 76.

DEANE: Charles, 43.

DEANNY: George, 293.

DEARING: John, 179, 191,
220, 245, 248.

DEARMAN - DEARMON: _____, 25;
Michael, 51.

DEBBINS: Galvain, 293.

DEBELL: William, 265.

DE BUTTS: _____, 82; John,
170; Rev. Lawrence, 19.

Deep Branch: 207.

Deep Run: 77, 268.

DELASHUMATE (see also
SHUMATE): Dan'l., 18.

DELGAM: John, 86.

DENNIS: James, 244;
Sally, 283; Samuel, 265.

DERGAN: Ann, 39; John 39.

Dettingen Parish: 85, 172.

DEVERS: James, 241.

DICKESON: Edward, 23.

DIGGES: Edward, 98, 110, 169,
194, 198, 221, 262, 293; Edward,
Jr., 277, 278; Elizabeth, 258;
Thomas, 110, 149, 150, 155, 189,
202, 239, 258, 262; Whiting, 286.

DILLARD: Major, 227.

DILLON: James, 260; Joseph, 260.

DINNASON: Horney, 191.

Dixon's Quarter: 56.

DOBIE: James, 124, 175.

DODD: Allen, 146; Benj., 103,
146; James, 146, 203, 212;
John, 146; Nathaniel, 18, 146w,
150i, 280, 293; Sarah, 146;
Sarah (Southard), 102.

DODRON: Betty, 168.

DODSON: Elijah, 34; Thomas, 23;
Abraham, 33w, 35i; Barbary, 33,
34,80; Enoch, 34, 80; Greenham,
34, 80w, 145i; Molly, 34;
Tabitha, 34.

DOGGETT: Benjamin, 99i.

DONALDSON: Daniel, 202, 275;
Stephen, 61, 87i; William, 85,
89.

DONIPHAN - DONAPHAN - DONEPHAN:
Joseph, 191, 196, 237; Mrs. Mary,
37, 44.

DOUDLE: James, 85.

DOUGHTY: Thomas, 151, 189, 288.

DOUGLASS - DUGLASS:
Hugh, 275; James, 23;
William, 275.

DOWDALL: Brawner, 195;
James, 85, 114, 127, 147,
256; Thos., 256.

DOWELL: Neamiah, 191.

Dowell's Run: 172.

DOWNING: John, 224.

DOWNMAN: Robert, 24.

DOWNS: Benjamin, 140,
295; Henry, 271.

DRAKE: Thomas, 272.

DRIM: William, 34.

DRUMMOND: Aaron, 23,
226; Ann, 41; James, 26,
40, 273; Joshua, 251;
Nancy, 41; Richard, 165;
Suckey (Shipp), 84;
William, 76i, 274.

DUFF: James, 31, 103.

DUFFEY: B., 303; Bn'rd.,
262; Bernard, 290, 303i.

DUGARD - DUGARDE: Dr.,
166; John, 75, 87i.

DULANY - DELANY: C., 78;
Charles, 225, 226;
William, 11, 14, 78.

DULIN: John, 89;
William, 11, 219, 236.

Dumfries: 135, 186, 191,
200, 225, 257, 261, 275,
276, 277.

DUNBAR: ____, 302;
Robert, 256, 274, 276, 279.

Dunbar & Vass: 293.

DUNCAN: Arch'd, 272, 292;
Catherine, 84; Charles, 14, 129,
132, 141, 175, 185, 189, 212,
230, 231, 250, 257, 279; Elias,
230, 263; Enoch, 230, 263;
Howsen (Housen), 223, 224, 266,
273, 285, 292, 293; James, 88,
228; John, 5, 13, 18, 97, 110,
127, 132, 141, 227, 230w, 292;
John, Sr., 263d; Joseph, 108,
150, 151, 223w, 224, 229i, 273,
292, 293; Lucinda, 230, 263;
Lydia, 223, 273w, 274i, 292,
293; Milly, 230, 263; Moses, 230,
263, 273, 293; Myrna, 223; Nancy,
144; Samuel, 147, Wilkey, 230,
231; William, 293; Willis, 230,
263.

Dunmore County, 1.

DYE: Fauntleroy, 249, 282, 290.

DYER: John, 155, 226.

- E -

EARL: Baylis, 61; Samuel, 4, 13,
14, 15, 171.

EASTHAM: George, 161, 267, 280,
294.

Eden & Co., 186.

EDGE: John, 44, 22; Siety, 44.

EDMONDS: Ann, 37; Betty, 38;
Charles, 152; E., 191; Elias, 9,
14, 15, 25, 38, 47, 55, 79, 84,
148w, 149, 170, 206, 237, 255(Sr.)
281; Elizabeth, 148; James, 255,
285, 292, 301; John, 38, 186, 196,
220, 233, 237, 255, 300i; Judith,
38, W., 189; William, 16, 38, 69,
100, 135, 151, 152, 194, 200, 272,
275, 303; Wm, Jr., 221, 255, 262,
274.

EDMONDSON: Thomas, 61.

EDWARDS: Betty, 197;
Edward, 106; Elizabeth,
168; Gerrard, 12, 27;
James, 27; John, 27, 50,
51, 99, 106, 281; Joseph,
25; Thomas, 198, 277.

EDZAR: Francis, 61.

Elk Garden, 102.

Elk Marsh Run: 92, 138.

Elk Run: 155, 157.

ELLIOTT - ELLITT - ELLETT
ELIOTT: (See also CUNDIFF)
Ann, 39, 152; Benj., 39,
59, 108, 134, 140; Elinor,
39, 152; Elizabeth, 112;
Jemima, 112; John, 108,
135, 198i, 227, 228;
Mary, 227; Molly, 112;
Mildred, 112; Lewis, 227,
228; Reubin, 52, 73, 112w,
113i, 163; Ruth, 112;
Sarah, 39, 119, 120; Thos.,
59, 112, 152, 228; William,
39, 58, 71, 108, 113, 135,
140, 152, 221, 226, 227,
299, 301.

ELLIS: Ann, 98; Jonathan,
98; John, 98w, 99i, 135;
Nathan, 199, 202, 230;
Owen, 98; Sarah, 55;
William, 98.

ELLZEY - ELLSEY: Nicholas,
140; William, 17, 20, 23,
151.

EMBREY - EMBRY: Ann, 191,
194w; Charles, 191; George,
266i; Robert, 191w, 194,
201i, 211d, 268; Thomas,
191, 211, 212 Jr., 194;
William, 212, 268.

EMMONS: Agatha, 263; James,
268, 276; Joseph, 48, 263, 264,
268, 276; William, 48, 263w,
264i, 268a, 275, 276a.

ENGLISH: Joseph, 293; Robert,
212.

ERVINS: Thomas, 275.

ESKRIDGE: Samuel (alias Kenner),
96.

ETHERINGTON - EDRINGTON:
Elizabeth, 84w, 92i; John,
37i, 43i.

ETHIS: Eb, 195.

EUSTACE: Isaac, 256, 257, 268,
272, 276; Mary, 209; William,
10, 33, 41, 42, 67, 88, 256;
William, Jr., 188, 209, 240.

EVAN: Humphrey, 67.

EVANS - EVINS: Thomas, 206;
Joseph, 228; Martha, 163.

EWELL: _____, 38, 207;
Bertrand, 56, 57; Ja., 52;
James, 151; Major, 151;
Solomon, 198, 202.

- F -

Fairfax County: 86. (Scott
land, 186)

FAIRFAX, THOMAS SIXTH LORD:
13, 25, 175.

Falmouth: 50, 61, 112, 302.

FARGARSON: Molley, 207.

FARROW: Alexander, 21, 60;
Ann, 207; Benj., 207; George,
61, 62, 228; Nimrod, 289.

FAUBION: Jacob, 50.

Fauquier Court House:
225, 279.

FEAGAN(S): Clery, 109;
Edward, 69, 109w, 113i,
206, 276, 288; Elizabeth,
109; Frances, 109; John,
109, 155, 222; Mary, 109,
288; Sarah, 109; Susanna,
109; William, 109.

FENNELL: Francis, 18.

FENNEN: Letice (Riley),
231.

FERGUSON: John, 32;
John H., 229,230; Lewis,
181.

FETHERINGSTON: Thos.,
155.

FEWELL - FEWEL: Henry,
166; Wm., 140.

FICKLIN - FICKLEN:
F., 302; Fielding, 261;
John, 261; Wm., 195.

FIDLER: Thos., 101.

FIELDING: Edwin, 141w;
Edward, 149i; Nancy, 141.

FIELD(S): Ann, 133;
Benj., 133; Elizabeth, 133;
Daniel, 132w, 137i; Fielden,
132; George, 132; Hannah,
133; John, 60, 81, 132, 163;
Lewis, 132; Margaret, 163;
Mary, 133; Milly, 133; Sarah,
133, 137.

Fincastle County; 102

FINCH: William, 121, 298,
303.

FINNIE: Ann, 12; Hannah, 12, 88;
John, 12w, 171, 291.

FISHBACK: Ann, 32, 285; Frederick,
7; James, 190; Jesse, 299; John,
6, 7, 36, 45, 54, 81, 117, 127, 132,
148, 167, 175, 187i, 207, 228, 279d,
295; Joseph, 54; Josiah, 99, 127,
132, 134, 150, 155, 160, 174, 175,
190, 232, 247, 285, 299i; Lucey,
225, 226; Mary, 285; Nanny, 156;
Patty, 280; Philip, 54, 134, 148,
291, 174, 232, 295; Sarah, 190, 279;
William, 220, 251.

FISHER: Richard, 201, 223, 224, 281,
294; Samuel, 201, 226, 303.

FITZGERALD: Kitty, 32; Wm., 145.

FITZHUGH: Dudley, 286; George,
286; Mary, 286; Thomas, 173, 174,
190, 206, 215, 291; Sarah Battaille,
286; William, 169, 173, 213, 286,
291.

FLEMING: James, 91.

FLETCHER: Aaron, 40, 41, 54, 55,
144, 224, 262; Elizabeth, 210;
John, 210, 223; Joshua, 77; Moses,
33; Patterson, 33; Richard, 223;
Sarah, 54; Thomas, 223w; 224i(Sr.);
William, 3, 4, 76.

FLINT: Valentine, 295.

FLORENCE - FLOWRENCE - FLOURANCE:
Daniel, 165; William, 251, 265.

FLOWERREE - FLOWEREE: D.,Sr., 211;
Daniel, 10, 17, 61, 68, 108, 126,
127, 132, 134, 135, 140, 190, 227;
Daniel, Jr., 285, 297; French, 233;
Major, 237; William 134.

FLOWERS: Andrew, 172.

FLYNN: Rachel, 258; Val., 135;
William, 258.

FOLEY: Bryant, 269;
Elizabeth, 269; Enoch,
269; James, 2, 14, 16, 19,
20, 23, 42, 44, 45, 47,
78, 135, 167, 185, 188,
269, 283, 294, 203, 248,
269w, 270, 279i; James,
Jr., 80; John, 269; Leah,
269; Lettuce, 269; Mary,
254; Molley, 269; Presley,
269; Sarah, 59; Thomas,
167, 188, 269, 284, 294;
William, 269.

FOOTE: Behethelm, 3;
Betty, 172; Celia, 72,
171; Elizabeth, 3, 33;
Frances, 3, 33; Gilson,
2, 3, 4, 20, 31, 33, 41i,
54, 55, 150; George, 2,
3, 4, 81, 33, 72w, 89i,
172, 230; Hannah, 54, 55;
Hesther, 72; Henry, 2, 3;
Margaret, 72; Mary, 2, 3,
22, 33; Richard, 2, 3, 4,
22, 40, 41, 54, 55, 72,
105w, 172, 284; Richard
Helm, 72; William, 2, 3,
4, 51i, 54, 55, 105, 222,
257, 276.

FORD: A., 245; George,
38, 228; Henry, 124; 283;
William, 227.

FOREMAN: John, 60;
William, 61.

FORRESTER - FORRISTER:
James, 290; John, 135, 247.

FORSYTH: _____, 25.

FOSHER: _____, 200.

FOSTER: Alexander, 295;
Jeremiah, 189.

FOWKE - FOOKES: Ann
Harrison, 53, 57; Chandler,
57, 116, 120; Elizabeth,
116, 120w, 125i; Enfield,

FOWKE (Con't.)
116, 120; George, 116, 120;
Gerard, 116; Jerrard, 25;
Mary, 53, 56, 116, 120; Robert
Dinwiddie, 116; Thos. Harrison,
57; William, 116, 120.

FOWLER: Anne, 139; Anne
(Bradford), 171; William, 171.

FOX: James, 226; John, 240,
259; Nancy, 252; S., 302.

FRANCIS: Alex'r., 200; Andrew,
200; Stephen, 284.

FRAYSER: Simon, 246.

FRAZIER: Daniel, 24w.

Frederick County: 15, 16, 22,
25, 28, 60, 237.

Fredericksburg: 77.

FREEMAN: Garrett, 210, 266,
293; Gollop (alias Duncan),
209; James, 35, 129; James, Sr.,
209w, 210 (Jr.), 212i; Margaret,
177, 209; Nathaniel, 210;
Salley, 209; William, 122, 129,
140, 193, 210; Willis, 268;
George, 268; Bennett, 268.

FRENCH: Daniel, 139, 181;
John, 111, 122, 181; Mason,
140, 295.

FRISTOE: John, 76, 77.

FROGG: John, 11.

FRYER: Jacob, 108.

FULTON: James, 300.

FURR: ___, 22; Edwin, 222;
Elizabeth, 133, 134; Ephraim,
60; Moses, 133; Thomas (alias
Johnson), 133w; William, 38.

Furrs Run: 260.

GAFNEY: James, 205.

GAINES: Byran, 166; Charles, 177; Robert, 151.

GALLANT: James, 61.

GALLIGHER: Bernard, 276.

GANER: Bryant, 135.

Gap Branch: 50.

GARNER: Aiana, 280; Ann, 33; Benjamin, 144, 193w, 194, 201i, 262; Charles, 70, 212, 285i; Daniel, 144i; Diannah, 193, 293; Elizabeth, 262; Jale, 293; James Withers, 262; Jemima, 262; Jesse, 262; John, 21i, 194; James, 262; Presley, 212, 293; S., 282; Sarah, 146; Smith, 273i; Vincent, 25, 34, 35, 194, 262w, 274; William, 262; Jonas, 262, 282.

GARRISH: Ben., 135.

GATES: John, 135.

GAUNT: John, 229, 230, 241, 281, 283.

GAUSOM: Fanny, 138.

GENN - GINN: James, 179, 191, 264.

GENT: Mary, 10, 20.

GEORGE: Aaron, 204i/a, 279; Abner, 279; Alvin, 189; Fanny, 279; Gabriel, 279; Joseph, 101, 156, 268, 280, 282; Pharnack,

GEORGE (Con't.): 21, 45, 81, 86, 165, 189, 201, 202, 203, 204, 259, 268i, 281a, 278; Peggy, 279; Presley, 279; Reuben, 279, 281; Wilmoth, 101, 278; Nicholas, 21, 35, 100w, 101, 104i, 110, 145; Margaret, 101; Nanny, 101; Matthew, 152; Elizabeth, 101; Lydia, 101; Tannack, 152; William, 101.

Georgetown, Md. (D.C.): 221.

Georgia: 286.

GERMAN: Michael, 108.

Germantown: 187.

GERRETT: Edward, 61.

GIBSON: Ann Grayson, 57; Capt., 87, 260; Davy, 256; George, 227; J., 264; John, 25, 53, 56, 204, 256, 257, 284; Jonathan, 2, 23, 28, 35, 53, 55, 57, 58, 65, 89, 99, 104, 126, 141, 156, 164, 171, 179, 204w, 256a, 276i; Jonathan Catlett, 57, 204; Margaret Catlett, 204; Mary, 204, 256; Robert, 159; S., 256; Sara, 256; Susannah, 56; Susanna Grayson, 204; Susannah H., 256; Thomas, 53, 56, 204, 240, 256, 257, 260, 282; Willia, 188, 301.

Gibsons Road: 249.

GILBERT: Elizabeth, 69.

GILCHRIST: _____, 186.

GILL: Presley, 254; Richard, 281.

GILLISON: ___ & Adie, 256; Ann, 56; James, 156, 209, 296(Sr.); John, 57, 209d, 296, 297; _____, 302.

GLASCOCK: ____, 227; Agatha, 225; Frances, 23; George, 132, 147, 211, 224, 226, 228, 235, 236, 288, 298; Gregory, 23, 89, 235; Hezekiah, 147, 233, 235, 251, 297, 298, 303; John, 23w, 147w, 148, 150i, 237, 245, 253, 284; Mary, 23; Peter, 228; Thomas, 23, 81, 126, 135, 147, 175, 186, 193, 225w, 226, 232i.

GLASS: Michael, 143.

Glebe Road: 85

GLENDENNY: G., 302.

GODFREY: Edmund, 60; (Edward, 61).

GODLEY: Edward, 274.

GOLDSMITH: Benjamin, 258; John, 221.

Goose Creek: 6,7,29,38,56, 57,60,86.

GORDON: B., 257, 282; George, 201, 274, 293; Samuel, 257, 282.

GRAHAM(E): Catesby, 284, 295; Celia, 229; Dr., 202; Duncan, 300a; George, 229, 37, 76; Joseph, 300; Nancy, 300; Original, 151; Reginald, 97, 98; Polley, 300; Richard, 171, 186; Robert, 261; Walter, 289; Wm., 300.

GRANT: George, 109, 139, 167, 295; John, 31w; Peter, 60, 91, 137, 143, 149, 153, 160, 178, 186, 187, 192, 197, 209, 211, 222, 238, 240, 243, 264; Susanna, 90, 160; Wm., 11, 41, 60, 68, 77, 88, 94, 110, 133, 141, 151, 172, 196, 227.

GRAY - GREY: Daniel, 170, 171, 200, 202, 233, 275; Garratt, Jr., 205; George, 233; James, 135, 228; Mr., 219; Nathaniel, 170, 206, 275.

GREAR: Elizabeth, 231.

Great Branch: 188.

Great Britain: 111, 172.

Great Mountains (Blue Ridge): 227.

Great Run: 188, 257.

GREEN: Ann, 151; Celia, 179; Elizabeth, 205; George, 169, 171; Isaac, 52; James, 140; John, 26, 68, 150, 151, 205, John, Jr., 151, 170; Thomas, 301; Timothy, 292, 293; Wm., 26, 150, 151, 256, 284; ____ & Slaughter, 150.

GREENFIELD: John, 28.

GREENWOOD: Daniel, 244, 292, 293; Nimrod, 293.

GREGORY: Richard, 275.

GRIFFIN: _____, 87; Helen, 285; William, 286.

GRIFFITH: Dennis, 258; Elijah, 257, 258, 295, 274; Evan, 21, 24, 67, 100, 109, 134, 257w, 258, 265i; Henry, 51; John, 155, 252, 257, 258; Peggy, 258; Sarah, 258, 295; Saraianne, 258; Willoughby, 257, 258.

GRIGSBY: Aaron, 221, 249; Ann, 117; Mrs. Anne, 186; Bayliss, 187, 233; Benjamin, 230; Eadey, 187; Enoch, 295; John, 45i, 61,62, 187w, 196i, 227, 233; James, 117; Lewis,

187, 233; Nathaniel, 187, 233;
Samuel, 45, 70, 81, 108, 117w,
126i, 135, 227, 294d; William,
117, 127i, 227, 228; Winnefred,
187.

GROGAN: Elizabeth, 105.

GRUBBS: Richard, 119; Thomas,
171; William, 68i.

GUNYON: William, 257.

GUTHRIDGE-GUTRICH-GUTRIDGE:
Allen, 283; Reuben, 283, 285,
301.

GUY: Charles, 83.

GWATHIN: James, 104.

- H -

HACKLEY: ____, 253; James, 210;
Lott, 14, 99, 165, 222, 226;
Mary, 210.

HADDUX - HADDOCKS: Charlotte,
133; Ezekiel, 264i.

HAINES: Simeon, 260i.

HALE: Joseph, 265, 276; Wm.,
185, 211, 221, 222, 264, 274.

HALEY: (See also: Healy-
Healey-Hailey): Honor, 227.

HALL: Cornelius, 284; Elizabeth,
37; Richard, 65w, 78i; Richard
Lingham, 30, 78i, 149; Robert,
228; Susannah, 138.

HAMBLETON: (See also: Hamilton);
Dorcus (Darkis), 235w; Presley,
235; William, 68, 171, 186i.

HAMBRICK - HAMRICK: James, 97;
Mary, 104; Patrick, 108; Wm.,
228, 300.

HAMILTON: Henry, 182, 197i;
Hugh, 66; James, 295; William,
182w, 186i, 200a.

Hamilton Parish: 1,2,5,11,17,
24,27,31,37,65,92,106,113,119,
120,131,132,133,139,157,167,
169; Glebe, 57.

HAMLET: William, 191.

HAMMIT: Hannah, 146.

Hampshire County: 22, 30.

HAMPTON: Benjamin, 61;
Charlotte, 64; Elizabeth, 29;
Frances, 192; Gale, 30; Henry,
189; Joanna, 64; Joseph, 260,
295, 303; Martha, 29, 30;
Mary, 192; Richard, 21, 29w,
301, 63, 64, 66, 79, 160;
Sarah, 29; Susannah, 64, 192;
Wade, 160; Wm., 29, 30, 43,
66, 79, 181, 201, 288, 293.

HAND: Thomas, 255; William,
4, 201.

HANER - HANOR: Harmon, 222;
Mary, 222; William, 200.

HANKS: William, 166.

HANNERS: Francis, 41.

HANNIBAL: Benjamin, 226.

HANSBROUGH: Morias, 73; Peter,
212; Sarah, 46; William, 46.

HANSON: Walter, 162.

HARDIN: George, 195; John, 7;
Martin, 2, 7, 17, 20, 21, 30.

HARDISTREE: Henndry, 291;
Susannah, 291.

HARDWICK: James, 36; William,
70.

HARMONS: Jno., 228.

HARPER: George, 295.

HARRELL-HARRILL: Daniel, 21, 44, 53; James, 21i; John, 21, 95; Moses, 21, 216.

HARRIS: George, 290i; Henry, 269; Jemima, 262; Matthew, 285; Richard, 167, 196, 199, 202; Samuel, 46, 61; Thomas, 99, 188, 196, 254, 256; William, 145, 218, 262.

HARRISON: Ann, 57; Benjamin, 53, 56, 57, 58, 65, 79, 83, 89, 184, 195, 204, 229, 256, 277w, 280i, 282, 284i; Burr, 199, 214, 228, 53, 55, 56, 57, 108; Col.: 41; Cuthbert, 56, 76, 103, 180, 295; Francis, 57; Jane, 71, 214; John P., 222, 224, 226, 260 (John Peyton), 264, 274; Lucy, 57; Matthew, 204 (Jr.), 277; Mary, 282, 284; Sarah, 57; Seth, 57; Thomas, 35, 53, 55w, 56, 57, 58, 65i, 195, 228; William, 35, 38, 40, 44, 46, 55, 57, 58, 71i, 214d, 227; William, Jr., 199d, 200a.

Harrison County: 174.

Harrison's Old Mill Dam: 172.

HARSLIKLE: _____, 151.

HARTE: William, 186.

HARWOOD: Thomas, 48.

HATHAWAY: Dolly, 174; Capt., 132; Elizabeth, 174; Francis, 174; Henry Lawson, 174; James, 63, 64, 95, 110, 119, 120, 151, 174, 178, 217, 302i; Jas., Sr., 285; Joanna, 63, 64; John, 97, 113, 126, 135, 140, 145, 160, 165, 174w, 175i,

226a, 295; Juday, 174; Molly, 174; Nancy, 174; Peggy Lawson, 174; Sarah, 174, 226; Sarepta, 174; Susannah, 174.

HAUS: John, 212.

HAVEN: Peter How White, 61.

HAWKINS: John, 132; Joseph, 232; William, 227, 228.

HAWSON: Matthew, 294.

HAYDEN-HAYDON: James, 169.

HAYMAKER: Addam, 24, 61.

HAYNIE: Charles, 24; Maximillam, 36.

HAYS: Moses, 25, 28.

HAZZELRIG: Samuel, 168.

HEADLEY-HEADLY-HEDLEY: James, 149, 185, 217w, 220i; John, 150, 151, 189, 290; Lucy, 217.

HEALE: William, 127, 140, 145, 160, 165.

HEALY-HEALEY-HALEY-HAILEY: Anthony, 179; Febea, 179; Honour, 190w, 193i; John, 60, 179w, 185i, 190, 191; Mary, 179, 191; Richard, 21; Roby, 195; William, 179.

HEARTWELL: William, 61.

HEATLY: William 39.

HEATON: John, 132i; William, 230i.

HEDENGRAN: Peter, 46.

HEDGMAN-HEDGEMAN: Peter, 176; William, 41.

HEDLEY: James, 275.

HEFLIN-HEFFERLIN-HEFFERLING:
Agathor, 276; Augustin, 228;
Martin, 268; Nancy (Hurst),
228; Simon, 73.

HELM: Ann, 64; Hester, 72;
Letty, 64; Lynaugh, 41, 72;
Thomas, 70, 156, 157, 164,
209, 268; Thomas, Jr., 72;
William, 196; _____, 56.

HENDERSON: Mr. H's store, 225;
____ & Gibson, 256; ____ & Co.,
292; Archibald, 23, 33; Henry,
85; John, 85; Samuel, 295;
_____, Fergerson & Gibson, 284.

HENDREN: John, 23.

HENNING: Robert, 277.

HENRY: Betty, 276; George,
268; Joseph, 143; Michael, 51.

HENSON: Robert, 212, 274, 290.

HERMMOND (See also Hermons):
John, 275.

HERNDON: John, 110, 189, 239,
243, 250, 261.

HERONOMOS: Francis, 61.

HERRINGDON: John, 284.

HEY: James, 191.

HICKMAN: John, 115, 212;
Joseph, 273.

HICKS: Kimble, 220.

HIGGINS: John, 155; Richard, 60.

HILL: Mary (Riley), 231.

HITCH-HICH: Christopher, 166,
188, 203, 254, 294; Rebechah,
166.

HITE: Abraham, 60; Elizabeth,
15; Isaac, 243; Jacob, 15, 28,
61; John, 61.

HITSON: William, 166.

HITT: Alice Katherine, 6;
Elizabeth, 47; Frankey, 233;
Harmon, 11, 47, 127, 8, 14,
81, 97, 190; Henry, 6, 48;
John, 47, 133i, 201; Joseph,
11, 47; Martin, 190; Mary, 8,
48; Peter, 7, 10, 20, 47i, 48,
169, 190; Sarah, 88.

HOARD: Thomas, 78.

HOCKMAN: Anne, 191, 192.

HODO: Peter, 158.

HOGAIN-HOGANS-HOGINS: Charles,
30, 31; Daniel, 13; J., 76;
James, 12; John, 42, 73, 85,
86, 222, 267; Margaret, 30w,
31i; Maryann, 85; Rawly, 167;
Thomas, 21, 113, 134; William,
12, 55.

HOGG: George, 25; Peter, 61.

HOLDER: Armistead, 291, 293;
David, 14.

HOLLIDAY: Samuel, 124.

HOLTON: Alexander, 124w;
Elizabeth, 124; William, 58,
124, 126, 135, 136, 139.

HOLTZCLAW: Archibald, 233;
Benj., 223, 224; Catharine, 233;
Eli, 233; Harman, 5, 6; Henry,
6, 7; Jacob, 5w, 6, 7, 10, 131,
16, 34, 149; Joseph, 5, 6, 169i,
233d; Josiah, 152; Milly, 33;
Salley, 233; Stephen, 233.

HOLMES-HOMES: E. E., 17; Edmond,
56, 143; James, 76, 85, 86, 147;
Thomas, 284.

HOMBEY: Michael, 61.

HONE: Betty, 122.

HONER(S)-HONOR: Harman, 76,77; F., 76.

HOOE: Henry D., 222; Henry Dade, 301; John, 280; John, Jr., 287; Col. Robert, 162.

HOOVER: Michael, 60.

HOPE: Henry, 189.

HOPEWOOD: _____, 302.

HOPPER: John, 12, 202, 275.

HORD: Peter, 166.

HORTON: Samuel, 274.

HOWELL: George, 228.

HOPKINS: David, 295.

HOPWOOD: James, 274.

HORNER: Dr., 189, 200, 201, 204, 221, 226, 232, 246, 257, 259, 279, 274, 278, 284; G. B., 293; William, 221, 238, 246, 259, 274, 275, 278, 302.

Horsepen Run: 211.

HORTON: Catherine, 205; William, 220.

HOTTON: Wm., 227.

HOW: Peter, 40.

HOWARD: John, 61.

HOWELL: Francis, 60.

HUBBARD: Ann, 148; Ephriam, 81, 108, 171, 186.

HUDNALL-HUDNALD: Jemima, 93; John, 47; Joseph, 2,14,33,142, 145, 166, 236; Thomas, 67.

Hudnall Branch: 211.

HUDSON: Dennis, 281, 288; Richard, 261, 279.

HUFFMAN: James, 290; William, 268.

HUGHES: Jean, 38; Thos., 44, 140, 228.

HUGHLETT-HULETT: Leroy, 73, 109, 128i.

HUME(S): Andrew, 117; Hannah, 88; James, 114; Margaret, 85; Robert, 245; William, 263i.

HUMPHRIES: Thomas, 268.

HUMSTON-HUMSTEAD: Edward, 16, 17, 18,29,35,65,200,248; Edward, Jr., 18; Susannah, 53; Thomas, 268.

Hunger Run, 6.

HUNT: Jacob, 212; William, 301.

HUNTON: Betty, 81; Hannah, 290; James, 166,197,204,232,268,269, 278,281,290; Judith, 81; Mary, 267; Mr., 151; Robert, 204,267; Thomas, 233,269,290,302; William, 46,71,75,80,81,112,166,181,193, 197,201,202,203,260,269; Wm., Jr., 179,204,232,233,268,278, 281,296.

HURMONS-HERMONS: James, 70; John, 70w,73i,108,140; Mary, 70,71; Susanna, 70.

HURST: Henry, 228,229; Jane, 229; Rosannah, 228w, 229, 230.

HUSK: Anne, 276.

HUTCHERSON: _____, 27;
Peter, 160.

HUTCHISON: John, 151; Joseph,
180; William, 228.

HUTTON: William, 108.

- I -

Indian Spring Savannah, 11.

INNES: Elizabeth, 172, 173.

Iphaweson: 114.

IRELAND: James, 152; Jane
(Burgess), 152.

ISLES: Absalom, 73.

ISRAEL: Sabbatiah, 145.

- J -

JACKMAN: Adam, 122; Hannah, 299;
Hester, 9; Joseph, 123,124;
Richard, 122; Thomas, 9,14,122w;
123; William, 123.

JACKSNAN: Richard, 60.

JACKSON: Francis, 148; Magdalen,
47; Molly, 280; Robert, 22;
Samuel, 275.

JACOBS: William, 268.

JAMEISON-JAMESON: Alex'r., 152;
David, 195.

JAMES: Agatha, 77; Benj., 87,88;
Dinah, 24,41,88; Elizabeth, 77,
142; George, 77,78; Hannah, 205;
James, 79,87w, 205; Margaret, 77;
Mary, 77; Molly, 77,78; John, 12,

JAMES (Con't.): 52,78,88,99,
1101,142,188,209,211,235,257,
260,266,276; Joseph, 192;
Suaannah, 88; Thomas, 77w,
78,85,87,88,89,991,124,281,289.

JANNEY-JANNY: Aquilla, 297;
Israel, 165.

Jefferson County, 170.

JEFFERSON: William, 290.

JEFFRIES: Alexander, 37,46;
Elizabeth, 233; JOSEPH, 221,
237,253,288,298; Joseph, Jr.,
206; Joseph, Sr., 206; Mary,
206; Misniah, 37; Sarah, 45.

Jeffries Branch, 177.

JENKINS-JEONKINS: Jekil, 58;
Josiah, 77; Susanna, 287;
William, 149.

JENNINGS: Augustine: 37,92w,
93,971,177,185,212,218,244,
249,257,263; Baylor, 92,268,
302; Betty,93,145; Berryman,
84,92,1321,141; Capt., 201;
George, 92,1891,221; Hannah,
92,93; Lewis, 92; Sally, 93;
Sarah, 268; Susanna, 141;
William, 92,93,99,131,139,158.

JETT: Anthony, 172; James,290;
John, 31,34; Thomas,241;
William, 9,10,191.

JIMMONS: John, 62.

JOHN: Jane, 296.

JOHNSON: Alten, 280; Bayly, 61,
135,212; C., 285; Betty, 47;
Bidy, 285; Baldwin, 286; George,
76, 279; Isaac, 10, 201,286w;
2971; James, 136, 2431; John,
72,124, 2671; Lydia, 286;
Margaret (Winn), 90;

JOHNSON (Con't): Martin, 165;
Moses, 47,107,180; Samuel, 279;
Smith, 191, 220i, 285a; Younger,
213; Alexander, 135; Hannah, 34;
Jeffry, 135w, 139i; Junis, 290;
Presley, 136; Sarah, 135, 136;
Thomas Furr (alias Johnson),
133w, 134i.

JOHNSTON: Aron, 15; Francis, 15;
Gedion, 278; Jemima, 270; Mary
(Peyton), 190; Nath'l., 293;
Nimrod, 259; Thomas, 4; Tunis,
293.

JOINIANSE: Joshua, 21.

JONES: Benj., 53; Betty, 63;
Brereton, 3,4,24,41,53,76,88,
253w,254; Charles, 73i, 199a;
Daniel, 51, 253; Darkes, 138;
Elijah, 199; Elisha, 199;
Elizabeth, 288; Gabriel, 24;
George, 63; 288; Henry, 46;
109; 254; John, 10,31,61,143i,
295; John Warner, 253; Joseph
H., 275; Lettice, 254; M.M.,
149; Robert, 253; Sarah, 276;
Solomon, 63,64; Thomas, 94,
284; William, 51,63,72,129,
145,169,226,254,263,264,268,
276,284; Wm. Sr., 268;
Willoughby, 33.

JORDAN: Nancy (Withers), 242.

JORDIN: Joseph, 195.

JUNYON: William, 193.

- K -

Kanawha River, 82.

KARR: Betsey, 287.

KEATING: Gerrard, 289;
Jemima, 289.

KEEBLE: Richard, 186,275.

KEEPORT: _____, 200.

KEER: Garland, 160.

KEITH: Alexander, 202,206,
269,271,275, 279; Betty, 178;
Catty, 269; Caty Gallahue,
178; Charlotte Ashmore, 178;
179; Isham, 82,178w,181i,183;
James, 28,268; John, 28,35,
95; Judith,177; John, 178,196,
227,228,237; Mary Isham,178;
Thomas, 71,82,135,149,166,179,
182,183,192,194,200,208,221,
228,243,252,261,264,266,268,
275,276; William, 269.

Keith & Blackwell: 41.

KELLEY-KELLY: John, 143w;
Joseph, 56,143; Sarah, 119;
Thomas, 143.

KEMP: Edward, 60, Elizabeth,
168.

KEMPER-KAMPER: Anne, 7, 292;
C-, 193; Caty, 292; Charles,
192,201,232,233,291,292; Elias,
292; Elizabeth, 292; Frederick,
158i; George, 212,278; Harman,
5; Herman, 62i; Henry, 7,29;
Jacob, 169, (Sr.: 192,292)
(Jr.: 292) John, 7,8,62,150,
169,192,201,233,236,281,291w,
292,293,295i; John Peter, 158,
183i,232a; Joseph, 291,292;
Juday, 174; Mary, 292; Peter,
62,131,139,140,155,166,193,201,
223,224,291,292; Phillies, 29;
Moses, 131,291; Solomon, 201;
Susannah, 291,292; Tilman, 291.

KENARD (See also Canard):
George, 89,108; Joshua, 289,290.

KENDALL: George, 275,283.

KENKENDAL: Abraham, 62.

KENNER: _____87; Betty, 299;
Francis, 95, 96; George Turberville, 21, 95, 96; Howson, 21,
23, 35, 41, 43, 53, 76, 95w, 96,
97; Judith, 216,217; Lawrence,
216; Lucy, 216; Margaret, 97;
R., 52; Rodham, 96, 131, 158,
216w, 217, 222i; Samuel Eskridge,
96; Susannah, 37, 96, 97; Robert,
131.

KENNERLY - KINNERLY: Randol, 25.

KENTON - Canton: John, 67; Mark,
23, 155 (Sr.); 227, 228 (Jr.);
Simon, 174; William, 52,53,134,
155,227.

Kentucky: 118, 180, 241, 247, 248,
258, 270, 271, 274, 285, 301.

KERNS - KERNES - KEIRNS: _____, 302;
Henry, 248; John, 42; William, 18,
208, 279.

KERR: Aseneth, 266; Betty, 265;
Darcus, 266; J., 249; James, 60,
105; John, 61,88,110,157,164,224,
232, 229, (Sr: 265w, 266i), 273,
(Jr., 266); Lucy 266; Peggy Smith,
266; Sarah, 266, 293, 292; Sarah
Crosby, 266; William, 266.

KEY: James, 95, 125.

KIBBLE: James, 259.

KIDWELL: Dorcus, 251; James, 251;
Mary, 251w; William, 251.

KINCADE: Dr., 261.

KINCHELOE: Cornelius, 36; Hannah
(Robinson), 128; John, 71, 140,
275, 290; William, 36, 71, 73,97,
140.

KINE(S): _____, 274;
John, 262.

King George County: 15, 38,
61, 117.

KING: George Harrison Sanford,
186; Isaac, 99i; Thomas, 43.

Kings Bridge (N.Y.): 80.

KINSY: Betsey M., 283.

KIRK: Elizabeth, 111, 164;
Patrick, 61; William, 79, 111w,
112, 164i.

KNOX: _____, 41; Elizabeth,
161; Jannet, 161; John, 161,
162, 24, 60; Robert, 161w,
165i; Robert Dade, 161; Rose
Townsend, 161, 162; William,
162.

Knox and Baillie: 162.

- L -

LAKE: Vincent, 228; William,
150, 228, 284.

LAMBERT: William, 24, 41,76,
77.

LAMBY: John, 61.

LAMKIN: _____, 294; George,
16, 24, 61; James, 239.

LANDMAN: Griffin, 279.

LANE: George, 284; James,
36,37; William, 135, 191,
228.

LANG: Alexander, 100.

LANGFIT: Philip, 295.

LINEH: Charles, 61.

LINGAN: Samuel, 66.

LITHGOW-LITHEOW-LITHCOE:
Alexander, 184,189; John, 76;
Mr., 77, 202.

LITTLE: Elias, 283.

Little River: 87,91,285.

LLOYD: James, 277; Joseph,
297,298.

LOCKART: John, 24.

LOFLANE: Daniel, 37.

LOMAX: _____, 27

Long Branch: 87

Long Ordinary (Fredericksburg):
77

LOTT: Jesse, 128.

Loudoun County: 6,7,36,38,86,
89,180,264.

LOVE: John, 275; Robert, 279;
Samuel, Jr., 264; William, 28,60.

LOVINGDER: (Widow), 152.

LOWRY: George, 249,268,274,276,
286,291,295.

LOWTHER: Thomas, 95.

LUCAS: Peter, 292,293.

LUCKETT: Ignatius, 240,287.

LUKINS: Manna (Rector), 234;
Peter, 233,234.

LUNCEFORD-LUNSFORD: Amos, 145i;
George, 128i.

LUTTRELL-LUTTERIL-LUTTRILL:
Abner, 93; Betsy, 93; Dinah,
93,94,225; Dolly, 93; Hannah,
93; James, 25,41,81,94; John,
22,25,41,76,94,196i,225;
Joshua, 199,202; Lott,93,224,
225; Lyddia, 93;Mary, 25,26,
93; Michael, 25, 93w, 97i,
225; Nathan, 93; Nimrod, 115;
Richard, 4, 25w, 26i, 32, 54,
90, 93, 94; Robert, 25, 26,
94, 225; Samuel, 25, 78;
Sarah, 25, 93; Simon, 284;
Susannah, 25; Unstiss, 25;
Winnefred, 167.

Lux, Boley & Russell: 232.

LYNN-LINN: Thompson, 240;
Fielding, 240; Francis, 240;
John, 239w, 295; Lewis, 239;
Nancy, 252.

- M -

McABOY: Peggy, 130.

McBEE: John, 139.

McCABE: George, 284.

McCARTY: _____, 168.

McCAVE: James, 166.

McCLANAHAN-McCLANAHAM: Andrew,
193; Gerard, 295; James, 81,
152, 266, 267, 276, 295, 301;
John, 284; Thomas, 17.

McCLAREN: Daniel, 302.

McCLUSKEY: Anne, 133.

McCOLLEY: Archibal, 279.

McCONKEY-McCONKY: Alex., 165,
268.

MARSON: Alexander, 282.

MARTIN: Benjamin, 222; Charles,
4,31,35,129,132,141,168w,1751,
223,261,244; Alexander Baill,
162; Col., 24,28; Elinor, 100;
Elizabeth, 100, 169; Enoch, 222;
Hosea,223; John, 94,99,102,139,
187,193,222,223,239,248,250,284;
Joseph, 152, Sr: 222w,223,2261;
Katharine,223; Nancy, 243;
Reuben, 169; Thomas, 28; Tilman,
8, 99w,100,1011; Verlinda,162.

Maryland (State): 19,27,161.

MASON: Ann, 86; John, 237;
Margaret, 168,244; Peter,283i;
Thompsnn, 264; William, 202.

MASSEY-MASSIE: Thomas, 212,300.

MASTERS: Ann (Robinson), 159.

MASTERSON: Ann, 189,243.

MATTHEW(S)-MATHEWS:
Benjamin, 293; Elizabeth, 36;
Edward, 2851; John, 37,54,
150,156,200,261,285w,286,2911;
Nathan, 288; Sally, 213.

MATTHIS: Alice, 36; Anna, 36;
Chichester, 36; Dudley, 36;
Elizabeth, 36; Griffin, 36;
Nancy, 36; Newman,37; Matthis,
36; Nancy, 36; Robert, 30,
36w, 37.

MAUZEY: Betty, 21,22,28,41,
76,77; Henry, 22,24,28,34,41,
44,76; Jemima, 273; John,
21w, 22,231,24,28,35,36,41,
76,77,146,147,169,201,204,218,
224,232,248,257,273,293,292,
301; Margaret (Peggy), 21,
22,28,41,76; Mary, 36w,40i,
41,44,78; Molly, 22,41,76,
77; Myrna, 223,224; Peter, 22,
36; Sally, 36,44,60,78,104,
153.

MAY: James, 183; John, 151.

MAYSON: Peggy, 275.

Medle Run: 43.

MELTON: William, 189.

MERCER: George, 61; James,
61; John, 56; Mr., 56.

MERCH: Nelson, 227.

METCALF: Bettse, 119,120;
Charles, 130,155,224,229,
236,260,240,295; Christopher,
811; Eliz'a, 274; John, 206,
23,44,52,71,110,264,275;
Sally, 280; William, 119,120,
174,175,200,206,232,244,264,
274,279,280,281,289,291.

Metcalf and Johnston: 275.

MILLAR: Will, 162.

MILLARD: William, 124w, 127i.

MILLER: Ann, 15; Elizabeth,
6; Harman, 6; Judith, 38;
Simon, 20,23,37w,38,44,148;
William, 25,41,76.

Mills:
     Harrison's, 172
     Blackwell, 177

MINOR: Armistead, 227;
John, 279.

MINTER: Anthony, 83,205,206,
288; Betsy, 206; Elizabeth,
83; Hannah, 50; Jacob, 50w,
511,65,83,151,171,203,205,
206; John, 65,83w,871,151,
189,203d,205a; Joseph, 43,
54,55,65w,671,83,150,151,
205,267; Mary, 65,83;
William, 65,83,203,205.

MISKELL: William, 95.

MITCHELL: John, 150i.

MIZNER: John, 189.

MODESETT: Charles, 189.

MOFFETT: Capt., 136; Daniel, 136; Jesse, 208,136; Henry, 4,14,228 (Jr., 124); John, 25,46,56,58,59,60,62,71,75, 89,108,126,129,134,152,163, 172,196,206,227,228,232,237.

MONDAY: Charles, 299; John, 303.

MONROE: Alexander, 169i, Daniel, 190i; Hugh, 283; John, 124,136,214,215,237, 244,301, (Rev., 212)

MONTER: Joseph, 150.

MONTGOMERIE: _____, 213; Thomas. 213.

MOORE: Cato, 131; Fra.,31, 54; Nathan, 271,274; Samuel, 60.

MORCY: John, 190.

MOREHEAD: Alexander, 34,268; Anne,170; Armistead, 142; Capt., 150; Charles, 4,30, 34,43,45,47,66,78,101,107, 112,128,142w,149i,164,268; Elizabeth, 142,268; James, 142; John, 30,34w,35i,76, 97,108,179,268,301,(Sr.,220) Joseph, 34; Kerenhappuch,142; Lidia (Nelson), 156; Lydia, 268;Mary, 101,143,268; Peggy, 268; Presley, 34,112,142,164, 275,293; Samuel, 268w,272i; Samuel B., 268; Turner, 66, 101,128,142,143,175,235,253, 262,275; Wm, 34,143; Wilmouth, 268.

MORGAN: Abel, 50,51; Alice,27; Anne,27; Abraham, 50; Benjamin, 27,34,232; Charles, 11,24,27w, 35,42i,48,60,109,117,142; Daniel, 62, 282; Elizabeth, 32; Enoch, 50,51; Grace, 51; Jeremiah, 218.185; James, 25i, 27,34; John, 10,27,32,48,202; Joseph, 32,120,126,137,139,141, 144,164i,218,219,245,259,301; Joshua, 24; Martha, 50,51; Mary, 27,51; Moses, 228; Randle, 50w, 511; Simeon, 200,218w,219; Simon, Sr.: 4,27,151,196,197, 231,235i; William, 21,27,34, 51,122,146,147,228,282,294.

MORLESS: Henry, 18.

MORIN: Joseph, 21.

MORRIEL: Benjamin, 36.

MORRIS: Benjamin, 37; Elizabeth, 136; Sanders, 266; William 149.

MORRISON: _____, 37, 257; Daniel, 113; Edward, 223.

MORSON: Arthur, 61.

MOSES: Wm. Healer, 155.

MOSS: Meredith, 86; Moses, 301; Nathaniel, 50, 152.

MOUNTJOY: Edward, 94,99,248; William, 284.

MULLEKIN: William, 205.

MURRAY-MURREY-MURRY: Dorcas,1; Enoch, 211; Francis, 211; George, 40; James, 2,20,81, 122,138w,145i; John, 39,77, 130,139,155;Mary,163; Mr., 202; Lydia, 138; Ralph, 41,138,139, 163,181,251; Reubin, 138,139; Sary, 114; Wm., 25,98,111,140.

MUSCHETT-MUSHITT-MURCHETT:
James, 104,186,191,202,206,
257, 290; John, 162; Mr., 243.

MUSE: Daniel, 275; Hudson, 275.

MYRES: Peggy, 301.

MYNATT: Richard, 24,34;
Sarah (Cummings), 44.

- N -

NALLE: William, 159; Jr.,193.

NALLS: Mary, 288; William,
155, Wm. Sr., 288; Wm. Jr.,
288.

NASH: Elijah, 80w.,
John, 81, 202; Mary, 171;
Travers, 189; William, 81.

NEALE: Anne, 154; Anstis,
166; Benjamin, 60,73,98,153,
(Jr. 99), 166w, 167i; James,
286; Jesse, 166; Joanah,
154; Joseph, 49,153w, 154,
155i; Judah, 154; Lewis,
134; Mary, 154,155,198;
Matthew, 78,154,155,198,
224,246,250,265,272,284;
Moses, 166.

Neale, Jameson & Co.: 232.

NEFF: Dr., 76; Henry, 24.

NEIGH: Ann, 286; Jacob,
286.

NEILL: Samuel, 284.

NEILSON: H., 185; Hugh,
264.

NELDON; Mr., 227.

NELSON: James, 451,215a,
227a; Benjamin, 224;
Catherine, 84; George, 264;
Hugh, 155; Jemima, 156;
Jesse, 156; John, 25,41,51,
55,73,75,76,99,101,145,
155(Sr.)w, 156,157,164i;
John, Sr., 205w, 218i;
John, Jr., 205,208; Joseph,
80,108,135,154,166,205,227,
302; Lettice, 156; Margaret,
156; Peggy, 76,77; Mary,
205; Thomas, 89,126,132,
156, 187,228; William, 89,
126,132,135,200,205,228,264,
275.

Nelson Co., Ky., 180.

NESBITT: White, 189.

NEVILLE-NEAVILL-NEVIL-
NEAVILLE: G., 290; Gabriel,
32; George, 23,24,32,63w,
64,681,151,264; Henry, 32;
James, 227; John, 20,31w,32,
76,227; Joseph, 13,18; Mary,
32,63; Robert, 31; Sarah,
122; Thomas, 32,135,302.

New York: 80.

NEWBLE: Peggy (Ash), 62,63.

NEWBY: Betty, 213; Eliza,
149; Henry, 149; (widow), 149.

NEWGENT - See: NUGENT

NEWHOUSE-NEWHOUS: Benjamin,
2321,259a; Jonathan, 275;
Polly, 259, 279,281.

NEWLAND-NEWLAN-NEWLON:
Daniel, 12; Jane, 12.

NEWMAN: John, 55.

NICHOLS: Elizabeth, 203;
Samuel, 203.

NICOLS: John, 461.

NIGHT: Epha, 189.

NOLAND: Rosanna, 60.

NORMAN: Benjamin, 280;
Clement, 4,21,24,166; Clemm,
191,245; Edward, 285,303;
Ezekill, 212; William, 8,20.

NORRIS: Dr., 189,202; John,
87,290; Septimus, 224,279,
302i; Thad's., 294,302;
William, 87,107,175,227,290.

NORTHCUT: Winny, 252.

North Fork of Licking (Ky.):
241.

Northumberland County: 95,
277.

NUGENT: Ann, 160w, 161i;
Charles, 257; Edward, 160,
192,203i,205d,212a,249d,
257 dower; Elizabeth, 212,
257; Frances, 257; Jale, 257;
Polly, 257; Thomas, 160, 192w,
196i,205,249,257.

NEWELL-NEWALL: Adam,112;
Benjamin, 124w,129i; John, 124;
Nancy, 124; Richard, 124.

O'BANNON: Andrew, 59,107,108,
180,195,236,238; Bacon, 171;
Benjamin, 59,80,108,139,295;
Bryan(t), 15w,161,58,59,108,
152,227; Elias, 270; Fanny
(Jennings), 93; Frances (Ashby),
62; George, 59,79w,80; Isham,
270,271,279; James, 270,271;
John, 14,15,16,19,20,23,38,42,
45,48,58w,61,71i,79,108,112,
126,127,135,181,185,187,194,
200,224,226,227,236,244,270w,

O'BANNON (Con't.)
John, 271, 273,275i,293,294.
Joseph, 187,224,227,236,251,
59,108,132, 270,271,279,294,295;
Mary, 107,108; Lydia, 224, 270,
271,273,293,292; Ruth (Burgess),
152; Samuel, 15,58,84,228;
Thomas, 15,58,84,108,295,228;
Sarah, 15,58; William, 15,23,
38,44,58,79w,108,135,227,270.

ODER-ODOR: Joseph, 48, 264,
268,276.

ODEN: Lydia, 300.

OGLISBY: Margit, 189.

Ohio River: 103, 241.

OLDAKER-OLDACRES: Abram, 245w,
248i; Hester, 245.

OLDHAM: George, 228; Richard,
71; Richard, Jr., 228.

OLIVER-OLLIVER: Hez'k., 284;
Hiss, 195; John, 302; Joseph,
261,268,280; Lewis, 195;
Reason, 268; Thomas, 261;
William, 302.

O'NEAL: Christopher, 190;
Honour, 190.

O'REAR-O'REER-OREAR:
Benjamin, 108; Daniel, 301;
John, 56; Sarah, 185.

Overall & Bronaugh: 293.

OWENS: Amelia, 258; James,
268; Jane, 67,239; Jeremiah,
67w,69i; John, 61,67,73,132,
155,180; Johnson, 80,155;
Joshua, 290,295; Mason, 252;
William, 21,132,134,155; Mr.,
76.

OWINGS: Jean, 219.

PHILLIPS: Abner, 45; Elizabeth, 120; William, 120,205,227,228.

PICKERING-PICKRING: Wm., 25.

PICKETT: Anna, 280,295; Anne, 100; Col., 202,204; Elizabeth, 28,29; George, 29,135; Hannah, 145; James, 281,291,295; James S., 280; John, 29,147,229; John S., 280; Martha, 280; Martin, 20,28,29,33,61,76,82,91,100,151, 166,178,189,200,201,206,212,214, 226,228,232,239,259,264,279,281, 290; Reuben, 28; Sanford, 280, 295; Sarah, 28,29; William, 20, 28w,29,107,112,132,140,158,167, 176,189,191,220,221,228,231, 280,281,291,292,293,295; Wm. S., 185,237; William Sanford, 130, 134,145,155,229,280w,290i,295a.

M. Pickett & Co., 238,257,275.

Pickett & Blackwell: 238,272, 294,278.

Pickett & Co.: 285.

PIERCE-PEARCE: Jacob Garrison, 32; John, 32,195,228; Judith, 197; Lydia, 32; Peter, 32w, 351, 195d; Robert, 295; Rosanna, 32, 195; Susanna, 32, 195.

PIERSON: Joseph, 281.

Pignut Ridge (Mt.): 38, 58,75, 122,218.

PINCHARD-PINCKARD: James, 127; Mildred, 146; William, 223.

PINKARD: William, 201.

PINKSTONE: Shadrack, 155.

PIPER: B., 129; Winifred, 207.

POOL: William, 268.

POPE: Ben, 76; William, 77, 85,97,154.

PORE: Mary, 168.

PORTER: Betty, 298,299; Charles, 24,299; Ebenezer, 273; Ebbin, 292,293; Edwin, 299; Eli, 298; Eve, 8; Hannah, 223,224,273; Jane, 219; John, 208,219,220,235, 238,239,299; Martin, 247, 299; Samuel, 8,151,226,274, 299; Thomas, 11,133,152,193, 215,226,298w,299,303i; William, 299.

POWELL: Col., 200,202; Kitty, 258; Levin, 165,264; Lewis, 61.

Powell & Harrison: 140.

Powell's Run (Prince William County): 183.

POWERS: _____, 174; Christian, 140.

POWLE: William, 276.

PRATT: _____, 285.

PRESTON: William, 14,42.

PRICE: Ann, 100; Bennitt, 34,51,72i,100w,110; Elizabeth, 100; Judith, 100; Thomas, 102.

PRICHARD: Peggy, 96; Stephen, 96; Thomas, 61.

PRICKETT-PRICHETT: Sam'l., 24, 25.

PRIEST: _____,40; Elizabeth, 157,158; Eneler, 114; Frances, 85; George, 114; John, 114; Mary, 250; Mason, 158; Peter, 250; Richard, 168,114;

PRIEST (Con't.):
Samuel,114; Sarah (Sary), 114,
167,250,251; Thomas, 26,32,51,
98,111,113,114,217,250w,251,
259i,272,301; William, 113w,
122i.

PRIMM: James, 202,243; John,
254; William, 69,253,254.

PRINCE: Hubbard, 98i.

Prince George Co., Md.: 265.

Prince William County: 3,5,6,9,
11,27,36,86,103,135,151,168,
172,183,246,261.

PRITCHETT: _____,246;
Jane, 10; William, 293.

PRUNTY: Anna (Carroll), 200;
David, 200,244.

PURCIFUL: Mrs., 240.

- Q -

QUAINTANCE: _____, 233,234;
Grace, 234; William, 234,235.

Quaintance vs. Rector: 234.

Quantico: 134.

QUARLES: Betty, 53,55;
Elizabeth Minor, 55; John, 55.

QUESENBERRY: Gracy, 229.

- R -

RAINS: Cornelius, 155.

RAILEY-RALEY-RAILY: Thomas, 23,
24,26,81,97,99,222.

RALLS: Edward, 73; John, 24,41,
76.

RAMEY: Absolem,12; Thomas,33.

RANDALL: Joseph, 295;
Richard, 140.

RANDOLPH: Col., 248; Robert,
213,215.

RANSDELL: Charles Morehead,
170; Chilton, 74,257,267,
280,294; Edward, 74,170;
John, 78,170; Margaret, 170;
Sarah, 170; Thomas, 74, 170;
206,217,225,227,233i,265i,
275; Wharton, 17,26,30,45,66,
67,74,78,79,149,150,151,170w,
164,171,178i (Jr., 175i);
William: 30,47,74w,151,170,
182i, 228.

Rappahannock Mt., 136.

Rappahannock River, 136.

RAWLINGS-RAWLINS: John, 237,
245; John Adams, 276.

RAWS: Abraham, 37.

READING-Ridding: William,
219,239. (See also
Reddin).

READY: James, 217.

REAVES: Elizabeth, 141.

RECTOR: Benjamin, 49,89,121,
127,134,263,273,284,288,297;
Catherine, 49,50; Caty, 298;
Charles, 49,128,228; Daniel,
49,228; Edward, 298; Eli, 298;
Elijah, 298; Elizabeth, 49;
Frederick, 49,121; Grace, 234;
Harmon, 48,49, 121,187w,189i,
(Jr., 121); Henry, 5,49,50,52,
121w,126i,128,253,298w,303i;
Jacob, 49,81,134,253i; James,
134; John, 16,20,49w,50,52i,
60,61,68i,121,129,171,234,
273,298, (Jr., 49,50,81i)

RECTOR (Con't.) Mary, 129,148, 156; Mary Ann, 298; Mary (Hitt), 48; Nancy, 298; Nathaniel, 20, 234, 292; Pency, 298; Sarah, 234; Spencer, 234, 298; William, 121,129,303.

REDD: Allen, 216; Joseph Bullett, 215,216; Permercis, 215; Pricilla, 215; Philip, 216; Susannah, 215, 216.

REDDIN-REDING-READING: Timothy, 10,20; William, 10,14,20.

REDDISH: John, 14.

REDMAN: George, 108; Jeremiah, 228; Richard, 3,13,18; Sarah, 32;

REDMOND: John, 166, 263i.

REED: Jacob, 155.

REEDER: Elijah, 103.

REID: James, 184.

REMO: Thomas, 275.

RENNOLD(S): James, 73w; John, 351; Margaret, 73.

RENO: Lewis, 33; Lila, 180; Mary, 180.

RENSE: _____, 40.

RHODAS: Mary, 19.

RICE: Bailey, 205; Benjamin, 151.

RICH: Daniel, 152i.

RICHARDS: William, 256.

Richards & Co.: 185.

Richmond County, Va.: 66, 267.

Richmond, Va.: 261.

RIDDLE-RIDDELL: John, 37, 54,55,61,73; Mr., 41.

Ridge Path: 25.

RIDLEY: John, 183.

RIGHT: James, 293.

RILE: Saly (Darnall), 45.

RILEY-RILAY-RILY: Catharine, 231; Charles, 231; Edward, 166,176,231; Eve, 176; George, 231; Hugh, 231; John, 135,228,231w,236, 239; Susannah, 231; Thomas, 231,256.

RIND: William, 150.

RINGO: _____, 233; Burtis (Bertice), 234; Hannah (Rector) 234.

RITCHIE: John, 74.

RIXEY: Richard, 185, 228, 245, 272,293,300.

ROACH: George, 179; Thomas, 281; William, 189, 243, 81,87.

ROBBIN: Elizabeth, 257; James, 257.

ROBERTSON-RoBERSON-ROBESON: Alice, 45; Ann, 112; James, 98; John, 24,37,44,98; Joseph, 99,113; Mesamilliam, 237; William, 33,202.

ROBIE: Peter, 140.

Robinson's Branch: 70

ROBINSON: Benjamin, 87,128, 159w,165,189,243a; Catherine, 128; Diannah, 279; Dixon, 159,160,189,214,243; Elesha, 159; Elijah,159, 189; Elizabeth, 199; Ely, 159; George, 159,160,189,243,278,293; Hannah, 128; James, 159; Jesse, 128; John, 128,151, 159, 199,222; Joseph, 52, 89,128w,132i,140; Lucy, 128; Lydda, 159; Martha, 128; Mary, 159,199; Maximillian, 128; Michael, Jr., 78; Molly, 128; Nancy, 128; Nath'l., 159,160,189; Peggy, 128; Stephen, 159; William, 14,128,150,171,199w.

Rock Run: 25.

ROGERS: Betty, 213; Charles, 52; Edward, 60,213,214; George, 30,43,74,83,95,149, 151,202,213w,214,2171,225, 265,266,267,268,278,281, 302; George, Jr., 149,193, 205,225; Henry, 243,244; Hugh,295; James, 15; John, 243w,244i; Mary, 244; _____ (Minter), 83; Robert, 250i; Sarah, 243; Stephen, 244.

ROLING: George, 24.

ROLLINS: John A., 284; 275. (See also: Rawlings)

RONAND: _____, 186.

ROOKARD: Elizabeth, 300; Hiram, 300; Nancy, 300; Robert Carter, 300; Sarah, 300; Thomas, 299w,300,303i.

ROSE: Robert, 290,293; Sarah, 139; Silas, 52.

ROSS: Alexander, 284;

ROSS (Con't): Hector, 75, 85; William, 284.

ROSSER: Benjamin, 133; Elizabeth, 137; George, 136, 137,158; Hannah, 137; John, 63,64,136w,137,139i,151; Letty, 137; Mary, 63,137; Richard, 136,137; Sally, 137; Sukey, 137; William, 136,137.

ROUSSAU-ROUSSAW-RUSAW: Betty, 37; Henry, 22,286,287; John, 22,24,41,79,286,287; Lydda,287; Margaret, 287; Prissilla, 286; Sarah, 287; W., 76; William, 2,22,25,26, 32,33,76,118,119,127,179,286w, 287,2911.

ROUTT-ROUT: Fanny, 187; James, 177,185,189,210,211,212,218, 250i,293; Jane,187; Peter,189, 249,263; Richard,187.

ROWLER: M., 61.

ROY: Thomas, 109,116,126,201, 232,289; Wil(e)y, 109,120,193, 201,217,232,235,239,240,243, 278,289,299,303.

RUSSELL: Ann, 76; Benjamin, 84,93; John, 33,149; Lucretia, 93; Mary, 9,247; William, 9, 14,47.

RUST: Benjamin, 126,127; Betty, 127; John, 89i,127,128,227,288i; Samuel, 108,127,196,237,295.

RUTH: S., 284.

RUTHERFORD: Robert, 61.

RUTTER: Hezekiah, 221.

RYCROFT: Thomas, 149.

Shenandoah County: 152, 156.

SHIPP: Betsy, 84; Coleby, 84;
John, 84w,85,89i,165,212;
Joseph, Sr., 212; Laban, 84,
85; Nancy, 84,165; Polly, 84;
Richard W., 84,85,165.

Short & Richards: 256.

SHULTZ: Benjamin, 245;
Joseph, 245.

SHUMATE (de la Shumate):
Anne, 169; Bailey,157; Daniel,
80,157,164i,180,220; Elizabeth,
296; James, 157; Jemima, 157;
John, 21,58,98,128,143,156(Sr.)w,
157,164i,187,188,211,256,272;
Joshua, 157; Judith, 157;
Lettice, 157; Mark, 263; Mary
(Dodson), 80; Mason, 188;
Molly, 253; Lewis, 296;
Tabitha (Dodson), 80; Thomas,
156,157,164,209,272; William,
2,157.

SHIRLEY-SHURLEY: Archibald,
80; James, 64; John, 64,275;
Richard, 152; Thomas, 151.

SIARS: (Siers-Syars-Sias):
James, 21,228; John, 14,16,20,
23,104w; John, Jr., 228; Mary,
104.

SIDDALL: John, 151.

SILMAN-SELMAN: Eleanor, 210;
Joseph, 177,210,212.

SIMMONS: Thomas, 140.

SIMMS: Francis, 254.

SIMPSON: Samuel, 21; Thomas,
283,284.

SINCLAIR-SINKLAIR-SINKLER:
Archibald, 288; Charity, 42;
Daniel, 42; Elizabeth, 42,247;

SINCLAIR: (Con't.): Horatio,
288; Isaac, 288; James, 42,
288,289; Jemima, 42; John, 13,
16,37,42w,45,76i,169,185,186,
288,289; Lydda, 288,289;
Margaret, 247; Mary, 42, Nancy,
288; Robert, 42; Sarah, 30, 42;
William, 42,193,265,288w,289,
290i; William Middleton, 288;

SINGLETON: Joshua, 127,236,239,
301; Robert, 151; Standley,227.

SINSEL: Sarah, 191.

SITHGOW: Wm. Alexander, 195.

SKINKER: George, 73; Thomas,
76,99,182; William, 192,280.

SLAUGHTER: ____, 246;
Cadwallader, 170; George, 133;
James, 79; John, 261.

Sleepy Creek (Hampshire Co.): 22.

SMARE: Sarah, 163.

SMEARER: John, 61.

SMITH: ____(Pickett), 280;
Abner, 194,219,236,238,283;
Alexander, 141,27; Andrew,281;
Ann, 121,123,153; Augustine, 2,
110i,120,248,256,274,284;
Charles, 25,60,76; Clater, 89;
Elizabeth, 90,121,270; Enoch,
219,220,238,239,273,293; Enoch
Oscar, 195; George, 18,186;
Guss, 256; H., 78; Hannah, 2,
123,281; Henry, 18; James, 2,
121,125,225,284,295; James D.,
274,239i; Jane, 2.27; Jesse,
166; John, 1,76,121,126i,134i,
152,153,157,160,161,166,167,
219,220,238,239,245,283,273,286;
John D., 261a; John William, 195,
261; Joseph, 4,46,81i,107,108,
117,120,125,166,191,194d,200,
219w,233,235(Jr.),236,238a,241,
265,280,295,301; Lewis, 2;

SMITH (Con't.): Martha, 90,125;
Mary, 1,54,90,160,161; Matthew,
121,125w,130i; Randolph, 192;
Rebecca, 123; Richard, 160,167;
Rowley, 87,166,219,220,238,239;
Ruth, 194,219,235; Susanna,121,
127i, 247; Thomas, 14,121,200,
215,221,227,263,273i,284,286;
Thomas A., 284; Wilhilmina,194,
219,238; William, 2,40,41,46,
113,121,125,134,136,165,197,
212,219,239,255,269,271,274,
275,281w,283i; Wm. Jr., 166;
Withers (Weathers), 243,260,
295.

SMITHEY: Susanna (Sukey),206.

SMOOT: Barton, 272; Betsy,272;
Charity, 272; Clahourn, 272;
Enoch, 272; Frances, 272;
John, 271w,272,284i,230; John,
Sr., 209; Leonard, 272; Lewis,
272; Mary, 272; Tomsen, 271;
William, 255,272.

SMOOTE: Leonard, 191.

SNAP(E): Laurence, 61;
Noth, 251.

SNELLING:Benjamin, 31,65w,
Elizabeth, 65; Samuel, 302;
William, 194.

SNICKERS: Edward, 60.

SNIDER: X'r., 135.

SON: John, 10.

South Carolina: 39.

South Run: 65.

SOUTHARD: Elizabeth, 102,103;
Francis, 102w,103,110i;
George, 102; Henery, 235;
Jemima, 103; John, 35,38,71;
Levi, 102; William, 102,289.

SPARK(S): Isaac, 10;
Winifred, 23.

SPARUM: James, 135.

Spaw Water Springs (Hamp-
shire County): 22

Speake & Kennedy: 62.

SPENNEY: James, 290.

SPICER: Randolph, 166.

SPILLER-SPILLAR: Philip,
54,55,184,277,280; Priss,
55.

SPILMAN: Elizabeth, 10;
Jacob, 10,17; John, 122.

SPITFATHOM: Benedict, 140.

Spotsylvania County: 77, 222.

Spring Gap Mt. (Hampshire
County):22

SQUIRES-SQUIERS: Ann, 105;
Elizabeth, 113; John, 98i,
113,140.

Stafford County: 36,86,105,
118,159,189,205,226,243,256.

STALLIARD-STEATARD: Joseph
Bullett, 215; Mary, 215;
Randolph, 216.

STAMPS: Ann, 46; George, 19;
Hannah, 19; John, 19; Mary.
19; Molly, 19; Thomas, 19w;
21i; Timothy, 19; William,
19, 45w,46 ,47i.

STANTON: William, 259.

STARKE: Cathrine, 41;
Elizabeth, 114; James, 114;
John, 158.

STARKS: James, 291.

STEELE: George, 151; Henry, 214,281; Samuel, 45,69,151, 165,203,206,214,217,265.

STEPHENS-STEVENS: Adam, 60, 76; Ann, 52; John, 136; Joseph, 61; Richard, 136; Robert, 52w, 54t,87,136,145; William, 52, 53,87,136.

STEPHENSON: Benjamin, 236; James, 193i; Peggy, 236. (See also: Stevenson)

STERMON: _____, 290.

STEVENSON: James, 212; Marthy, 212; William, 197i; 212a.

STEWART: (See also Stuart) Allen, 119,302; Betty, 119; Charles, 119; Elizabeth, 285, 302; George William, 189; H., 264; Helen, 119,302; James, 24,47,79,119w,120,133, 193,232,262,285,302a; James, Jr., 19,103; James,Sr., 285; Jane, 119,120,303; John, 119, 133,227,302; Mary, 119,302; William, 36,103,108,119,182, 267,302.

STINSON: Elizabeth, 189; James, 189w,190,272; John, 189; Leannah, 189; Mary, 189; Samuel, 264; Sarah, 189.

STOCKLAN: Joseph, 34.

STONE: Benjamin, 39; Menoah, 155, 206; Thomas, 5,51.

STRANGE: Cloe (Cornwell), 75.

STRIBLING-STRIPLING: Taliaferro, 60,61.

STRICKLAND: Joseph, 52.

STRICKLER: _____, 61.

STRINGFELLOW: Henry, 150; Robert, 222,226,266,276.

STRODE: John, 279.

STROTHER-STRAWTHER: Benjamin, 163; James, 97i, 301; Lewis, 283; Reuben, 113,128,163,296, 301; William, 99,228; S., 191.

STUART: _____, 237; William, 220,222.

Stuart and Marshall: 200

Stuart and Muschett: 256.

STURDY: William, 32.

SUDDUTH-SUDDOTH-SUDITH: Alse, 246; Ann, 125; Frances, 292; Francis, 122,247,293,294; George, 247,302; I., 200; James, 253; Leanner, 235; Mary, 235,247; William, 239, 246w,247,290; John, 39,125, 152.

SULLIVAN: Anne, 229; Elizabeth, 229; George, 44,71,100i,229d; John, 229; Owen, 229.

Summerduck Run: 191,211.

Summer Dusk: 161.

SUMMERS: Isbell, 85.

SUTHARD: John, 97.

SUTPHIN: Christopher, 66.

SUTTELL: William, 155.

SUTTLE-SUTTEL: Sarah, 262; William, 151, 202, 262.

TODD: Nathaniel, 27.

TODS: James, 140.

TOLLE: Anne, 211; George, 105,
211; Jonathan, 105; Roger,
105w, 110i, 295; Sary, 105;
Stephen, 91,105,211w, 217i;
Susannah, 105.

TOMKIES: Morgan, 196.

TOMLIN-TOMBLIN: John, 30,67,74,
87,150,152,267d, 275,205,206,
303; John, Jr., 175; John, Sr.,
266i; Samuel, 267; William, 83,
267.

TOOLE: James, 140.

TOWARD: Warner, 5.

TOWLES: Henry, 52.

Town Run: 72,152,172.

TRACEY: George, 182.

TRIPLETT: Anne, 241; Benedicte,
241; Betty Hedgman, 241;
Frances Amelia, 241; Francis,
61,108,129,157,161,191,231,
241w,2451,246a,290; Hedgman,
241;Mary, 166; Reuben, 224;
Robert, 241; Thomas, 24,245,
246; William, 31,241.

TROUTVINE: Jacob, 61.

TRUMAN: James, 290.

TULLOSS-TULLOS-TILLIS:
Ann, 88; Joshua, 40,60,252,
255,268; Richard, 2,4,13;
Rodham, 24,30,34,40,41,87,
141,252.

TUPMAN: Francis, 39.

TURBERVILLE: George, 131,290.

Turkey Run: 285.

TURLEY: Margaret, 148;
William, 122,129,140,253,283.

TURNBULL: Robert, 192.

TURNER: Capt., 114; Edward,
98,105,113,133,165,217,296,
301; Hezekiah, 46,69,76,94,
109,115,129,165,171,187;
John, 201,236,279,278,295;
Mary, 105; Richard, 296;
Samuel, 275.

TUTT: Benjamin, 60.

TUTTLE: John, 284; William
294,295.

TWENTYMEN: Alender, 9;
Benjamin, 9; Edward, 9,10,14;
Elizabeth, 9; John, 9.

Tyger River: 174.

TYLER: Charles, 200; Mary,
311,54,55; Mr., 54.

- U -

UNDERWOOD: Margaret, 122;
William, 4.

UTTERBACK: Agness, 187;
Charles, 187,284; Elizabeth,
188; Harmon, 197,290; Henry,
10,20,121,187; John, 68,127,
150; Nimrod, 246.

USTICE: Isaach, 189.

- V -

VANN: William, 76,77.

VAN SWERINGEN: Capt., 60.

VINNELL: John, 72.

WEST: Benjamin, 222,232,264;
Edward, 34; Ignatius, 222w,
266i,232; Jane, 240; John,
201,279; Sally, 242; Sibly,
89; Thomas, 140; William, 61.

WESTALL: Mary, 188.

Westmoreland County: 66, 275.

WHARTON: Samuel, Jr., 210.

WHEATLEY:Ann, 124; Elizabeth,
244; George, 18,244,261,287i;
Heathey, 244; James, 27,88,
150,244i,261,279a,280,302;
John, 124,127,244,260i,261,
280; Joseph, 18,255i,261,
302a; Landon, 244; Lawson,
244; Leannah, 124; Lucretia,
261; Lucy, 261; Mary, 124,
146,244,302; Sarah, 124;
Sukey, 244; William, 18,244.

WHITE: Ann, 37; Carr, 160;
Celia (Seley), 235; David,
22; James, 128,222,281;
John, 185,187,303; Mrs.,
81; Nathaniel, 60; Pleasant,
37w,40i; Thomas, 91;
William, 37,108,151,159,160,
165,179,189,214,227,243,259;
Wm. Jr., 202.

WHITING: Betty, 126; Francis,
68,126,168,213; John, 168w,
170i; Thomas, 251,295,290.

WHITLEY: William, 89,248.

WHITTEDGE: Thomas, 57,76.

WHITTON: _____, 302.

WIATT: John, 170.

WICKLIFF: David, 131,260.

WICKS: Jean, 167.

WIGGINTON: John, 145;Mary,301.

WILKERSON: Eliza, 54.

WILLBOURN: Edward, 5.

WILLIBY: John, Jr., 228.

WILLIAMS: Ann,31,176;
Benj., 133; Catherine, 176;
Charles, 231; Elijah, 176,
177; Frances, 205,257;
George, Jr., 177; George, Sr.,
176w,1771,185,209; John,31,
176; John P., 282; John
Pope, 140; Jo's., 33;
Joseph, 166; Margett, 231;
Nath'l., 33,41; Paul, 18,
21,27,70,88,97,110,127,
129,146,169; Pope, 122;
Richardson, 176; Thomas,
62,257; Toughler, 280;
William, 176,177,210;
Zelah, 284.

Williams Gap: 6.

WILLIAMSON: Elizabeth, 146;
James, 66; John Pope, 193;
Mary, 66; Richard, 280.

WILLIS: Francis, Jr., 131;
Rich, 126; William, 290.

WILLOUGHBY: Benjamin, 20,23,
73; John, 20,21,24,134i,155.

WILLS: Humphrey, 60,61;
John, 268.

WILSON: Alex., 195; Cumber-
land, 275; George, 186;
John, 195, 284,295.

WILTON: John, 61.

WILY-WILEY: Allen, 6;
Eve, 6,7.

Winchester, Va.: 22. 274,278.

WINKFIELD: Honer, 296w.

WINN: Betty, 242; Hannah, 91,
242.243; James, 61,90,91;
John, 62,90; Margaret, 90,
91,264; Minor, 90w,91,99i,
108,113,125,132,152,185,
227,237,242,243,264a,275,
279,295,299; Richard, 90;
William, 90.

WITHERS: Abijah, 254;
Benjamin, 242; Cain, 203,
264; Centhy, 203; Enoch,
185,200,203,206,226,242,
264,293; Enoch K., 170,
171,229,262,267,273,292,
303; Elizabeth, 203,209,
254; Elijah, 293; George,
249; George Washington,
144,147,217,218; Hannah,
203; James, 28,60,144w,
145,146i,147,181,188,194,
201,203,209i,212,226,243,
262,266,273,281,282,289,
290,292,293; Jemima, 145,
147; Jesse, 201; John, 144,
145,147,188,194,201,203,
212,242,243,249d,273,274,
281,283,292,293; John (son
of old field), 266;
Joseph, 191,221,241,242,
245; Lewis, 255,264,292;
Lucy, 203; Matthew Keen,
242; Pattey, 203; Rose,
223,224; Sally, 203; Sithey,
203; Thomas, 35,203,242w,
243,281,283; William, 35,
145,147,200,203,207,242,
243,249,272,292.

WOOD-WOODS: _____,25;
Bailey, 172; Benjamin, 60;
Dickerson/Dickason, 46,181,
198,199,204,209,245,272,
284,297; Eliza, 54,55;
General, 185; James, 21,60,
72,256,267; John, 26,41,74,
90,172,192,229,256; Nem, 41;
Peter, 41,76,256; Samuel, 26,
76,81; Sarah, 20,41; Robert,
191,201,24; Thomas, 61;
William, 61,256,267,272,284.

WOODFORD: Catesby, 167,171,
212,213w,215i; John, 213;
Mark, 213; Mary, 212,213;
William, 213.

WOODROW-WODRON: Alexander,
17,60,61,62;

Woodrow & Nelson: 28,30,34,
61,62.

Wodron, Nelson & Foster: 61.

WOODRUFF: Owen, 284.

WOODSIDE: John, 161,196;
William, 161,192,196,287,
294.

WOODYARD: Lewis, 124,227.

WREN: Isaac, 265; John, 265.

WRIGHT: Betsey, 208; Elizabeth,
208; George, 60; James, 45,
78,84,138,190,208,228,250,
227,228,243,248,255,257,261,
274,284,302; John, 9,13,16,
37,42,84,92,97,110,208w,
211i; Joseph, 9w,11i,14;
Mary, 208,223; Reubin, 129;
Rosamond, 208; William, 16,
120,208.

- Y -

Yates & Lovel: 200.

YEATES: Joshua, 38.

YOAKUM: George, 60.

YOUNG: Bersheba, 85; Betty,
129; Bryan, 206; Chris, 41,
76; James, 61; James, 23,32,
73,295i; Margaret, 264;
Reginald, 60; Senet, 76;
Patience, 206; Original, 24,
58,74,76,77,85,86,97,115,
116,119,125,127,167,168,171,
195,205,216,218,225,229,256;
William: 129,206w,211i,216,221a,
268,

www.ingramcontent.com/pod-product-compliance
Lightning Source LLC
Chambersburg PA
CBHW060138280326
41932CB00012B/1558